Northern Ireland
A Chronology of the Troubles
1968–1999

Northern Ireland
A Chronology of the Troubles
1968–1999

Paul Bew
and
Gordon Gillespie

THE SCARECROW PRESS, INC.
LANHAM, MARYLAND, 1999

SCARECROW PRESS, INC.

Published in the United States of America
by Scarecrow Press, Inc.
4720 Boston Way
Lanham, Maryland 20706

http://www.scarecrowpress.com

First edition published in Ireland in 1993. This revised and updated edition published simultaneously in Lanham, Maryland, by Scarecrow Press, and in Dublin, Ireland, by Gill & Macmillan, 1999.

ISBN 0-8108-3735-8

British Library Cataloguing in Publication Information Available

Library of Congress Cataloging-in-Publication Data Available

Manufactured in Ireland

Dedicated to the memory of
Sam Gillespie

Contents

Introduction to the First Edition

For a quarter of a century Northern Ireland has been locked in a bitter conflict centred around a constitutional dispute in which the majority of the population wish to remain within the United Kingdom and a minority would prefer that Northern Ireland was incorporated within the Republic of Ireland (Éire). Already over 3,000 people have lost their lives due to political violence in a small territory inhabited by only one and a half million people; worse, there is no end in sight.

By the end of 1992 the 'talks process', intended to lead to an accommodation between peaceful unionists and nationalists, the political representatives of 90 per cent of the Northern Irish population, had collapsed. While some of the participants on both sides displayed significant good will in an effort to reach a compromise, in the final analysis the gap between the aspirations of the two communities was unbridgeable.

The talks had excluded Sinn Féin, the political wing of the Provisional IRA (which has 10 per cent of the vote in Northern Ireland) because of its refusal to condemn Irish Republican Army violence, the single most potent agent of death in 'the Troubles'. In 1992 several leading Sinn Féin strategists had enunciated some unusual themes—one might almost say themes which were nearly revisionist with respect to republican orthodoxy—indicating, for example, surprising doubts about the wisdom of coercing the unionist community into a united Ireland. But, by the end of the year, these discussions within the republican movement seemed to have stopped and Sinn Féin, which had been dismayed by the unexpected re-election of the Conservative Party in Britain, was buoyed up by the triumph of Bill Clinton in the United States. Sinn Féin President Gerry Adams made it clear that he now hoped that the international criticism of Britain's role in Northern Ireland would grow. In the event President Clinton initially at least, displayed considerable caution in his attitude toward Northern Ireland. The IRA still retained a substantial capacity to continue a terrorist campaign but it should be noted that in 1992, for the first time, loyalist terrorists killed more people than the IRA. Sectarian antagonism and instability appeared to be growing once again, although it had yet to reach the horrendous levels of the 1970s.

While no one can predict the end of the Troubles with confidence, the last quarter of a century has seen enormous change in Northern Ireland.

The key demands of the Civil Rights movement of 1968–9 have long been met. The Northern Ireland parliament at Stormont, controlled by the Ulster Unionist Party, which was seen by many as being too slow to reform its anti-Catholic and anti-nationalist ethos, has been replaced by a system of direct rule from London. The Anglo-Irish Agreement of 1985 has given the Dublin government a voice in the affairs of Northern Ireland. The effects at some levels have been quite dramatic. For example, direct rule has transformed employment patterns in government service. Twenty years ago Professor Donnison reported (*New Society*, 5 July 1973) that only five per cent of Northern Irish civil servants between the grades of assistant principal and deputy secretary were Catholics, then 33 per cent of the overall population. In 1992 it was reported that Catholics were actually over-represented in the civil service whilst the government set a target of 25 per cent Catholic representation for senior posts (currently 17.1 per cent) for the end of 1996. It was widely believed on all sides that the government's target would be met. The Catholic middle class is increasingly perceived to be a growing force in Northern Irish society, but there remains the obdurate reality of a substantial Catholic urban ghetto community which tends to support Sinn Féin.

The figures for state employment are of great importance because direct rule has not been able to prevent the regional decline of the Northern Ireland industrial sector: at the beginning of the Troubles over 40,000 were unemployed; by 1993 the figure was over 100,000. A Catholic male is still more than twice as likely to be unemployed as a Protestant. This problem has remained much as it was despite 20 years without Unionist rule. It is worth noting, however, that a relatively low difference in under-representation in jobs creates a large difference in unemployment. Catholics form 38 per cent of the economically active population; the Catholic share of jobs is 32 per cent for males and 37 per cent for females.

Thanks, at least in part, to fear of the IRA Catholics are reluctant to take up more than a small fraction of jobs in the security sector, although the government is desperately anxious to encourage this process. Ironically, the Catholic share of jobs in the Royal Ulster Constabulary today is less than that achieved by the old 'Orange' regime of Stormont premier Sir James Craig. This is so despite the professed hopes of Peter Barry in 1985, then Irish Minister for Foreign Affairs, that the Anglo-Irish Agreement would make it easier for Catholics to join the RUC. Again, with even heavier irony, the IRA's campaign has allowed many thousands of unionists, who would have been rendered jobless by the decline of Belfast's traditional blue-collar industries, to find alternative, well paid, in local terms, employment (an average of £33,000 a year with overtime) in the security forces. The interaction of the direct rule machine and violence has, therefore, produced a complex and uneven effect on the socio-economic landscape of Northern Ireland.

Politically, too, direct rule has had major effects. Because locally elected institutions have virtually no power they have become marginal and often attract people of relatively low calibre. Interestingly, direct rule's framework combined with the IRA's activities has actually made the Protestant population subjectively more British. In 1968 20 per cent of Protestants thought of themselves as Irish as opposed to British or 'Ulster'; by 1989 this figure had fallen to 3 per cent. Over the same period the number of Protestants describing themselves as British rose from 39 per cent to 68 per cent (Stringer and Robinson, p. 25). In 1969, 326 Northern Irish students obtained their higher education in the rest of the United Kingdom compared to 359 who went to the Republic. In 1989, 2,550 went to Britain while only 184 went to universities in the South.

On the other hand, support for Gaelic culture in the Catholic community has also grown; the 1991 census reveals that 10 per cent of the population claim to know some Irish despite, or perhaps because of, independent Ireland's complete failure to revive the Irish language.

The picture broadly emerges, therefore, of two starkly opposed communities. The unionist community has, at least for the moment, turned away from extravagant, bombastic gestures—as a symptom Dr Ian Paisley's Democratic Unionist Party has been in decline since 1981. Nevertheless, it remains in its instinctive mental focus as sharply removed from any sympathy with Irish nationalism as ever. Substantial sections of the nationalist community remain as aggrieved and resentful of the status quo as at any time in their history; the force of this, at times millenarian, emotion is reduced only by the widespread knowledge in both communities that the subvention from the UK Exchequer amounts to £6,400 per annum for every family of two adults and two children in the province.

The outline of a widely acceptable solution is tragically not yet in place. The intractability of the problem remains its most marked feature.

In this work we have attempted to outline the key developments of the last quarter of a century and to allow the various actors to speak for themselves. The shape of 'the Troubles' was largely moulded in the first five to seven years of the conflict and the sections which include our comments on significant events over the last 25 years reflect this with a large number of defining incidents occurring between 1968 and 1974 and fewer after that date. We hope that there will be no need for a sequel to this volume in another quarter century.

Introduction to the Second Edition

As we concluded the first edition of this work in 1993, the Troubles remained an endemic part of Northern Ireland life. Rather than end the chronology with a reference to another murder, however, we sought to provide something more optimistic by quoting the words of Mother Teresa of Calcutta during a visit to Belfast on 3 June of that year: 'Together let us do something beautiful for God, bring peace, bring love, bring joy. Let us forget any hurt. Where there is holiness, there is joy, there is unity, there is peace.' Five years later some of these sentiments appeared to have taken root among Northern Ireland's hardened political cynics.

The Downing Street Declaration of December 1993 was undoubtedly a turning-point. The declaration opened the way for paramilitaries to join political negotiations on the future of Northern Ireland, provided they 'permanently' renounced violence. The British government accepted the principle of self-determination for the people of Ireland; the Irish government accepted that this self-determination could take the form of Irish unity only when a majority in Northern Ireland supported that choice. The British government refused to be a persuader for a united Ireland but did become a persuader for an 'agreed Ireland'—a Northern Ireland based on equality between the two major traditions with a new set of cross-border linkages. The projected detail of these cross-border links would be spelt out in the Frameworks Document of 1995.

The IRA declared a cease-fire on 31 August 1994, but frustration at what republicans perceived as foot-dragging by the British government, allied to internal tensions, led the IRA to end that cessation with the Canary Wharf bomb in London in February 1996. The cease-fire was, however, to be restored in the late summer of 1997, and the renewed cease-fire led to the inclusion of Sinn Féin in the talks process and subsequently to the Belfast Agreement of 1998.

The Belfast Agreement at last appeared to have provided the political framework for a settlement that had eluded politicians for thirty years. Most parties could legitimately claim that they had achieved some, though by no means all, of their goals. Few claimed either total victory or total defeat. The key to the agreement was, perhaps, realism. The Belfast Agreement represented a historic compromise between the two main traditions and was supported by 71 per cent of those who voted in a referendum on the package in Northern Ireland as well as by over 90 per cent in the Republic. The Downing Street Declaration had provided the guiding themes for this accommodation; but the theme of 'permanence' continued to nag away at the political subconscious of Northern Ireland. Despite all the undoubted progress, the granite-like intractability of the issue of paramilitary weapons remained, and beneath it perhaps the central question of the peace process: had the paramilitaries really made a permanent renunciation of violence? By the spring of 1999 the answer was still unclear.

It should be noted that security statistics given at the end of each year have been revised in line with changes made in the RUC Chief Constable's report of 1994.

Acknowledgments to the First Edition

We would like to thank Diana Kirkpatrick, Donna McCleary and Alan McMillan of the main library at Queen's University Belfast for their help (and patience) in attempting to answer some of the obscure questions posed by the authors during the preparation of this work. We should also like to thank Colin Coulter for similar reasons.

Acknowledgments to the Second Edition

In addition to those mentioned above, we would like to thank Norma Menabney of the Main Library at Queen's University and our colleagues in the School of Politics, Sydney Elliott, Richard Jay, Patrick Maume, and Rick Wilford. We would also like to thank Serif for permission to use material from our chronology *The Northern Ireland Peace Process, 1993–1996.* Those requiring fuller details of what might be called the 'first peace process', from the gathering momentum of the Hume-Adams and party political talks to the Canary Wharf bomb, will find additional details of those years in that work.

List of Abbreviations

CLMC	Combined Loyalist Military Command
DCAC	Derry Citizens' Action Committee
DHAC	Derry Housing Action Committee
DUP	Democratic Unionist Party
EEC	European Economic Community
FEA	Fair Employment Agency
FEC	Fair Employment Commission
GAA	Gaelic Athletic Association
GOC	general officer commanding (British army)
HMG	her majesty's government (the British government)
ICJP	Irish Commission for Justice and Peace
ICTU	Irish Congress of Trade Unions
IIP	Irish Independence Party
INLA	Irish National Liberation Army
IPLO	Irish People's Liberation Organisation
IRA	Irish Republican Army (usually refers to Provisional IRA)
IRSP	Irish Republican Socialist Party
LAW	Loyalist Association of Workers
LVF	Loyalist Volunteer Force
NICRA	Northern Ireland Civil Rights Association
NILP	Northern Ireland Labour Party
NIO	Northern Ireland Office
NUM	New Ulster Movement
PD	People's Democracy
PR	proportional representation
PUP	Progressive Unionist Party
RIR	Royal Irish Rangers; Royal Irish Regiment
RUC	Royal Ulster Constabulary

SAS	Special Air Service
SDLP	Social Democratic and Labour Party
UDA	Ulster Defence Association
UDP	Ulster Democratic Party
UDR	Ulster Defence Regiment
UFF	Ulster Freedom Fighters
UK	United Kingdom
UKUP	United Kingdom Unionist Party
UPNI	Unionist Party of Northern Ireland
USC	Ulster Special Constabulary (also known as B Specials)
UTV	Ulster Television
UUAC	United Unionist Action Council
UUUC	United Ulster Unionist Council
UUUM	United Ulster Unionist Movement
UUUP	United Ulster Unionist Party
UVF	Ulster Volunteer Force
UWC	Ulster Worker's Council

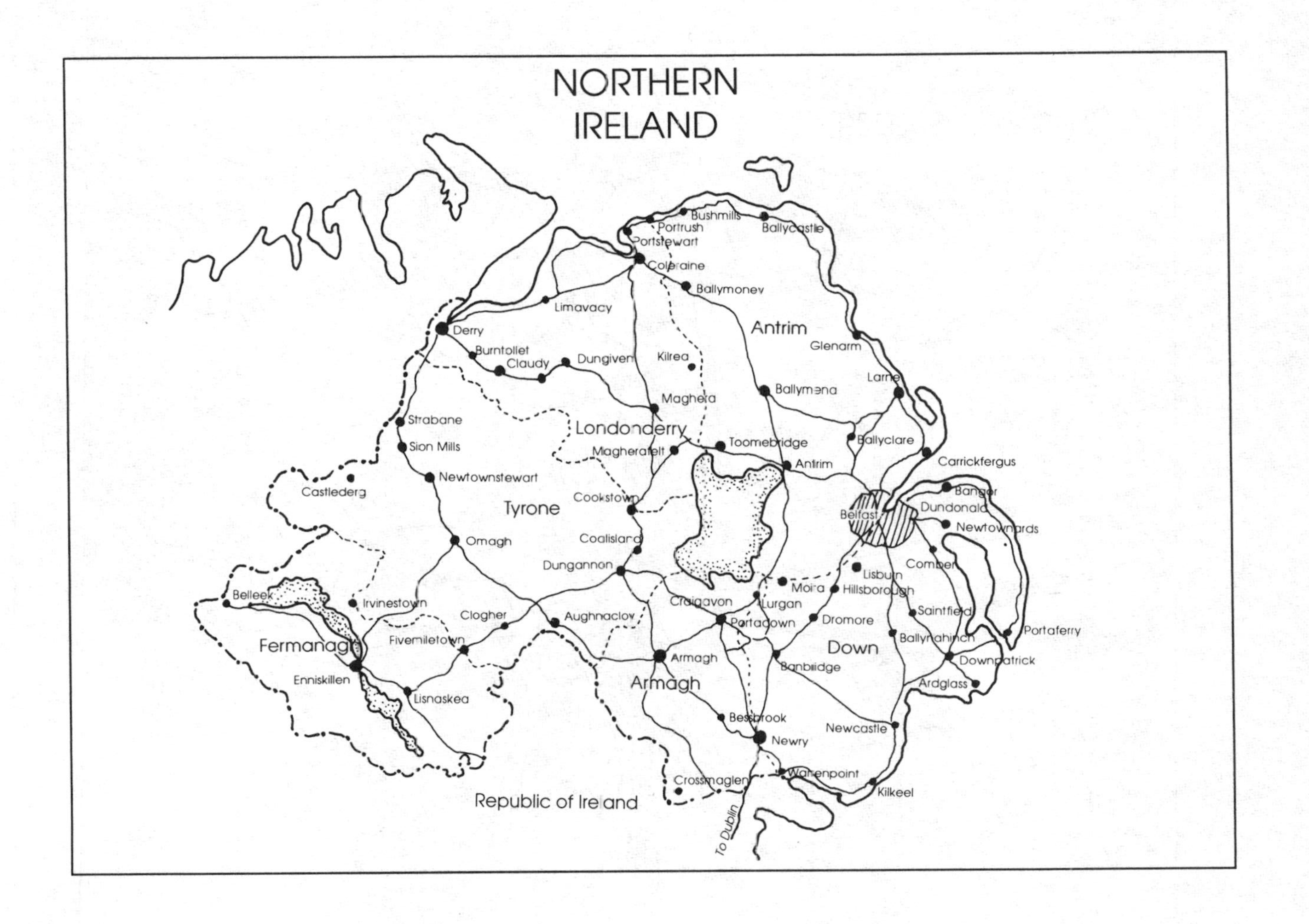

NORTHERN IRELAND
Antrim
Londonderry
Tyrone
Fermanagh
Armagh
Down
Republic of Ireland
To Dublin
Portrush
Bushmills
Ballycastle
Portstewart
Coleraine
Ballymoney
Limavady
Derry
Burntollet
Claudy
Dungiven
Kilrea
Glenarm
Larne
Ballymena
Maghera
Strabane
Sion Mills
Toomebridge
Magherafelt
Ballyclare
Carrickfergus
Antrim
Newtownstewart
Castlederg
Cookstown
Bangor
Dundonald
Belfast
Newtownards
Omagh
Coalisland
Dungannon
Comber
Lisburn
Moira
Hillsborough
Belleek
Irvinestown
Craigavon
Lurgan
Clogher
Aughnacloy
Saintfield
Portadown
Dromore
Portaferry
Fivemiletown
Ballynahinch
Down
Downpatrick
Fermanagh
Armagh
Banbridge
Enniskillen
Ardglass
Lisnaskea
Bessbrook
Newcastle
Newry
Warrenpoint
Crossmaglen
Kilkeel

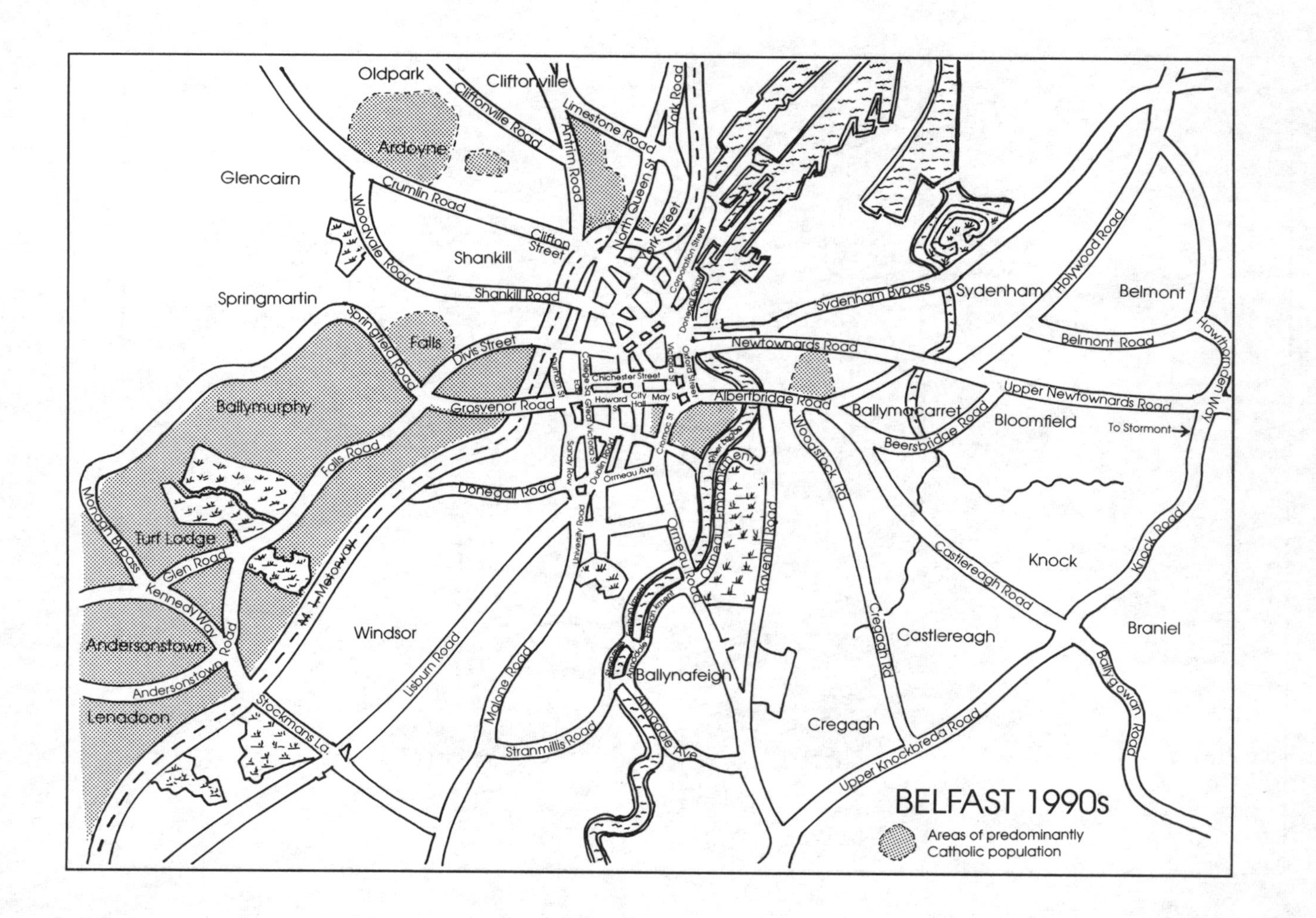
BELFAST 1990s
Areas of predominantly Catholic population
Oldpark
Cliftonville
Cliftonville Road
Ardoyne
Glencairn
Crumlin Road
Woodvale Road
Antrim Road
Limestone Road
York Road
North Queen St
York Street
Corporation Street
Donegall Quay
Clifton Street
Shankill
Shankill Road
Springmartin
Springfield Road
Falls
Divis Street
Ballymurphy
Grosvenor Road
Falls Road
Donegall Road
Turf Lodge
Glen Road
Monagh Bypass
Kennedy Way
Andersonstown
Andersonstown Road
Lenadoon
Stockmans La
M1 Motorway
Windsor
Lisburn Road
Malone Road
Stranmillis Road
University Road
Sandy Row
Dublin Road
Great Victoria St
College Sq
Durham St
Chichester Street
Howard St
City Hall
May St
Victoria St
Oxford Street
Cromac St
Ormeau Ave
Ormeau Road
Ormeau Embankment
Ravenhill Road
Annadale Ave
Ballynafeigh
Cregagh
Cregagh Rd
Castlereagh
Castlereagh Road
Upper Knockbreda Road
Woodstock Rd
Albertbridge Road
Newtownards Road
Ballymacarret
Beersbridge Road
Bloomfield
Upper Newtownards Road
To Stormont
Sydenham Bypass
Sydenham
Holywood Road
Belmont
Belmont Road
Hawthornden Way
Knock
Knock Road
Braniel
Ballygowan Road

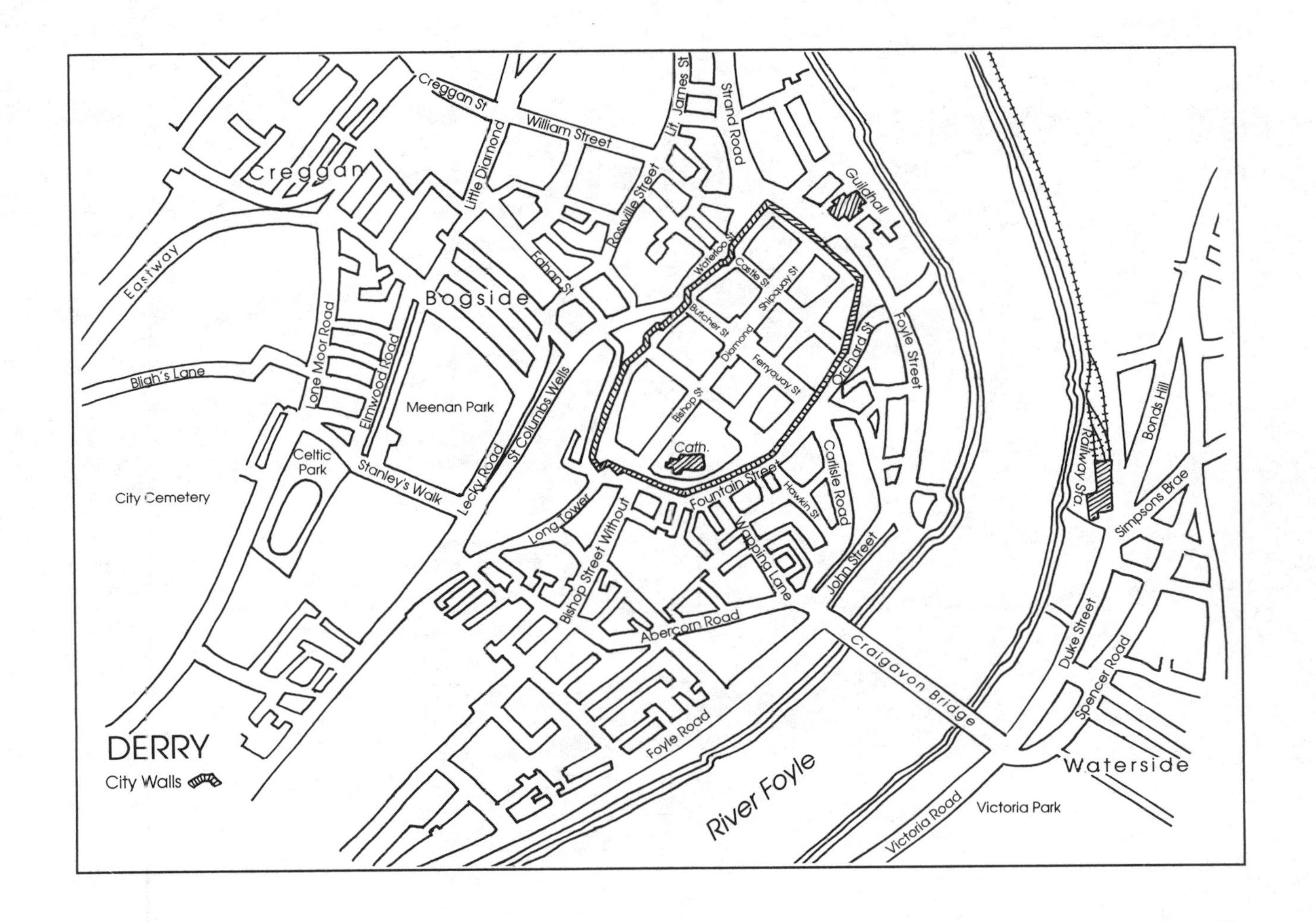
Creggan St
William Street
Lit. James St
Strand Road
Guildhall
Creggan
Little Diamond
Rossville Street
Eastway
Fahan St
Waterloo St
Castle St
Shipquay St
Bogside
Butcher St
Diamond
Foyle Street
Orchard St
Ferryquay St
Bligh's Lane
Lone Moor Road
Elmwood Road
Meenan Park
St Columbs Wells
Bishop St
Bonds Hill
Cath.
Carlisle Road
Railway Sta.
Celtic Park
Stanley's Walk
Lecky Road
Fountain Street
Hawkin St
City Cemetery
Long Tower
Bishop Street Without
Wapping Lane
John Street
Simpsons Brae
Abercorn Road
Duke Street
Craigavon Bridge
Spencer Road
Foyle Road
DERRY
City Walls
River Foyle
Waterside
Victoria Road
Victoria Park

1967

1 February The Northern Ireland Civil Rights Association is formed. It calls for a universal franchise for local government elections (instead of one based on rate-payers) and the ending of the company vote ('one man, one vote'); the re-drawing of electoral boundaries to end gerrymandering; the introduction of laws to end discrimination in local government employment; a compulsory points system for public housing to ensure fair allocation; the repeal of the Special Powers Act; and the disbanding of the wholly Protestant police reserve, the Ulster Special Constabulary (B Specials). From the outset many Protestants believe that the NICRA is merely a front for the IRA, which at this time is almost non-existent. In 1972, however, the Scarman Report (para. 2.8) notes that 'several of its [NICRA's] prominent members were Republicans and there were various links with IRA personalities.' Many Protestants believe that the ultimate goal of the NICRA is not civil rights but a united Ireland.

11 December The Prime Minister of Northern Ireland, Terence O'Neill, meets the Taoiseach, Jack Lynch, at Stormont, the seat of the Northern Ireland Parliament. Snowballs are thrown at Lynch's car by Protestant clergymen as it passes the Carson statue on the way in, and he is barracked by Rev. Ian Paisley and his supporters as he drives through the gates of Stormont when leaving. In contrast, however, with the antagonism aroused by the visit of the previous Taoiseach, Seán Lemass, in 1965 (which took place on O'Neill's personal decision and without consultation with other members of the Northern Ireland Cabinet), O'Neill has the support of his colleagues. Discussions centre on trade, tourism, and electricity supply.

1968

January Unemployment is viewed as one of the major problems in Northern Ireland: 40,000 people (7.8 per cent of the working population) are out of work, though this falls to 36,000 (7.0 per cent) by December.

8 January Terence O'Neill visits Dublin to continue discussions begun the previous month in Belfast. Again non-contentious issues, such as cultural exchanges and precautions against foot-and-mouth disease, are the subject of discussion; a joint statement says that both governments will do their best to promote co-operation in these areas. By the end of the year most of the work that had gone into normalising relations between the North and the South has been undone by the course of events.

22 March John Brooke defeats the challenge of an Independent Unionist to win the Lisnaskea by-election for Stormont. He succeeds his father, Viscount Brookeborough, the former Prime Minister of Northern Ireland.

16 May The Ulster Unionists retain the City of Londonderry constituency at Stormont in a by-election.

20 June A number of squatters are evicted from council houses in Caledon, Co. Tyrone, by the RUC. One of the houses had been allocated to a nineteen-year-old Protestant woman, the secretary of a local Unionist politician. The Nationalist MP for East Tyrone at Stormont, Austin Currie, who had occupied the house to draw attention to the problem of discrimination in the allocation of housing, is one of those evicted.

3 July 150 members of Derry Housing Action Committee, formed in March, stage a sit-down at the opening of the extension to the Craigavon Bridge in Derry. Éamonn McCann, one of the committee's leading members, later says that 'by this time our conscious, if unspoken, strategy was to provoke the police into over-reaction and thus spark off mass reaction against the authorities' (*War in an Irish Town,* p. 35).

31 July Lord Grey of Naunton (Governor of the Bahamas since 1964) is appointed to succeed Lord Erskine of Rerrick as Governor of Northern Ireland. With the abolition of the post after the introduction of direct rule in 1972, he will be the last person to hold the position.

24 August After agreeing to a proposal from Austin Currie, 2,500 people take part in an NICRA march from Coalisland to Dungannon to protest against discrimination against Catholics. A loyalist counter-demonstration leads to a ban on a rally in Dungannon that had been planned for the end of the march. In the wake of this comparative success the NICRA agrees to another march in association with DHAC, this time in Derry.

5 October Rioting breaks out after a confrontation between civil rights marchers and the RUC in Derry. The march, in protest against discrimination in housing and employment, was banned on 3 October by the Minister of Home Affairs, William Craig, under the Public Order Act, on the grounds that there was likely to be a clash with an Apprentice Boys parade planned for the same time. Despite the ban, the demonstration—attended only by between 200 and 400 people—goes ahead. It forms at the railway station in the Waterside, whereupon the RUC stop a van with loudspeakers and charge its three occupants, members of the NILP, with incitement to break the ban. At the front of the march are Eddie McAteer (leader of the Nationalist Party at Stormont), Austin Currie, Gerry Fitt (Republican Labour MP at Stormont and Westminster), and three British Labour Party MPs.

When the march reaches an RUC road-block scuffles break out, leading to arrests; several people, including Fitt, McAteer, and Currie, are injured. There is a sit-down in front of the RUC, and an impromptu meeting is held. It is at this point, as some of the crowd begin to sing 'We Shall Overcome', that the RUC order the crowd by loudspeaker to disperse, though the announcement is shouted down by some of the marchers.

As some of the demonstrators begin to move again, trouble flares up once more. Members of the Young Socialists throw placards at the RUC, who advance on them with batons. The demonstrators are unable to retreat because of a second cordon behind them, which advances on the marchers and begins to attack them with batons. The County Inspector of the RUC orders the police to halt, but despite this they continue to advance on the demonstrators. After the march has been broken up, some of those involved cross the River Foyle to the city centre and reassemble at the Diamond, where another confrontation with the RUC takes place. Another section of the crowd marches to the Guildhall, from where they are forced to the Diamond and eventually dispersed. By now the original march is all but forgotten as a battle develops between the RUC and youths from the Bogside estate. Two days of rioting in Derry end with the police using armoured cars, high-pressure water-hoses and baton charges in an attempt to restore order. About a hundred demonstrators and several members of the RUC are injured.

As the clashes continue over the next few weeks, community relations turn sour. On 15 October Eddie McAteer announces that his party will no longer act as the official opposition (a role it accepted after Lemass's visit to Belfast in 1965), but so far there is no permanent withdrawal from Stormont. At the trial of the marchers arrested in Derry it emerges that they had broken no law until they had been ordered to disperse by the RUC; and whether many of them could have heard this order above the background noise is debatable. *Fortnight* was later to comment on the events of the day: 'In later years the events of October 5th 1968 were polished into simplified propaganda versions, but the whole affair was a series of blunders. The violence resulted from inadequate planning and leadership by the organisers of the march, and from stupidity and a breakdown of control on the part of the authorities. But the greater share of blame lies with those who had the greater power—the Minister of Home Affairs and the Royal Ulster Constabulary' (*Fortnight*, October 1988).

The Derry Civil Rights March

The events in Derry on 5 October 1968 opened up the modern Ulster crisis. The television coverage—especially the work of the RTE cameraman Gay O'Brien—changed the course of Northern Ireland history. The media gave widespread coverage to the unrestrained batoning by the RUC of demonstrators, including MPs, without 'justification or excuse' (according to the Cameron Commission). The perception rapidly developed that something was rotten in the state of Northern Ireland. Cocooned in their devolutionist shell, the Unionists found it difficult to defend the peculiarities of their system to outsiders. For the first time in their careers the leadership, used to easy victories and stability, found themselves having to deal with a real crisis—complicated, it has to be said, by the confused cross-currents of student radicalism.

Irish neutrality during the Second World War had weakened nationalism's credibility in London. The arrival of the welfare state in the North contrasted with mass emigration from the Republic in the fifties; these developments provided the circumstances that bred a generation of complacent Unionist politicians that believed, wrongly, that it held all the political and economic cards. In particular it was a political generation used to easy and unproblematic relations with London. Furthermore, in 1966, after forty years of independence, the population of the Republic (at 2.88 million) was less than it had been in 1926 (2.97 million), while that of the part of Ireland still 'unfree' was larger (1.25 million in 1926, 1.48 million in 1966). Slow to see the positive implications for the Republic of the Lemass revolution in economic strategy, the Unionist leaders felt that economic trends remorselessly strengthened unionism while at the same time undermining the logic of nationalism.

The response of Brian Faulkner (Minister of Commerce) to the events in Derry reflected these assumptions. While William Craig had responded by claiming simply that the NICRA had been infiltrated by the IRA and that 'majority opinion in the IRA Council was communist,' Faulkner stressed the economic advantages of the status quo. 'All the lurid accusations and every bit of sensational political mud-slinging rebounded not only on Orange and Unionist Ulstermen but endangered the pay packets of every Nationalist citizen of Northern Ireland as well.' He added: 'For industrialists there was no Unionist Ulster, no Nationalist Ulster, no West or East of the Bann. There was only Northern Ireland as a place within which the man who builds a factory could count on finding stability, fair dealing and common sense.' This was a picture of Northern Ireland that was already rapidly ceasing to exist. As Faulkner acknowledged in the same speech, 'unfortunately for Northern Ireland, the attempt to equate Nationalism with civil rights ... was an effective one in the eyes of the world.' A new possibility—direct rule—was already opening up. Within two days of the Derry fracas, O'Neill was telling reporters: 'We might get back to a situation of 1912, when a Liberal government tried to interfere in Irish affairs.'

9 October A student demonstration takes place in Belfast against the 'police brutality' of 5 October. Afterwards People's Democracy, a left-wing student group, is formed. The aims of PD are 'one man, one vote'; an end to the gerrymandering of electoral areas; freedom of speech and assembly; repeal of the Special Powers Act; and fair allocation of jobs and housing.

Derry Citizens' Action Committee is formed, bringing together five protest organisations that already exist in the city. Ivan Cooper is chairman of the committee and John Hume vice-chairman.

16 October Over 1,300 students march to Belfast City Hall in support of civil rights.

19 October A sit-down protest is held at the Guildhall in Derry, organised by DCAC.

25 October The New University of Ulster, controversially sited in the mainly Protestant town of Coleraine rather than the predominantly Catholic city of Derry, opens with four hundred students. Numbers are predicted to rise to five thousand by 1980, though in fact this number is not reached until the 1990s.

30 October During a semi-official visit to London, Jack Lynch publicly calls for the ending of partition to resolve the unrest in Northern Ireland.

2 November DCAC members march from Waterside railway station in Derry to the Diamond. The RUC prevent clashes with loyalists.

4 November Terence O'Neill, William Craig and Brian Faulkner meet the British Prime Minister, Harold Wilson, for talks in London. Wilson warns the Unionists that if reforms are not continued the government might consider the 'complete liquidation of all financial agreements with Northern Ireland.' His line is at least partly moulded by pressure from some of his own MPs (Paul Rose, Stan Orme and Kevin McNamara among them) involved in the Campaign for Democracy in Ulster, who press him to play a greater role in Northern Ireland's affairs. After the meeting, Wilson states that there will be no transfer of Northern Ireland to the Republic without the consent of the Northern Ireland Parliament, a repetition of the pledge given in 1949 in the wake of the Republic of Ireland Act.

What was perceived as the 'green' tinge of the Labour Party's attitude towards Northern Ireland is to be a recurring theme over the next twenty-five years and, given Unionist suspicions of the Labour Party's intentions, an important element in destabilising the political situation at crucial moments.

5 November In the House of Commons, Harold Wilson says he wants an impartial inquiry into the events of 5 October. He supports O'Neill but calls for early changes in the local government franchise.

6 November The Ulster Unionists retain South Antrim in a Stormont by-election.

9 November A loyalist march to the Diamond in Derry is led by Rev. Ian Paisley and Major Ronald Bunting.

13 November William Craig bans all marches in Derry from the following day until 14 December.

16 November In Derry up to fifteen thousand people take part in a march organised by DCAC, thus breaking the ban on demonstrations imposed two days earlier. Some marchers later go to the Diamond and take part in a sit-down protest.

18 November There are marches by dockers and factory workers in the centre of Derry. The following day, after further demonstrations, the chairman of DCAC, Ivan Cooper, calls for a halt to spontaneous marches. The next day Protestants clash with civil rights supporters in Derry, leading to twenty-four people (twelve of them policemen) being injured.

22 November The Northern Ireland government issues a five-point reform programme: a new system for the allocation of houses by local authorities is to be established, an ombudsman is to be appointed to investigate complaints, and a Development Commission is to take over the powers of Londonderry Corporation. The Special Powers Act will also be abolished as soon as it is safe to do so (in the following years both the Northern Ireland and later the British government will continue to insist that emergency powers cannot be removed while the terrorist campaign continues). On the contentious issue of the local government franchise, the Northern Ireland government announces the ending of the company vote but takes no immediate decision on enfranchising those who are not ratepayers.

The planned reforms cause widespread dissension within the Stormont Cabinet, with William Craig calling for tougher action against civil rights demonstrators. Nevertheless, by the end of the year Terence O'Neill's reform package appears to have gone some way towards easing Catholics' sense of grievance.

Complete stability had not been re-established, however. As the Scarman Report was to comment (para. 1.4–1.9), 'the Government was faced with a familiar dilemma. If it stood firm it attracted violent opposition. Yet to promise reform under threats to law and order was a recipe to encourage further demonstrations and counter-demonstrations, and to increase rather than diminish the risk of confrontations between minority groups and the police ... The reform programme had left opposition activists dissatisfied, but at the same time it had evoked hostility from some Protestants. While the Catholic minority was developing confidence in its power, a feeling of insecurity was affecting the Protestants. They became the more determined to hold their traditional summer parades, particularly those in Londonderry and Belfast. In these circumstances sectarian conflict was to be expected, unless the police were strong enough to prevent it. But the police were not strong enough.'

30 November An NICRA march in Armagh is halted by a loyalist crowd led by Rev. Ian Paisley and Major Ronald Bunting, who then take over the centre of the town. In January 1969 Paisley and Bunting are sentenced to three months' imprisonment on charges of unlawful assembly.

2 December Commenting on the communal tensions raised by the marches, William Craig says: 'It has been by the grace of God that civil war has not already been created in Northern Ireland. The temperature is at a boiling-point that I have never known in my lifetime. One of these days one of these marches is going to get a massive reaction from the population. Ordinary decent people have been at boiling-point for some time. It's not just Mr Paisley' (quoted in *Keesing's Contemporary Archives,* p. 23207).

4 December There is violence in Dungannon after a civil rights march when demonstrators clash with loyalists.

9 December In an attempt to go over the heads of his Cabinet critics and appeal directly to the public for support, Terence O'Neill makes a television and radio broadcast in which he appeals for calm and says: 'Ulster stands at the crossroads. I believe you know me well enough by now to appreciate that I am not a man given to extravagant language. But I must say to you this evening that our conduct over the coming days and weeks will decide our future ... These issues are far too serious to be determined behind closed doors or left to noisy minorities. The time has come for the people as a whole to speak in a clear voice. For more than five years now I have tried to heal some of the deep divisions in our community. I did so because I could not see how an Ulster divided against itself could hope to stand. I made it clear that a Northern Ireland based upon the interests of any one section rather than upon the interests of all could have no long-term future. Throughout the community many people have responded warmly to my words. But if Ulster is to become the happy and united place it could be, there must be the will throughout our province, and particularly in parliament, to translate these words into deeds ... There are, I know, today some so-called loyalists who talk of independence from Britain—who seem to want a kind of Protestant Sinn Féin. These people will not listen when they are told that Ulster's income is £200 million a year but that we can spend £300 million, only because Britain pays the balance ... Rhodesia, in defying Britain from thousands of miles away, at least has an air force and an army of her own. Where are the Ulster armoured divisions and the Ulster jet planes? ... Unionism armed with justice will be a stronger cause than Unionism armed merely with strength ... What kind of Ulster do you want? A happy and respected province in good standing with the rest of the United Kingdom? Or a place continually torn apart by riots and demonstrations and regarded by the rest of Britain as a political outcast?' (quoted in *Keesing's Contemporary Archives,* p. 23207).

The following day the *Irish News* calls the speech 'one of the clearest statements of policy to date,' which 'pleased the broad masses of moderate intellectual opinion coming as it did amid the wave of Civil Rights demonstrations, and the strong differences existing in his own party.' The writer also comments, however, that 'there remained a feeling of disappointment on the one man one vote statement which would clear the streets of Civil Rights demonstrations.' The article also cited the sympathetic reaction to the speech of the Catholic Primate, Cardinal William Conway, and the Nationalist Party leader, Eddie McAteer. In the wake of the speech DCAC announces a suspension of marches until 11 January.

Buoyed by apparently overwhelming public support for his policy, O'Neill sacks Craig on 11 December and appoints William Long in his place. Long retains his position as Minister of Education.

10 December The *Belfast Telegraph* prints a coupon on its front page that says, 'I approve of Captain O'Neill's broadcast and support his efforts to heal the divisions in our community.' The newspaper asks readers to cut it out and send it to them to show their support for O'Neill. The coupon is printed again on the following day.

12 December A meeting of Unionist MPs at Stormont gives overwhelming support to Terence O'Neill and his policies, though four MPs abstain.

20 December People's Democracy announces that it intends to undertake a protest march from Belfast to Derry. It makes the extravagant claim that the march is modelled on the march from Selma to Montgomery in the United States in 1965 led by Martin Luther King. Realising that the demonstration will increase loyalist fears, both Nationalist and NICRA leaders denounce the march. A week later the loyalist leader Major Bunting ominously warns the marchers to avoid 'loyalist' areas.

By the end of the year Terence O'Neill's prestige seems high. The 'I back O'Neill' campaign receives over 150,000 letters and telegrams of support, requiring a special post room to be set up at Stormont to deal with the letters. On 29 December O'Neill is voted 'man of the year' by the readers of the *Sunday Independent,* while the Co. Donegal Sinn Féin leader Séamus Rodgers concedes that the civil rights movement has achieved more in a few weeks 'than decades of IRA activities.'

1969

1 January Against the advice of the NICRA, about forty members of People's Democracy begin a four-day march from Belfast City Hall to Derry. The marchers are harried by loyalists at various places along the route. On 4 January, when the number of marchers has grown to several hundred (accompanied by eighty policemen), they are attacked by about two hundred loyalists at Burntollet Bridge, near Derry. The loyalists, including off-duty members of the Ulster Special Constabulary, use stones, bottles, sticks and iron bars to attack the demonstrators; thirteen later receive hospital treatment. Bernadette Devlin described the incident: 'We came to Burntollet Bridge, and from lanes at each side of the road a curtain of bricks and boulders and bottles brought the march to a halt. From the lanes burst hordes of screaming people wielding planks of wood, bottles, laths, iron bars, crowbars, cudgels studded with nails, and they waded into the march beating hell out of everybody … What had been a march was a shambles. The first few rows had managed to put a spurt on when the attack came, had got through the ambush, and were safely up the road. The rest of us were all over the place. The attackers were beating marchers into the ditches, and across the ditches into the river … A few policemen were at least trying to stop us from being killed, but the others were quite delighted that we were getting what, in their terms, we deserved. I went rampaging up the road saying that if I had my way, not one solitary policeman who was at Burntollet would live to be sorry for what he had done' (*The Price of My Soul,* p. 139–41).

The arrival of the marchers in Derry and the subsequent entry of the RUC into the Bogside leads to further conflict. On 3 March an inquiry, under Lord Cameron, is begun into the reasons for violence since October 1968. Its report later finds the RUC 'guilty of misconduct which involved assault and battery [and] malicious damage to property.' The PD later decide to give up marching in Northern Ireland, because, in the words of a leading member, Eamonn McCann, 'the civil rights campaign must acknowledge that it had failed in its primary task of building bridges to the Protestant working class. We have alienated them [Catholics] from their Protestant neighbours more than ever before.'

The People's Democracy March

Years after the event, one of the organisers of the march, Michael Farrell, wrote: 'The march would be the acid test of the government's intentions. Either the government would face up to the extreme right of its own Unionist Party and protect the march from the "harassing and hindering" immediately threatened by Major Bunting, or it would be exposed as impotent in the face of sectarian thuggery, and Westminster would be forced to intervene, reopening the whole Irish question for the first time in 50 years. The march was modelled on the Selma–Montgomery march in Alabama in 1966, which had exposed the racist thuggery of America's deep South and forced the US government into major reforms' (*Northern Ireland: The Orange State,* p. 249).

The failure of the Unionist government to handle the march was arguably one of the gravest mistakes of the Troubles. There was little support for the march at the outset—only a few dozen left Belfast—and proscribing it might have brought little reaction. Having allowed the march to go ahead, the government should have provided professional policing. The consequences of the loyalist attack on the (to them) extremely provocative march transformed the situation and strengthened the hostility of many Catholics to the state. It could be argued that the march marks the pivotal point at which the Troubles changed from being primarily about civil rights to being about the more ancient disputes concerning national and religious identities. The attitude of People's Democracy was perhaps naïve. The dubious nature of the comparison between Northern Ireland and the southern United States would be revealed in the following years. The marchers believed that they were participating in a protest for civil rights; in reality they had helped unearth layers of animosity and hatred that had remained at least partly buried over the previous decades.

11 January There is serious rioting, particularly in Derry and Newry, after a PD march weakens O'Neill's authority.

23 January The Minister of Home Affairs, William Long, bans a civil rights march due to leave from Belfast City Hall on 25 January.

24 January The Minister of Commerce and Deputy Prime Minister, Brian

Faulkner, who is not convinced of Terence O'Neill's policies, resigns from the government, to be joined two days later by William Morgan, Minister of Health and Social Services. Despite this, groups are also being set up to support the reform process. In January the New Ulster Movement is formed as a pressure group for promoting moderate and non-sectarian policies. It calls for the creation of a community relations commission and the centralised control of public housing. The movement will later play a major role in the formation of the middle-ground Alliance Party of Northern Ireland.

30 January In the wake of the ministerial resignations, twelve Unionist backbenchers issue a demand for the removal of Terence O'Neill in order to keep the party united.

3 February O'Neill responds to this criticism by announcing the dissolution of Parliament and calling a general election for 24 February.

24 February The Stormont general election, called the 'crossroads election' by Terence O'Neill, takes place. After decades of a rigid and seemingly unchanging party political system dominated by the Unionists and Nationalists, with the more recent challenge of the NILP in Belfast, the range of candidates is dazzling. In some constituencies the Unionist Party supports the Prime Minister and selects a pro-O'Neill candidate, while constituencies that oppose O'Neill choose candidates with a similar outlook but who are also official Unionist candidates. Thus some unofficial Unionists support O'Neill's mildly reformist policies, while some official Unionist candidates oppose them. The civil rights platform is represented by a number of candidates, while a more extreme position is taken by People's Democracy. At the other end of the political spectrum Protestant Unionists also stand in opposition to O'Neill's plans for reform.

The election throws up a number of new names who are to dominate the politics of Northern Ireland over the next twenty-five years. In Bannside, O'Neill successfully defends his seat against Rev. Ian Paisley (Protestant Unionist) and the PD activist (and later writer) Michael Farrell. In Foyle, John Hume, standing as an independent, wins the seat from the Nationalist leader Eddie McAteer. The civil rights campaigner Eamonn McCann stands for the NILP in the same constituency. With a turn-out of just under 72 per cent, the election returns 39 Unionists: 24 official

Unionists and three unofficial Unionists who support O'Neill, 10 official Unionists opposed to O'Neill, and two undecided. The Nationalists lose three seats to civil rights candidates but still retain six seats; Republican Labour wins two seats in Belfast, as does the NILP. The most significant outcome of the election is that it emphasises the divisions within unionism, with official Unionist supporters of O'Neill taking 31.1 per cent of the poll and unofficial Unionist supporters another 12.9 per cent, compared with anti-O'Neill official Unionists' 17.1 per cent. O'Neill still appears to be in control, but the election has not isolated his critics, as he had hoped.

20 March Opposition members at Stormont are suspended after a sit-down protest during the debate on a Public Order Bill. The protest begins after Unionists vote to close the debate during a speech by John Hume. Hume and seven others, including Ivan Cooper and Paddy Devlin, sit on the floor of the chamber singing 'We Shall Overcome' and refuse to resume their seats. After a thirty-minute suspension of the sitting the eight members and an NILP member, Vivian Simpson, who had joined them, still refuse to leave. They eventually withdraw one at a time and are suspended for a week.

17 April In a by-election brought about by the death of George Forrest, the Unionist MP for Mid-Ulster, Bernadette Devlin, standing as a unity candidate, is elected to Westminster by defeating the former MP's widow. The turn-out is almost 92 per cent. At the age of twenty-one Devlin becomes the youngest woman ever elected to the House of Commons and the youngest MP for half a century.

19 April There is rioting in Derry when a planned civil rights march from Burntollet to Derry is banned by the government because of fears that a loyalist counter-demonstration will lead to violence.

21 April In the wake of a series of terrorist attacks on public buildings and utilities, the army sends 1,500 troops to take responsibility for guarding vital installations. There are several attacks on Belfast's main source of water supply, the Silent Valley reservoir, which were believed to have been carried out by the IRA but in fact were the work of the Ulster Volunteer Force, a loyalist paramilitary group attempting to destabilise O'Neill and end the reform programme.

22 April In her first speech in the House of Commons, Bernadette Devlin breaks with tradition to deliver a controversial attack on the 'arch-Tories of Ireland', north and south. 'The question before this house, in view of the apathy, neglect and lack of understanding which this house has shown to these people in Ulster which it claims to represent, is how in the shortest space it can make up for fifty years of neglect, apathy and lack of understanding. Short of producing miracles, such as factories overnight in Derry and homes overnight in practically every area in the north of Ireland, what can we do? If British troops are sent in I should not like to be either the mother or sister of an unfortunate soldier stationed there. The honourable member for Antrim North [Henry Clark] may talk till doomsday about "our boys in khaki," but it has to be recognised that the one point in common among Ulstermen is that they are not fond of Englishmen who tell them what to do.

'Possibly the most extreme solution, since there can be no justice while there is a Unionist Party, because while there is a Unionist Party they will by their gerrymandering control Northern Ireland and be the government of Northern Ireland, is to consider the possibility of abolishing Stormont and ruling from Westminster. Then we should have the ironical situation in which the people who once shouted "Home rule is Rome rule" were screaming their heads off for home rule, so dare anyone take Stormont away? They would have to ship every government member out of the country for his own safety' (*Hansard,* fifth series, vol. 782, col. 287–8).

23 April The Northern Ireland government announces that it will accept universal adult suffrage in local government elections, conceding the civil rights demand of 'one man, one vote.' Major James Chichester-Clark, the Minister of Agriculture, resigns in protest, claiming that the timing of the reform is wrong.

28 April As it becomes increasingly clear that Terence O'Neill has failed to rally the Unionist Party around him, he resigns as Prime Minister and is succeeded on 1 May by James Chichester-Clark. In an attempt to reunite the party, Chichester-Clark brings Brian Faulkner back into the Cabinet as Minister of Development. John Taylor and John Brooke, both O'Neill critics, receive junior government posts in the Ministry of Home Affairs and Ministry of Commerce, respectively. Chichester-Clark declares that he will continue O'Neill's policies—including the changes in the local government franchise—and also concedes that local government boundaries will be redrawn by an independent commission. As a result the civil rights movement eases off on its campaign of agitation, and peace appears to be returning. The damage to community relations has already been done, however, and Protestants increasingly come to believe that the civil rights movement is merely a front for old-style Irish nationalism.

6 May An amnesty is announced for all offences connected with demonstrations since 5 October 1968.

10 May In an interview with the *Belfast Telegraph* following his resignation, Terence O'Neill says: 'It is frightfully hard to explain to Protestants that if you give Roman Catholics a good job and a good house they will live like Protestants, because they will see neighbours with cars and television sets. They will refuse to have eighteen children. But if a Roman Catholic is jobless and lives in a most ghastly hovel, he will rear eighteen children on national assistance. If you treat Roman Catholics with due consideration and kindness they will live like Protestants, in spite of the authoritarian nature of their church.'

21 May James Chichester-Clark and members of the Northern Ireland government meet Harold Wilson and the Home Secretary, James Callaghan, in London.

24 June As part of the series of reforms within Northern Ireland, the Parliamentary Commissioner Act (Northern Ireland) becomes law. The role of the Commissioner, who is independent of the Northern Ireland government, is to investigate complaints of maladministration against government departments.

12 July Serious rioting occurs throughout Northern Ireland. In Belfast, Orange marchers are attacked with bottles at Unity Flats, while their attackers wave Tricolours. In Derry another Orange parade is attacked by youths from the Bogside; police are later stoned and shops looted. At Dungiven an Orange hall is attacked, and in Lurgan there are sectarian clashes for the second consecutive day.

13 July Speaking to a crowd of about five thousand at Loughgall, Co.

Armagh, Rev. Ian Paisley says: 'I am anti-Roman Catholic, but, God being my judge, I love the poor dupes who are ground down under that system' (quoted by Deutsch and Magowan, *Northern Ireland: A Chronology of Events, vol. 1,* p. 34).

16 July Samuel Devenney, a 42-year-old taxi-driver from Derry, dies from injuries after he was beaten on 19 April by members of the RUC who attacked and batoned him in his home while they were pursuing rioters in the Bogside. He received internal injuries and suffered a heart attack and, though treated in hospital, never recovered. In November 1970 the Chief Constable, Sir Arthur Young, says there is a 'conspiracy of silence' among members of the RUC over the identity of those involved in the incident.

While Samuel Devenney is regarded by some as the first victim of the Troubles, others claim that Francis McCloskey, a 67-year-old man from Dungiven found lying by the roadside on the night of 13 July, had been struck by a police baton. He died the following day. In 1994 the RUC includes Mr McCloskey in the official list of those killed in the Troubles.

1 August At a time when the Troubles are about to break out, RUC strength is just over 3,000. The Ulster Special Constabulary has 8,500 part-time and approximately 100 full-time members. By 1991 the RUC will have almost 8,500 members, with a full-time reserve of 3,000 and a part-time reserve of 1,500.

12 August Sectarian rioting in July and early August had been contained by the police, but on 12 August a parade by the Apprentice Boys of Derry leads to a riot as the marchers pass the Bogside. Early in the evening about a thousand policemen with armoured vehicles and water cannons enter the Bogside to try to contain the rioting. The rioters throw stones and petrol bombs from behind barricades and drive the police back towards the city centre. By midnight, however, the RUC, using CS gas, have advanced again and reached the centre of the Bogside. Commenting on the use of tear gas, the Deputy Inspector-General of the RUC (and later Chief Constable), Graham Shillington, says the police 'would have been completely overrun and there would have been a great deal of damaged property ... Our chaps are still dead tired. We haven't got the manpower to keep these groups apart.'

The success of the police is short-lived, and the 'Battle of the Bogside' will eventually lead to the erection of more permanent barricades in nationalist working-class areas in Belfast and Derry and the creation of 'no-go' areas, where the police and army are unable to operate. The 'Free Derry' area of the Bogside becomes the most famous.

As rioting spreads to other areas it quickly deteriorates into open sectarian conflict, as Protestant fears are raised that the existence of Northern Ireland is under threat. In Belfast, fires destroy hundreds of houses, leaving thousands of people, most of them Catholics, homeless. In 1972 the Scarman Report will estimate that 1.6 per cent of all households in Belfast were forced to move in July, August and September 1969; 1,505 of these are Catholic and 315 Protestant. The report suggests that 5.3 per cent of all Catholic households and 0.4 per cent of Protestant households in Belfast were forced to move in the three months after June 1969. In 1974 a report by the Community Relations Commission will estimate that 60,000 people in Belfast, more than 10 per cent of the city's population, will have been forced to move by February 1973. In general, Catholics are forced out of east and north Belfast and Protestants out of west Belfast.

13 August As rioting continues, the Taoiseach, Jack Lynch, makes a television broadcast in which he announces that Irish army field hospitals would be set up near the border. 'It is clear now that the present situation cannot be allowed to continue. It is evident that the Stormont government is no longer in control of the situation. Indeed the present situation is the inevitable outcome of the policies pursued for decades by successive Stormont governments. It is clear also that the Irish government can no longer stand by and see innocent people injured and perhaps worse.'

14 August With the RUC exhausted after several days of rioting, all USC members are told to report to the nearest police station for duty. More importantly, the British government agrees to the request of the Northern Ireland government for troops to be used, and a company of the Prince of Wales's Own Regiment goes on duty in Derry. With the widespread deployment of British troops the increased involvement of the London government in Northern Ireland matters becomes inevitable.

The deployment of troops leads to Lieutenant-General Sir Ian Freeland, General Officer Commanding troops in Northern Ireland, becoming Director of Operations in security matters on 28 August. The position of GOC is to remain one of the most important posts in Northern Ireland until at least the late seventies, when the policy of 'police primacy' leads to the RUC taking the lead in security matters instead of the army.

In Armagh, John Gallagher, a thirty-year-old father of three, is shot dead after rioting had broken out at the end of a civil rights demonstration. No-one is charged in connection with his death, though the shot that killed him is believed to have been fired by a member of the Special Constabulary. John Gallagher is considered at that time the first 'official' victim of the Troubles.

Nine-year-old Patrick Rooney, shot in the head at his home at Divis Towers, Belfast, is the first child killed in the Troubles. Herbert Roy (26) and David Linton (48) die during riots on the Crumlin Road. They are the first Protestants to be killed during the Troubles.

The Arrival of British Troops

The decision to send in troops was taken in the middle of August 1969. They were well received in nationalist areas. Nevertheless, as early as 11 September the Home Secretary, James Callaghan, was confiding to Richard Crossman: 'Life was very bleak ... there was no prospect of a solution. He had anticipated [that] the honeymoon wouldn't last very long and it hadn't. The British troops were tired and were no longer popular and the terrible thing was that the only solutions would take ten years, if they would ever work at all' (Crossman, *Diaries of a Cabinet Minister, vol. 3,* p. 636). The full intractability of the conflict was becoming tragically clear to British policy-makers; the outline of the modern Ulster crisis was already in place. Was there any realistic way of avoiding this tragic impasse? Harold Wilson had always insisted that the arrival of troops would imply accompanying constitutional change: the implementation of direct rule. Nevertheless, it remained a fact that for most British policy-makers on the Northern Ireland Committee of the Cabinet the arrival of troops—which was postponed for as long as possible—was the minimum possible form of intervention by the British state.

It is arguable that the decision to send in the troops, while leaving the Stormont regime intact, was the greatest mistake of British policy during the Troubles. The effect was to allow the Provisional IRA to present the British army as the tool of the 'Orange' Stormont Ascendancy regime. The Provisionals also had the great advantage that they had a realistically achievable transitional objective: the abolition of Stormont. Austin

Currie, one of the leading nationalist politicians of his generation, was later to argue powerfully that the British government 'should have taken that extra step and suspended Stormont. Had that happened in 1969 then I believe that a lot of the trouble and a lot of the deaths that occurred after that could have been avoided.' In reply, Callaghan explained the position of the British government: 'Public opinion would not have been ready. We would not have been in a position to handle the situation. We did not have enough understanding of it at that time.' Callaghan in fact had favoured further political reform, but the Defence Secretary, Denis Healy, insisted that Chichester-Clark should be pushed 'only as far as he wanted to go.' It is also worth noting that the original British decision in 1921 to establish devolved arrangements for Northern Ireland—against the wishes of many Unionists—rather implied that the elected government of Northern Ireland should be allowed to sort out its own problems.

15 August The Third Battalion of the Light Infantry Regiment takes up duty in west Belfast. Fifteen-year-old Gerald McAuley, shot near Bombay Street, Belfast, is the first member of the IRA to be killed in the Troubles.

19 August The British and Northern Ireland governments meet in London for two days and issue a joint policy statement that comes to be known as the Downing Street Declaration. It says that the United Kingdom government reaffirms 'that nothing which has happened in recent weeks in Northern Ireland derogates from the clear pledges made by successive United Kingdom governments that Northern Ireland should not cease to be a part of the United Kingdom without the consent of the people of Northern Ireland ... The Border is not an issue.' It continues by saying that affairs in Northern Ireland are entirely a domestic United Kingdom matter and that troops will be withdrawn when law and order has been restored. The British government welcomes reforms in the Northern Ireland local government franchise, in local government areas and in the allocation of public housing and the creation of a Parliamentary Commissioner for Administration and machinery for considering citizens' grievances as demonstrating the 'determination of the Northern Ireland government that there shall be full equality of treatment for all citizens. Both governments have agreed that the momentum of internal reform should be maintained.'

It concludes: 'The two governments ... have reaffirmed that in all legislation and executive decisions of government every citizen of Northern Ireland is entitled to the same equality of treatment and freedom from discrimination as obtains in the rest of the United Kingdom, irrespective of political views or religion.'

As a sign of the growing involvement of the British government in Northern Ireland matters, the statement also announces the appointment of two senior British civil servants as liaison officers at Stormont. The relationship between the British and Northern Ireland civil servants is far from ideal; the British have some documents marked *UK eyes only* to exclude Northern Ireland civil servants from information.

22 August The *Irish Times* suggests that 'a decade of direct rule by Westminster might change the North so much that, ideologically, the Nationalist position of the population might drop out of the tradition of Irish nationalism ... If Westminster were to use the North as an example of a new federal system of government, money, ideas and energy would be poured in to such an extent [that] the standard of living for everyone could rise so high that the rest of Ireland would be left behind.'

26 August Oliver Wright and Alec Baker, two English civil servants, arrive in Belfast to act as liaison officers with Stormont.

27 August The Home Secretary, James Callaghan, visits Northern Ireland for talks with the Unionist government and other groups. He puts pressure on the Stormont government to introduce further reforms, including the reconstruction of the RUC (the Hunt Committee had been appointed to look into this the previous day). The Northern Ireland government sets up a tribunal under Lord Justice Scarman to inquire into the course of events that had led to the riots and, on 29 August, at the end of the meeting with Callaghan, commits itself to further reforms, particularly in the area of government administration.

29 August An article in the *Spectator* compares James Chichester-Clark to Gustáv Husák, the submissive leader who had replaced Alexander Dubček in Czechoslovakia. 'Certainly there is no need to abolish Stormont and revert to direct Westminster rule so long as Major Chichester-Clark is prepared to play Husák to Whitehall's Kremlin ... all that can be done now is to reaffirm that the border is a permanency … and then to hope that within this secure context, the forces of reason will, gradually, once more begin to prevail over those of unreason.'

9 September James Chichester-Clark announces a decision by the army to erect a 'peace line' in parts of Belfast to keep Protestants and Catholics apart and help contain rioting.

12 September The Cameron Report into disturbances in Northern Ireland is published. It says (para. 142): 'The conclusions at which we arrived after the evidence was heard and considered, that certain at least of the grievances fastened upon by the Northern Ireland Civil Rights Association and its supporters, in particular those which were concerned with the allocation of houses, discrimination in local authority appointments, limitations on local electoral franchise and deliberate manipulation of ward boundaries and electoral areas, were justified in fact is confirmed by decisions already taken by the Northern Ireland government since these disturbances began.'

9 October The British Home Secretary, James Callaghan, pays a second visit to Northern Ireland for two days of discussions with the Stormont government. The meetings end with a communiqué setting out a list of commitments to further reforms regarding the police, legal system, and administration. The Northern Ireland government agrees to establish a central housing authority and to re-examine local government reform in the light of this decision and to keep under review the adequacy of laws against incitement to hatred.

The communiqué also accepts the recommendations of the Hunt Report on the police in Northern Ireland, which is also published on 10 October. The Hunt Committee recommends that the RUC become an unarmed civilian force and that the B Specials be replaced by a new RUC reserve and a locally recruited part-time military force under the control of the British army. The legislation bringing the Ulster Defence Regiment is passed by Parliament in London in December.

While most Catholics welcome the changes, Protestants remain at best sceptical and at worst hostile to what are seen as concessions made in the face of nationalist coercion. The recommendations of the report lead to two nights of rioting by loyalists on the Shankill Road, and on 11 October Constable Victor Arbuckle (29) becomes the first policeman to be killed in the Troubles. He is shot and killed on the Shankill Road, probably by the UVF.

Another area covered by the 10 October communiqué is that of fair employment for all sections of the community, a problem that will prove to be the most intractable of the demands made by the civil rights movement. In the public sector the Unionist government addresses the question of fair employment by extending the powers of the Parliamentary Commissioner for Administration from April 1970 to cover personnel matters in the Northern Ireland Civil Service. It also obtains declarations of equality of employment opportunity from public bodies and local authorities; and the new Ministry of Community Relations is charged with ensuring that public employers adopt approved employment procedures. A commission is established in June 1970 to review local government appointment procedures, and on 22 June 1971 Brian Faulkner announces that those tendering for government contracts will be required to give an undertaking that they will not practise discrimination in the performance of the contract.

Even at this time it is apparent that the most difficult area of the fair employment issue lies in the private sector. In August 1971 a Northern Ireland government paper notes: 'Account has to be taken of practical problems in a wide variety of different locations and circumstances. It is important to distinguish discriminatory practices as such from the whole complex of factors—such as accidents of location, the particular blend of industrial skills required in the labour force, or traditional methods of recruitment—which affect the balance of employment in any given concern' (*A Record of Constructive Change*).

10 October Sir Arthur Young, Commissioner of the City of London Police, becomes Chief Constable of the RUC, at the personal request of Harold Wilson. He is appointed to introduce the reforms recommended by the Hunt Report; but while he attempts to create a force that will be acceptable to all sections of the community he does so at a time when violence is beginning to increase rapidly. Unionists feel, therefore, that he is unduly soft on republicans.

29 October In line with a commitment given in the 29 August communiqué to designate a minister to have special responsibilities for community relations, an act establishing the Ministry of Community Relations becomes law. The first minister, the Unionist MP Dr Robert

Simpson, is appointed in the first instance a Minister of State (junior minister) in the Prime Minister's Department; on taking up the post he resigns from the Orange Order and the Masonic Order. The department is charged with monitoring action to put the policy contained in the joint communiqués into effect and with advising other departments on community relations aspects of their work, assisting the Community Relations Commission, and administering payments to projects designed to improve social amenities in urban areas suffering from social deprivation.

25 November As part of the reform programme agreed on 29 August the Commissioner for Complaints Act (Northern Ireland) becomes law. The Commissioner for Complaints deals with the grievances of individuals against local councils and public bodies. The Commissioner is independent of the government and reports to the Northern Ireland Parliament (there is no similar position in either the Republic or Britain).

Another commitment given in the August communiqué, to ensure the proper representation of minorities by fair electoral laws, practices and boundaries and the appropriate inclusion of minority representatives to appointed posts, is largely met by an act that had been introduced before the Downing Street Declaration. The Electoral Law Act (Northern Ireland) institutes universal adult suffrage for local elections (instead of restricting the vote to ratepayers, as before). The same act introduces votes for all at the age of eighteen in both parliamentary and local elections.

28 December The split in the IRA and the birth of the Provisionals is signalled by a statement from the 'Provisional Army Council' that says: 'In view of the decision by a majority of delegates at an unrepresentative convention of the IRA to recognise the British, Six-County and 26-County parliaments, we, the minority of delegates at that convention ... do hereby repudiate that compromising decision and reaffirm the fundamental Republican position ... The adoption of the compromising policy referred to is a logical outcome of an obsession in recent years with parliamentary politics with the consequent undermining of the basic military role of the Irish Republican Army. The failure to provide the maximum defence possible of our people in Belfast is ample evidence of this neglect' (quoted by O'Clery, *Phrases Make History Here,* p. 131).

DEATHS ARISING FROM THE TROUBLES: 14. SHOOTINGS: 73. BOMBS PLANTED: 10. FIREARMS FOUND: 14. EXPLOSIVES FOUND: 102 kg (225 lb).

1970

By January 1970 the British government appears to believe that the Northern Ireland problem has been resolved by the reform programme. As a result, by February three of the eight extra army units have returned to Britain. This does not reflect the situation on the ground, where relations between Protestants and Catholics continue to deteriorate.

11 January At the Sinn Féin ardfheis in Dublin the republican movement openly splits when a majority of delegates (though not the two-thirds required to change policy) vote in favour of taking seats in the Belfast, London and Dublin parliaments in future. Consequently, 257 supporters of the 'Provisional Army Council' walk out and set up their offices in Kevin Street, Dublin, while Official Sinn Féin maintains its offices in Gardiner Place. Two leading commentators on the Provisional IRA (Bishop and Mallie, *The Provisional IRA,* p. 137) noted: 'The nomenclature, with its echoes of the 1916 rebels' provisional government of the Irish Republic, reflected the delegates' belief that the irregularities surrounding the extraordinary convention [of the IRA the previous year] ... rendered it null and void. Any decisions it took were revocable. They proposed to call another convention within twelve months to resolve the leadership of the movement. Until this happened they regarded themselves as a provisional organisation. Ten months later, after the September 1970 Army Council meeting, a statement was issued declaring that the "provisional" period was now officially over, but by then the name had stuck fast.'

The Marxist Officials, who favour political participation, become known as the 'Stickies', because their Easter lilies during commemorations of the Easter 1916 Rising are self-adhesive; the Provisionals' Easter lilies continue to be affixed with a pin.

26 March The Police Act (Northern Ireland) comes into effect. Under the act the Northern Ireland government accepts the principle of a civilianised and unarmed police force and establishes a Police Authority representative of the whole community. The act also establishes a volunteer reserve force, the RUC Reserve, which at the outset consists of 1,500 men.

29 March In Derry 5,000 demonstrators take part in an Easter Rising commemoration march that stops outside the city's main police station. Part of the crowd tries to break down the main gates of the station, with the result that twelve soldiers are injured and seventeen people are arrested. Soldiers later seal off the Bogside estate in Derry after clashes with rioters.

1 April The Ulster Defence Regiment (UDR), inaugurated to replace the B Specials (disbanded on 30 April), becomes operational. The regiment has a strength of 4,000, with a target of 6,000. It is envisaged that the UDR will assist the regular army by guarding installations, carrying out patrols, and operating check-points and road-blocks; it is not to be used in crowd control.

3 April Following three nights of rioting in Ballymurphy in Belfast, which sees the extensive use of CS gas during the first major clash between nationalists and the British army, the GOC, Sir Ian Freeland, announces a new 'get tough' policy and warns that anyone manufacturing, carrying or throwing a petrol bomb is liable to a maximum of ten years' imprisonment. 'What's more, they are liable to be shot dead in the street if, after a warning, they persist.' The riots also lead to the expulsion of Protestants from the New Barnsley estate nearby, leading Austin Currie to comment that 'the minority in Northern Ireland were rapidly throwing away the huge amount of international good will which they had earned over the past eighteen months' (*Irish Times,* 3 April 1970). The arrival of 500 more soldiers brings the total in Northern Ireland to 6,500.

16 April Two Stormont by-elections return Ian Paisley (standing as a Protestant Unionist) for the Bannside constituency formerly held by Terence O'Neill and William Beattie (also Protestant Unionist) for South Antrim. The by-elections have been described as 'probably the most vital in the history of the Stormont House of Commons' (Flackes and Elliott, *Northern Ireland: A Political Directory,* p. 365), as they accentuate increasing unionist dissatisfaction with the reforms carried out under Chichester-Clark.

21 April The Alliance Party of Northern Ireland is formed, with the aim of uniting Protestants and Catholics on a platform of moderate policies. One of the party's most prominent members, Oliver Napier, a Catholic solicitor from Belfast, becomes leader of the Alliance Party in 1972. Unlike existing 'centre' parties, such as the NILP and smaller Ulster Liberal Party, Alliance concentrates almost entirely on Northern Ireland problems and, with no past reputation to hinder it, quickly acquires the 'moderate' vote at the expense of the other parties.

28 May In Dublin the former Minister for Finance Charles Haughey and former Minister for Agriculture Neil Blaney appear in court in connection with a plot to smuggle arms to the IRA in the North. They deny any involvement and are released on bail. Blaney is cleared of gun-running charges on 2 July and Haughey on 23 October. The defence argued that the guns had been imported as part of an officially sanctioned operation for the Irish army.

29 May The Macrory Report on the reform of local government is completed. The committee, headed by Sir Patrick Macrory, recommends the abolition of the old system of local government based on the six counties and their replacement with twenty-six district councils. The new system would also establish area boards to control health, education and library services. In December the Unionist government at Stormont announces that it will accept the recommendations.

While this centralisation seemed reasonable from a purely functional point of view, the drawback was that Macrory intended the Northern Parliament to run the newly centralised services. With the introduction of direct rule in 1972 control of these services and the power to nominate members to the new boards passed to the Secretary of State and his ministers. Locally elected representatives, of whatever political persuasion, would retain little influence. While they did keep control of the functions of the new district councils, this amounted to little more than responsibility for refuse collection, public toilets, and crematoria and cemeteries—'bins, bogs, and burials,' as it came to be known. The abolition of Stormont was thus to deprive Unionists (as well as the other parties) of any real power either at the provincial or the local level of government. The lack of democratic accountability to the people by those who controlled these newly centralised services would come to be called the 'Macrory gap'.

18 June The Westminster general election returns a Conservative government led by Edward Heath. In Northern Ireland the Ulster Unionist Party wins only eight of the twelve seats, despite taking 54.3 per cent of the poll. Ian Paisley is elected MP for North Antrim and Frank McManus (Unity) for Fermanagh-South Tyrone. Gerry Fitt and Bernadette Devlin hold West Belfast and Mid-Ulster, respectively. The NILP, with almost 100,000 votes (12.6 per cent of the poll) fails to win a seat.

22 June Bernadette Devlin's appeal against a six-month prison sentence for her part in the disturbances in the Bogside area of Derry in August 1969 is dismissed. On 26 June she is arrested at a road-block on her way to a meeting and taken to Armagh Women's Prison. Supporters claim she had intended to give herself up later. Following the arrest there is severe rioting that evening in Derry, where a crowd pelts troops with stones and petrol bombs before the soldiers use CS gas to break up the riot.

26 June The daughters of an IRA man killed in a premature explosion in Derry are the first women to die in the Troubles.

27 June Fierce rioting occurs in north and east Belfast. In the first sustained military action by the Provisional IRA, snipers enter the grounds of St Matthew's Catholic Church on the lower Newtownards Road and fire onto the road for five hours in the course of prolonged intercommunal rioting. During the day five Protestants and a Catholic are shot dead and twenty-six people are wounded. The following day about five hundred Catholic workers are expelled from the Harland and Wolff shipyard in east Belfast by Protestants.

28 June The Northern Ireland Prime Minister, James Chichester-Clark, says that a serious situation has developed and that stern measures will be taken to deal with gunmen. The army commander, General Sir Ian Freeland, warns that anyone carrying a gun is liable to be shot.

1 July Reginald Maudling pays his first visit to Northern Ireland as British Home Secretary. Bombarded by conflicting demands and opinions from those he meets, he gratefully boards the plane back to London and remarks, 'For God's sake bring me a large Scotch. What a bloody awful country!' (Sunday Times Insight Team, *Ulster*, p. 213).

Stormont passes the Criminal Justice (Temporary Provisions) Act, creating a mandatory prison sentence for rioting. On the following day the Prevention of Incitement to Hatred Act is also passed.

3 July A curfew lasting thirty-four hours (except for a two-hour break to allow shopping) is imposed on the (Catholic) Lower Falls area of Belfast, covering approximately fifty streets. An army helicopter circles overhead, warning people that they will be arrested if they remain on the streets. A search of the area conducted by the army during the curfew uncovers 100 firearms, 100 home-made bombs, 250 lb of explosives, 21,000 rounds of ammunition, and 8 two-way radios. Residents claim that the soldiers have caused unnecessary damage, have stolen property and abused locals during the searches. During the curfew gun battles break out between the army and both wings of the IRA, resulting in five civilians being killed (two of them snipers) and sixty people (including fifteen soldiers) being injured.

The curfew is often seen as the turning-point in relations between the Catholic working-class community in Belfast and the British army, in that the operation so soured relations that the army would no longer be seen as the protectors of the Catholic community. At the same time the failure of the army and police to defeat the IRA and prevent 'no-go areas' being established encourages the growth of paramilitary groups in Protestant working-class areas.

6 July The Irish Minister for External Affairs, Dr Patrick Hillery, visits Belfast secretly and tours the Falls Road area. Chichester-Clark issues a statement saying that he deplores this act, especially at a time of such tension. In London the Foreign Secretary, Sir Alec Douglas-Home, calls the visit a diplomatic discourtesy.

Growing fears that Orange parades to be held on 13 July (as 12 July is a Sunday) could lead to widespread rioting and deaths lead Maudling to formally request Orange leaders to call them off. They refuse, saying that to do so would do more harm than good. As a result, large-scale military preparations are made, with 11,300 soldiers and 3,000 RUC and UDR men on duty. Despite these fears the parades, involving 100,000 Orangemen, pass off peacefully.

Throughout the summer the Provisionals continue a bombing campaign aimed at allowing them to set the agenda for nationalist politics. They also predict that the collapse of the Stormont government would be the first step towards a united Ireland.

16 July A bomb explodes in a bank in High Street, Belfast, injuring thirty people.

23 July The Stormont government bans all public processions until January 1971.

30 July A fresh spate of rioting leads to a youth being shot dead by the army. The incident leads to rioting in Catholic areas of Belfast between 2 and 4 August.

31 July The army uses rubber bullets (officially called 'baton rounds') for the first time during a riot on the New Lodge Road, Belfast. The rounds are six inches long, weigh five ounces, and have a range of fifty yards, but they are not intended to be lethal. 55,000 have been fired by 1975, when hard plastic rounds replace the earlier rubber versions.

2 August The Stormont government increases the reward offered for information leading to the arrest of terrorists from £10,000 to £50,000. The increased reward fails to produce any result.

12 August Two RUC constables are killed at Crossmaglen by a booby-trap bomb in a car.

21 August The Social Democratic and Labour Party is formed, with Gerry Fitt from Belfast as party leader and John Hume from Derry as deputy leader. Reformist in nature, the SDLP is nevertheless committed to a united Ireland as its long-term, and arguably chief, objective.

26 August The Minister of Home Affairs, Robert Porter, resigns from the Cabinet for health reasons; Chichester-Clark assumes responsibility for Home Affairs himself. John Taylor, a staunch critic of the reformist wing of the Unionist Party, is appointed Minister of State in the Ministry of Home Affairs, which is responsible for the police. James Chichester-Clark hopes to placate the right wing of the Unionist Party by making this appointment.

4 September One IRA man is killed and another injured when a bomb they are placing at an electricity transformer in Belfast explodes prematurely.

15 September RUC members vote narrowly in favour of remaining unarmed. As attacks on the police continue, however, this policy is slowly broken down, and the RUC is eventually fully rearmed.

23 September Sir Arthur Young resigns as Chief Constable of the RUC to return to his duties as Commissioner of the City of London Police. He is succeeded by his deputy, Graham Shillington, in November.

26 September There is rioting in the (Protestant) Shankill Road area of Belfast, lasting four nights and resulting in buses and cars being burned and 200 civilians and 100 soldiers and police being injured. The trouble begins after youths supporting Linfield Football Club attack the (Catholic) Unity Flats as they return from a football game.

1 October At the British Labour Party's annual conference the NILP unsuccessfully calls for a merger of the two parties.

During October the NICRA threatens to go back on the streets, claiming that local government reforms are being deliberately delayed. Chichester Clark says that the legislation on the local government franchise is being prepared and that an electoral system based on proportional representation is being considered.

21 October Bernadette Devlin is released from prison, having served four months of her sentence.

30 October Riots in the (Catholic) Ardoyne area of Belfast lasting three nights involve anti-personnel bombs being used against soldiers.

17 November Graham Shillington is sworn in as Chief Constable of the RUC.

By the end of the year, despite hardening attitudes and the calls of the former Unionist ministers Harry West and William Craig for a tougher security policy, Chichester-Clark seems to have strengthened his position.

DEATHS ARISING FROM THE TROUBLES: 25. SHOOTINGS: 213. BOMBS PLANTED: 170. FIREARMS FOUND: 324. EXPLOSIVES FOUND: 305 kg (670 lb).

1971

January The split between the Official and Provisional IRA works its way onto the streets, with the Provisionals gaining control in almost all areas except the Lower Falls district of Belfast.

10 January Four men are tarred and feathered by the IRA for breaking and entering and for peddling drugs.

13 January Riots break out in the (Catholic) Ballymurphy estate, Belfast; two days later riots also start in Ardoyne.

23 January There is rioting in the (Protestant) Shankill Road area of Belfast.

3 February Soldiers searching for arms are attacked by women, leading to riots and gun battles on the Crumlin Road and in Ardoyne, Belfast. On the following day Lieutenant-General Vernon Erskine-Crum succeeds Sir Ian Freeland as army commander in Northern Ireland; however, he suffers a heart attack twelve days later and dies in hospital on 17 March. On 2 March he is replaced by Lieutenant-General Harry Tuzo, who proves to be a controversial appointment in that he plays a greater political role in Northern Ireland affairs than any other army commander.

6 February On the New Lodge Road, Belfast, machine-gun fire from the Provisional IRA kills Gunner Robert Curtis of the 32nd Battery, Royal Artillery; he is the first British soldier to die in the Troubles while on duty. On 15 May the Provisional gunman who killed Curtis is shot dead during an exchange of gunfire with the British army in Belfast—by coincidence, he is killed in Curtis Street (Bishop and Mallie, *The Provisional IRA,* p. 176).

8 February A five-year-old girl is knocked down and killed by an army vehicle, leading to a fresh wave of riots.

With rioting continuing and the British army apparently unable to resolve the situation quickly, public opinion in England begins to move towards the view that troops should be withdrawn, apparently under the impression that the Troubles could be contained within Northern Ireland and would no longer concern them.

9 February Two BBC engineers and three building workers are killed by a land mine near the transmitter on Brougher Mountain, Co. Tyrone.

13 February The wearing of military-style uniforms by 'subversive organisations' is banned by the Stormont government.

25 February The Housing Executive Act (Northern Ireland) becomes law, requiring that the building and allocation of all public authority houses be the responsibility of the Northern Ireland Housing Executive, rather than local councils and the Northern Ireland Housing Trust. In 1970–71 a record total of 13,000 new houses was built; the plan for 1970–75 called for a total of 73,500 new houses, at a cost of £300 million.

26 February Two unarmed RUC men are machine-gunned to death in an IRA attack in Alliance Avenue, Belfast. On 28 February members of the RUC are issued with flak jackets and bulletproof vests, and on 1 March police in some areas are reissued with guns to protect themselves. In March the IRA begins a systematic plan of bombing police stations and attempts to murder off-duty RUC men and their families.

8 March The feud between the Provisional and Official wings of the IRA breaks out into a gun battle in Leeson Street, Belfast.

9 March Three off-duty soldiers, two of them brothers, aged seventeen and eighteen, are lured from a pub by members of the Provisional IRA and murdered on the outskirts of Belfast. The suspected killers are later tracked down by Scotland Yard but escape to the Republic. The widespread revulsion at the incident increases loyalist pressure on James Chichester-Clark to pursue a tougher security policy, including the complete rearming of the police, the creation of a 'third force', and the introduction of internment.

The incident also gives an identity to gangs of loyalist youths called 'tartan gangs', who adopt tartan scarves as a 'uniform' in memory of the three Scottish soldiers, each gang with its own distinctive tartan. The gangs become involved in clashes with rival gangs of Catholic youths and in attacks on Catholic homes and property in many towns. Confrontations with the police and army and attacks on the homes of policemen are also fairly common occurrences. The gangs are particularly strong in east Belfast. During a five-day period in late April and early May 1972 tartan gangs become involved in intermittent clashes with both Catholic youths from the Short Strand area and with the RUC. Vanguard representatives finally succeed in calming the situation after talks with gang members and the police. As time passes, however, the tartan gangs increasingly fall under the influence of the paramilitary Ulster Defence Association.

16 March James Chichester-Clark flies to London to discuss the deteriorating security situation with Edward Heath, but with London fearful of alienating Catholic opinion, he receives no help. On 20 March he resigns after the British government responds to a set of demands for a tougher security policy, including the military occupation of no-go areas, by promising only an extra 1,300 soldiers. Three days later Brian Faulkner becomes Prime Minister when he defeats William Craig by twenty-six to four in a vote by Unionist MPs. Faulkner's Cabinet, announced on 25 March, includes Harry West as Minister of Agriculture and the former NILP Stormont MP David Bleakley as Minister of Community Relations.

23 March As part of the reform of local government the Local Government Boundaries Act (Northern Ireland) becomes law. The act provides for the appointment of a Boundaries Commissioner to recommend boundaries and names for the twenty-six new district councils and the electoral districts and wards into which they will be divided.

10 April In Belfast there are two separate marches by republicans to commemorate the Easter Rising. The first, organised by the Provisional IRA, attracts a crowd of about seven thousand, while a later march by the Official IRA has approximately half that number.

13 April IRA gunmen fire on a crowd returning from an Orange parade, leading to fierce rioting in mainly Protestant east Belfast.

25 April The census is held. The results will show the population of Northern Ireland to be 1,519,640, with 477,921 (31.4 per cent) describing themselves as Catholics, 405,717 (26.7 per cent) as Presbyterians, 334,318 (22.0 per cent) Church of Ireland, 71,235 (4.7 per cent) Methodist, and 87,938 (5.8 per cent) belonging to other denominations; 142,511 (9.4 per cent) had no religious affiliation or did not reply to the question.

13 May In line with the October 1969 commitment to relieve the RUC of responsibility for prosecutions and to establish a system of independent public prosecutors, Faulkner announces the government's intention to appoint a Director of Public Prosecutions for Northern Ireland, responsible to the Northern Ireland Attorney-General, who in turn will be responsible to the Northern Ireland Parliament.

14 May The Ulster '71 exhibition planned to celebrate the Jubilee of Northern Ireland is opened by the Lord Mayor of London, despite fears that it would have to be abandoned in the face of civil unrest. The exhibition proves remarkably successful and attracts 700,000 visitors before it closes in September.

25 May Sergeant Michael Willets of the Parachute Regiment dies saving two adults and two children after a bomb is thrown into Springfield Road police station. Sergeant Willets is awarded the George Cross posthumously. In March 1985 Sergeant Willets' medal is sold for £20,250.

13 June Orangemen defy a ban and march through the mainly Catholic village of Dungiven, leading to a clash with the army and police that is eventually broken up by the use of rubber bullets and CS gas.

22 June Brian Faulkner announces a plan to involve all parties in a parliamentary committee system at Stormont, with key chairmanships going to members of minority parties. He states: 'It must be recognised that any concept of participation [by nationalist parties] will be hollow which does not recognise the duty to participate in bearing the burdens of the state as well as enjoying its advantages, and that no duty is more important than to mount a united opposition to terrorism' (*NI Parliamentary Debates,* vol. 82, col. 8). The scheme is welcomed with some enthusiasm by the SDLP but is undermined within weeks when the party withdraws from Stormont.

8 July There are severe riots in Derry after two men, who the army claim were armed, are shot dead. On 12 July, John Hume announces that unless there is an impartial inquiry into the circumstances of the two men's deaths the SDLP will withdraw from Stormont. When no inquiry is forthcoming the SDLP withdraws on 16 July. They then proceed to set up an 'Assembly of the Northern Irish People' and call for a campaign of civil disobedience, including the non-payment of rent and rates and the withdrawal of Catholics from public bodies.

11 July As the traditional Orange celebrations approach, the IRA steps up its terror campaign to provoke Protestant-Catholic confrontations in an attempt to bring about direct rule, which they see as a first step towards a united Ireland. There are large explosions in central Belfast, but only nine people are injured, and the parades on 12 July pass off peacefully. With the IRA campaign seemingly beyond the government's control, fears of a 'Protestant backlash' continue, putting pressure on the authorities to take some action. At the same time nationalist leaders threaten that there will be outright rebellion if internment is introduced. By early August, with no sign of a reduction in civil disorder, the British government finally accedes to Faulkner's request to introduce internment.

9 August 'Operation Demetrius' brings the introduction of internment without trial. In a series of dawn swoops the army attempts to arrest 452 men, though only 342, mainly from the Official IRA, are captured. Of those arrested, 105 are released within two days; the rest are detained.

In a statement announcing the move, Brian Faulkner says: 'I have therefore decided after weighing all the relevant considerations, including the views of the security authorities, and after consultation with Her Majesty's government in the United Kingdom, to exercise where necessary the powers of detention and internment vested in me as Minister of Home Affairs ... We are, quite simply, at war with the terrorist, and in a state of war many sacrifices have to be made' (quoted in *Keesing's Contemporary Archives,* p. 24912). The Taoiseach, Jack Lynch, says the introduction of internment is 'deplorable evidence of the political poverty of Ulster's policies.'

16 August In Belfast the chief of staff of the Provisional IRA, Joe Cahill, gives a press conference at which he says only thirty IRA men have been interned.

Internment

The introduction of internment brought an upsurge in violence, both in the short term and the medium term. Some of those killed on 9 August included Father Hugh Mullan—the first priest killed in the Troubles—

who was shot while administering the last rites during rioting in Belfast. Private Winston Donnell, shot at a road-block near Strabane, was the first UDR member to be killed. As Northern Ireland sat on the brink of civil war, Protestants were forced out of the Ardoyne area of Belfast, setting fire to 200 houses as they left rather than have them occupied by Catholics. Women and children leaving the area came under machine-gun fire. Two thousand Protestants were left homeless, while 2,500 Catholics left Belfast for refugee camps set up in the Republic. In the following days barricades were erected in Catholic working-class areas and the Official IRA engaged in a gun battle with the army in Belfast.

By 12 August twenty-two people had been killed and up to seven thousand people (the majority Catholics) left homeless as houses were burned to the ground. In the year as a whole, 34 people had been killed before the introduction of internment but 140 died after that date. While internment in itself provided limited, if any, security benefits, the social and political reaction it created far outweighed this. As a result, violence increased for the rest of the year, and the SDLP refused to become involved in political talks while internment continued. It is clear, however, that the main winners from the introduction of internment were the Provisional IRA, as their chief chroniclers wrote. 'The militancy of the young men of Derry, Belfast and an increasing number of rural areas was deepened by the experience, to the point where some of the Provisional leaders believed that a full-scale encounter with the British forces was now feasible. More significantly they had been handed an endlessly productive mine of propaganda. Internment succeeded in uniting the IRA's fiercest enemies inside the Catholic community behind them and lent some credence to their claims to legitimacy.' (Bishop and Mallie, *The Provisional IRA*, p. 189).

The intensity of the reaction also made it difficult for the British government to openly consider direct rule at that time, as this was the goal the IRA proclaimed as an intermediate step towards a united Ireland. Despite this, as Faulkner's gamble visibly failed and the British army found itself the target of vastly increased Catholic animosity, the introduction of direct rule was widely expected. By October 1971 even Ian Paisley was declaring that it was imminent. The events of Bloody Sunday on 30 January 1972 only increased the perception that direct rule from Westminster was only a matter of time.

18 August In Strabane the army shoot dead a deaf mute man who they claim was armed.

19 August The British Minister of Defence, Lord Carrington says that some news reporting by the BBC is 'below the standard of fairness, and accuracy, which we are entitled to expect.' His criticism of what he sees as political bias by the BBC is one of the first blows in what is to become a long-running battle with successive governments over the media's coverage of the Troubles.

31 August In the wake of allegations that those arrested when internment had been introduced had been ill-treated, the Northern Ireland government sets up a Committee of Inquiry under Sir Edmund Compton to look into the charges.

1 September A series of explosions over two days results in thirty-nine people being injured by IRA bombs in towns throughout Northern Ireland. An explosion in Belfast on 2 September destroys the offices of the Ulster Unionist Party.

5 September The Army Council of the Provisional IRA produces a set of constitutional proposals centred on the idea of Dáil Uladh—a nine-county Ulster assembly—in an attempt to show their concern for Protestant susceptibilities. They state: 'No compromise can be made on the basic quest for an independent 32-county Irish Republic. But it is equally true that Protestant and Unionist fears of being swamped in the Republic must be considered. Their fears could be adequately satisfied if they formed a large part, possibly a majority, in an Ulster regional parliament' (*Republican News,* 11 September 1971).

The Provisionals' belief that a British declaration of intent to withdraw from Northern Ireland will lead Protestants to negotiate is increasingly at odds with actual conditions, where Protestant paramilitary groups were mobilising and Catholics were being killed in a campaign of sectarian assassinations.

6 September William Craig and Rev. Ian Paisley address a crowd of almost twenty thousand at Victoria Park, Belfast, and demand a 'third force' to defend Ulster.

7 September In Derry, fourteen-year-old Annette McGavigan is shot dead when she is caught in cross-fire between the army and the IRA in the Bogside. At the time she is considered the hundredth victim of the Troubles.

12 September Cardinal Conway and five Catholic bishops denounce the IRA and criticise internment. In the statement, Cardinal Conway attacks the 'small group of people who are trying to secure a united Ireland by the use of force ... Who in their sane senses wants to bomb a million Protestants into a united Ireland?'

27 September A two-day meeting begins at Chequers, the British Prime Minister's country residence in Buckinghamshire, involving the British, Irish and Northern Ireland Prime Ministers to discuss matters of common concern.

30 September A Provisional IRA bomb explodes in a bar in the Shankill Road area, killing two men and injuring thirty others. The incident, which is condemned by the Official IRA, leads to sectarian clashes the following day.

During September the Ulster Defence Association is established by the merging of a wide range of Protestant vigilante and paramilitary groups; it assumes the motto 'Law before violence'. For many loyalists the abolition of the B Specials in April 1970 has created a gap in Northern Ireland's defences that the newly formed Ulster Defence Regiment has failed to fill. Meanwhile violence and the mass movement of people to areas that they consider safe continues. In the middle of this chaos Protestant vigilante groups had sprung up in the Belfast area, which merge in the formation of the UDA. The organisation has an overwhelmingly working-class membership, is organised on military lines, and at its peak in 1972 has a membership of between forty and fifty thousand men. The great majority have full-time jobs and play little part in the day-to-day running of the organisation, performing such functions as manning barricades and attending meetings only occasionally; the hard core, however, are often unemployed and spend their time either working for the UDA or frequenting local pubs and clubs.

The UDA provides a medium through which the frustrations of young working-class loyalists can be channelled by manning barricades and taking part in marches and demonstrations. The sight of thousands of UDA men—usually wearing masks or sun-glasses, bush hats, and combat jackets—marching through the centre of Belfast becomes a common one in 1972. The breakdown in social services at local level also leaves a gap that is often filled by the paramilitaries (both loyalist and republican), who assume control of functions ranging from the setting up of their own drinking-clubs to the allocation of housing.

But if the UDA provides certain benefits for working-class Protestants in boosting morale and providing a way for them to show their frustration, there is clearly a more sinister side to many of its activities. The UDA uses kangaroo courts to administer its own justice to those who break its rules, and severe beatings are handed out in 'romper rooms' to those found guilty. Racketeering is another element that emerges early in the UDA's history. And from the outset there is always a section that sees the organisation as little more than a front for attacking Catholics.

7 October 1,500 more soldiers are sent to Northern Ireland to help meet a deteriorating security situation.

23 October The army shoot dead two women in a car in the Falls Road area of Belfast after they say they had been fired on. The following day three youths are shot dead by soldiers in Newry after they attempt to rob a man lodging cash in a night safe.

27 October G. B. Newe, a Catholic, is appointed Minister of State in the Prime Minister's Department at Stormont by Brian Faulkner; he is the first Catholic to hold a ministerial position in the Northern Ireland government. Basil McIvor succeeds David Bleakley as Minister of Community Relations. Bleakley had resigned on 26 September in protest at the introduction of internment and the failure to introduce new political initiatives.

30 October After the collapse of negotiations earlier in the year between Ian Paisley, William Craig and members on the right wing of the Unionist Party to form a new party, Paisley and the Unionist dissident Desmond Boal announce the formation of the Democratic Unionist Party, which will be 'on the right on constitutional issues and on the left on social issues.' The DUP will become a combination of evangelical Protestants living mainly in rural areas and linked to the Free Presbyterian Church and Boal's apparent social radicalism appealing to the working-class constituency in Belfast. The inaugural meeting of the new party takes place in the Ulster Hall, Belfast.

31 October An IRA bomb explodes at the Post Office Tower in London.

1 November There is an upsurge in IRA activity, with two RUC detectives being shot dead by the IRA while they are investigating a burglary in the Andersonstown area of west Belfast. On 7 November two off-duty soldiers are shot dead by the IRA in Armagh, and on 11 November two RUC men are shot dead in north Belfast. On the same day Protestant distrust of the intentions of the British Labour Party towards Northern Ireland is demonstrated when 20,000 workers go on strike in protest at the visit of the shadow Home Secretary, James Callaghan.

11 November In the third incident of its kind during the week, a seventeen-year-old Derry girl has her hair shorn and ink poured over her for 'fraternising' with British soldiers.

12 November The Northern Ireland government announces that the RUC is to be armed with automatic weapons in order to protect police stations.

16 November The Compton Report on press allegations of brutality against detainees is published. It concludes that individuals had not suffered physical brutality but that there had been 'ill-treatment'. There had not been torture but there had been 'in-depth' interrogation, involving hooding, forcing detainees to stand with their arms against walls for long periods, and the use of 'white noise' and food and sleep deprivation to cause confusion. While the committee had investigated charges made by forty detainees, only one gave evidence to the committee.

In the introduction to the report the Home Secretary, Reginald Maudling, writes (para. 14): 'As regards the initial arrests it is clear from the report that there were very few complaints and those there were had, in the Committee's view, very little substance. The record of events reflects great credit on the security forces, who carried out a difficult and dangerous operation in adverse circumstances with commendable restraint and discipline. The more serious allegations which the Committee were able to investigate relate to the subsequent interrogation in depth of 11 individuals. Here again the Committee have found no evidence of physical brutality, still less of torture or brain-washing. Their findings about physical ill-treatment do, however, raise certain questions about the detailed application of the general rules governing interrogation.'

19 November Two IRA escapers from Crumlin Road Prison in Belfast are arrested in a car approaching the border dressed as Catholic priests. They are accompanied by monks from the Cistercian monastery at Portglenone, Co. Antrim, which leads to the monastery being searched by soldiers.

25 November In the House of Commons the Labour Party leader, Harold Wilson, makes a statement on Northern Ireland in which he says: 'Many of us on this side of the house owe part of our political education to the reproductions of the Will Dyson cartoon in the old *Daily Herald* in 1919. Honourable members opposite will know of it too. It was a cartoon of the statesmen of Versailles and a child tragically labelled "Class of 1940". The words said by one of the statesmen were: "Curious, I seem to hear a child weeping." We are Versailles fifty years later—that is Belfast and Derry today, and we have to pause in our own conflicts and ponder what it means. That child crying today wears the insignia of the class of 1980, the class of 1990, the class of all the years there are to come.' (*Hansard,* fifth series, vol. 826, col. 1584).

Wilson then announces his 'fifteen-point plan' for a solution to the Irish problem. Working on the assumption that the effects of the introduction of internment on Catholic politics required a fresh response from the British government, he states: 'I believe that the situation has now gone so far that it is impossible to conceive of an effective long-term solution in which the agenda at least does not include consideration of, and which is not in some way directed to finding a means of achieving, the aspirations envisaged half a century ago, of progress towards a united Ireland ... A substantial term of years will be required before any concept of unification could become a reality, but the dream must be there. If men of moderation have nothing to hope for, men of violence will have something to shoot for' (*Hansard,* fifth series, vol. 826, col. 1586).

Wilson suggests that progress towards a united Ireland would have to be based on Protestant consent and take place over a period of approximately fifteen years. He makes no attempt, however, to explain how or why this consent from Protestants would be forthcoming. The Taoiseach, Jack Lynch, calls the plan 'highly important' but rejects Wilson's idea that the Republic should rejoin the Commonwealth.

29 November In the House of Commons the Home Secretary, Reginald Maudling, announces that up to £50 million will be made available to a new

Northern Ireland Finance Corporation to assist businesses temporarily in difficulty over the next three years.

4 December McGurk's bar in North Queen Street, Belfast, is bombed by the UVF. Fifteen people, including the owner's wife and daughter, are killed and thirteen are injured; another person dies later. This is the greatest loss of civilian life resulting from a single incident until the Omagh bombing of August 1998.

6 December A member of the Salvation Army is killed in an IRA bomb explosion in Belfast.

11 December Four people, including a seven-month-old boy, die when a bomb explodes in a crowded shop on the Shankill Road, Belfast.

12 December A Unionist senator, Jack Barnhill, is murdered by the Official IRA at his home in Strabane. Twenty-two people have been killed in the past eight days.

Relations with the Republic continue to deteriorate throughout the year, with both the Provisional and Official IRA operating openly from their Dublin offices. The British army comes under fire from the Republic on several occasions while 'cratering' border roads in an attempt to slow the easy access of terrorists from the South. Two customs officers, a soldier and a woman are killed in separate incidents as a result of gunfire from the Republic.

DEATHS ARISING FROM THE TROUBLES: 174. SHOOTINGS: 1,756. BOMBS PLANTED: 1,515. FIREARMS FOUND: 716. EXPLOSIVES FOUND: 1,246 kg (2,750 lb)

1972

1 January An editorial in the *Irish Press* says: 'In the North the Catholics have said we've had enough ... The IRA are the hard cutting edge of their grievances and, horrible though many of the deeds which have been done in the North are, the IRA continue to draw support ... Indeed, attempting a settlement without the IRA would be like America ending the Vietnam War without reference to the Viet Cong.'

3 January An IRA bomb explodes in Callender Street, Belfast, injuring over sixty people, including many children.

17 January Seven internees being held on the *Maidstone* in Belfast Lough escape after swimming across the Musgrave Channel, seizing a bus, and escaping into the Markets area.

22 January Despite a ban on parades, civil rights marchers hold parades in Armagh and Magilligan, Co. Derry, where a second internment camp had been opened days earlier. A fight breaks out when soldiers try to prevent them marching towards the camp.

27 January There are gun battles between the army and the IRA at Forkhill, Co. Armagh, along the border with the Republic. Soldiers fire over a thousand rounds.

30 January Thirteen men, all apparently unarmed, are shot dead and seventeen are wounded by the Parachute Regiment in Derry. Another man dies later. The shooting begins at the end of a civil rights rally attended by nearly ten thousand people when part of the crowd try to climb over a street barrier and are forced back by the army with rubber bullets and spray from a water-cannon. More than a hundred youths throw stones and iron bars at the soldiers, and a running battle continues for more than ten minutes.

It has never been established who fired the first shot. Major-General Robert Ford (Commander of Land Forces) later denies that the army fired first and says: 'There is absolutely no doubt that the Parachute Battalion opened up only after they were fired on.' Some claim that a loyalist sniper opened fire as Bernadette Devlin was about to speak to the crowd.

In August 1973 the inquest returned an open verdict on those killed by the army. Nevertheless, for nationalists the events of the day were summed up by the coroner, Hubert O'Neill, when he described the killings as amounting to 'sheer unadulterated bloody murder.'

Bloody Sunday

The events of 30 January 1972 created a wave of anger that swept through the Catholic community. In an interview with RTE the following day John Hume captured the mood of the time by saying: 'Many people down there [the Bogside] feel now that it's a united Ireland or nothing.' In a debate in the House of Commons, Bernadette Devlin, speaking of the Home Secretary, Reginald Maudling, said: 'The minister has stood up and lied to the house. Nobody shot at the paratroops, but somebody will shortly ... I have a right, as the only representative in this house who was an eyewitness, to ask a question of that murdering hypocrite.' She then ran across the chamber, pulled Maudling's hair, and slapped his face. Later she said: 'I didn't shoot him in the back, which is what they did to our people' (Hansard, fifth series, vol. 830, col. 37–43).

Reaction in the Republic was equally hostile, with the *Irish Press* saying: 'If there was an able-bodied man with Republican sympathies within the Derry area who was not in the IRA before yesterday's butchery there will be none tonight.' The Irish ambassador to Britain was recalled in protest at the events of the previous day, and on 1 February the Minister for Foreign Affairs, Dr Patrick Hillery, arriving in New York on his way to speak to the United Nations, said: 'From now on my aim is to get Britain out of Ireland' (quoted by O'Clery, *Phrases Make History Here,* p. 142).

The repercussions of the Derry killings continued on 2 February, when, after a series of anti-British demonstrations throughout the day, the British embassy in Dublin was burned down after it was attacked by a crowd of more than twenty thousand. In the wake of the incident the *Irish Press* wrote: 'At every level, constitutional or otherwise, it must be realised that a united national effort must be made to press on to the ending of the present Stormont regime and the withdrawal of British troops ... On the non-constitutional plane, it must be realised that all the forces united against British policy must realise that the shared objective can be lost if we fall to fighting amongst ourselves as the disturbances at the British Embassy last night underlined. It gave the gardaí a distasteful job, but they were right to make every effort to protect the embassy. Failure to do this for a diplomatic mission, however unpopular, would reduce us in the eyes of the world to the low levels the British themselves are now plumbing.'

Amid the torrent of international criticism of Britain as a result of the killings, Edward Heath announced the setting up of a tribunal of inquiry into the shootings in Derry, to be headed by Lord Chief Justice Widgery. Perhaps most importantly, Bloody Sunday was also the final straw for the British government as far as Stormont was concerned, and in the wake of the incident it decided that London had to assume control of the security forces, a decision that would bring about the end of the Stormont regime.

9 February The former Northern Ireland Minister of Home Affairs, William Craig, launches Ulster Vanguard as a ginger group within the Ulster Unionist Party and as an umbrella movement for the right wing of unionism. Vanguard feeds on loyalist discontent with both the Stormont and London governments and takes an uncompromising stance from the beginning. On 18 March, at a rally attended by 60,000 people in Ormeau Park, Belfast, Craig warns that 'if and when the politicians fail us, it may be our job to liquidate the enemy' (Deutsch and Magowan, *Northern Ireland: A Chronology of Events, vol. 2,* p. 163). He also threatens to form a provisional government in Northern Ireland if London tries to impose a political settlement to which Protestants are opposed.

A committee of British Privy Councillors headed by Lord Parker reports on the methods used to interrogate detainees and in particular the five techniques associated with 'in-depth interrogation': hooding, food deprivation, sleep deprivation, being forced to lean against a wall by the fingertips for long periods, and the use of 'white noise' to cause disorientation. Of the three-man committee, Lord Parker and a second member hold that the techniques can be justified under exceptional circumstances, but the third member, Lord Gardiner, disagrees, saying (para. 21): 'The blame for this sorry story, if blame there be, must lie with those who, many years ago, decided that in emergency conditions in colonial-type situations we should abandon our legal, well-tried and highly successful wartime interrogation methods and replace them by procedures which were secret, illegal, not morally justifiable and alien to the traditions of what I still believe to be the greatest democracy in the world.' The Prime Minister, Edward Heath, later announces that the interrogation techniques will not be used again.

22 February A 50 lb bomb in a stolen car placed by the Official IRA explodes at Aldershot military barracks, headquarters of the sixteenth Parachute Brigade, killing five women workers preparing meals in the kitchen, a gardener, and Captain Gerry Weston, a Catholic priest in the army. The Official IRA says its attack is a response to the deaths on Bloody Sunday.

25 February The Stormont Minister of State for Home Affairs, John Taylor, survives a murder attempt by the Official IRA in Armagh. They believed incorrectly—that Taylor had been one of the main advocates of internment.

4 March The Abercorn Restaurant in Belfast is bombed by the IRA. Two people are killed and 130 injured, including two sisters who were shopping for a wedding dress, both of whom lost both legs.

20 March Six people are killed and more than a hundred injured by a 100 lb car bomb exploded by the Provisional IRA in Lower Donegall Street, Belfast. Not only is no warning given but a hoax call deliberately leads shoppers towards the area where the bomb is planted. Two off-duty policemen are killed as they try to lead people towards what they believe is a safe area.

24 March The Conservative Prime Minister, Edward Heath, announces the suspension of the Stormont government for one year after it refuses to accept losing control of law and order powers to London. In the House of Commons, Heath says: 'The United Kingdom government remain of the view that the transfer of this responsibility to Westminster is an indispensable condition for progress in finding a political solution in Northern Ireland. The Northern Ireland government's decision therefore leaves us with no alternative to assuming full and direct responsibility for the administration of Northern Ireland until a political solution to the problems of the province can be worked out' (*Hansard,* fifth series, vol. 833, col. 1860). Later, in a television broadcast, Heath claims that the new arrangements will create the opportunity for a 'fresh start'. Addressing himself primarily to Catholics, he continues: 'Now is your chance. A chance for fairness, a chance for prosperity, a chance for peace, a chance at last to bring the bombings and killings to an end.'

In his letter of resignation, Brian Faulkner writes that the transfer of security powers to London 'is not justifiable and cannot be supported or accepted by us. It would wholly undermine the powers, authority and standing of this government.' The introduction of direct rule deprives the Unionist Party of control of the administrative apparatus of Northern Ireland. Henceforth administration is controlled by a newly created government department, the Northern Ireland Office. The suspension of Stormont is welcomed by the Irish Government, which re-establishes diplomatic relations with Britain.

26 March William Whitelaw, Leader of the House of Commons, is designated the first Secretary of State for Northern Ireland. Lord Windlesham and Paul Channon are appointed Ministers of State and David Howell Under-Secretary.

27 March William Craig's Vanguard movement organises a two-day work stoppage in protest at the abolition of Stormont. The 48-hour strike proves relatively successful: public transport is stopped, power supplies are cut off, and most large industries close. The strike and a 100,000-strong unionist rally at Stormont the following day help to relieve some of the immediate tension by giving Protestants an opportunity to express their opposition to the British government's actions.

Commenting on the suggestion by the new Northern Ireland Office that an advisory commission of individuals picked by the Secretary of State should be set up to help govern Northern Ireland, Brian Faulkner says: 'Northern Ireland is not a coconut colony and no coconut commission will be able to muster any credibility or standing' (quoted by O'Clery, *Phrases Make History Here,* p. 144).

28 March The last sitting of the Northern Ireland Parliament takes place at Stormont. The suspension of Stormont marks the end of a system of government that has lasted for fifty years. In its place the Conservatives introduce direct rule from London, with a Secretary of State for Northern

Ireland, assisted by a group of junior ministers, to carry out the functions that had previously been performed by the Unionist government at Stormont. The Northern Ireland (Temporary Provisions) Bill is introduced in the House of Commons on 27 March, receives its second reading the following day, goes through the committee stage on 29 March, and is passed by the House of Commons nineteen hours later, after an all-night sitting. By 1 p.m. on 30 March the bill has become law.

The new Secretary of State, William Whitelaw, makes it clear that he sees direct rule as a stop-gap and presents the prorogation of Stormont as a chance for a new beginning. He suggests that the intervening year be used for political dialogue. Whitelaw's optimism is not justified, for the introduction of direct rule is viewed by most Catholics in Northern Ireland as a political victory and by most Protestants as a defeat, serving only to enhance community divisions. Though the suspension of Stormont creates support for political negotiations within the Catholic community, as the new conditions seem more favourable to them, the Provisionals' fear of losing the initiative to the SDLP leads them to continue their campaign. On the Protestant side the introduction of direct rule is seen by many as a first step towards a British withdrawal and strengthens the hand of paramilitaries and hard-line politicians.

The prorogation of Stormont also creates difficulties with regard to democratic representation and accountability. Northern Ireland legislation, which has previously been debated at length in (a greatly under-used) Stormont, is now largely dealt with by the use of Orders in Council at Westminster, which are simply voted through without discussion, often against the wishes of all Northern Ireland MPs (particularly on economic matters). The shadow Home Secretary, James Callaghan, also points out that the new Secretary of State has 'almost dictatorial powers,' a position strengthened by the changes in local government introduced as a result of the recommendations of the Macrory Report of 1970, which advocated that many local services be run from Stormont. The Secretary of State thus controls all the principal areas of administration affecting the day-to-day life of the people of Northern Ireland.

The effective abolition of Stormont also marks a sea change in the administration of Northern Ireland at the provincial level, for although the personnel of the Northern Ireland Civil Service remain, policy development is now controlled by British civil servants seconded to Northern Ireland. The administrative system thus becomes increasingly dependent on the British Parliament and government.

An inconsistency emphasised by the introduction of direct rule is the fact that Northern Ireland's twelve Westminster MPs represent many more constituents than the average British MP. The 'reduction' in the number of Northern Irish MPs had been seen as a quid pro quo for the fact that Northern Ireland had its own Parliament, which dealt with many of its own affairs and should therefore have a smaller say in London, where many decisions affected purely British matters. With the abolition of Stormont this argument was no longer relevant. While the Northern Ireland (Temporary Provisions) Bill is being debated, the North Down MP, Jim Kilfedder, points out that he represents 123,000 constituents, compared with the average of 60,000 in England and 50,000 in Scotland.

The Introduction of Direct Rule

In February 1972 a Unionist Cabinet minister told a journalist: 'Look, let's face it, Ted Heath regards us as his doorstep Cyprus. Don't be surprised by anything that happens—I won't.' The *Economist* declared at the beginning of 1972: 'Ministers have made little secret of their belief that the most satisfactory solution in the end would be if a political solution were created over the years in which the Protestant majority in the North would come to recognise a future for itself in a united Ireland.' Encouraged by such sentiments, the Provisional IRA proclaimed that 1972 would be the 'year of victory'. Indeed, the fact that the Provisionals were so obviously aiming for direct rule was the main factor in delaying its implementation. However, by the end of March, Heath moved to strip away security powers and then to prorogue Stormont. The Parliament of Northern Ireland met for one last time on 28 March 1972. There is no doubt that when the end came for Stormont it was due to a British perception that the United Kingdom could not continue to suffer the damaging international perception that it was linked to militarism in the North. There was not, however, any deep or profound consensus about future policy beyond that point.

For the Provisionals, direct rule was a victory. They declared that it 'places us in a somewhat similar position to that prior to the setting up of partition and the two statelets. It puts the "Irish Question" in its true perspective—an alien power seeking to lay claim to a country for which it has no legal right.' In fact the real significance of direct rule lay elsewhere: its introduction represented the definitive end of the 'Orange state'; it allowed the British government the space to introduce a strategy of reform 'from above.' Loss of control of the local state also helped generate a long period of disarray and confusion in unionist politics; indeed, for almost a decade it was marked by the rise of Ian Paisley and the DUP and the weakening of the Ulster Unionist Party. It was to take almost two decades for the Unionist Party to re-establish itself as the dominant force in Protestant politics. The introduction of direct rule was the most decisive moment of the crisis; it is the *sine qua non* for all later developments, including the Anglo-Irish Agreement, which is, in effect, merely a 'green' appendage to the direct rule machine.

6 April The Scarman Report, examining the causes of the violence of the summer of 1969, is published. It concludes that the disturbances arose from a mixture of social, economic and political factors. It finds that the RUC had been seriously at fault on a number of occasions but rejects accusations that it had co-operated with Protestants to attack Catholics.

14 April The worst day of violence since direct rule was imposed sees twenty-three explosions in places throughout Northern Ireland.

18 April The report of the committee headed by Lord Widgery, investigating events in Derry on 'Bloody Sunday', concludes: 'There would have been no deaths in Londonderry on 30 January if those who organised the illegal march had not thereby created a highly dangerous situation in which a clash between demonstrators and the security forces was almost inevitable ... Each soldier was his own judge of whether he had identified a gunman. Their training made them aggressive and quick in decision and some showed more restraint in opening fire than others. At one end of the scale some soldiers showed a high degree of responsibility; at the other ... firing bordered on the reckless ... None of the deceased or wounded is proved to have been shot whilst handling a firearm or bomb.'

22 April Eleven-year-old Francis Rowntree from west Belfast is the first person to die as a result of injuries caused by a plastic bullet.

13 May Loyalists bomb a bar in west Belfast, injuring more than sixty people.

14 May *Republican News* says that the Provisional IRA car bomb campaign which has been running since early in the year is aimed at 'striking at the colonial economic structure' and making Northern Ireland too expensive for the British to govern. However, the indiscriminate and horrifying effects of such bombs serve only to damage support for the Provisionals.

17 May The Provisional IRA open fire on workers as they leave Mackie's engineering factory in west Belfast. The factory has an almost entirely Protestant work force.

21 May Eight people are shot dead in gunfire between the (Catholic) Ballymurphy and (Protestant) Springmartin estates. British paratroops move into the area to try to separate the two sides, armoured cars drive between the firing lines, and soldiers take up position facing both directions. After dark the battle intensifies, with street lights being turned out and groups of vigilantes hijacking vehicles, setting them on fire and using them to barricade streets.

25 May The Official IRA kidnap and kill William Best, a nineteen-year-old member of the Royal Irish Rangers home on leave in the Creggan area of Derry. As he wandered round the area meeting his friends he was picked up and taken to a shop in Meenan Park for 'questioning'. Later he faced a 'trial' and was then murdered. The man who presided over this 'trial' said: 'Once we had him there was nothing we could do but execute him. Our military orders after Bloody Sunday were to kill every British soldier we could. They didn't say anything about local soldiers. He was a British soldier and that is all there was to it' (McCann, *War and an Irish Town,* p. 107). Best was driven to an area of waste ground near William Street with a hood over his head. He was told to get out and walk straight ahead; after he had taken a few steps he was shot in the back of the head.

The killing of a local man by the Official IRA, even one in the British army, outrages local opinion. The day after the murder four hundred mothers march to Official Sinn Féin's Derry offices and launch a vitriolic attack on those there. In the wake of the incident the SDLP calls on nationalists who had boycotted public offices to end their protest. On 29 May the incident leads the Official IRA to call a permanent halt to its military campaign. The Provisionals, who had also condemned the killing, continue theirs.

11 June Colonel Gaddafi of Libya, speaking at a rally in Tripoli, says that he has supplied arms to 'the Irish revolutionaries who are fighting Britain.'

A sectarian gun battle in the Oldpark area of Belfast leads to two Catholics, a Protestant and a soldier being killed.

13 June The Provisionals invite William Whitelaw to meet them in 'Free Derry', without the ending of internment as a precondition. He rejects the offer, but the move allows the SDLP (who had also previously refused to talk while internment continued) to meet him for talks in London on 15 June. John Hume and Paddy Devlin of the SDLP had met the Provisionals in Derry on 14 June, when the IRA leaders outlined their conditions for talks with the British: the granting of political status to republican prisoners, an independent witness to the meeting, that the meeting not be at Stormont, and that there be no restriction on who the Provisionals name as part of their team. The SDLP members pass on the proposals to Whitelaw, who agrees to all of them (Bishop and Mallie, *The Provisional IRA,* p. 225).

By 19 June, when the SDLP meet Whitelaw again, a group of IRA prisoners in Crumlin Road Jail have gone on hunger strike, demanding that they be treated as prisoners of war and be accorded special privileges. Under pressure from the SDLP, and fearful of the impact of the hunger strike on Catholic opinion, Whitelaw concedes 'special category' status, allowing more visits and the use of civilian clothes, for eight republican and forty loyalist prisoners. While Whitelaw believes at the time that the concessions are 'fairly innocuous,' the decision is to have an impact that is to last for the next two decades and to culminate in the 1981 hunger strike (Whitelaw, *The Whitelaw Memoirs,* p. 94).

22 June In a statement, the Provisional IRA says it will suspend its activities from 26 June, 'provided that a public reciprocal response is forthcoming from the armed forces of the British crown.' As a result of the cease-fire it hoped there would be 'meaningful talks between the major parties in the conflict.'

30 June In response to the continuation of republican 'no-go' areas, and fearful of British concessions to the IRA, the UDA begins erecting no-go areas in Protestant districts.

3 July In an incident at Ainsworth Avenue, Belfast, the UDA and British troops come face to face in a conflict over the erection of street barricades that would have included a number of Catholic families within a Protestant 'no-go' area. The UDA's numbers force the government to make concessions on the issue, and the army sets up a permanent check-point of its own.

7 July William Whitelaw and other British ministers meet members of the Provisional IRA at the home of the Minister of State at the NIO, Paul Channon, in London. The IRA delegation includes Séamus Twomey, Seán Mac Stiofáin, Dáithí Ó Conaill, Gerry Adams, Ivor Bell, and Martin McGuinness. Adams, who was being detained, was released into the custody of Paddy Devlin of the SDLP in order to attend the meeting. The Provisionals' main demand is a British withdrawal from Northern Ireland by 1975, leading Whitelaw to write later: 'The meeting was a non-event. The IRA leaders simply made impossible demands which I told them the British government would never concede. They were in fact still in a mood of defiance and determination to carry on until their absurd ultimatums were met' (Whitelaw, *The Whitelaw Memoirs,* p. 100). Whitelaw admits to the meeting on 10 July.

13 July Three soldiers and a civilian are killed as the IRA ends its two-week cease-fire. On the following day four civilians and a soldier are killed.

18 July In Belfast a sniper kills the hundredth soldier to die in the Troubles. In London the leader of the Labour Party, Harold Wilson, meets the same IRA group that Whitelaw met on 7 July.

21 July The IRA sets off twenty-six bombs in Belfast, including one in Oxford Street bus station, killing eleven people and injuring 130. Some of the bodies are so badly destroyed that parts have to be collected in plastic bags. An NIO spokesman dubs it 'Bloody Friday'. Later that evening Francis Arthurs, a Catholic, is kidnapped and taken to a social club in the Shankill Road area, where he is severely beaten, stabbed repeatedly, then shot, and his body dumped. His murder is believed to be committed by some of those later involved in the loyalist murder gang known as the 'Shankill Butchers'.

31 July The biggest British military operation since Suez, 'Operation

Motorman', ends 'no-go' areas in Belfast and Derry. Twelve thousand soldiers with bulldozers and tanks smash their way into the 'no-go' areas in an attempt to restore government control. In Belfast the UDA helps soldiers dismantle barricades in Protestant areas, and, to a lesser extent, Catholics do the same in their areas. While the army was reputed to have prepared for up to forty civilian casualties, only two youths are shot dead and two injured during gun battles in Derry. No soldiers are injured. The army fails, however, to capture any IRA members, despite a series of raids, though twenty-four people are arrested for illegal possession of arms and explosives.

Three IRA car bombs explode in Claudy, killing eight people.

9 August There is severe rioting on the first anniversary of the introduction of internment.

22 August Nine people are killed by an explosion at a customs post at Newry when a bomb explodes prematurely; among those killed are the three IRA men who planted the bomb.

2 September A bomb explodes at the Ulster Unionist Party offices in Glengall Street, Belfast, causing severe damage to adjoining buildings.

20 September The SDLP publishes a policy document, *Towards a New Ireland,* which calls for joint British and Irish sovereignty over Northern Ireland, a treaty between Britain and the Republic, and a declaration of intent by the British government to work for Irish unity.

25 September The Darlington Conference on political options for Northern Ireland, called by the Secretary of State, takes place over the next three days. Whitelaw holds discussions with some of the Northern Ireland parties in the hope of finding agreement on a future form of government. Only the Ulster Unionist Party, Alliance and the NILP bother to attend, while the SDLP boycotts the conference in protest at the continuation of internment. The conference achieves little. Even without the SDLP there is no agreement on what shape a future Northern Ireland government should take.

16 October A fifteen-year-old boy is killed when he is run over by an army vehicle during the second day of rioting in Protestant areas of east Belfast.

After the incident a UDA statement says that the 'British Army and the British government are now our enemies.' The following day loyalist gunmen open fire on the army in several areas of Belfast.

19 October At a meeting of the right-wing Monday Club in the House of Commons the leader of Vanguard, William Craig, says he can mobilise eighty thousand men to oppose the British government. 'We are prepared to come out and shoot and kill. I am prepared to come out and shoot and kill. Let us put the bluff aside. I am prepared to kill, and those behind me will have my full support' (quoted by O'Clery, *Phrases Make History Here,* p. 147).

30 October Despite the failure of the Darlington Conference, the NIO produces a discussion paper, *The Future of Northern Ireland.* It states Britain's commitment to the Union for as long as the people (previously the Parliament) of Northern Ireland wish it. But it also introduces two new ideas. On the question of what form a future Northern Ireland government should take the discussion paper says (para. 79): 'There are strong arguments that the objective of real participation should be achieved by giving minority interests a share in the exercise of executive power.' Because the discussion paper contains a wide range of ideas and options it is not clear that the government is in effect calling for a power-sharing government of both unionist and nationalist parties. The discussion paper also refers to the 'Irish dimension' of the Northern Ireland situation, the first time this phrase has been used in an official document. These new elements of British policy cause concern among many unionists about the government's long-term objectives in Northern Ireland.

2 November In the Dáil the Fianna Fáil Government introduces a bill for a referendum which removes the special position of the Catholic Church from the Constitution of Ireland.

5 November William van Straubenzee replaces Paul Channon as Minister of State at the NIO. David Howell is promoted to Minister of State. Peter Mills is appointed Under-Secretary.

19 November The Provisional IRA leader Seán Mac Stiofáin is arrested in Dublin. He goes on a hunger and thirst strike and is later transferred to hospital. On 26 November, after he has been sentenced to six months' imprisonment, shots are fired when IRA men dressed as priests and hospital orderlies make an abortive attempt to release him. Mac Stiofáin eventually calls off his hunger strike.

20 December The report into the legal procedures required for dealing with terrorist cases—the Diplock Report—is published. The report concludes: 'The main obstacle to dealing effectively with terrorist crime in the regular courts of justice is intimidation by terrorist organisations of those persons who would be able to give evidence for the prosecution if they dared.' Commentators later suggest that between January 1972 and September 1974 at least one witness to a terrorist trial was murdered and that 482 refused to give evidence out of fear (Steven Greer and Anthony White, *Fortnight,* 21 April–4 May 1986). The Diplock Report recommends that 'trials of scheduled offences should be by a Judge of the High Court, or a County Court Judge, sitting alone with no jury, with the usual rights of appeal.' The recommendations for the controversial 'non-jury' courts are later included in the Emergency Powers Act (1973).

The most bloody year of the troubles. DEATHS ARISING FROM THE TROUBLES: 470. SHOOTINGS: 10,631. BOMBS PLANTED: 1,853. FIREARMS FOUND: 1,259. EXPLOSIVES FOUND: 18,819 kg (41,490 lb). PERSONS CHARGED WITH TERRORIST OFFENCES (from 31 July 1972): 531.

1973

1 January Ireland and the United Kingdom become members of the European Economic Community, a development that implies closer co-operation between Britain and the Republic in the future, with unpredictable consequences for Northern Ireland. Some nationalists perceive entry to the EEC as a way of undermining the border and bringing about a united Ireland; some unionists are wary of entry to the EEC for the same reason.

28 January There is serious rioting in Derry on the anniversary of Bloody Sunday.

1 February Lieutenant-General Sir Frank King succeeds Sir Harry Tuzo as army commander in Northern Ireland.

2 February Rioting breaks out in Protestant areas of east Belfast.

3 February Two loyalists are detained in connection with the murder of a Catholic man on his way to work. That evening 2,000 people, including members of the UDA and Vanguard, gather at Templemore Avenue in east Belfast and march to Castlereagh RUC station to demand the release of the two detained men. A spokesman says that unless the men are released they will not accept responsibility for the crowd's actions.

5 February It is announced that the two men arrested on suspicion of murder are to be held under the Detention of Terrorists Order, making them the first Protestant internees. In response, loyalists call for a general strike for 7 February under the auspices of the United Loyalist Council, a body set up in October 1972 to co-ordinate the policies and actions of the Loyalist Association of Workers (LAW), the UDA, and several other loyalist paramilitary groups. The Vanguard Party is dragged into supporting the strike in the paramilitaries' wake.

6 February Brian Faulkner calls on Protestants to resist the loyalist strike, but by 6 p.m. electricity cuts begin to hit Belfast.

7 February Belfast and many other areas suffer a complete electricity blackout. There are reports of workers being intimidated to prevent them going to work; some shops are forced to close by gangs of men carrying cudgels. Because there is no transport or electricity, schools close at midday. RUC stations in Belfast are picketed throughout the day, and violence erupts in the afternoon when Willowfield and Donegall Pass RUC stations are attacked by crowds of loyalists. Elsewhere shops are set on fire, and Lavery's bar in Bradbury Place is burned down. A firefighter is shot dead by a loyalist sniper as he helps put out a fire at the top of Sandy Row. Shots are fired at the army in Paulett Avenue, off Albertbridge Road; the army returns fire and kills two men. A Protestant is found shot dead near the New Lodge Road, and a Catholic is shot dead by the army in the Lower Falls Road area. St Anthony's Catholic Church at Willowfield is ransacked by a gang of youths, and a Catholic home for mentally handicapped children at Whiteabbey is also attacked.

The LAW leader Billy Hull congratulates loyalists on their response to the strike and says that 'the power of the grass roots' can no longer be ignored (Deutsch and Magowan, *Northern Ireland: A Chronology of Events, vol. 2,* p. 270). During the day five people have been killed, seven wounded by gunfire, and twenty others injured. There have also been thirty-five cases of arson, eight explosions, and a total of sixty-eight arrests.

The LAW Strike

The great majority of unionists were appalled by the events of 7 February, and the loyalist organisations were forced to back down. Less than a week later, on 12 February, the executive committee of the Loyalist Association of Workers issued a statement condemning the 'lawless hooliganism and vandalism' that had taken place during the strike (Deutsch and Magowan, *Northern Ireland: A Chronology of Events,* vol. 2, p. 271–2).

Though the strike lacked the widespread support among Protestants that was to characterise the May 1974 strike—in fact there was a strong middle-class reaction against the violence that occurred throughout the day the stoppage nevertheless showed that loyalist workers had the industrial power to bring Northern Ireland to a standstill.

In the aftermath of the February strike LAW fell apart. Some members remained suspicious of Hull's NILP background; there were personality clashes between LAW members; and Hull had also clashed with the leader of Vanguard, William Craig, in August 1972, when he had considered turning LAW into a working-class loyalist party. Poor organisation also played a part in LAW's demise. Money that was paid by LAW members was sent to the central fund, but because records were poorly kept, cash was easily siphoned off by individuals for their own use. When this became known the organisation's credibility among workers was badly undermined. The general public condemnation of the February strike was the final straw for the organisation, and by the middle of the year the LAW had in effect ceased to exist.

15 February Albert Browne, a member of the UDA, is found guilty of murdering a member of the RUC in October 1972 and is sentenced to death—a mandatory sentence for the killing of a police officer under the Criminal Justice Act (Northern Ireland) (1966). On 6 April the sentence is commuted to life imprisonment by the Secretary of State, William Whitelaw, to run concurrently with a 25-year sentence imposed for the attempted murder of a second policeman and for possession of firearms. The death penalty is later abolished as part of the Emergency Provisions Act.

17 February Speaking in the Ulster Hall, the leader of Vanguard, William Craig, says: 'Much though we wish to maintain the Union we should all be seriously thinking of an independent dominion of Ulster.'

1 March In a general election in the Republic, Fianna Fáil loses power for the first time in sixteen years; a coalition Government of Fine Gael and the Labour Party is formed.

8 March The 'border poll' promised by Edward Heath at the time of the suspension of the Stormont parliament is held to determine the constitutional position of Northern Ireland. The poll offers the alternatives 'Do you want Northern Ireland to remain part of the United Kingdom?' and 'Do you want Northern Ireland to be joined with the Republic of Ireland outside the United Kingdom?' The result is a vote of 591,820 (57.5 per cent of the electorate) in favour of retaining the Union while 6,463 vote for unity with the South. There are almost 6,000 spoiled votes. The fact that most nationalists boycott the poll means the turnout is less than 60 per cent.

Car bombs at the Old Bailey and the Ministry of Agriculture building in

London kill one and injure nearly 250 people. Two other car bombs are defused. On 14 November nine people are found guilty of planting the bombs. Eight of them are sentenced to life imprisonment. Six of the eight convicted admit to being in the Provisional IRA.

20 March The government issues its White Paper *Northern Ireland Constitutional Proposals.* It calls for a Northern Ireland Assembly of about eighty members elected by proportional representation from multi-member constituencies. Concerning the composition of a future Northern Ireland government, it states (para. 52) that 'it is the view of the government that the executive itself can no longer be solely based upon any single party, if that party draws its support and its elected representation virtually entirely from only one section of a divided community.' The Secretary of State is to act as a mediator between the parties to discover whether an Executive can be set up that would command 'widespread support' in the community.

Problematic as the concept of a power-sharing government involving unionists and nationalists might be, even more ambitious are the proposals for relations with the Republic. The White Paper repeats the aspirations of the earlier discussion paper, *The Future of Northern Ireland* (para. 78): that it is 'clearly desirable that any new arrangements for Northern Ireland should, whilst meeting the wishes of Northern Ireland and Great Britain, be so far as possible acceptable to and accepted by the Republic of Ireland.' It points out areas of mutual interest where a Council of Ireland might prove useful, such as tourism, regional development, electricity, and transport. It also outlines the course the British government intends to take on the 'Irish dimension'. After the Assembly elections the British government will hold talks with the Government of the Republic and representatives from Northern Ireland at a conference to discuss the acceptance of the present status of Northern Ireland, effective consultation and co-operation, and the provision of a firm basis for concerted action against terrorism.

Assuming that these talks are successful and that agreement is reached, an Executive can be established, to which the Secretary of State would devolve responsibility for areas such as social security, education, industry, agriculture, and planning. The British also hold out the hope of control over security being handed over to the Executive at an unspecified date in the future. Thus the British pursue a carrot-and-stick approach. The unionists would regain responsibility for many of the areas they had controlled under the Stormont Parliament (security being the main exception), but to do so they must share power with a nationalist party, and come to an understanding with the Republic. Ironically, the White Paper itself points out the flaw in the arrangement when it states (para. 111): 'If a Council is to be set up not merely as a statutory concept, but as a useful working mechanism in North-South relations, it must operate with the consent of both majority and minority opinion in Northern Ireland, who have a right to prior consultation and involvement in the process of determining its form, functions and procedures.'

27 March Faulkner wins an important vote in the Ulster Unionist Council (the governing body of the Unionist Party) when it turns down, by 381 votes to 231, a motion to reject the White Paper. Nevertheless there are grave misgivings about the contents of the White Paper, and on 30 March some of the defeated minority within the party, led by William Craig, leave the Unionist Party to form the Vanguard Unionist Progressive Party.

If the close links between Vanguard and the paramilitary UDA were one factor that was to differentiate it from other unionist parties, another was its somewhat ambivalent position towards the maintenance of the Union. Craig summed up this attitude by stating: 'We would prefer to maintain the Union but the desire must be reciprocated, and pledges must be accompanied by a powerful parliament in Northern Ireland to resist all attacks and to defeat the inevitable recurring terrorist onslaughts virtually guaranteed to take place by the success of the present [IRA] attack. If there is not to be this strength in the United Kingdom we would prefer to be outside the United Kingdom, seeking no special treatment but expecting at least the same consideration as the anti-British South when it opted out' (quoted by Rose, *Northern Ireland: A Time of Choice,* p. 40–41). This attitude contrasts sharply with that of the DUP, which at this time welcomes direct rule as a step towards full integration with Britain and as a further buffer against a united Ireland.

Though Vanguard undoubtedly enjoyed the support of a significant section of unionism, other sections, generally the more prosperous and less radical groups, will have nothing to do with the movement. They fear that Craig's extreme views will further alienate the British government from unionism, perhaps even to the extent of forcing unionists into considering an independent 'Ulster'. The position is not made easier by the frequent sight of Craig travelling to Vanguard rallies in an open car and with a motorcycle escort provided by the Vanguard Service Corps, the paramilitary organisation linked to the movement.

10 April Believing that the political vacuum can only help the terrorists, the government pushes ahead with its political plans at almost breakneck speed and introduces the Northern Ireland Assembly Bill. It becomes law on 3 May. The Northern Ireland Constitution Bill is introduced on 15 May and becomes law on 18 July.

The main question the Assembly election poses is whether enough members who support the White Paper will be returned to make it workable. The Alliance Party is fully committed to the government's proposals; the DUP and Vanguard reject the proposals entirely; and the SDLP give a qualified acceptance, provided internment is ended and the proposed Council of Ireland is given substantial powers. The crucial question is whether a large enough section of the Ulster Unionist Party will give its support to the proposals to make them viable. Faulkner attempts to hold his party together by putting his reputation on the line and by fudging the issue of power-sharing. In April and May he tours the local Unionist associations, drumming up support for his line, and he orders the committee drawing up the Unionist Party's manifesto for the Assembly election to draft it in such a way that it will not automatically prevent them from joining an Executive that included the SDLP if that were the price to be paid for a devolved government. This course of action is later interpreted either as an astute political move by those supporting power-sharing or, by those who oppose it, as underhanded and misleading and as Faulkner's excuse to regain power at any cost. On 8 May the carefully worded policy statement says: 'We are not opposed to power-sharing in government, but we will not be prepared to participate in government with those whose primary aim is to break the union with Great Britain.' The interpretation of what is meant by the 'primary aim' of a party will be crucial in giving Faulkner room to negotiate in order to achieve a devolved government.

22 April Dáithí Ó Conaill, one of the leaders of the Provisional IRA, makes an appearance at a demonstration to mark the Easter Rising of 1916 but manages to evade capture by the police.

30 May The first elections for the twenty-six new district councils are held. The single transferable vote form of proportional representation is used for the first time in Northern Ireland since 1929.

The first election since 1970 sees many party names appearing on the ballot paper for the first time, including the DUP, Vanguard, Alliance,

SDLP, and Republican Clubs (Sinn Féin). Despite this the turn-out is a modest 68.1 per cent, as the election is mainly seen as a trial run for the Assembly elections. Of the 526 seats available, Ulster Unionists take 233 (with 41.4 per cent of the first-preference vote), the SDLP 83 (13.4 per cent), Alliance 63 (13.7 per cent), and a combination of Loyalist Coalition, Vanguard and DUP candidates 70 (14.1 per cent). The NILP wins only 4 seats, with 2.5 per cent of first-preference votes, fewer than the Republican Clubs, with 7 seats and 3.0 per cent.

With the district council elections out of the way, the contest for the Northern Ireland Assembly begins. On the unionist side the divisions between those who generally support the government's proposals (still called pro-White Paper unionists, even though the White Paper has partly been superseded by the Northern Ireland Assembly Act) and those opposed to the proposals are becoming clearer. The anti-White Paper unionists stand as Vanguard Unionists, Democratic Unionists or Loyalists and put forward fifty candidates. Forty-four 'Official Unionist' and twelve 'Unionist' candidates are nominated by Ulster Unionist constituency associations, but not all of these support Faulkner's line, and their outlook often reflects that of local associations opposed to the government's policies.

Faulkner emphasises the division among Unionist candidates by stating that only those who accept the party pledge to support the White Paper can be endorsed. Ulster Unionist candidates are therefore called either 'pledged' or 'Official Unionist' if they support the Faulkner line and 'unpledged' or simply 'Unionist' if they are against the White Paper. The division splits the party from top to bottom, and on 8 June Rev. Martin Smyth, Vice-President of the Unionist Council, tells the twelve 'unpledged' candidates that they will not be disowned by the party, showing that opposition to the White Paper exists at the 'tree-tops' as well as at the grass roots.

5 June Lord Windlesham is replaced by Lord Belstead at the NIO and as government spokesman on Northern Ireland in the House of Lords. David Howell is promoted to Minister of State at Stormont.

12 June Six pensioners aged between sixty and seventy-six are killed when a bomb explodes outside an off-licence in Coleraine. In the run-up to the election, violence continues unabated: there are clashes between the army and loyalists in Belfast and continuing sectarian killings, some of them committed by a new group, the 'Ulster Freedom Fighters', later revealed to be a section of the UDA. Armed men break into the home of a Vanguard candidate and UDA vice-chairman, Tommy Herron, and shoot dead his brother-in-law. On 21 June a mentally handicapped Protestant boy is found shot dead in west Belfast; the Provisional IRA say they are responsible for the murder. North Belfast proves a particularly dangerous area. Youths attack the home of an SDLP candidate, shots are fired at the home of a Unionist candidate, and on 26 June the SDLP leader Gerry Fitt's election agent, Paddy Wilson, and a woman travelling in his car are stabbed to death by the UFF. On the same day, in Derry, the Provisional IRA murders a Pakistani civilian who supplied sandwiches and tea to soldiers, claiming he was an 'army spy'.

14 June In the House of Commons the shadow Foreign Secretary and former Home Secretary James Callaghan speaks of Britain 'reconsidering' its position if the majority in Northern Ireland 'sabotaged' the Assembly; 'Britain cannot bleed for ever,' he says (*Hansard,* fifth series, vol. 857, col. 1750). On 23 June the Labour Party leader, Harold Wilson, threatens a 'reappraisal' of the relationships between Britain and Northern Ireland if the main principles of the White Paper are rejected.

28 June The Assembly elections are held. The extent of public interest in the new Assembly, aided by good weather, leads to a turn-out of 72 per cent (only the 1970 and 1983 Westminster elections have produced higher turn-outs in the last twenty years). Queues form at several polling stations in the morning and evening as people vote on their way to work or on returning home. Two busloads of pensioners on holiday in Co. Donegal return home to vote before resuming their holiday. As usual, the day is not untouched by violence. There are explosions in Magherafelt and Derry, the army deals with bombs in Belfast and Newry, and there are several shooting incidents: a soldier is wounded in Eliza Street, Belfast, and another in the Creggan in Derry. Shots are fired at a polling station, St Patrick's Hall in Pennyburn, Derry, as people queue to vote, and three mortar shells are fired at a polling station in Roden Street, Belfast. No-one is injured in either incident.

The election result appears to give a clear majority to the parties favouring the White Paper. Nominally there are 24 pro-White Paper 'Official' Unionists (with 29.3 per cent of valid first-preference votes), along with 19 SDLP members (22.1 per cent), eight Alliance Party (9.2 per cent), and one NILP (2.6 per cent), a total of 52. The anti-White Paper group consists of eight Democratic Unionist (10.8 per cent), seven Vanguard (10.5 per cent), and three West Belfast Loyalists (2.3 per cent), as well as eight 'Unionists' (8.5 per cent), a total of 26 members.

A closer look at the attitudes of the Official Unionist members reveals a less comfortable position for Faulkner. Austin Ardill and Jim Kilfedder, both Official Unionists, are in fact strongly opposed to the government proposals, and several others are less than enthusiastic. David McCarthy, another 'Official' Ulster Unionist, is killed in a car accident on 15 July, and Nat Minford will be elected Speaker of the Assembly, making him ineligible to vote. On the other side of the coin, of those elected as 'Unionists' only Leslie Morrell joins the Faulknerite group. Thus, as the Assembly finally gets under way, Faulkner can count on only 21 votes, while 27 unionists and loyalists are opposed to the White Paper. Added to this, the PR system of voting shows that lower-preference votes in the election had gone away from the moderate 'centre' parties rather than towards them, suggesting that attitudes are hardening.

31 July The first meeting of the Northern Ireland Assembly takes place.

6 August At his trial in Dublin, Kenneth Littlejohn, one of two brothers arrested during a bank robbery in the Republic, claims he is working for the Secret Intelligence Service (MI6) to infiltrate the Official IRA. He is later sentenced to twenty years' imprisonment. The British government refuses to comment on the allegations.

12 August The RUC uses plastic bullets for the first time during a riot.

29 August Two IRA bombs explode in Solihull, Warwickshire, and an incendiary device is found in Harrod's department store in London. On 10 September two more bombs explode at London railway stations, and on 23 September a soldier is killed in Birmingham when a bomb he is trying to defuse explodes.

16 September The vice-chairman of the UDA, Tommy Herron, is found shot dead in a ditch on the outskirts of Belfast. It is later suggested that his murderers were either British soldiers working under cover or (more likely) a rival faction within the UDA. It is rumoured that Herron had been involved in racketeering.

24 September The Irish Minister for Foreign Affairs, Garret FitzGerald, announces to the General Assembly of the United Nations that the two national governments have agreed on the formation of an Executive, the reform of the RUC and the civil service, and the creation of a Council of Ireland.

3 October Faulkner states that his supporters will not participate in a power-sharing Executive unless they hold the majority of seats, but he does not completely rule out the possibility of a power-sharing Executive.

5 October Representatives of the Ulster Unionist Party, the Alliance Party and the SDLP meet for talks at Stormont Castle under Whitelaw's chairmanship. The main topic is the formation of an Executive from the three parties represented. Whitelaw is not optimistic at the prospects for success and tells his staff to be ready for an early lunch adjournment, in the hope that the break would ease tensions and improve personal relations. Whitelaw's culinary planning appears to have the required effect, and the talks begin to make headway (Whitelaw, *The Whitelaw Memoirs,* p. 115). While the parties disagree on policing, internment, and a Council of Ireland, they are able to find other areas on which there is common ground. Significantly, the SDLP declares that it accepts the Northern Ireland Constitution Act and that it is prepared to call for an end to the rent and rates strike if agreement can be reached. Sub-committees are set up to discover areas of agreement and disagreement.

9 October The Unionist, Alliance and SDLP groups meet again at Stormont and issue a statement saying that they have reached broad agreement on an economic and social programme. Even so, antagonism between the conservative Roy Bradford and socialist Paddy Devlin has delayed agreement in this relatively uncontentious area.

16 October The three parties meet again and manage to secure a measure of agreement on law and order issues, though the question of policing, and in particular the name to be given to the police force, is to remain one of the last to be resolved.

If the omens for a power-sharing Executive are brighter, there is a price to be paid. Faulkner's grip on the Unionist Party is becoming increasingly tenuous, and from early October his leadership is openly questioned by

Unionists hostile to the idea of a deal with the SDLP. On 8 October, Harry West's 'unpledged' Unionists call for Faulkner's resignation as Unionist Party leader over the issue of power-sharing, and on 11 October Herbert Whitten, one of the 'pledged' Unionists, publicly declares his opposition to power-sharing. On 23 October the party's Standing Committee gives its support to a policy that will allow Unionist members of the Assembly to take part in a power-sharing Executive, but only by a vote of 132 to 105. While Faulkner declares himself pleased with the outcome, the comparatively close result also gives the unpledged Unionists reason to be optimistic as well.

25 October In the Assembly a member of Vanguard, Glen Barr (who is also a senior UDA member), makes what is considered to be the first 'Ulster nationalist' speech at Stormont. He says: 'I have no intention of remaining a British citizen at any price. The price being put on British citizenship under the Constitution Act is too much to bear. It has got to be borne in mind that Ulstermen have more pride than to accept a piece of white paper that has been thrown across the Irish Sea at them ... An Ulsterman's first allegiance must be the state of Ulster. True Ulstermen must reject anything which in any way indicates that Ulster is going to be put into a united Ireland. True Ulstermen must therefore reject the Constitution Act. Let it be put on record that I stand here as an Ulster Nationalist' (*Northern Ireland Assembly Debates,* vol. 1, col. 618–19).

31 October Members of the Provisional IRA hijack a helicopter and force the pilot to land in the exercise yard of Mountjoy Prison, Dublin, where they pick up three IRA prisoners, including the Chief of Staff, Séamus Twomey, and fly them to freedom. Twomey is later recaptured in Dublin in December 1977.

1 November Jamie Flanagan becomes Chief Constable of the RUC in succession to Sir Graham Shillington. He is the first Catholic to hold the post.

By late November, agreement on the formation of an Executive has stalled on the issues of law and order and the composition of the Executive itself. The Unionist Party is clearly split on whether or not to follow Faulkner's policy on power-sharing. A meeting of the Ulster Unionist Council on 20 November turns down, by the narrow margin of 379 to 369, a proposal to reject power-sharing. Whitelaw meanwhile puts pressure on the Faulknerite, SDLP and Alliance members and sets a deadline of 21 November for them to reach agreement on the formation of an Executive.

By the morning of 21 November, Whitelaw is pessimistic about the chances of success and he rings Heath to warn him that agreement is unlikely. On that day talks between Whitelaw and the three parties last for ten hours. During this time Whitelaw speaks privately to Fitt and Hume and eventually persuades them that the name of the Royal Ulster Constabulary must remain unchanged.

The last sticking point is the composition of the Executive itself. At the afternoon meeting Whitelaw tells the representatives that he is prepared to alter the Northern Ireland Constitution Act to allow greater flexibility in the number of Executive members, and that the number of members holding office outside the Executive is also open to discussion. These changes allow a situation where the Unionists can hold a majority in the Executive itself, but office-holders who are not members of the Executive will even up the balance for the other parties.

Finally, agreement is reached. The Executive will consist of eleven members, six of whom will be Faulknerite Unionists, four SDLP, and one Alliance. There will also be four non-voting members: two SDLP, one Unionist, and one Alliance.

22 November The formation of the Executive is announced. While politicians in Britain and the Republic generally welcome these developments, loyalists are outraged. Ian Paisley is in the United States, and it is left to his deputy, William Beattie, to call the agreement 'the greatest betrayal since Lundy' (Deutsch and Magowan, *Northern Ireland: A Chronology of Events, vol. 2,* p. 356), a sentiment echoed in statements by other loyalists.

The following day Whitelaw receives a warm welcome in the House of Commons as he presents the details of the agreement. He notes that the principal matter outstanding is the Council of Ireland and says that talks between British, Irish and Northern Ireland representatives will soon take place on this issue. At the same time he warns: 'We have set out upon a very difficult operation. There are those in this house and outside who are convinced and determined that we should fail. They are, clearly, entitled to pursue their aims by constitutional means. But let there be no illusions in this house or anywhere else: they are not entitled to blur that line between constitutional action and force' (*Hansard,* fifth series, vol. 864, col. 1587).

Details of the posts to be held by each of the parties and of who is to hold them are soon announced. Faulkner is to be Chief Executive and Gerry Fitt Deputy Chief Executive. For the Unionists, Herbie Kirk will be in charge of Finance; Roy Bradford, Environment; Basil McIvor, Education; Leslie Morrell, Agriculture; and John Baxter, Information. The non-voting Unionist is the Chief Whip, Major Lloyd Hall-Thompson. For the SDLP, John Hume will be Minister for Commerce; Austin Currie in charge of Housing, Development, and Local Government; and Paddy Devlin of Social Security. Ivan Cooper and Eddie McGrady, in charge of Community Relations and Planning and Co-ordination, respectively, are the two non-voting SDLP members. The Alliance representatives are Oliver Napier, in charge of the Office of Law Reform, with Bob Cooper, the party's non-voting member, at Manpower Services.

23 November Loyalists react angrily to the announcement that a power-sharing Executive has been agreed. Craig says that they are 'going to make this executive unworkable'; and as the date for the next meeting of the Assembly approaches, the political temperature increases. Paisley meanwhile rejects an offer from Whitelaw to meet him for discussions, because the loyalists have not been invited to participate in talks with the Irish and British governments and members of the Executive. These talks will be crucial to the overall settlement, as power will not be devolved to the Executive until the details of the Irish dimension have also been worked out.

28 November The meeting of the Assembly deteriorates into a verbal assault by some of the loyalists on the members-designate of the Executive. The Speaker suspends the meeting twice, but within five minutes of its resumption loyalist members once more begin shouting, 'Traitors, traitors. Out, out!' at Faulkner and his supporters. The Speaker adjourns the Assembly for the day.

Late November and early December 1973 are dominated by the Sunningdale Conference. Apart from disrupting the Assembly, loyalist politicians have been unable to make much impact on political developments. They argue that they should be invited to take part in the Sunningdale talks because, they represent a significant section of public opinion in Northern Ireland, and the government's own White Paper has stated that 'the leaders of elected representatives of Northern Ireland opinion' will be invited to the tripartite conference. The power-sharing parties and the Irish Government, however, fear that the loyalists will disrupt the talks and disclose details of the negotiations before they are completed; they therefore oppose their involvement in negotiations. As a result the British government fudges the issue of the pledge given in the White Paper and refuses the loyalists an invitation to participate.

*Ian Paisley and William Craig, as party leaders, are eventually to be asked to Sunningdale to give their views to the conference, but not as participants. Paisley angrily rejects the government's offer and later comments: 'We were simply invited to go and put our point of view and, having received the lunch, to be removed and taken away. We were to have the same privilege as the catering staff, apart from the fact that we were going to be allowed to go in and say something before we had this wonderful lunch' (*Northern Ireland Assembly Debates, *vol. 1, col. 1488, 14 December 1973).*

29 November As the Sunningdale conference approaches, the Northern Ireland parties involved in the conference outline their positions. For the Unionists, Faulkner says he expects the Republic to end its territorial claim to Northern Ireland as a prerequisite of the talks. Two days later, at the SDLP conference, Fitt says it will be impossible for the Executive to work in close co-operation while internment continues. For the Alliance Party, Oliver Napier states: 'There will not be a Council of Ireland which in any way undermines Northern Ireland's position within the United Kingdom because the Alliance Party will not agree to it' (Deutsch and Magowan, *Northern Ireland: A Chronology of Events, vol. 2,* p. 360).

3 December Francis Pym is appointed Secretary of State for Northern Ireland in succession to William Whitelaw. An exhausted Whitelaw is recalled to London to become Secretary of State for Employment; Heath hopes that Whitelaw can achieve another political coup and do a deal with the National Union of Mineworkers to restrict pay increases. The removal of Whitelaw at this time has often been seen as a mistake, in that it removed a person who had been closely involved with local affairs for almost two years and replaced him with one with comparatively little knowledge of Northern Ireland. Whether Whitelaw's presence at Sunningdale would have made any difference to the outcome is debatable; Whitelaw himself believes it made no difference and that in some ways a fresh face was an advantage (Whitelaw, *The Whitelaw Memoirs,* p. 123). Nevertheless, the abiding impression given by Whitelaw's departure is that Northern Ireland's interests have once more been sacrificed in favour of national demands.

In the long term, events taking place outside Northern Ireland are to have a greater impact than the change of personnel at the NIO. Following an overtime ban by the coal-miners on 12 November, Heath declares a national state of emergency, which places restrictions on the use of electricity. At the same time the outbreak of war in the Middle East in October leads to huge increases in the price of oil and adds to the general air of crisis.

As the tripartite conference approaches, loyalists begin organising in opposition. The 'unpledged' Unionists, led by Harry West, announce the formation of a new group, the Ulster Unionist Assembly Party. Later that evening they hold a joint meeting with Vanguard and the DUP at the Ulster Hall in Belfast. The following day Paisley storms out of his first meeting with Pym after being told that loyalists were not to be invited to participate in the Sunningdale talks.

5 December At a meeting of the Assembly, fighting breaks out in the chamber. Four leading Faulknerite members—Lloyd Hall-Thompson, Basil McIvor, Peter McLachlan, and Herbie Kirk—are physically attacked by Vanguard and DUP members as the police attempt to remove the loyalists. Five of the seven Ulster Unionist MPs at Westminster announce their decision to support West rather than Faulkner.

6 December The tripartite conference at the Civil Service Staff College at Sunningdale Park in Berkshire begins, and continues until 9 December. It is the first conference since 1925 at which heads of government from Britain and both parts of Ireland are present. The British representatives include Edward Heath (Prime Minister), Sir Alec Douglas-Home (Foreign Secretary), Peter Rawlinson (Attorney-General), and Francis Pym. The Irish representatives include Liam Cosgrave (Taoiseach), Garret FitzGerald (Minister for Foreign Affairs), and Conor Cruise O'Brien. The SDLP delegation consists of Fitt, Hume, Devlin, Currie, McGrady, and Ivan Cooper; the Alliance Party is represented by Napier, Glass, and Bob Cooper. Faulkner, Bradford, Morrell, McIvor, Kirk and Baxter represent the Unionists.

The objective of the conference is to put flesh on the ideas for the 'Irish dimension' that had been outlined in the White Paper. Faulkner, desperately needing to win concessions to bolster his position, presses the Irish Government to scrap articles 2 and 3 of the Constitution of Ireland, which claim jurisdiction over Northern Ireland. Cosgrave refuses, on the grounds that it would require a constitutional referendum, which might be defeated by the Fianna Fáil opposition. Instead he offers a declaration 'that there could be no change in the status of Northern Ireland until a majority of the people of Northern Ireland desired a change in that status' (Sunningdale communiqué, para. 5). The only other area where Faulkner could claim to have made any headway for unionists was in the extradition of terrorist suspects from the Republic to Northern Ireland. Again the Irish Government argues that extradition presents them with legal difficulties under the Constitution but agrees to the setting up of a joint British and Irish commission 'to consider all the proposals put forward at the conference and to recommend as a matter of extreme urgency the most effective means of dealing with those who commit these crimes' (Sunningdale communiqué, para. 10).

The main area where agreement is reached is the formation of a Council of Ireland. The council will have representatives from Northern Ireland and the Republic and will consist of a Council of Ministers and a Consultative Assembly. The Council of Ministers is to be made up of seven members of the Executive and seven members of the Irish Government (though other, non-voting members could also be included) and is to have 'executive and harmonising functions and a consultative role.' As a concession to unionists it is agreed that the Council of Ministers will only be able to take decisions on a unanimous vote. The Consultative Assembly, with thirty members from the Assembly and an equal number from the Dáil, will have 'advisory and review functions'. There will also be a permanent secretariat for the council, which will 'service the institutions of the Council and ... supervise the carrying out of the executive and harmonising functions and the consultative role of the Council' (Sunningdale communiqué, para. 7).

On the same day, a rally attended by 600 delegates from Unionist Party constituency associations, Vanguard, the DUP and the Orange Order is held in the Ulster Hall in Belfast, and the United Ulster Unionist Council is formed to oppose power-sharing.

The power-sharing majority within the Assembly and the fact that Faulkner is still leader of the Unionist Party disguise the fact that the Faulknerite line now faces the threat of becoming the minority view in the unionist community. Faulkner clearly requires significant gains on the questions of security and the Republic's recognition of Northern Ireland from the Sunningdale conference if he is to sell the package to unionists.

The SDLP, meanwhile, having overturned its own commitment not to participate in any Northern institution while detention without trial remains, is looking for movement by the British government on the issue of internment as well as a strong Irish dimension. Whether these potentially conflicting demands can be successfully reconciled is open to question.

Sunningdale

The flaw in the Sunningdale Agreement was that those involved in it had completely different views of what it entailed. Faulkner saw the Council of Ireland as an advisory body and raised few objections to its dealing with the 'harmonisation' of cross-border issues such as tourism, transport, agriculture, and electricity, which he believed was 'necessary nonsense' (Faulkner, *Memoirs of a Statesman,* p. 237).

Some members of the SDLP had a different opinion of what the Council of Ireland would mean. 'The general approach of the SDLP to the talks was to get all-Ireland institutions established which, with adequate safeguards, would produce the dynamic that could lead ultimately to an agreed single state for Ireland. That meant, of course, that SDLP representatives would concentrate their entire efforts on building up a set of tangible executive powers for the Council which in the fullness of time would create and sustain an evolutionary process' (Paddy Devlin, *The Fall of the Northern Ireland Executive,* p. 32).

The British government was also partly responsible for creating this situation. By failing to define clearly those areas that the Council of Ireland would control and those that it would not, it succeeded in inflating nationalist aspirations while at the same time raising loyalist fears of the council as the means of forcing them into a united Ireland.

In retrospect, it is clear that the Faulknerite Unionists were the principal losers at Sunningdale, though they were under pressure from almost all the other parties involved in the talks to give ground. When Faulkner came out strongly against the Southern government having any say on the police, Heath joined the SDLP and the Irish government to pressure him into accepting that the Council of Ireland would be consulted with regard to the composition of the new police authority. In return Heath gave a largely meaningless pledge in the Sunningdale communiqué to discuss the devolution of responsibility for policing 'as soon as the security problems were resolved and the new institutions were seen to be working effectively.'

In its immediate aftermath, the conference seemed another triumph for consensus politics. It is evident, however, that the groups involved in the conference, buoyed by their earlier successes, failed to recognise the strength of opposition building up within a unionist community that was increasingly feeling that it was being railroaded into a united Ireland. For the SDLP, Gerry Fitt was hardly involved in the details of the talks, and it could be argued that a closer involvement on his part might have provided a more realistic outcome. Similarly, the British government, and Heath in particular, seemed insensitive to Faulkner's weakening position. It is here that Whitelaw's experience might have made a difference, for he would surely have been aware of the difficulties Faulkner would face in selling the deal on his return to Northern Ireland. At the same time a promise by Heath to the SDLP that he would phase out internment and begin releasing detainees as soon as possible also failed to materialise (Paddy Devlin, *The Fall of the Northern Ireland Executive,* p. 39). This left the SDLP to concentrate on the apparent benefits of the Council of Ireland, a policy that served only to further heighten unionist fears of the Sunningdale deal. The Irish Government also promised more than it was eventually able to deliver, and of the Irish delegation only Cruise O'Brien seemed aware of the likely barriers to progress that had been erected at Sunningdale.

The Unionist representatives at the conference were also partly responsible for their own downfall. The only experienced negotiators on their side were Faulkner and Bradford, and they arrived at the conference remarkably unprepared. As a result there was some truth in the accusation levelled at them by their loyalist opponents that the Faulknerites had been out-manoeuvred and out-negotiated at Sunningdale.

10 December Loyalist paramilitaries react to the Sunningdale agreement by forming the Ulster Army Council, an umbrella group for the most important loyalist paramilitary groups (including the UDA and UVF), and say they will support loyalist politicians who oppose moves towards a Council of Ireland (Deutsch and Magowan, *Northern Ireland: A Chronology of Events, vol. 2,* p. 362). With the UUUC and loyalist workers also planning action to wreck the Sunningdale agreement, the Northern Ireland Executive is, from the outset, working against the clock to establish its credentials. While it seems that the Sunningdale package, with a Council of

Ireland and the offer of an end to internment, helps bring nationalists in from the political wilderness, this has been achieved only by creating conditions that alienate a substantial proportion of the unionist community.

28 December In an open letter to the people of the Republic in the *Irish Times* the Alliance leader Oliver Napier asks: 'Do you really want a Council of Ireland? ... The Council of Ireland hangs by a thread ... if you do nothing in the next few weeks, history will judge you and its judgement will be harsh and unforgiving.'

DEATHS ARISING FROM THE TROUBLES: 252. SHOOTINGS: 5,019. BOMBS PLANTED: 1,520 (explosions: 1,007). FIREARMS FOUND: 1,313. EXPLOSIVES FOUND: 17,426 kg (38,420 lb). CASES OF INTIMIDATION: 3,096. PERSONS CHARGED WITH TERRORIST OFFENCES: 1,418.

1974

1 January The Northern Ireland Executive takes office. However, as the NIO withholds the power to implement changes in economic or security policy, the new regime quickly becomes bogged down in horse-trading and achieves little or nothing in the five months of its existence.

4 January The Ulster Unionist Council—the governing body of the Ulster Unionist Party—rejects the 'proposed all-Ireland Council settlement' in the Sunningdale Agreement by 427 votes to 374. In the wake of the decision Brian Faulkner resigns as Unionist Party leader on 7 January.

8 January David Howell is withdrawn from the NIO because of the responsibilities devolved to the Executive.

16 January In the High Court in Dublin Mr Justice Murnaghan states that the view that 'Northern Ireland could not be reintegrated into the national territory until and unless a majority of the people of Northern Ireland indicated a wish to become part of a united Ireland [was] no more than a statement of policy' (quoted by O'Clery, *Phrases Make History Here,* p. 155). The ruling further undermines Faulkner's position with unionists, and as a result he flies to Dublin for urgent talks with the Taoiseach, Liam Cosgrave, in an attempt to patch up the situation.

17 January In a speech at Trinity College, Dublin, the SDLP Assembly member Hugh Logue says that the Council of Ireland is 'the vehicle that would trundle Unionists into a united Ireland.'

22 January Loyalist politicians disrupt the Assembly. The mace is seized and passed from hand to hand, and police forcibly eject eighteen loyalist members. On the same day Harry West is appointed leader of the Ulster Unionist Party in succession to Brian Faulkner.

1 February Cosgrave and seven of his ministers fly to Hillsborough for a meeting with members of the Executive. It is agreed to set up working groups of Northern and Southern civil servants to investigate what 'executive functions' the Council of Ireland could have. The report from the

Northern civil servants presented to Faulkner at the end of the month recommends that the Council of Ireland have responsibility only for tourism, conservation, and 'aspects of animal health.' Where electricity generation and distribution is concerned the report notes: 'The Chairman of the Northern Ireland Electricity Service has pointed out that possible adverse staff reactions ... could cause serious disruption. It has been suggested that the public in the North who are opposed to a Council might take the excuse to withdraw payment of bills.' The Executive is now so divided that Faulkner withholds the report for two months.

The UUUC begins preparing for the seemingly imminent general election by pasting up posters saying DUBLIN IS ONLY A SUNNINGDALE AWAY.

4 February A bomb planted on a coach carrying soldiers and their families explodes near Bradford, killing eleven people. Some of the bodies are thrown 250 yards from the scene of the explosion. On 4 November Judith Ward (later proved innocent) is jailed for thirty years for causing the explosion.

7 February Edward Heath calls a general election for 28 February. During meetings of the Cabinet the Secretary of State for Northern Ireland, Francis Pym, argues against calling the election. The Executive is only beginning to find its feet, and Pym fears that an election will lead to its destruction. Eventually he is forced to concede that an election is inevitable because of the deteriorating economic situation in Britain.

Announcing that there will be no coalition pact between the Executive parties, Faulkner declares: 'Our candidates will rout those Unionists aligned with paramilitary associations' (Deutsch and Magowan, *Northern Ireland: A Chronology of Events, vol. 3,* p. 14). Faulkner's position is weakened, however, by the question mark that still hangs over the Sunningdale agreement.

In Dublin Kevin Boland appeals to the Supreme Court against the High Court's dismissal of his case that the agreement is unconstitutional. The appeal is unanimously rejected on 22 February.

12 February An IRA bomb explosion in Buckinghamshire injures ten people.

15 February Ulster Unionist, Vanguard and DUP leaders meet at Stormont and select six Unionist, three Vanguard, two DUP and one Independent

Official Unionist (Jim Kilfedder) as agreed UUUC candidates. Elements of the SDLP meanwhile remain unhappy that the party is involved in the Executive at all while internment continues. Partly as a result of this, the SDLP commits itself to fielding a candidate in all twelve constituencies. When nominations close, forty-eight candidates have been named. The twelve UUUC, twelve SDLP, three Alliance and four NILP representatives are joined by seven Pro-Assembly (Faulknerite) Unionists, four Republican Clubs (Sinn Féin) candidates, two Independent Labour, two Unity, one Independent Socialist (Bernadette McAliskey), and one Independent Republican (Albert Price, father of the Price sisters convicted of planting car bombs in London in March 1973, who are on hunger strike in Brixton Prison over their demand to be transferred to a prison in Northern Ireland).

The election emphasises divisions among the power-sharing groups while providing a source of unity for those who oppose the Sunningdale agreement. Including the pro-agreement NILP, a single UUUC candidate faces two candidates who support power-sharing in West Belfast, North Antrim, South Antrim, Armagh, North Down, Fermanagh-South Tyrone, and Mid-Ulster, three who support power-sharing in East Belfast and North Belfast, and, in the most extreme case, four in South Belfast. In only two constituencies, South Down and Londonderry, are those in favour of power-sharing represented by a single (SDLP) candidate. Faulkner advises his supporters to abstain from voting in areas where there is no pro-Assembly Unionist candidate rather than vote for Alliance or the SDLP.

16 February The election heralds an increase in tension between loyalists and the police and army. There is rioting on the Newtownards Road in Belfast, resulting in a Protestant being shot dead and two men being seriously injured when an army patrol opens fire.

23 February Taxi-drivers hijack buses and seal off the Shankill Road in protest against alleged army harassment.

25 February There is more rioting in east Belfast after one of those injured on 16 February dies. Cars and buses are hijacked and set alight, and soldiers open fire with rubber bullets. All this takes place against a background of an increase in the number of bombings throughout Northern Ireland, including an explosion at the Alliance Party's offices in Belfast on 25 February.

As the election approaches, the Irish government attempts to support

Faulkner by making conciliatory speeches in the Dáil. The Taoiseach, Liam Cosgrave, states that the Council of Ireland is 'not a way of achieving unity either by stealth or against their [unionists'] wishes' (*Dáil Debates,* vol. 270, col. 1538). The Dáil rejects Neil Blaney's motion calling for a reassertion of a resolution passed in 1949 protesting against partition; instead it accepts, by 73 votes to 68, Cosgrave's amendment that 'the aspiration towards a united Ireland can be achieved only by peaceful means and with the consent of a majority of the people of Northern Ireland' (*Dáil Debates,* vol. 270, col. 1679). The Fianna Fáil opposition votes against the amendment.

28 February The election is the fourth time that voters in Northern Ireland have gone to the polls in less than a year. In Britain the main election issues are the miners' strike, inflation, and rising prices. In Northern Ireland the only issue that matters is the Sunningdale agreement. In effect the election will be a referendum on power-sharing and the Council of Ireland. The UUUC manifesto leaves voters in no doubt about what is the main issue: 'In Britain they are asking, Who Governs Britain? We In Ulster ask Who Governs Ulster? The Irish Republic—the IRA—the SDLP—a Council of Ireland?'

As polling takes place, more than 30,000 soldiers and police are on duty. In some areas ballot boxes are transported by armoured car. In Derry an oil-tanker is hijacked and bombs damage two shops. A land mine found 200 yards from the home of Austin Currie in Coalisland is defused by the army. Gunmen fire at soldiers guarding a polling station in Andersonstown, Belfast, though no-one is injured. There are twelve explosions in Belfast that evening, with a man being killed at the Red Star bar in Donegall Quay. There are also explosions in Glengormley, Whiteabbey, and Lurgan, and a land mine is defused at Carnlough, Co. Antrim.

In west Belfast, where Gerry Fitt stands against two other nationalist candidates—Albert Price and John Brady (Republican Clubs)—a close result is expected. John McQuade of the DUP is the UUUC candidate, while Billy Boyd stands for the NILP.

Loudspeaker vans tour the Falls Road area announcing that Gerry Fitt will be disqualified from taking his seat in the House of Commons because he is a member of the Northern Ireland Executive (Deutsch and Magowan, *Northern Ireland: A Chronology of Events, vol. 3,* p. 22); this is untrue but is typical of the many dirty tricks that take place in the constituency. In the end Fitt retains his seat with a majority of just over two thousand votes ahead of McQuade, the smallest majority of the twelve seats. Fitt is the only non-UUUC candidate to win a seat.

When the polls close it is found that the turn-out, at 68.9 per cent, is lower than any other region in the United Kingdom and lower than in the 1970 general election (76.6 per cent). People are obviously becoming tired of elections, but fewer polling stations were used, for security reasons (even so, three polling stations were fired on during the day), while the risk of violence may have made many people afraid to go out to vote. The result gives UUUC candidates eleven of the twelve seats, with 51.1 per cent of valid votes cast. Gerry Fitt holds West Belfast for the SDLP, which wins 22.4 per cent of the vote; Pro-Assembly Faulknerite Unionists receive 13.1 per cent, and Alliance 3.2 per cent. The result in effect destroys the legitimacy of the Executive in the Protestant community.

The 1974 General Election

It is impossible to speculate how many seats the power-sharing parties would have won with fewer candidates, since, for example, many SDLP voters would not have voted for a Faulknerite Unionist under any circumstances, and vice versa. Nevertheless it was perhaps tactically inept for the SDLP to field candidates in constituencies such as East Belfast and North Down, or for a pro-Assembly Unionist to stand in Fermanagh South Tyrone. Fielding fewer candidates might not have won them any more seats, but by putting forward so many it increased the feeling that the Executive was disunited. While there were some areas where the rigid Protestant-Catholic divide would have made no difference to the outcome, it was surely nothing short of suicidal for the power-sharing parties not to have agreed a single candidate in areas such as South and East Belfast, where a Faulknerite Unionist might well have won a seat.

The Executive leaders' reaction to the result was fatalistic, Faulkner claiming that it represented unionist fears about the unknown expressed 'in that term Sunningdale,' while Gerry Fitt noted that 'the election has come too soon for the people of Northern Ireland to really begin to understand what Sunningdale really means.' Ian Paisley, on the other hand, led the calls for fresh Assembly elections. 'We want the British government to have a general election on the Ulster assembly and for a new Northern Ireland executive to present itself to the people' (Deutsch and Magowan, *Northern Ireland: A Chronology of Events, vol. 3,* p. 23). Ironically, Kevin Boland's appeal against the Sunningdale agreement was finally dismissed by the Supreme Court on the same day, 1 March.

The February 1974 general election brought about a sea change in the fortunes of the Northern Ireland Executive, for it exposed—as many of those involved in the power-sharing experiment feared it would—the unpopularity of the Sunningdale agreement with Protestant voters. After the election it was impossible for the Faulknerites to claim realistically that they represented the majority of unionist opinion.

While the election result did not kill off the Sunningdale agreement, it provided loyalist opponents with the mandate they needed to support their actions aimed at ending power-sharing and, more importantly, stopping the Council of Ireland.

4 March The Liberals reject Heath's offer of a coalition with the Conservatives, and Heath resigns as Prime Minister. A minority Labour Party government is formed.

The Unionist pro-Assembly group decides that no further steps should be taken towards the ratification of the Sunningdale agreement. There will be no Council of Ireland unless articles 2 and 3 of the Constitution of Ireland are repealed. At the same time the SDLP continues to insist that there can be no 'watering down' of the Sunningdale agreement.

5 March Merlyn Rees becomes Secretary of State for Northern Ireland. In the following days Stan Orme, a long-time Unionist critic and friend of Gerry Fitt, is appointed Minister of State and Lord Donaldson Under-Secretary.

9 March Two thousand supporters of the UUUC march to Stormont and proclaim their intention of bringing down the Executive.

13 March In an attempt to undo some of the damage caused by the High Court's ruling on the Boland case, Cosgrave declares in the Dáil: 'The factual position of Northern Ireland is that it is within the United Kingdom and my Government accept this as a fact. I now therefore solemnly reaffirm that the factual position of Northern Ireland within the United Kingdom cannot be changed except by a decision of a majority of the people of Northern Ireland' (*Dáil Debates,* vol. 271, col. 8).

20 March The RUC shoot dead two British soldiers by mistake on a country road at Mowhan, Co. Armagh. They were said to be returning from leave; the Secretary of State, Merlyn Rees, denies that they were part of an undercover operation.

23 March A new loyalist group, the Ulster Workers' Council, issues a statement threatening widespread civil disobedience unless fresh Assembly elections are held.

4 April Rees states his intention of removing the ban on the UVF and Sinn Féin and phasing out internment.

8 April Rees and Orme meet representatives of the UWC in an 'angry, disjointed meeting' at Stormont. Rees later sends a confidential minute to Wilson expressing his scepticism about Sunningdale (Rees, *Northern Ireland: A Personal Perspective,* p. 59). Two days later Rees expresses his concerns about Sunningdale at a full Cabinet meeting and warns of the danger of political collapse. Wilson asks a group of ministers to prepare contingencies.

18 April Wilson visits Northern Ireland for talks with police and army commanders, members of the Executive, trade unionists and church leaders and says that there can be no alternative to the Sunningdale agreement.

20 April A twenty-year-old Catholic man, a former internee, is shot dead in Belfast. At the time he is considered the thousandth 'official' victim of the Troubles.

23 April In a speech at Newcastle-under-Lyme the Defence Secretary, Roy Mason, says: 'Pressure is mounting on the mainland to pull out the troops; equally, demands are being made to set a date for withdrawal.' Though later retracted, the statement causes concern both in Northern Ireland and the Republic.

The UUUC begins a three-day conference at Portrush to work out policies and tactics for bringing down the Executive. The conference, attended by UDA representatives and by Enoch Powell, demands an immediate Assembly election and threatens strikes if this does not occur.

26 April After its conference in Portrush the UUUC calls for a Northern Ireland regional parliament within a federal United Kingdom.

2 May The European Commission on Human Rights begins hearing the charges of torture against the British government brought by the Irish government over the treatment of prisoners in Northern Ireland.

Six Catholics are killed and eighteen injured in an explosion at the Rose and Crown pub on the Ormeau Road, Belfast. Private Eva Martin (29), shot dead in Clogher, is the first woman UDR member to be killed.

10 May The UWC issues a statement calling for fresh elections to the Assembly. The UWC is not seen as a serious threat by the authorities, because of the failure of earlier strikes by the LAW and low turn-outs at loyalist demonstrations against Sunningdale.

14 May The Assembly rejects, by 44 votes to 28, a motion condemning power-sharing and the Council of Ireland. At 6:08 p.m. Harry Murray and Bob Pagels of the UWC inform the press at Stormont that a strike will begin in protest at the Assembly's support of Sunningdale and that electricity output will be reduced from 725 to 400 megawatts.

After the first few days the strike is run by a co-ordinating committee chaired by the Vanguard Assembly member and UDA member Glen Barr. The committee has a core of between thirteen and fifteen members and includes political leaders (Ian Paisley, William Craig, and Harry West), loyalist paramilitary leaders (including Andy Tyrie of the UDA and Ken Gibson of the UVF), and UWC leaders. The stoppage is characterised by power cuts, the use of a system of 'passes' issued by the strike committee to workers in 'essential services', allowing them to pass barricades and purchase petrol, and by restrictions on the opening hours of shops on the 'advice' of the strikers.

In London the Northern Ireland (Emergency Provisions) Act (1973) (Amendment) Order, legalising the UVF and Sinn Féin, is passed without debate.

15 May The UWC calls for a general work stoppage. The strike begins with power cuts and factory closures. Many workers, including those in Harland and Wolff, go on strike; supporters of the Executive claim there are threats of car-burning by paramilitaries in order to close the shipyard. Larne is 'cut off' by armed men. Stan Orme meets members of the UWC accompanied by Craig, Paisley, John Laird and three 'armed observers' at Stormont.

16 May In the House of Commons, Merlyn Rees says that Northern Ireland MPs will have to face up to the question whether 'their loyalism will lead them to come up against British troops ... There is a political strike taking place at present with the aim of bringing about early elections. Because it is a political fight this gives me a great deal of freedom in how I deal with various matters under it. I regret that there is a great deal of intimidation. My information is that when factory meetings were held, to which often only small numbers of people went, the vote was not decisive, but that it was the intimidation afterwards by groups and bands that was keeping the strike together. This is a political and not an industrial strike' (*Hansard,* fifth series, vol. 873, col. 1446).

Stan Orme says that from 1 January to 30 April 1974 seventy-four people have been killed and that claims for compensation for damage to property amount to about £102 million (*Hansard,* fifth series, vol. 873, col. 1442).

17 May Twenty-two people are killed and over a hundred injured when three car bombs explode during the rush hour in Dublin. Five others are killed and twenty injured by a car bomb in Monaghan. The eventual death toll of thirty-three is the greatest number of people killed in any one day of the Troubles. Three girls are among those killed in Dublin: one of them is decapitated; the bodies of the other two are fused together by the heat of the blast. Two of the three cars used in the Dublin bombings had been stolen earlier in Protestant areas of Belfast, and all four cars had Northern Ireland registrations. Both the UDA and UVF deny responsibility for the bombs, but the press officer of the UDA and of the strike co-ordinating committee, Sammy Smyth, says, 'I am very happy about the bombings in Dublin. There is a war with the Free State, and now we are laughing at them.'

Leaving Stormont Castle after talks with Rees, the leader of Vanguard, William Craig, says the Secretary of State is highly irresponsible in refusing to negotiate with the UWC. He warns that Northern Ireland is slipping quickly into a disastrous situation and that essential services could collapse within hours.

19 May Rees announces a state of emergency under section 40 of the Northern Ireland Constitution Act (1973).

20 May In the House of Commons Stan Orme says: 'We will not negotiate with the Ulster Workers' Council. We have listened to what it had to say at a meeting. What it is asking for is not negotiable' (*Hansard,* fifth series, vol. 874, col. 38).

In a half-page advertisement in the *News Letter,* unionist politicians call for support for the strike.

Seemingly unaware of the unionist grass-roots backing for the stoppage, the Executive declares that 'support for the strike was based on a false understanding of Sunningdale. Once this had been removed by a clear agreed statement from the Executive support for the strikers would diminish' (minutes of Executive meeting, quoted by Bew and Patterson, *The British State and the Ulster Crisis,* p. 65).

Séamus Mallon, chairman of the SDLP Assembly party, says that in view of Roy Bradford's suggestion the previous day that the Secretary of State should negotiate with the UWC, Bradford should no longer be allowed to continue as a member of the Executive.

21 May A back-to-work march is led by the General Secretary of the Trades Union Congress, Len Murray, but only two hundred take part. The marchers are pelted with eggs and tomatoes by supporters of the strike. Trade unionists claim that people wanting to join the march had been prevented from doing so by paramilitaries barricading housing estates.

At a Cabinet meeting Rees points out 'the impossibility of the task.' In the House of Commons, Wilson states: 'This is not only a political strike; it is a sectarian strike which is aimed at destroying decisions taken by this House of Commons, both as regards power-sharing, and by the elected Assembly. It is being done for sectarian purposes, having no relation to this century but only to the seventeenth century' (*Hansard,* fifth series, vol. 874, col. 184).

22 May The Executive agrees to the Council of Ireland being 'phased in'. SDLP Assembly members vote 11 to 8 against the revised plan but after talks with Orme agree to accept the changes. John Hume produces a fuel oil plan left over from an industrial dispute for discussion in the Executive.

23 May In the House of Commons Merlyn Rees says: 'It is a matter of regret to me that certain members of this house should attempt to set up a provisional government in Northern Ireland by issuing their own ration books and so on, and then come here and draw pay as democrats. That makes me a little sick' (*Hansard,* fifth series, vol. 874, col. 616). Ian Paisley challenges Rees to name the MPs or withdraw the remark; Rees replies: 'The honourable gentleman cannot have double standards and be a democrat here and a demagogue in Northern Ireland' (*Hansard,* fifth series, vol. 874, col. 618). Parliament later adjourns for the Whit recess, supposedly until 10 June.

Rees discusses the oil plan and informs Wilson that implementing it would involve using the army.

The report of the Anglo-Irish Law Enforcement Commission is published. It recommends an 'extra-territorial' method of bringing terrorist suspects to trial in the part of Ireland where they were arrested, no matter where the offence had been committed.

24 May At Chequers, Harold Wilson holds talks with Brian Faulkner, Gerry Fitt, and Oliver Napier. Wilson is accompanied by the Defence Secretary, Roy Mason, the Attorney-General, Sam Silkin, and the Northern Ireland Secretary, Merlyn Rees. Faulkner says that although the strikers are in control he feels the situation can still be saved by strong government action. Later the British Cabinet holds a special meeting at which it is apparently agreed that troops can go in to the power stations if Rees so decides. It is also suggested that the army might attempt to run petrol stations and oil supplies. The army leadership in Northern Ireland, however, is reluctant to use the army to confront the strikers. With the senior ranks of the NIO holding a similar opinion, it seems unlikely that Wilson will risk confrontation with loyalists to defend the Executive.

25 May At 10:15 p.m. Harold Wilson makes a television and radio broadcast about the situation. He describes the strike as 'a deliberate and calculated attempt to use every undemocratic and unparliamentary means for the purpose of bringing down the whole constitution of Northern Ireland so as to set up a sectarian and undemocratic state, from which one-third of the people would be excluded.' The strike is being run by 'thugs and bullies', he says. 'The people on this side of the water, British parents, British taxpayers, have seen their sons vilified and spat upon and murdered. They have seen the taxes they have poured out almost without regard to cost—over £300 million a year this year with the cost of the army operations on top of that—going into Northern Ireland. They see property destroyed by evil violence and are asked to pick up the bill for rebuilding it. Yet people who benefit from this now viciously defy Westminster, purporting to act as though they were an elected government, spend their lives sponging on Westminster and British democracy and then systematically assault democratic methods. Who do these people think they are?'

One of the loyalist politicians on the strike co-ordinating committee has been warned by contacts in London that leaders of the strike are to be arrested immediately after Wilson's speech, and as a result the co-ordinating committee goes to ground in east Belfast. In the event no attempt is made to arrest them, and they return to their headquarters in Hawthornden Road, Belfast, the following day.

27 May The army takes over twenty-one petrol stations throughout Northern Ireland; in response the UWC steps up strike action by threatening further power cuts. In the afternoon Paddy Devlin and Ivan Cooper of the SDLP, who had been in Dublin for talks with members of the Irish government, are forced to turn back at Dromore on their way north and return to Dublin. Their car is surrounded by a crowd blocking the road; Cooper later claims that although an RUC vehicle been nearby the police did not come to their assistance.

28 May As the crisis comes to a head, a situation report from the Executive's Emergency Co-ordinating Unit makes the following assessment:

'Electricity—supplies are expected to cease during this afternoon.

'Water—situation not much changed. The supply with some interruptions is being provided. If the electricity supply fails there will be difficulties but the service expects to be able to provide a supply for two or three days. The public can best help by not wasting water. If there are problems the public will be informed.

'Sewerage—the service is coping at the moment. There is an increasing incidence of pollution due to untreated sewerage in some areas but the public health authorities are keeping a tight watch on the position.'

Brian Faulkner resigns as Chief Executive, in effect ending the Assembly, after Rees refuses to meet the UWC. Explaining the decision of the Unionist members of the Executive to resign, he says: 'It is ... apparent to us from the extent of support for the present stoppage that the degree of consent needed to sustain the Executive does not at present exist. Nor, as

Ulstermen, are we prepared to see our country undergo, for any political reason, the catastrophe which now confronts it. That is why I have recommended this morning, on behalf of myself and my Unionist colleagues, that some sort of dialogue between government and those confronting it should now take place but the Secretary of State was unable to accept this recommendation. We have therefore offered our resignations to the Secretary of State and have advised him to explore at once the possibility of constructing a new administration on a basis which will command general public confidence.'

At 2 p.m. Rees issues a statement saying: '(*a*) The Secretary of State today received and accepted the resignation of Mr Brian Faulkner, Chief Executive Minister, together with those of Unionist members in the Northern Ireland Administration. (*b*) Under the terms of the Constitution Act 1973 there is now no statutory basis for the Northern Ireland Executive. (*c*) Arrangements exist for the continued Government of Northern Ireland in accordance with the Northern Ireland Constitution Act. In particular, the Secretary of State remains responsible for the preservation of law and order.'

Several hundred farmers line the route to Stormont in a massive tractor demonstration, and others block the Upper Newtownards Road in east Belfast. They carry placards and banners saying JAW JAW NOT WAR WAR and REES MUST TALK WITH UWC. Loyalist Assembly members, including John Taylor, Glen Barr, and Ian Paisley, address the farmers from the Carson monument. As news of the collapse of the Executive becomes known, Protestants celebrate by dancing and lighting bonfires in the streets of Belfast and throughout Northern Ireland.

Two IRA prisoners in Parkhurst maximum security prison, Isle of Wight, are reported to be suffering from the effects of a hunger strike. Francis (Frank) Stagg and Michael Gaughan have been refusing food since 30 March. The Home Office says that since that date the prisoners have been fed intermittently whenever it was necessary to preserve their health.

29 May With the threat of the Council of Ireland removed, Protestant support for the strike evaporates, and most people begin returning to work. Despite protests from many of their followers, UWC strike leaders decide to call off the stoppage.

In the wake of the strike a Cabinet sub-committee chaired by Wilson is set up to discuss possible future options for Northern Ireland. The sub-committee, which meets for the next three months, examines all possibilities, including British withdrawal from Northern Ireland, re-partition, and the creation of a *cordon sanitaire* along the border. The committee rules out all three options, on the grounds that they would only make matters worse.

30 May The Assembly is prorogued (it is officially dissolved on 29 March 1975). A columnist in the *Evening News* (London), Lord Arran, writes: 'I loathe and detest the miserable bastards … savage murderous thugs. May the Irish, all of them, rot in hell' (quoted by O'Clery, *Phrases Make History Here*, p. 159).

The UWC Strike

It is impossible to explain the degree of Protestant support that existed for the UWC strike without considering the impact of the events that preceded it on the unionist community: the civil rights demonstrations, the outbreak of sectarian conflict, the perceived hostility of the Irish government towards Northern Ireland, the apparent inconsistency of British government policy, the role of nationalist political leaders in bringing about the abolition of Stormont, and the continuing IRA campaign. Most unionists perceived the course of events from 1968 to 1973 as one of continual political retreat, if not defeat. Given this fact, it was unlikely that the Protestant community would accept the same people who had been instrumental in undermining the Stormont regime as part of a local administration, especially since members of the SDLP, with the Council of Ireland in mind, still talked as if a united Ireland were only months away.

While most Catholics were happy with the Sunningdale agreement, Protestants were at best ambiguous about power-sharing, while most were hostile towards the Council of Ireland. In short, for Protestants the Sunningdale deal was too much and too soon. It may have copperfastened SDLP involvement in the Executive, but it also ensured that most unionists would have nothing to do with it.

Whether the power-sharing Executive could have survived without the Irish dimension hammered out at Sunningdale is a debatable but entirely hypothetical question, since the power-sharing Executive and the Irish dimension were both parts of a single package: there was no option of accepting some parts of the agreement while rejecting others. The February general election was therefore of crucial importance to the future of the Sunningdale agreement, for it was as close to a referendum on the settlement as local voters were likely to get, and the result was clear. Unionists overwhelmingly rejected it. In their eyes, the Irish Government had failed to meet the commitments given at Sunningdale on extradition, recognition of Northern Ireland, and improved security.

The only real question then was whether the Executive would collapse from internal or external pressures. The fact that the *coup de grâce* was delivered by the UWC strike was to have unfortunate long-term consequences for the chances of an internal Northern Ireland political settlement, as an important section of the main nationalist party, the SDLP, was left permanently embittered by the manner in which the Executive ended and with the abiding belief that if only the British government had 'faced down' the strikers in the first few days of the stoppage the Sunningdale agreement would have succeeded. The most likely outcome of such a policy would have been a hardening of unionist resolve to oppose the settlement, with the Executive coming to a bloody end rather than merely collapsing. Nevertheless the strike undoubtedly hastened the 'greening' of the SDLP, with the party increasingly looking outside Northern Ireland in the hope of achieving political progress rather than attempting to resolve the problem primarily within the confines of Northern Ireland itself.

31 May At a press conference in Stormont Merlyn Rees says: 'There is a strong feeling of Ulster nationalism growing, which will have to be taken into account and which it would be foolish to ignore.' Rees and the NIO also believe that a new working-class consciousness is beginning to emerge within Northern Ireland.

The opposition of the Provisional IRA to the Sunningdale agreement leads them to believe that they can reach agreement with loyalists involved in the strike. A statement says: 'The loyalist workers are now capable of throwing up their own leaders and will not, in future, be led by the nose by middle-class, careerist politicians or the landed gentry of Ulster Unionism.'

Republicans meanwhile, still contending that Ireland is partitioned only to serve British self-interest, become euphoric over limited overtures of detente from loyalist paramilitaries. On 28 June one leading republican says: 'The fight is almost over. The British troops are ready to withdraw.' By July the Provisionals also believe that the British intend to set up a Northern Ireland Constitutional Convention to produce recommendations that will prove unacceptable to them, thus preparing British public opinion for withdrawal from Northern Ireland.

3 June Michael Gaughan dies in Parkhurst prison on the sixty-fifth day of his hunger strike.

8 June After six months the Price sisters end their hunger strike in Brixton Jail.

17 June The IRA bombing campaign in England continues when a 20 lb bomb explodes at the 900-year-old Westminster Hall in London, injuring eleven people. On 14 July there are bombs in Manchester and Birmingham, and on 17 July another bomb at the Tower of London kills one person and injures forty-one others.

19 June In the wake of a three-day conference of loyalist paramilitaries, which supports negotiated independence for Northern Ireland, a statement from the Provisional IRA says: 'There is evidence that the working-class Protestants who comprise the paramilitary groups are strongly socialist in their thinking. This bodes ill for traditional Unionist politicians ... who have exploited the loyalist working class on the basis of sectarianism. This development could have far-reaching effects, if they realise, as they must surely do in time, their community of interest with the depressed Catholic working class' (quoted by Bew and Patterson, *The British State and the Ulster Crisis,* p. 79). *Republican News* (22 June 1974) is less certain, however, about 'a significant change in the mentality of the Orange colonists who have for 180 years been the major agents in upholding English imperialism in Ireland.'

22 June An unarmed Catholic man is shot dead by a soldier in Strabane. The following day a member of the Life Guards Regiment becomes the first soldier to be charged with murder during the Troubles.

27 June Roland Moyle (Minister of State) and Don Concannon (Under-Secretary) are appointed to the NIO to help run functions that had previously been devolved to the Executive.

3 July In response to an offer from the UDA leader Andy Tyrie to negotiate with the Provisional IRA, a Belfast Sinn Féin leader, Máire Drumm, says they are ready to sit at the conference table with representatives of the UWC. The continuation of detente between the Provisionals and loyalist paramilitaries is aided by their shared concern on the issue of internment.

Loyalist and republican prisoners in the Maze develop an unofficial compromise, and are encouraged in this by the government. The NIO minister Stan Orme later admits to having been involved in round-table negotiations involving republican and loyalist leaders in the Maze (*Irish News,* 28 June 1976).

4 July A White Paper, *The Northern Ireland Constitution,* sets out a scheme for the election of a Constitutional Convention to draft an agreed plan for the government of Northern Ireland. It says: 'In recent months various groups within the community have shown an increased desire to participate in the political process and a growing belief that they can best find for themselves political relationships which will be acceptable to them. The government believes it is essential that participation in these processes should take place not only between like minded groups but equally between groups which hold apparently strongly opposed views.' The White Paper does not spell out whether groups supporting paramilitary organisations will be included. It also maintains the basic concepts of the 1973 settlement: there must be some form of power-sharing; any proposals must be acceptable to 'the people of the United Kingdom as a whole,' while 'Northern Ireland unlike the rest of the United Kingdom shares a common land frontier and a special relationship with another country, the Republic of Ireland. Any political arrangement must recognise and provide for this special relationship. There is an Irish dimension.' Officially at least the government appears not to recognise that the Irish dimension is dead for the foreseeable future.

6 July At a conference in Oxford, NIO ministers and members of the former Executive meet the chairman of the UWC, Harry Murray. Disagreements within the UWC lead to Murray leaving the organisation shortly afterwards.

9 July In the House of Commons, Rees announces the gradual phasing out of internment.

16 July The Taoiseach, Liam Cosgrave, votes against his own government's Contraception Bill on a matter of conscience, helping to defeat the bill by 75 votes to 61.

20 July The UDA resigns from the UWC and the Ulster Loyalist Central

Co-ordinating Committee and invites representatives of the Catholic community to hold talks with them.

22 July The British government announces that it is to acquire a majority shareholding in the Harland and Wolff shipyard.

14 August The Provisional IRA leadership, convinced that the British government has decided to use the Convention as a cover for the withdrawal from Northern Ireland, states: 'The deliberate inaction and vagueness of British government policy is designed to increase uncertainty among loyalists and Unionists and to encourage them to take up entrenched positions. When the time comes for the Loyalist/Unionist elements to make agreed proposals to the British government the hard-line group's proposals will be unacceptable. The time will then be right for the British government to make its appeal to British public opinion ... The Pilate-like washing of hands will be ceremoniously carried out and will be heartily endorsed by the mass of British people ... A dignified withdrawal is then possible with little loss of face and considerable financial benefit to the British taxpayer' (quoted by Bew and Patterson, *The British State and the Ulster Crisis,* p. 81).

2 September Rees launches a new policing scheme, which includes the expansion of the RUC, the RUC Reserve, and the UDR, but there is to be no 'third force' or home guard along the lines being demanded by unionist politicians.

3 September Enoch Powell is adopted as the Ulster Unionist candidate for South Down.

4 September Brian Faulkner launches the Unionist Party of Northern Ireland.

In a statement in the *Irish Times* the SDLP continues to dispute the underlying causes of the UWC strike and insists instead that Britain declare that 'it will remain in Northern Ireland only until such time as agreed institutions of government are established which allow the people of Ireland, north and south, to live together in harmony and peace.' The 'greening' of the SDLP also results from their fear that the failure of the Executive will lead Catholic support to move from them towards the Provisionals. As a result, the party increasingly adopts a more nationalist approach.

12 September There are demonstrations in Belfast by supporters of both loyalist and republican prisoners, protesting about food and parole. Trouble in the prisons continues intermittently in the following months.

16 September A judge, Rory Conaghan, and a magistrate, Martin McBirney, are killed by the IRA in Belfast, signalling an intensification of the IRA's campaign in Northern Ireland and the beginning of a bombing campaign in Britain. At the same time there is an upsurge in sectarian murders committed by loyalists.

5 October Five people are killed and fifty-four injured when IRA bombs explode without warning in two pubs in Guildford, Surrey. Further explosions occur in the centre of London on 11, 22 and 28 October, when a bomb explodes under the car of the Sports Minister, Denis Howell. In 1976 the 'Maguire Seven' are wrongly convicted of making the bomb used in Guildford.

10 October The British general election returns the Labour Party to power with an overall majority of three seats. The UUUC wins ten of the twelve 12 Northern Ireland seats, but the Unionist leader Harry West is defeated by the compromise nationalist candidate, Frank Maguire. The UUUC receives 58 per cent of the vote, the SDLP 22 per cent, and Alliance 6 per cent, while Faulkner's recently formed UPNI attracts only 3 per cent; the turn-out is 69 per cent. The *Times* (London) comments: 'Ulster voters have retreated to their sectarian stockades at the polling booths as never before.' The result makes the prospect of any agreement on the proposed Convention seem remote, and there are suggestions that it be dropped altogether. Conversely, the suspicion that the British government is about to announce withdrawal from Northern Ireland is never far from the surface.

During October there is pressure from Northern Ireland politicians to have Merlyn Rees removed from Northern Ireland, because of the growing political instability resulting from what are perceived as the political machinations of the NIO.

15 October Huts in the Maze Prison are burned down by republican prisoners in protest against new restrictions on visitors. Soldiers are flown in to the prison by helicopter to put down the riot. There is also trouble at Magilligan and Armagh prisons and in nationalist areas of Belfast.

22 October James Molyneaux is elected leader of the UUUC MPs in the House of Commons.

6 November Thirty-three republican prisoners escape from the Maze Prison through a tunnel. One is killed and the rest are recaptured.

7 November One person is killed and twenty-eight injured by an IRA bomb planted in a pub in Woolwich, London.

9 November In a series of incidents around Belfast, four Catholics are shot dead and a Catholic and a Protestant wounded. The former LAW leader Billy Hull and a former UDA leader, Jim Anderson, are wounded in what is believed to be a loyalist attack on the Crumlin Road in Belfast.

14 November In Coventry an IRA man, James McDade, is killed when a bomb he is planting explodes prematurely. The Provisional IRA's plans to hold McDade's funeral in Birmingham are dropped and he is buried in Belfast instead. The body is flown to Dublin after staff at Belfast Airport refuse to handle his coffin. McDade's death is later seen as the reason for the IRA's bombing of the Birmingham pubs a week later.

21 November Nineteen people are killed and 182 injured by bombs planted by the IRA at the Mulberry Bush and Tavern in the Town pubs in Birmingham. Two other people die later. Five men who left Birmingham after the bombings are later arrested.

25 November In the wake of the Birmingham pub bombs the government introduces the Prevention of Terrorism Act, which permits detention without charge for seven days and expulsion from Britain. Introducing the bill in the House of Commons, the Home Secretary, Roy Jenkins, says: 'These powers … are draconian. In combination they are unprecedented in peacetime. I believe they are fully justified to meet the clear and present danger' (*Hansard,* fifth series, vol. 882, col. 35). The act becomes law four days later. On 5 December it is extended to Northern Ireland.

8 December The Irish Republican Socialist Party emerges after a split in Official Sinn Féin; by March the following year it claims seven hundred members, including its founder, Séamus Costello, and the former MP

Bernadette McAliskey. In 1975 the organisation develops a military wing, the Irish National Liberation Army, which attracts some members from the Provisional IRA who are unhappy with the truce.

10 December Talks between Protestant churchmen and six members of the Provisional IRA Army Council take place in Feakle, Co. Clare. Their strategy is to 'try and strengthen the "doves" in the army council' (Gallagher and Worrell, *Christians in Ulster, 1968–80,* p. 97). The clergymen leave a series of proposals for the Provisionals to consider as the basis for a permanent cease-fire, and the Provisionals set out their demands. The Provisionals then call a temporary cease-fire to allow the government to reply to the proposals. On 12 December one of the churchmen, Dr Butler, the Anglican Bishop of Connor, says: 'We were all most impressed with their attitude, with their fairmindedness, and we were so pleased to find that they were talking seriously and deeply and with great conviction and had listened very carefully to what we had to say' (*Irish Times,* 13 December 1974).

20 December The Provisional IRA declares a temporary cease-fire, to last from 22 December to 2 January.

22 December Government officials conduct talks with Provisional Sinn Féin lasting until 17 January. By the end of 1974 an announcement of British withdrawal from Northern Ireland seems, to some observers, to be imminent.

The IRA plant a bomb at the home of the former Prime Minister Edward Heath in London.

DEATHS ARISING FROM THE TROUBLES: 220. SHOOTINGS: 3,208. BOMBS PLANTED: 1,113 (explosions: 669). INCENDIARIES: 270. FIREARMS FOUND: 1,236. EXPLOSIVES FOUND: 11,848 kg (26,120 lb). CASES OF INTIMIDATION: 2,453. PERSONS CHARGED WITH TERRORIST AND SERIOUS PUBLIC ORDER OFFENCES: 1,374.

1975

2 January The Provisional IRA extends its cease-fire to 17 January. Early in the year secret talks between officials of the NIO and members of the Provisional IRA lead to a truce. The IRA believes that the UWC strike in May 1974 has brought about radical changes in British policy and that the truce will be a first step towards British withdrawal.

7 January A meeting between Rees and a DUP delegation breaks up after arguments over the nature of government dealings with the Provisional IRA concerning the cease-fire. By mid-January it has become known that the Secretary of State, Merlyn Rees, has authorised discussions between NIO officials and Sinn Féin.

17 January The 25-day break in the IRA campaign comes to an end. Rees denounces the action, saying, 'I will not be influenced by any views which are backed by the bomb and the bullet.'

27 January Four bombs planted by the IRA explode in London. Nineteen people are injured in another explosion in Manchester.

30 January The Gardiner Report, examining measures to deal with terrorism in the context of civil liberties and human rights, recommends that detention without trial be maintained as a short-term necessity but that it be controlled by the Secretary of State, not the judiciary. It also recommends that special-category status be ended.

5 February A discussion paper on power-sharing, *The Government of Northern Ireland: A Society Divided,* is published. In the House of Commons, Merlyn Rees announces that 'H blocks' are to be built at the Maze Prison while a new prison is being built at Maghaberry, Co. Antrim.

9 February The Provisional IRA announces an indefinite cease-fire, to begin the following day.

11 February 'Incident centres', manned by Provisional Sinn Féin, are set up to monitor the cease-fire in liaison with British government officials. The incident centres come to symbolise the truce itself. The president of Provisional Sinn Féin, Ruairí Ó Brádaigh, calls them 'the very legs on which the truce stands,' while Máire Drumm says they constitute a 'power base for Sinn Féin' (Bew and Patterson, *The British State and the Ulster Crisis*, p. 66).

The Provisional IRA outlines the twelve points they say the British government has agreed to:

1. The release of a hundred detainees within three weeks.
2. The phasing out of internment within a specific period.
3. Effective withdrawal of the army to barracks, meaning three to four thousand soldiers returning to Britain within six months.
4. An end to the system of arrests and screening and large-scale searches in Catholic areas.
5. The establishment of incident centres, manned by Sinn Féin members and connected with an incident room at Stormont, to monitor the cease-fire.
6. Provision for 'army-to-army' discussions at local level.
7. The ending of military check-points and road-blocks at the edge of Catholic areas.
8. Immunity from arrest for specific people.
9. Firearms licences for specific people.
10. No immediate attempts to introduce the RUC or UDR to Catholic areas.
11. A formal cease-fire agreement to be drawn up by the British.
12. Further talks to take place between IRA leaders and senior British representatives.

The Truce

The relationship between the government and the IRA during the cease-fire is highly contentious. Though the NIO consistently rejected claims that they had done a deal with the Provisionals, when Dáithí Ó Conaill was arrested in Dublin in September and the Gardaí recovered what appeared to be a copy of a twelve-point peace agreement, the British government took the unusual step of formally denying the authenticity of the document.

The IRA felt that the negotiations undertaken during the truce would lead to a British withdrawal from Northern Ireland, though they believed that the British could not admit to this publicly. At the same time the discussions between government officials, including the most senior civil servant in Northern Ireland, Sir Frank Cooper, aroused the fears of other groups in the North, from the UDA to the SDLP.

The president of Sinn Féin, Ruairí Ó Brádaigh, gave his view of the period in the *Irish Times* (30 April 1992). 'Resulting from Feakle, a unilateral truce by the Irish Republican Army was declared and observed from December 22nd 1974, until January 16th 1975. Following the expiration of this and renewed army activity by both British forces and the IRA, talks were entered into—at the request of the British—for three weeks and the outcome was a bilateral truce on written terms from February 10th, with monitoring mechanisms in place.

'The Republicans were in receipt of a message from the British over the Christmas period that "HMG wished to devise structures of disengagement from Ireland." The bilateral truce lasted until September 22nd that year with various near-breaking points along the way. Truce-monitoring meetings and separate political meetings took place right through from February to September between "HMG representatives" and those of the "Republican movement", as they variously called themselves.

'The representatives offered to deliver a permanent ceasefire in return for a public British government declaration that it would quit Ireland by a date to be negotiated. The discussions failed and the bilateral truce failed even though the British Secretary of State of the time, Merlyn Rees, admitted afterwards in a letter to the London *Times* in July 1983 that the cabinet sub-committee dealing with Ireland had "seriously considered" withdrawal …

'The truce failed for three reasons: (*a*) the loyalist death squads immediately embarked on the greatest assassination campaign of innocent Catholics up to [that time]; (*b*) the Dublin government indicated to the British that a withdrawal must not be contemplated ("Dublin was becoming increasingly twitchy at the continuation of the truce and the talks," the British representative said) and a key republican leader, Dáithí Ó Conaill, was singled out and hunted down by them in early July; and (*c*) finally in the outcome the British did not deliver on their promise of the previous Christmas.'

At least some of the Provisionals' twelve points undoubtedly operated. Seven 'incident centres' were set up, security activity in Catholic areas was scaled down, and leading Provisionals were apparently not arrested when spotted by the army. In effect the British government acquiesced in a high IRA profile in, if not control of, certain areas. Labour Party politicians and NIO officials later claimed that the purpose of the truce was to divide the Provisional leadership and to create the conditions for ending internment and for criminalising the Provisionals. Some observers believe this to be a retrospective rationalisation of the situation.

18 February The new leader of the Conservative Party, Margaret Thatcher, appoints Airey Neave opposition spokesman on Northern Ireland, in place of Ian Gilmour.

20 February A feud breaks out between the Official IRA and the INLA. The chairman of the recently formed Whiterock IRSP, allegedly shot by the Official IRA in Belfast, is one of the first victims.

21 February Sir Robert Lowry, Lord Chief Justice of Northern Ireland, is named chairman of the Constitutional Convention.

The Irish Republican Information Service in Dublin announces that the Provisional IRA in Belfast is operating as a 'temporary police force' in republican areas, under the control of the incident centres. Belfast Sinn Féin later repudiates this.

27 February An IRA gunman shoots dead a London policeman at point-blank range. In the police sweep that follows, an IRA bomb-making factory is discovered in Hammersmith.

15 March The UVF murder two UDA men after a dispute in a bar in York Road, Belfast, sparking a feud between the two paramilitary groups. Between 10 and 21 March there are four shooting incidents in the feud between the INLA and the Official IRA, leading to three men being wounded, and nine incidents in the feud between the UVF and UDA, leaving two dead and seven wounded.

16 March Reserve Constable Mildred Harrison (26), killed in a bomb explosion at a public house in Bangor, is the first policewoman to die in the Troubles.

18 March The Price sisters are moved to Armagh Prison.

25 March Harold Wilson visits Northern Ireland and announces that 1 May will be polling-day for the Convention.

26 March Stanley Orme announces that the Harland and Wolff shipyard is to be nationalised.

2 April The bombing of a travel agency in Belfast marks the first breach of the truce by the Provisional IRA, which claims that the British have already violated it. At Easter the Provisionals in Newry close the town's incident centre and begin a series of attacks on the army and police. Using the title of 'South Armagh Republican Action Force', they begin a series of sectarian attacks.

5 April Five Protestants are killed by an explosion at the Mountain View Tavern on the Shankill Road, Belfast, and two Catholics are killed at McLaughlin's pub on the Antrim Road. A total of nine people are killed and seventy-nine injured in the series of bomb attacks.

12 April Five Catholics are killed in an explosion at the Strand Bar in the Short Strand, Belfast.

14 April In the House of Commons, Rees says that a loyalist gunman tried to kill him in 1974.

28 April An Official IRA leader, Billy McMillen, is shot dead in Belfast during the continuing feud between the Official IRA and INLA.

1 May The elections for the Constitutional Convention are held. With a turn-out of 65.8 per cent, the UUUC (with one Independent Loyalist, Hugh Smyth), who had advocated 'British parliamentary standards'—i.e. majority rule—wins 47 of the 78 seats, with 54.8 per cent of first-preference votes; the SDLP wins 17 seats, with 23.7 per cent of the first-preference vote, Alliance wins 8 seats (9.8 per cent), the UPNI wins 5 seats (7.7 per cent), and the NILP wins one seat (1.4 per cent). It is the seventh poll to be held in Northern Ireland in just over two years.

With the elections giving an overall majority to a Unionist coalition standing on a platform of opposition to power-sharing and an Irish dimension, there appears to be no possibility of accommodation. However, the truce between the government and the IRA helps generate apprehension in both blocs about Britain's intentions, and as a result both groups prove more pliable than might have been expected. The most significant expression of this is the suggestion of an emergency coalition by William Craig, who claims that the SDLP had originally suggested the idea. Although the plan appears to have considerable support, it is undermined when Ian Paisley, who originally appeared to favour the idea, comes out against it so as to prevent a split in the DUP.

5 May The Fair Employment (Northern Ireland) Bill is introduced in the House of Lords. Its purpose is to establish an agency to promote equality of opportunity in employment and to make discrimination on the grounds of religion or political opinion illegal.

8 May The first meeting of the Northern Ireland Convention takes place.

15 May In the House of Commons, Merlyn Rees claims that an upsurge in violence is due to internal republican feuds and sectarian murders, suggesting that there is no connection with the truce. While the truce means that the Provisionals need to re-channel the activities of their volunteers, leading to attacks on the Official IRA and Sinn Féin and on commercial premises, the increase in violence is also partly created by loyalist fears concerning the direction of the government's policy.

5 June A referendum is held to decide on whether the United Kingdom should continue to be a member of the EEC. In Northern Ireland the referendum throws up some unlikely allies, with the SDLP, Alliance, UPNI and NILP calling for a 'yes' vote and the DUP, Official Sinn Féin and Provisional Sinn Féin supporting a 'no' vote. The Ulster Unionists and Vanguard take no position. The referendum sees the lowest turn-out of any region of the United Kingdom, but, somewhat surprisingly, the vote in Northern Ireland goes in favour of continued EEC membership: 52 per cent in favour, 48 per cent against.

11 June Harold Wilson carries out a Cabinet reshuffle. Merlyn Rees stays in Northern Ireland, despite rumours that he might be replaced.

18 June A bill to amend the Northern Ireland Emergency Provisions Act (1973) is introduced in the House of Commons. The Secretary of State is to control detention instead of commissioners.

23 June The *Sunday Times* prints an article by John Whale that states: 'An epic change is being accomplished in Britain's relationship with N. Ireland. British withdrawal is becoming a fact. The lightening of the Ulster murk is now just perceptible ... What withdrawal means is the renunciation by the Westminster government of the attempt to wield power in N. Ireland ... It can be said to have begun in March 1972 when a Conservative administration discovered (as the army has still not quite discovered) that it did not have the power to beat the IRA militarily. The movement took a leap forward under the new Labour government in May 1974, at the time of the UWC strike, when ministers perceived that the most careful and equitable British originated solution could not be made to work ... The central fact about British policy ... is that the government has made the clear-eyed decision to have no policy, because it has no power to enforce one ... The British government has triumphantly completed that part of the necessary psychiatric therapy which consists in alienating the patient's affections ... The ultimate release from the problem of conflicting loyalties will be the emergence of a genuine N. Ireland identity. It is already detectable. Both Dr Paisley and Mr Fitt ... have already proclaimed their loyalty as Ulstermen on the floor of the Convention. An odd fate has overtaken the Provisionals. The theologians have a phrase for it: realised eschatology—that condition where the long-dreamt dream of the final fulfilment turns out to have become a reality here and now. The nub of the Provisionals' dream is an Ireland without British influence. Now they have it ... It has not happened in quite the way they expected it, and it will not have the consequences they once looked for: but these things never do.'

11 July The prosecution in the Birmingham bombing trial concedes that the six men accused were seriously assaulted while in custody. Though convicted, the 'Birmingham Six' are later proved to be innocent.

14 July In the House of Commons, Rees outlines the government's response to the IRA's proposals. The size and frequency of army patrols have been reduced, and questioning and searching of homes have been scaled down. No interim custody orders have been signed since the cease-fire began. The scaling down is to continue, and if there is a permanent cessation of violence security will be reduced to 'a peace-time level'. If violence ended, detainees would be progressively released. Rees says that discussions have taken place with the UDA and UVF and that the same opportunities existed for both the Provisional and Official IRA.

17 July Four soldiers are killed by a Provisional IRA bomb at Forkhill, Co. Armagh. The IRA claims that the murders are in retaliation for the killing of two Catholics earlier in the month.

31 July Three members of the Miami Showband from Dublin are murdered in a UVF attack near Newry. Two UVF men are killed in the same incident when a bomb they are planting explodes prematurely.

July Inter-party talks are held during the Convention recess and continue into August.

1 August Lieutenant-General Sir David House replaces Sir Frank King as army commander. During the next two years the army increasingly takes a back seat to the RUC in security matters. Of more immediate concern is the fact that the cease-fire with the IRA is in effect over.

10 August An 'anti-internment festival' at Dunville Park, Belfast, deteriorates into rioting and gunfire between the IRA and the army. Two children are killed in the cross-fire and eight people are wounded. The incident reflects the Provisional leadership's increasing difficulty in controlling its own grass roots.

13 August Five people are killed and nearly forty injured in a Provisional IRA attack on a bar on the Shankill Road believed to be used by members of the UVF.

29 August Éamon de Valera, former Taoiseach, former President of Ireland, and principal author of the Constitution of Ireland, dies at the age of ninety-two.

1 September Four Protestants are murdered at an Orange hall in Newtownhamilton, Co. Armagh, when it is attacked by a faction of the

Provisional IRA using the name 'South Armagh Republican Action Force'. Two masked men enter the packed hall and fire into the crowd, killing four people and injuring seven others.

2 September At an 'Irish Forum' in the University of Massachusetts at Amherst, the UDA expresses its support for the idea of an independent Northern Ireland.

5 September A bomb at the Hilton Hotel in London kills two people and injures sixty-three.

8 September The idea of a voluntary coalition for Northern Ireland put forward by the leader of Vanguard, William Craig, is repudiated by the UUUC, leaving Craig isolated. A resolution moved by Ian Paisley against 'republicans taking part in any future Cabinet in Northern Ireland' is passed by 37 votes to one, with only Craig voting against. Though Craig receives the support of the Central Council of Vanguard on 11 October, on the following day his former deputy, Ernie Baird, and eight other Convention members resign from Vanguard to form the United Ulster Unionist Movement. On 24 October Craig and his three remaining supporters in the Convention are expelled from the UUUC.

12 September Harold Wilson is forced to issue a statement denying reports that the Conservative Party is asking for Rees to be replaced as Secretary of State.

18 September Unemployment figures show 54,977 (11 per cent of the work force) out of work, an increase of 20,000 on the previous year.

22 September Bombs explode in towns throughout Northern Ireland. With the Provisional IRA claiming responsibility for some of the blasts, the truce is exposed as a façade.

3 October The UVF is again proscribed after twelve people die as a result of revenge attacks the previous day. The UVF says it carried out the attacks to show its 'utter disgust and displeasure at the failure of the civil and military authorities to take effective counter-terrorist action following recent IRA bombings.'

In the Republic a Dutch businessman, Dr Tiede Herrema, is abducted. His kidnappers threaten to kill him unless three republican prisoners are released.

9 October One person is killed and twenty injured in an explosion outside Green Park tube station in London.

21 October Gardaí surround a house in Monasterevin, Co. Kildare, where Dr Herrema is being held captive.

22 October At the Old Bailey in London, Paul Hill, Patrick Armstrong, Gerard Conlon and Carole Richardson, found guilty of causing explosions in Britain in October 1974, are sentenced to life imprisonment. The 'Guildford Four' will be found not guilty after a retrial in 1990.

23 October A car bomb outside the home of the Conservative MP Hugh Fraser in London explodes, killing a passer-by.

29 October The feud between the Official IRA and the Provisionals breaks out into open conflict. On 31 October, Séamus McCusker, a senior Provisional Sinn Féin member, is shot dead. By 11 November ten people have been killed in the feud.

4 November Rees announces that special-category status will not be accorded to those convicted of terrorist crimes committed after 1 March 1976. The decision arouses more protest from loyalist groups than from republicans, who believe a British withdrawal is just around the corner in any event.

6 November A seventeen-day siege in Monasterevin ends when Eddie Gallagher and Marian Coyle surrender. Dr Herrema is released unharmed.

7 November The UUUC report is endorsed by the Northern Ireland Constitutional Convention by a vote of 42 to 31. The report calls in effect for a return to the 'majority rule' system, modified by a series of all-party scrutiny committees similar to those suggested by Faulkner in June 1971. On the two key issues of power-sharing and the Irish dimension, the report states: 'The selection and dismissal of ministers should be at the discretion of the [Northern Ireland] Prime Minister, who should not be compelled to include members of any particular party or group. That no country ought to be forced to have in its Cabinet any person whose political philosophy and attitudes have revealed his opposition to the very existence of that state. External relations should be the responsibility of the government at Westminster in consultation with the government of Northern Ireland. Good neighbourly relations should be welcome but that imposed institutionalised associations with the Republic of Ireland should be rejected.'

10 November The Provisional IRA in Derry, who oppose the cease-fire, 'close' the incident centre in the city by blowing up the building in which it is situated.

11 November Four men are killed in the continuing feud between the Provisional and Official IRA.

12 November Announcing the closure of the remaining incident centres, Rees says that they serve 'no useful purpose. The Provisionals claim they are still in contact with government representatives.

14 November The Conservative Party leader, Margaret Thatcher, visits Northern Ireland.

17 November Rees meets local parties over three days to discuss power-sharing, policing and finance and decides to recall the Convention. Talks with the parties continue into 1976.

18 November Two people die and twenty-three are injured in an explosion in a London restaurant caused by an IRA bomb.

22 November Three soldiers are shot dead by gunmen at a border observation post in south Armagh.

27 November Ross McWhirter, a supporter of conservative causes, is killed by republican gunmen in London.

5 December Announcing the end of detention without trial, Rees says: 'As from today no-one is held under a detention order. The rule of law will be imposed impartially and firmly through the courts. Those who are guilty of crimes against the community will be arrested, charged and brought before the courts. If they are found guilty they will serve the sentences appropriate to their crimes. This is not merely right but infinitely better than relying on a system which has to be renewed every year' (quoted in *Keesing's Contemporary Archives,* p. 27762). Only 73 people (57 of them Provisionals) are held in detention; of these, 27 are also serving prison sentences. The last 46 detainees not serving sentences are released. Between August 1971 and December 1975, 1,981 people were detained; 107 of these were loyalists, the rest republicans.

6 December After a car chase and gun battle through the West End of London, IRA gunmen burst into a flat in Balcombe Street, where they take a married couple hostage. The four men then barricade themselves and their two hostages into one room. The area is evacuated, and police marksmen surround the flat. A telephone link is later set up, and a series of negotiations is begun (conducted on the police side by Detective-Superintendent Peter Imbert, later Commissioner of the Metropolitan Police.) The IRA men demanded an aircraft to take them and the two hostages to Ireland. The police refuse the terrorists' demands for food but allow water, which is lowered to them from the flat above.

The Balcombe Street siege ends six days later when the IRA men give themselves up without harming the hostages. They are later questioned about the murders of a London policeman in February and the murder of Ross McWhirter in November.

9 December A *Daily Telegraph* opinion poll shows that 64 per cent of people in Britain want troops withdrawn from Northern Ireland, compared with 55 per cent in 1974 and 34 per cent in 1972.

DEATHS ARISING FROM THE TROUBLES: 247. SHOOTINGS: 1,803. BOMBS PLANTED: 635 (explosions: 363). INCENDIARIES: 56. FIREARMS FOUND: 820. EXPLOSIVES FOUND: 4,996 kg (11,015 lb). CASES OF INTIMIDATION: 1,483. PERSONS CHARGED WITH TERRORIST AND SERIOUS PUBLIC ORDER OFFENCES: 1,197.

1976

4 January Two Catholics are murdered at their farmhouse near Whitecross, Co. Armagh, and another three Catholic men are killed by loyalist gunmen at Ballydugan, Co. Down.

5 January Ten Protestant workers are murdered at Kingsmills, Co. Armagh, by the 'Republican Action Force' (a cover name for the local IRA) as they return from work in a works minibus. The bus is stopped and the driver (a Catholic) is separated from his passengers, who are then machine-gunned. As a result of the killings Rees increases the number of soldiers in the area; this includes the first official deployment of the SAS, on 7 January. A squadron of the SAS had helped patrol the streets of Derry and Belfast when soldiers were first used in Northern Ireland in 1969 but had not operated under cover. One of the SAS's first operations takes place in March when they snatch an IRA commander, Seán McKenna, from his home in the Republic and hand him over to an army patrol in the North (Smith and Ripley, *Inside the SAS*).

12 January In the House of Commons, Merlyn Rees announces that the Convention is to be reconvened for four weeks from 3 February to consider specific matters he has laid down: power-sharing, finance, and law and order. Rees sees the central issue as Cabinet membership for the SDLP. Harold Wilson says that a united Ireland is neither a practical proposition nor a solution that any British party would wish to impose, emphasising the government's wish to ease itself out of the truce. Sinn Féin's leadership is still divided over the truce, and early in the year a shake-up in the Provisional leadership sees Seán Mac Stiofáin return to the Army Council.

15 January The first all-party security meeting on Northern Ireland is held in London, with the Prime Minister, Harold Wilson, in the chair.

21 January Gerry Fitt warns the Northern Ireland Committee of MPs in the House of Commons that some tenants' associations in Belfast are dominated by paramilitaries.

23 January The cease-fire ends, but contacts between the government and the Provisional IRA are maintained. While giving them an air of legitimacy, the truce divides the Provisionals. One IRA man notes that even if troops are withdrawn from Northern Ireland and detainees released they are no further towards a united Ireland than they had been in 1969. The Provisionals are also divided over the effect of the truce on the campaign against internment, some seeing the attempt to maintain the cease-fire as detracting from the campaign to end internment immediately.

3 February The Constitutional Convention reconvenes. Inter-party talks chaired by Sir Robert Lowry continue until 23 February.

12 February There are talks between the UUUC and the SDLP in the Convention, but no agreement on SDLP involvement in a Northern Ireland Cabinet. As far as Rees is concerned, the Convention is finished.

The IRA hunger-striker Frank Stagg dies in Wakefield Prison. The government had refused to transfer him to a prison in Northern Ireland. Stagg's death leads to rioting in west Belfast and bomb attacks in Derry the following day.

18 February Wilson suggests to Rees a meeting of British and Northern Ireland politicians in London.

29 February There are riots in Catholic areas against the ending of further admissions to special-category status.

3 March The last sitting of the Convention takes place. Unionists push through their report calling for a return to majority rule. On 5 March the Constitutional Convention is dissolved.

10 March The Irish government refers the case against Britain over treatment of prisoners to the European Court of Human Rights.

A former UDA spokesman, Sammy Smyth, is killed by gunmen at his sister's home in Belfast.

16 March Harold Wilson announces that he is resigning as Prime Minister.

18 March The effective end of the cease-fire comes with an army raid on the Falls Road incident centre, followed four days later by the resignation of Sinn Féin's Belfast organiser.

25 March In the House of Commons, Rees announces a policy of 'police primacy', making the RUC the leading element of the security forces. He says: 'I and ministerial colleagues in other departments ... are now examining the action and resources required for the next few years to maintain law and order, how best to achieve the primacy of the police, the size and the role of locally recruited forces, and the progressive reduction of the armed forces as soon as it is safely practicable' (*Hansard,* fifth series, vol. 908, col. 647).

26 March The Prevention of Terrorism Act (1976) comes into effect in Northern Ireland.

30 March The NICRA calls off its rent and rates strike after almost five years; it had originally begun as a protest against internment.

March Unemployment reaches 11 per cent, an increase of nearly half on the previous year. By June, 54,000 are unemployed, a post-war record.

5 April James Callaghan becomes Prime Minister. Stanley Orme and Lord Donaldson are moved out of Northern Ireland, and James Dunn and Ray Carter are brought in. Don Concannon is promoted to Minister of State.

1 May Kenneth Newman becomes Chief Constable of the RUC, succeeding Sir Jamie Flanagan. Newman pushes the policy of police primacy, which leads to a deterioration in police-army relations for a number of years.

5 May Nine IRSP members escape from the Maze Prison through a tunnel.

6 May Eight SAS soldiers are arrested in the Republic after what is claimed to be an accidental crossing of the border.

15 May Four RUC men are killed in two IRA attacks. Loyalist attacks on the same day lead to six Catholic men being killed and many more injured. The following day an RUC reservist and two Protestant men are killed by the IRA; on 17 May a Catholic man is shot dead in Derry; and on 18 May two Protestant brothers are killed by the IRA. Rees says he will not replace the 1,000 troops withdrawn before the upsurge in violence, as this is counter to the policy of establishing the primacy of the police.

22 May The UVF announces a three-month cease-fire.

4 June Ian Paisley leaks news of five meetings between the Ulster Unionists and SDLP held since March. On 7 June the UUUC votes against further talks between the two parties.

5 June Seven Catholics and two Protestants are killed and over seventy people injured in a spate of bombings and shootings in the Belfast area. The following day it is announced that 200 more soldiers are to be brought to Northern Ireland.

14 June In the House of Commons, Rees reveals that a committee has been set up to look at the problem of 'securing greater effectiveness of the police in enforcing the rule of law' (*Hansard,* fifth series, vol. 913, col. 50). The statement indicates an about-turn by the government. Having dealt with the Provisionals for a year and allowed them to impose their standards of order on many Catholic areas, Rees now says the security problem is one involving 'small groups of criminals.'

2 July Rees announces the results of the security inquiry to the House of Commons. Proposals include increasing the size of the RUC, new specialised investigation teams, greater flexibility, expanded training facilities, encouraging support from Catholics, and greater use of the RUC Reserve. The package adds up to a policy of police primacy.

21 July The British ambassador in Dublin, Christopher Ewart-Biggs, is killed when a land mine explodes under his car. Merlyn Rees was supposed to have been in the same car.

29 July In the House of Commons, Rees states that there have been no talks between government officials and Provisional Sinn Féin since early in the year.

8 August Republican rallies are held to commemorate the anniversary of the introduction of internment. In a speech Máire Drumm, a vice-president of Sinn Féin, says that, in the struggle for special-category status, 'if it is necessary [Belfast] will come down stone by stone, and if it is necessary other towns will come down, and some in England too' (quoted by O'Clery,

Phrases Make History Here, p. 168). Rees says that no action is taken towards prosecuting the speaker because reporters refuse to co-operate.

9 August The home of the SDLP leader Gerry Fitt home is broken into by a republican mob; Fitt forces them out at gunpoint. Later he recounts: 'For a few seconds I was faced with a crowd who were actually in my bedroom. I had a revolver in my hand and I pointed it at them ... The thoughts that went through my head at that time all in the space of a few seconds were: "Gerry, this is how you die"; secondly, "I hope to God you don't get my wife and young daughter"; and thirdly, "I hope to God I don't have to pull this trigger and kill someone myself" (quoted by O'Clery, *Phrases Make History Here,* p. 168).

10 August Two of Anne Maguire's children are killed and a third injured by a gunman's getaway car in the Andersonstown area of Belfast. The driver had been shot dead by soldiers, leading the car to run out of control and mount the pavement, where it crushed the children against a fence. The third child died on the following day. The youngest of the children was a six-month-old boy who was in his pram at the time of the accident.

12 August More than a thousand women in Andersonstown demonstrate in favour of peace, and on 14 August a second meeting attracts a crowd of ten thousand. These are the first of a number of rallies that lead to the launching of the Women's Peace Movement (later called the Peace People) at a 20,000-strong rally attended by both Protestants and Catholics in Ormeau Park on 21 August. A declaration of the Peace People is read out, which calls for the right to 'live and love and build a just and peaceful society.' They reject the 'use of the bomb and the bullet and all the techniques of violence.' One of the leaders of the new movement, Mairéad Corrigan, an aunt of the Maguire children, says: 'Everybody has failed so far to get the two sides together and to bring us peace. I believe it is time for the women to have a go and see what the women of both sides, working together, can do.' There are further marches and rallies on 28 August, when 25,000 people march along the Shankill Road to Woodvale Park, and in September, when further rallies are held throughout Northern Ireland and in Liverpool and Glasgow. The Peace People demonstrations are the first since the outbreak of the Troubles where large numbers of ordinary Protestants and Catholics have marched together in Belfast.

18 August Brian Faulkner announces his retirement from political life. On 13 September he is succeeded as leader of the UPNI by Anne Dickson, the first woman to lead a political party in Ireland.

1 September The Irish government declares a state of emergency, which allows suspects to be held for seven days without being charged.

2 September The European Commission on Human Rights announces its findings in the case brought by the Republic against Britain on the treatment of IRA suspects in 1971. It finds that the 'deep interrogation' techniques used constitute a breach of the European Convention on Human Rights 'in the form, not only of inhuman and degrading treatment but also of torture.'

10 September In a Cabinet reshuffle, Roy Mason becomes Secretary of State for Northern Ireland, with Merlyn Rees becoming Home Secretary. Roland Moyle is replaced by Lord Melchett. The Mason period accentuates a serious discrepancy in British government policy. On the one hand it points out the benefits of direct rule by 'impartial' British ministers and makes adverse judgments on local politicians, while at the same time it needs to hold out the promise of a return of power in the future to the same politicians it has spent part of the time denigrating.

15 September Kieran Nugent, a members of the Provisional IRA, is the first prisoner convicted of terrorist activities not to be accorded special-category status. When he enters the 'H Blocks' at the Maze Prison (so called because of the shape of the buildings) he refuses to wear a prison uniform and wraps himself in a blanket to distinguish himself from those convicted of non-terrorist crimes (often referred to as 'ordinary decent criminals' or ODCs). The so-called blanket protest over the restoration of special-category status will eventually develop into the hunger-strikes.

27 September At his first press conference as Secretary of State, Roy Mason stresses the importance of the economy over the political or security situations. 'Unemployment, little new investment, too many businesses closing down, these are the questions that must receive priority' (*Times,* 28 September 1976).

In the sixties the establishment of manufacturing plants belonging to national and international companies had offset the decline in Northern Ireland's traditional employers: agriculture, textiles, and shipbuilding. As the world recession begins to bite in the early and mid-seventies and many of the new manufacturing plants begin to close, the peripheral location of Northern Ireland, together with the continuing Troubles, only increases the likelihood of factories in Northern Ireland being chosen as the ones to close. The economic decline also has implications for the question of fair employment, as Catholics continue to be over-represented in the lower-paid, unskilled and semi-skilled areas of employment, which are likely to be most severely affected.

As Northern Ireland is unlikely to attract substantial foreign investment while these conditions continue, it is suggested that the state should take a greater role in creating and supporting jobs. Restrictions in public spending in Britain, however, mean that this never happens. While the Labour Party government (and future Conservative governments) would take pride in pointing out the higher rate of public spending per head in Northern Ireland compared with Britain, they fail to reflect on the fact that greater spending is needed to compensate for past under-funding and the greater need in Northern Ireland because of higher unemployment, the greater proportion of family dependants, poorer housing, poorer health conditions, and lower living standards in general. In effect the Mason era does little more than ease the worst excesses of public spending cuts in the United Kingdom.

10 October The founders of the Women's Peace Movement are attacked by a mob in the (Catholic) Turf Lodge area of Belfast. The death of a thirteen-year-old boy a week earlier, after he had been hit by a plastic bullet fired by a soldier, led to rioting in the area and the denunciation of the Peace Movement by republicans. Despite the growth of the Peace Movement, the response of the government—to patronise it and use it as an ideological weapon against the Provisionals—merely lends credence to republican statements that it is pro-British.

28 October Máire Drumm is shot dead while she is a patient in the Mater Hospital, Belfast.

27 November Betty Williams and Mairéad Corrigan, joint founders of the Peace Movement, lead a 30,000-strong march for peace through London. The march and rally at Trafalgar Square are attended by Jane Ewart-Biggs, widow of the British ambassador to Ireland killed by the IRA, the Archbishop of Canterbury, Cardinal Basil Hume (the most senior member of the Catholic Church in Britain), and the American singer Joan Baez. A number of republican supporters involved in a counter-demonstration chant 'Troops out!'

1 December The Fair Employment Act comes into effect. It makes it illegal to discriminate in employment on religious or political grounds and also establishes the Fair Employment Agency.

3 December Dr Patrick Hillery becomes President of Ireland.

At the end of 1976 the Chief Constable of the RUC, Kenneth Newman, reports that many Provisional IRA units have been removed and that there were twice as many charges against IRA members as in 1975 (Taylor, *Beating the Terrorists?* p. 80–1).

DEATHS ARISING FROM THE TROUBLES: 297. SHOOTINGS: 1,908. BOMBS PLANTED: 1,192 (explosions: 664). INCENDIARIES: 236. FIREARMS FOUND: 736. EXPLOSIVES FOUND: 9,849 kg (21,715 lb). CASES OF INTIMIDATION: 1,216. PERSONS CHARGED WITH TERRORIST AND SERIOUS PUBLIC ORDER OFFENCES: 1,276.

1977

As the Labour Party's majority disappears early in the year, the Leader of the House, Michael Foot, holds discussions with the leader of the Unionist Party in the House of Commons, James Molyneaux. In return for more seats (something opposed by the SDLP and the Irish government, on the grounds that it is a move towards integration) and some form of 'administrative devolution', the Unionists would not oppose the government.

14 January The *New Statesman* says: 'The Irish will have to be left to sweat it out for a while if they are to come to their senses.' The statement is symptomatic of the fact that British government attempts either to extricate itself from Northern Ireland or to completely appease Catholic grievances by assuming control of the administration of Northern Ireland have failed.

29 January Seven bombs planted by the IRA explode in the West End of London.

2 February Jeffrey Agate, the English manager of the Du Pont factory in Derry is shot dead by the IRA. The killing is followed by a series of attacks on prominent businessmen. On 14 March James Nicholson, a Yorkshire businessman, is murdered while on a day visit to the Strathearn Audio plant in west Belfast.

4 February The police discover an IRA bomb factory in Liverpool.

10 February IRA members involved in the siege in Balcombe Street, London, are found guilty of six murders.

28 February The *Irish Times* publishes details of a report drafted by the Orange Order on the question of British withdrawal from Northern Ireland. The report dismisses the fears of withdrawal as groundless and says: 'On every side there is growing acceptance of the Ulster case for increased representation in the Commons ... In the absence of a devolved government here Westminster has apparently accepted her responsibility to govern, and if Mr Mason's remarks are to be believed, the intention is to govern well.'

3 March Brian Faulkner dies after he is thrown from his horse while out riding.

11 March Twenty-six members of the UVF are jailed for a total of more than seven hundred years.

2 April The Conservative Party spokesman on Northern Ireland, Airey Neave, says that Provisional Sinn Féin should be proscribed.

17 April The Catholic Primate of All Ireland, Cardinal William Conway, dies.

25 April The United Unionist Action Council, led by Ian Paisley with Ernie Baird of the UUUM and supported by the UDA and UWC, announces that it will call a strike in May to protest against government security policy and to demand the return of a majority-rule government in Northern Ireland. The UUAC issues an ultimatum to the Secretary of State, giving him seven days to meet their demands. Mason makes much of the impact another strike would have on the economy and promises that enough soldiers and police will be made available to maintain the law.

As the deadline draws closer, both sides attempt to gather support. On 30 April DUP leader Rev. Ian Paisley says he will quit politics if the strike fails, while on 1 May 1,200 extra soldiers are brought into Northern Ireland and RUC leave is cancelled. Families stock up on supplies in preparation for a repeat of the May 1974 strike.

3 May The UUAC strike is launched amid conflicting claims and a well-orchestrated propaganda campaign by the NIO. The government says there is massive intimidation to try to get people to support the strike. Conditions are considerably different from 1974 when there was widespread fear among Protestants that Britain was about to withdraw from NI. By 1977 this fear has largely receded and as a result the strike is criticised by Ulster Unionists, Vanguard and the Orange Order. On 4 May the UUAC is dissolved as a result of the strike.

A majority of Belfast's shipyard workers vote against the strike. Most people go to work as usual despite threats of intimidation. The RUC reports that it has removed 300 road blocks, arrested twenty-three people and received 1,000 complaints of intimidation in the first three days. The success of the strike comes to depend on the attitude of the Ballylumford power station workers who supply two-thirds of NI's electricity. The power workers are put under pressure by both sides and twice refuse pleas from the UUAC to shut down the generators, saying that they will continue to produce power as long as other workers ignore the strike. On 6 May Ballylumford workers openly refuse to support the strike meaning that electricity supplies can be maintained and factories stay open, although the port of Larne is closed. As the stoppage fails to make any impact the strikers become more desperate. On 9 May there are demonstrations and road blocks in support of the strike. Paisley joins farmers in Ballymena who have blocked roads into the town with tractors and farm machinery. The government moves heavy troop reinforcements and armoured vehicles toward the town in a show of strength. The police take no action at the time but later arrest Paisley and Baird and charge them with obstruction before releasing them again. On 12 May sailings from Larne resume and on 13 May the UUAC strike is called off. Paisley claims the strike had been a success. Secretary of State Roy Mason tells Ulster workers that they can stand 'ten feet tall'. During the strike three people had been killed and forty-one RUC officers injured. On 15 May the RUC says that 115 have been charged with offences committed during the strike.

Secretary of State Mason is later to recall: 'I didn't intend Paisley and his cohorts to be able to run over the Secretary of State and direct rule and HMG. That would have been the last straw for us wouldn't it? So I was determined that wasn't going to happen. There was a lot of intimidation, a lot of villainy. They intimidated the Ballylumford power station workers on telephones at home, their wives and their families, those that were wanting to go on night-shift, to keep them back from the night-shift. They blasted a petrol station, killed a petrol station attendant because he was selling petrol against their wishes, then they killed a bus driver to take all the buses off the streets, which they succeeded in doing until that man had been buried. Then to try and stop the petrol being moved round the city they shot a tanker driver; they didn't kill him, they injured him. It was at a crucial time that as well, towards the end of the strike as our intelligence was reporting, and on what we thought was the final day the tanker drivers came to see me at Stormont Castle en masse. They were now going to call a tanker strike because one of their chaps had been shot and we kept them there all that day.

'Our intelligence was the strike was going to crumble that night. We couldn't have a hiccup; we couldn't allow the tanker drivers to go back to their branches and call out a strike, so we held them there for discussions, bringing in the General, bringing in the Chief Constable, my Minister of State Don Concannon, who played a superb part in that, and myself, one by one, discussing matters with them, security and their future, bringing in fish and chips from the city in order to feed them and keep them there and we held them long enough into the evening so that their branches couldn't be reported to and at 11 o'clock that night the strike collapsed.

'There was another very interesting episode in that strike and that was trying to keep the Ballylumford power station at work. Now of course you knew that these are all Paisley's men, a third of them were with him to the hilt, a third were very doubtful, a third I think wanted to work. So I brought twenty-seven shop stewards to Stormont Castle representing every grade in the power station, white collar, blue collar, the lot, right up to management and I addressed them on the security situation in the province. I outlined the steps of improving security in the province. At the end of the day I presented a paper to them of the steps which I intended to take. I had them run off and signed each one individually, gave one to every shop steward and they went and reported back and they carried on working. That saved the station.

'... He was a coward, Paisley, went to Ballymena and he barricaded his town with all his farmer friends, with agricultural vehicles and their tractors. I took off in my helicopter from Stormont Castle that day, singing as I rose into the air "Don't cry for me Ballymena", and I went across the top of the city and there, looking down, like High Noon in the street were Paisley's men across the road. Fifty yards down the RUC stretched across the road, megaphones in hand, talking to each other and now and again one man walked from each side to converse and go back again. That went on all day. At five o'clock in the morning, in spite of representations made to me not to do it, we arrested Paisley.' (Lord Mason interviewed in *The View from the Castle*, BBC NI 1988).

The UUAC Strike

While the main reason for the failure of the UUAC strike was the general lack of support from the unionist community the government's reaction was more planned and decisive than it had been in 1974. Secretary of State Roy Mason was excused from cabinet duties and stayed in Northern Ireland throughout the strike. A daily briefing was held in an operations room at Stormont every morning involving the Secretary of

State, the army GOC and the Chief Constable while the NIO also successfully played a delaying game with the electricity workers whose support was crucial to the success or failure of the stoppage.

Taken together with the 1974 UWC strike, the 1977 strike indicated several things about the nature of the loyalist strike tactic—that where unionists were united in opposing a political solution which required their participation then that solution was unlikely to succeed; at best the British government would find it difficult to impose its will in such circumstances. However, the strikes also showed that it was only in extreme cases, when the very existence of Northern Ireland was felt to be threatened, that such unionist unity existed, and even then intimidation was often required to keep the doubters in line. What the 1977 strike had shown, and what had been lost in the loyalist wave of euphoria which followed the 1974 strike, was that while unionists could destroy a settlement which required their involvement they could not dictate the terms of their own to the British government. In 1974 the strike leaders had failed to achieve their goal of fresh Assembly elections and failed to change government policy in the long term. In 1977 the UUAC strike failed to force the Labour government to implement the report of the Constitutional Convention. In 1985 a Conservative government would go one step further and ignore unionist opinion completely in an attempt to bring about a solution. In retrospect, however, it is apparent that this policy has also proved extremely limited in creating greater political stability.

14 May Captain Robert Nairac, a British army officer working under cover, is overpowered by seven or more men in a bar in Co. Armagh and taken prisoner by the Provisional IRA. The IRA later says it has interrogated and killed an SAS officer. Despite being tortured, Nairac apparently gave away no information (Hamill, *Pig in the Middle,* p. 216). He was later posthumously awarded the George Cross, the highest decoration awarded in peacetime.

18 May District council elections are held. As a result of the abortive UUAC strike the UUUC has splintered and the main unionist parties stand against each other in an election for the first time since 1974. With a turn-out of 57.9 per cent (down more than 10 per cent on the previous council elections in 1973), the Ulster Unionist Party take 29.6 per cent of first-preference votes (178 seats) and the DUP 12.7 per cent (74 seats). Other unionist groupings do poorly, with Baird's UUUP receiving 3.2 per cent (12 seats), the UPNI 2.4 per cent (six seats), other Loyalists 2.4 per cent (11 seats), and Vanguard 1.5 per cent (five seats). Alliance dominates the 'centre' with 14.4 per cent (70 seats); the NILP receive only 0.8 per cent of first preference votes (one seat). On the nationalist side, the SDLP strengthens its position by taking 20.6 per cent (113 seats), compared with Nationalist and Unity candidates with 1.5 per cent (six seats) and the Republican Clubs (Sinn Féin) with 2.6 per cent (also six seats).

25 May Callaghan announces that an all-party Speaker's Conference will consider the case for more Northern Ireland seats in the House of Commons. The Labour Party's willingness to concede increased representation for Northern Ireland will help produce a more pronounced nationalist response from the SDLP.

3 June Nine members of the UVF from Coleraine are jailed for a total of 108 years for terrorist offences after the longest trial in Northern Ireland legal history. By mid-summer, violence from loyalist sources has virtually dried up as a result of the RUC's breaking up of UVF gangs.

8 June Mason announces the withdrawal of the army's 'spearhead battalion' but says that RUC strength will be increased by 1,200 to 6,500 and the full-time UDR to 2,500. New anti-terrorist squads will also be set up.

16 June In the Republic the coalition government loses the general election, mainly over the handling of the economy. The new Fianna Fáil government, led by Jack Lynch, is openly critical of continuing direct rule in the North.

27 July Four people are killed in Belfast as part of a feud between the Official and Provisional IRA.

5 August Fire-bombs cause damage estimated at £1 million in Belfast and Lisburn. Six shops, two garages and an office block are destroyed.

10 August Despite an IRA campaign to prevent her visit by threats of bombing and riots, the Queen pays a two-day visit to Northern Ireland as part of her silver jubilee. It is her first official visit to Northern Ireland for eleven years. On the second day of her visit a small bomb explodes at the New University of Ulster in Coleraine shortly after the Queen had left. Nationalist leaders criticise the visit as 'insensitive', because it comes on the day after the anniversary of the introduction of internment. Members of the SDLP refuse to attend a reception held in her honour.

25 August An SDLP policy document calls for greater emphasis on the Irish dimension in response to what it sees as an integrationist policy by the British government. The adoption of this document leads Paddy Devlin to resign as chairman of the party, and he is later expelled, leaving Gerry Fitt as practically the only member of the leadership with a Belfast background.

30 August In the United States, President James Carter, under pressure from the Irish-American lobby, urges a new initiative tied to the nebulous promise of American investment. He says: 'A peaceful settlement would contribute immeasurably to stability in Northern Ireland and so enhance the prospects for increased investment. In the event of such a settlement, the US government would be prepared to join with others to see how additional job-creating investment could be encouraged, to the benefit of all the people of Northern Ireland' (quoted in *Keesing's Contemporary Archives,* p. 28700).

28 September The Taoiseach, Jack Lynch, and Prime Minister James Callaghan, meet in London. A joint communiqué issued later refers to the aim of getting a 'devolved system of government in which all sections of the community could participate.'

September is the first month since 1968 in which no civilians are killed as a result of the Troubles.

5 October Séamus Costello, founder and leader of the IRSP, is murdered in Dublin. Both the Provisional and Official IRA deny carrying out the killing. It is the first time the leader of a political party has been murdered in the Republic.

7 October The Irish Independence Party, led by Fergus McAteer and the former MP Frank McManus, is formed in Belfast. The IIP poses the first real political challenge to the SDLP's domination of nationalist politics.

Added to this, the lack of sympathy for the SDLP's position shown by Mason merely speeds the SDLP's swing towards a traditional nationalist position.

The Chairman of the Northern Ireland Prison Officers' Association is shot dead in Belfast.

10 October It is announced that Betty Williams and Mairéad Corrigan, founders of the Peace People, are to be awarded the Nobel Peace Prize. The award is actually that for 1976, for which they were nominated by members of the West German parliament. As the nominations arrived after the closing date, the award was a surprise. The £80,000 prize that goes with the award later becomes a source of controversy within the movement.

11 October Lenny Murphy, later revealed as the leader of the loyalist murder gang known as the 'Shankill Butchers', is found guilty of possession of firearms and jailed for twelve years.

14 October Tomás Ó Fiaich, an academic from St Patrick's College, Maynooth, and a native of Crossmaglen, is appointed to the vacant See of Armagh.

1 November Lieutenant-General Timothy Creasey succeeds Sir David House as army commander in Northern Ireland.

21 November Roy Mason produces a 'five-point plan' for the government of Northern Ireland. He suggests partial devolution as an intermediate stage towards the establishment of a legislative body with a wide range of powers. The plan is not dissimilar to Molyneaux's scheme for administrative devolution and consequently is not taken seriously by the SDLP.

26 November Following the split over the issue of voluntary coalition government for Northern Ireland the previous year, William Craig announces that Vanguard will cease to function as a political party. When the party dissolves on 25 February the following year most of the party's members, including Craig himself, join the Ulster Unionists.

30 December The *Irish Times* reports Roy Mason as saying, 'The tide has turned against the terrorists and the message for 1978 is one of real hope.'

DEATHS ARISING FROM THE TROUBLES: 112. SHOOTINGS: 1,081. BOMBS PLANTED: 535 (explosions: 366). INCENDIARIES: 608. FIREARMS FOUND: 563. EXPLOSIVES FOUND: 1,728 kg (3,810 lb). CASES OF INTIMIDATION: 3,039 (2,301 during UUAC stoppage in May). PERSONS CHARGED WITH TERRORIST AND SERIOUS PUBLIC ORDER OFFENCES: 1,308.

1978

6 January The optimism of the government concerning its ability to defeat the IRA is reflected in an article in the *New Statesman* that says of the Secretary of State for Northern Ireland, Roy Mason: 'It may be that he has broken the fighting capacity of the Provisional IRA.'

8 January In a television interview the Taoiseach, Jack Lynch, calls for a British declaration of intent to withdraw from Northern Ireland and suggests that he might eventually offer an amnesty to IRA prisoners in the Republic. The statement is supported by many nationalists in the North, including the Catholic Archbishop of Armagh, Tomás Ó Fiaich, who says: 'I believe the British should withdraw from Ireland. I think it is the only thing that will get things moving' (*Irish Press,* 16 January 1978). The comment prompts Ian Paisley to describe Ó Fiaich as 'the IRA's bishop from Crossmaglen'.

11 January The FEA publishes a report showing that Catholic men are two-and-a-half times as likely to be out of work as Protestant men.

13 January The Guildhall in Derry is badly damaged by an IRA bomb, seven months after being reopened following repairs carried out as a result of fire-bombing in July 1972.

18 January The European Court of Human Rights in Strasbourg delivers its ruling on the 1976 findings of the European Commission on Human Rights regarding the treatment of IRA suspects by Britain in 1971. It rejects the commission's use of the word 'torture', because the interrogation techniques used 'did not occasion suffering of the particular intensity and cruelty implied by the word torture.' Instead it says the suspects suffered 'inhuman and degrading treatment.'

7 February In the *Irish Times* the SDLP states that it is 'the British dimension which is the obstacle keeping us away from a lasting solution.'

8 February A booby-trap car bomb kills a member of the UDR and his ten-year-old daughter at Maghera.

15 February Reiterating the policy of an 'agreed Ireland'—first proposed by the SDLP in September the previous year—as an alternative for the British government after the maintenance of the status quo or withdrawal from Northern Ireland, John Hume says: 'The third option open to the British government is to declare that its objective in Ireland is the bringing together of both Irish traditions in reconciliation and agreement' (*Irish Times,* 16 February 1978).

17 February Twelve people, all Protestants, are killed and twenty-three are injured by an IRA incendiary bomb at the La Mon House Hotel in Castlereagh, Co. Down. Four hundred were in the building at the time. Cans of petrol were attached to the bombs, sending fire sweeping through a dining-room. Members of the staff had begun to clear the hotel after an anonymous telephone warning when the bomb exploded on a windowsill outside the dining-room. Many guests jumped from windows with their clothes on fire. The RUC later distribute thousands of leaflets with photographs of the remains of those killed. There have already been a hundred explosions throughout Northern Ireland so far in 1978.

18 February Twenty men are arrested in connection with the La Mon bombing and murders.

25 February Gerry Adams is charged with membership of the IRA. He is freed on 6 September when a judge rules that there is insufficient evidence to prove he is a member of the organisation.

3 March A woman civilian searcher and a soldier are killed in Belfast city centre when a gunman in fancy dress mingles with students during the university rag-day procession and shoots the two dead.

16 March A Provisional IRA man, Francis Hughes, is arrested after a gun battle near Maghera in which a soldier is killed.

7 April There are increasing signs that the bipartisan approach to Northern Ireland in the House of Commons is breaking down when the Conservative Party spokesman on Northern Ireland, Airey Neave, says that power-sharing is no longer 'practical politics' and that a future Conservative government will support the Ulster Unionists' proposals for an upper tier to local administration.

19 April The Prime Minister, James Callaghan, says that Northern Ireland's representation in the House of Commons will be increased as part of a general redistribution of seats. Northern Ireland eventually gets seventeen seats, a decision bitterly attacked by the SDLP leader, Gerry Fitt.

1 June David Cook of the Alliance Party is installed as Belfast's first non-Unionist Lord Mayor as a result of a dispute between Unionist councillors.

17 June The IRA ambush an RUC patrol car near Crossmaglen. One policeman is killed and the second, Constable William Turbitt, kidnapped. The following day Father Hugh Murphy, a Catholic priest, is abducted from his home in Ahoghill, Co. Antrim. The kidnappers say they will return Father Murphy in the same condition as the kidnapped RUC man. After appeals by Protestant ministers (including Ian Paisley) Father Murphy is released unharmed. The body of Constable Turbitt is discovered in a derelict house on 10 July. In December three members of the RUC are charged with kidnapping Father Murphy and, with two other policemen, of murdering a Catholic shopkeeper in Ahoghill in 1977.

19 June The leader of the Conservative Party, Margaret Thatcher, visits Northern Ireland and holds meetings with a variety of groups. She promises that a future Conservative government will form a 'regional council structure' in Northern Ireland along the lines suggested by the Ulster Unionists.

21 June Soldiers kill three IRA bombers and a passer-by in an ambush at a post office depot in north Belfast. The risks involved in such activities by the army are illustrated on 11 July when soldiers kill a youth who has returned to a terrorist arms cache that he has discovered and reported to the police.

2 August Three days after a visit to the Maze Prison, Cardinal Ó Fiaich says of the conditions resulting from the 'dirty protest' that 'one would hardly allow an animal to remain in such conditions, let alone a human being.' His remarks are welcomed by Provisional Sinn Féin and the SDLP. More than three hundred republican prisoners are refusing to wear prison clothes or follow prison regulations in a protest aimed at restoring special-category status to those convicted of terrorist offences. The prisoners wear only blankets and smear the walls of their cells with their own excreta, creating a health hazard both for themselves and the prison staff. A republican propaganda campaign that portrays the British government as being entirely responsible for the conditions is particularly successful in the United States, where contributions to the IRA increase dramatically.

Roy Mason announces that the De Lorean Motor Company is to open a sports car factory in west Belfast. The government is to provide £56 million, out of a total cost of £65 million. John De Lorean has previously failed to get the financial backing he seeks in the Republic, Puerto Rico, or the United States. The acquisition of the De Lorean project is looked on as something of a coup, though doubts remain over technical problems, the cost of transporting the cars to America, the fierce competitiveness of the American sports car market, and the fact that the factory is to be established on the edge of an area with a high level of republican activity.

14 August The *Daily Mirror* announces its support for a British withdrawal from Northern Ireland.

27 August Up to ten thousand people take part in a march from Coalisland to Dungannon to mark the anniversary of a similar civil rights march ten years earlier.

During August, Amnesty International claims that suspects at Castlereagh RUC detention centre in Belfast have been ill-treated. The allegation is rejected by the Chief Constable, Kenneth Newman. Mason later promises an inquiry into RUC practice and procedure during interrogations.

5 October Betty Williams, Mairéad Corrigan and Ciarán McKeown say they are stepping down as leaders of the Peace People.

6 October A part-time UDR captain is killed at the Newry cattle market. He is the only army casualty in the months of September and October.

8 October The tenth anniversary of the Derry riots that marked the deterioration of the civil rights campaign into one of sectarian conflict sees more rioting in Derry after the RUC permit a Sinn Féin demonstration to pass through the (Protestant) Waterside district of the city. Seventy RUC men are injured while dispersing a loyalist counter-demonstration organised by Ian Paisley.

12 October One woman is killed and two others injured when a bomb explodes on the Dublin–Belfast train.

Having suffered a number of setbacks in the previous two years and with declining support among Catholics, the IRA has reorganised into smaller units, which pay much greater attention to their own security. A mislaid British army intelligence document of 2 November entitled 'Northern Ireland: Future Terrorist Trends' comments: 'We see no prospect in the next five years of any political change which would remove PIRA's raison d'être.' The report observes that 'there is a stratum of intelligent, astute and experienced terrorists who provide the backbone of the organisation … our evidence of the calibre of rank-and-file terrorists does not support the view that they are merely mindless hooligans drawn from the unemployed and unemployable.' The report notes that while 'there is seldom much support even for traditional protest marches, by reorganising on cellular lines, PIRA has become much less dependent on public support than in the past and is less vulnerable to penetration by informers.'

11 November Tom Pendry becomes an Under-Secretary at the NIO.

14 November Having regrouped and stockpiled arms and explosives, the Provisional IRA launches a fresh bombing campaign. Thirty-seven people are injured as car bombs explode almost simultaneously in Belfast, Derry, and several large towns throughout Northern Ireland. Over the next week more than fifty bombs explode.

26 November In a continuing series of attacks on prison officers, Albert Miles, Deputy Governor of the Maze Prison, is shot dead by the IRA at his home in north Belfast.

1 December IRA bombs explode in eleven towns throughout Northern Ireland.

12 December The wives of three prison officers and a postman are injured by exploding parcel bombs in Belfast and Lisburn.

17 December IRA bombs explode in Liverpool, Manchester, Bristol, Coventry, and Southampton.

20 December In the wake of IRA bombs in a number of British cities, police leave in London is cancelled and more than two thousand uniformed officers are drafted into the West End in a bid to prevent a pre-Christmas IRA bombing campaign.

21 December In Crossmaglen three soldiers are machine-gunned to death by IRA men in a passing van while people do their Christmas shopping.

DEATHS ARISING FROM THE TROUBLES: 81. SHOOTINGS: 755. BOMBS PLANTED: 633 (explosions: 455). INCENDIARIES: 115. FIREARMS FOUND: 393. EXPLOSIVES FOUND: 956 kg (2,110 lb). CASES OF INTIMIDATION: 513. PERSONS CHARGED WITH TERRORIST AND SERIOUS PUBLIC ORDER OFFENCES: 843.

1979

20 February Eleven members of the loyalist murder gang known as the Shankill Butchers are convicted of 112 offences, including nineteen murders. They receive a total of forty-two concurrent life sentences.

16 March The Bennett Report is published. The three-man committee headed by an English judge, Judge Harry Bennett, was set up by the Secretary of State, Roy Mason, to examine allegations of ill-treatment at interrogation centres. The report goes beyond its terms of reference and says there have been cases where medical evidence shows that injuries sustained in police custody were not self-inflicted. The government accepts two major recommendations: that closed circuit television cameras be installed in interview rooms, and that suspects have access to a solicitor after forty-eight hours. Almost all the other recommendations are later accepted by the incoming Conservative government.

28 March The abstentionist MP for Fermanagh-South Tyrone, Frank Maguire, goes to the House of Commons for a crucial vote of confidence in the Labour Party government, but does not vote. He comments: 'You could say I came over to London to abstain in person' (quoted by O'Clery, *Phrases Make History Here,* p. 180). The SDLP leader, Gerry Fitt, also refuses to support the government, which is defeated by 311 votes to 310.

30 March Airey Neave, the Conservative Party spokesman on Northern Ireland and a close friend of Margaret Thatcher, dies after a bomb explodes under his car as he drives out of the underground car park at the House of Commons. Neave had advocated a strong security line to combat republican terrorists and would almost certainly have become Secretary of State for Northern Ireland after the election in May. The Conservative manifesto for the general election says: 'In the absence of devolved government we seek to establish one or more elected regional councils with a wide range of powers over local services.' With the death of its author, however, no serious attempt is made to implement the proposals.

16 April A prison officer is shot dead as he is leaving a church after his sister's wedding at Clogher.

17 April Four RUC men are killed in an IRA bomb explosion at Bessbrook. It is the largest explosion up to this time.

19 April A prison officer is killed and three others wounded by gunmen outside Armagh women's prison.

3 May The Conservative Party, led by Margaret Thatcher, wins the general election. In Northern Ireland the turn-out is 68.4 per cent, and seats change hands in three constituencies. In East Belfast, in a close contest, Peter Robinson (DUP) receives 15,994 votes and defeats the sitting MP, William Craig (15,930 votes); Oliver Napier (Alliance) receives 15,066 votes. In North Belfast, John McQuade wins the seat for the DUP from the new Ulster Unionist candidate, Cecil Walker, by just under a thousand votes. In North Down Jim Kilfedder retains his seat despite having resigned from the Ulster Unionist Party and facing opposition from a Unionist candidate. In Fermanagh-South Tyrone, Austin Currie stands as an Independent SDLP candidate, but the split nationalist vote is offset by a split in the unionist vote between Ernie Baird (UUUP) and Raymond Ferguson (Ulster Unionist), and Frank Maguire retains his seat.

Humphrey Atkins ('Humphrey Who?' asks the *Sunday News,* 6 May 1979) becomes Secretary of State, with Michael Alison and Hugh Rossi as ministers of state and Lord Elton, Philip Goodhart and Giles Shaw under-secretaries.

10 May An American judge rules that IRA suspects accused of bombing Ripon Barracks in Yorkshire cannot be extradited to Britain.

7 June The first elections to the European Parliament are held. In Northern Ireland thirteen candidates stand for three seats (elected by PR), with Northern Ireland as a single constituency (in the rest of the United Kingdom the 'first past the post' system is used). The election centres on individuals rather than parties, and Ian Paisley is elected on the first count with 170,688 first-preference votes (29.8 per cent of valid votes). John Hume also polls well and receives 140,622 first-preference votes (24.6 per cent), less than three thousand below the quota needed. The two Unionist candidates do poorly by comparison: John Taylor receives 68,185 votes (11.9 per cent) and Harry West 56,984 (10.0 per cent). Oliver Napier (Alliance), Jim Kilfedder (Ulster Unionist) and Bernadette McAliskey

(Independent) receive between 30,000 and 40,000 first-preference votes each, while the remaining candidates (including David Bleakley and Paddy Devlin) receive fewer than 10,000 votes each. On the second count no-one is elected. Hardly surprisingly, John Hume gets only 55 of Paisley's surplus vote and fails to reach the quota. On the third count, with the elimination of the six lowest candidates and the transfer of their votes, John Hume is elected and McAliskey eliminated. The fourth count sees Napier eliminated and the fifth, West. The transfer of West's votes leads to the election of John Taylor on the sixth count. The turn-out (valid votes) is 56.9 per cent.

The massive personal vote for Paisley in the European election and the poor Alliance showing do not augur well for any government initiative.

2 July Humphrey Atkins announces the banning of the INLA.

12 July The new Prime Minister, Margaret Thatcher, attacks the BBC after it broadcasts an interview with a member of the INLA. Confrontations between the government and the broadcasting media continue through the eighties and into the nineties.

2 August An IRA land mine kills two soldiers, bringing the total of army deaths since 1969 to 301.

27 August In the Irish Republic the Queen's cousin, 79-year-old Earl Louis Mountbatten, and three other people die after their 30-foot boat is blown up by an IRA bomb at Mullaghmore, Co. Sligo. Mountbatten's fourteen-year-old grandson, a seventeen-year-old boatman and the Dowager Lady Brabourne are also killed in the explosion. Mountbatten, who had been supreme commander of allied forces in South-east Asia during the Second World War and later the last British Viceroy of India (the Indian government announced a week of mourning for him), had spent every August in Mullaghmore for the past thirty years and never had a bodyguard. Thomas McMahon and Francis McGirl are charged with the murder of Lord Mountbatten on 30 August. In November McMahon is sentenced to life imprisonment for murder. McGirl is acquitted on the same charge.

A few hours after the Mountbatten murders, eighteen soldiers are killed in an IRA bomb blast at Narrow Water near Warrenpoint, Co. Down. A 500 lb bomb planted in a lorry loaded with hay is detonated by the IRA as an army convoy drives past, killing six members of the Parachute Regiment.

A second explosion in the same area damages a helicopter carrying members of a 'quick reaction force' from the Queen's Own Highlanders, killing twelve solders including the commanding officer Lieutenant-Colonel David Blair. A gun battle breaks out between the soldiers and IRA men firing from the Irish Republic. During the shooting an innocent civilian is killed on the Republic's side of the border. The incident brings the army's greatest loss of life in any one day of the Troubles.

The events of 27 August are followed by an upsurge in the number of Catholics killed in sectarian murders. At the same time in the United States a campaign is being orchestrated by the 'Four Horsemen'—'Tip' O'Neill, Speaker of the House of Representatives, Senator Edward Kennedy, Senator Daniel Moynihan, and Governor Hugh Carey of New York—to force Britain to undertake a political initiative in Northern Ireland. This campaign culminates in a decision by the State Department at the end of August to suspend the sale of hand-guns to the RUC (the RUC buys weapons from Germany instead). This action causes great concern to the British government, as the United States has generally remained uncritical of British policy in Northern Ireland.

30 August It is announced that the RUC complement is to be increased by 1,000 men, to 7,500.

7 September James Molyneaux becomes leader of the Ulster Unionist Party, in succession to Harry West. Molyneaux had been leader of the Ulster Unionist MPs in the House of Commons since October 1974.

30 September On a visit to the Republic Pope John Paul II addresses an audience of 250,000 at Drogheda and makes an appeal for an end to violence in Ireland. 'To all of you who are listening, I say: do not believe in violence; do not support violence. It is not the Christian way. It is not the way of the Catholic Church. Believe in peace and forgiveness and love; for they are of Christ. On my knees I beg of you to turn away from the paths of violence and to return to the ways of peace. You may claim to seek justice. I too believe in justice and seek justice. But violence only delays the day of justice. Violence destroys the work of justice … do not follow any leaders who train you in the ways of inflicting death. Those who resort to violence always claim that only violence brings about change. You must know that there is a political, peaceful way to justice.'

2 October Replying to the Pope's speech, the IRA says: 'In all conscience we believe that force is by far the only means of removing the evil of the British presence in Ireland ... we know also that upon victory, the Church would have no difficulty in recognising us' (quoted by O'Clery, *Phrases Make History Here,* p. 182).

The former head of the Secret Intelligence Service (MI6), Sir Maurice Oldfield, is appointed to the new post of security co-ordinator for Northern Ireland in an attempt to improve relations between the RUC and the army.

25 October In a move primarily designed to ease American pressure, and despite there being no support for a new political initiative, Atkins announces that he will be calling a conference of interested parties to discuss possible paths to devolution.

2 November The Gardaí seize weapons worth £500,000 sent from IRA sympathisers in the United States.

13 November Reacting to the growing use of socialist-sounding rhetoric by Provisional Sinn Féin, William Deedes writes in the *Daily Telegraph*: 'The Provisional IRA are determined, confident, ruthless and far more ambitious. Their aim is no longer "Brits Out" but as Adams has recently proclaimed quite openly, a Marxist revolution in all Ireland.'

20 November The government publishes a consultative document, *The Government of Northern Ireland: A Working Paper for a Conference,* which states that the aim of the talks is to achieve 'the highest level of agreement ... which will best meet the immediate needs of Northern Ireland.' The paper rules out discussion of Irish unity, confederation, independence, or the constitutional status of Northern Ireland. It also says that direct rule is not a 'satisfactory' basis for the government of Northern Ireland. Although the White Paper rules out discussion of the Irish dimension, Atkins is later forced to concede the principle of parallel talks, which allows the SDLP to raise the question in order to obtain their participation.

22 November The White Paper brings about a split within the SDLP and the resignation of its leader, Gerry Fitt, who wishes to continue discussions with the unionists even without the Irish dimension. In his resignation statement Fitt says: 'Nationalism has been a political concept in Ireland over many, many years but I suggest that it has never brought peace to the people of the six counties. I for one have never been a nationalist to the total exclusion of my socialist ideals' (*Belfast Telegraph*, 22 November 1979). John Hume, who refuses to accept exclusion of the Irish dimension, replaces Fitt as leader of the SDLP. Hume's accession to the leadership marks the advent of a more nationalist mood in the party as a whole, providing few signs of optimism for the Atkins initiative.

1 December Lieutenant-General Sir Richard Lawson succeeds Sir Timothy Creasey as army commander in Northern Ireland.

5 December Jack Lynch resigns as Taoiseach and is succeeded by Charles Haughey six days later.

12 December Twenty-four IRA suspects are arrested in cities throughout England in an attempt to foil a bombing offensive.

16 December Five soldiers are killed, four by a land mine outside Dungannon and one by a booby-trap bomb.

23 December A member of the RUC Reserve is shot dead in an ambush in Co. Monaghan while on his way to buy Christmas turkeys.

DEATHS ARISING FROM THE TROUBLES: 113. SHOOTINGS: 728. BOMBS PLANTED: 564 (422 explosions). INCENDIARIES: 60. FIREARMS FOUND: 300. EXPLOSIVES FOUND: 905 kg (1,995 lb). CASES OF INTIMIDATION: 446. PERSONS CHARGED WITH TERRORIST AND SERIOUS PUBLIC ORDER OFFENCES: 670.

1980

1 January John Hermon becomes Chief Constable of the RUC in succession to Sir Kenneth Newman.

4 January Three UDR members are killed and four others injured by a 1,000 lb booby-trap bomb, bringing the 'official' death toll to more than two thousand.

7 January As part of the 'Atkins talks', a constitutional conference involving the DUP, Alliance and SDLP gets under way. The Ulster Unionists refuse to take part, claiming that the talks are little more than a gimmick. Enoch Powell, the MP for South Down, goes further and says that the talks are designed to separate Northern Ireland from the United Kingdom. There is disagreement on the agenda at the outset as the SDLP insists on discussing issues outside the remit of the conference; as a result a parallel conference is convened to discuss these issues. The DUP in turn refuses to become involved in this parallel conference. Though the talks continue intermittently for several months, there seems little chance of any worthwhile agreement between the parties, particularly in the absence of Northern Ireland's largest party, the Ulster Unionists.

The IRA shoot dead a policeman inside Seaview football ground in north Belfast during an Irish League match.

13 January Three people are killed and two injured in a blast caused by an incendiary device on a train travelling between Belfast and Lisburn.

17 January The MP for North Down, James Kilfedder, launches the Ulster Progressive Unionist Party; the name is later changed to Ulster Popular Unionist Party.

21 January Anne Maguire, mother of the three children whose deaths sparked the formation of the Peace People in 1976, is found dead; she is believed to have committed suicide. The Maguires emigrated to New Zealand to try to start a new life but had returned because of homesickness.

10 February After rumours of serious disagreements among members of the executive committee of the Peace Movement, Betty Williams, one of the founders, resigns for family reasons. On 5 March a former chairman of the Peace People, Peter McLachlan, also resigns. One of the sources of disagreement is the attitude the movement should take towards republican prisoners in the Maze Prison.

16 February The IRA shoot dead a British army colonel in Germany. On 1 March another soldier is critically injured.

20 February The government and liberal press begin endowing Ian Paisley with statesmanlike qualities, believing that he is about to become involved in a new political deal. In the *Guardian* a senior British official says: 'It's because he smells power that he is a totally changed man ... Paisley's always been a wrecker but now he is trying to build something.' Three days later the *Economist* echoes this sentiment: 'Mr Paisley seems to be becoming more moderate now that he sees the possibility of becoming top dog in the province.' At the same time the Ulster Unionists are castigated in the same quarters for refusing to become involved in the talks.

11 March The remains of the German industrialist and consul, Thomas Niedermayer, who had been kidnapped in December 1973, are found in a rubbish tip in west Belfast. An earlier extensive search in November 1978 had revealed nothing.

24 March The 'Atkins talks' end without any significant agreement.

26 March Atkins announces the phasing out of special-category status from 1 April for those convicted of terrorist offences, irrespective of when the crime was committed. At this time there are 443 special-category prisoners. An earlier decision in March 1976 denied special-category status to those sentenced after that date, and in April 1980 a further NIO decision denied the status to those charged after that date no matter when the crime was committed.

Since 1976 there has been a growing campaign of non-co-operation by prisoners on the issues of wearing prison clothes, doing prison work, freedom to associate with other prisoners and to organise recreational facilities, and remission of sentences. Protests began with prisoners refusing to wear prison clothes, but by late 1977 the campaign had also begun to involve the refusal to wash or use toilet facilities and the smearing of cells by prisoners with their own excrement and food. In February thirty women in Armagh Jail had joined the 'dirty protest' in an attempt to step up the campaign to regain political status. The propaganda aspect of the protest is also of importance, particularly to the Irish-American audience, and a great deal of effort is expended by republicans in an attempt to make the NIO appear responsible for the condition of the cells, though these are regularly steam-cleaned by the prison authorities in order to maintain hygiene.

3 April Three members of the staff of Kincora Boys' Home in east Belfast are charged with acts of gross indecency against some of those staying there. There are accusations that military intelligence, senior civil servants and some loyalists have been involved in, or are aware of, the events that took place in the home.

20 May In the House of Commons on the eve of a meeting with the Taoiseach, Charles Haughey, Margaret Thatcher says: 'The future of the constitutional affairs of Northern Ireland is a matter for the people of Northern Ireland, this government and this Parliament and no-one else' (*Hansard,* fifth series, vol. 985, col. 250).

4 June John Turnley, chairman of the Irish Independence Party, is shot dead near his home in Carnlough, Co. Antrim.

5 June Courtauld's viscose fibre plant at Carrickfergus closes.

16 June Sir Brooks Richards, a deputy secretary in the Cabinet Office, becomes security co-ordinator in succession to Sir Maurice Oldfield, who resigns because of poor health.

19 June A report by the European Commission on Human Rights rejects a case brought by Kieran Nugent and three other former republican prisoners that conditions during the 'dirty protest' are inhuman, on the grounds that the conditions are self-inflicted and 'designed to enlist sympathy for their political aims.' The commission also claims that the British government is being 'inflexible'. In the wake of the decision the IRA steps up its campaign of attacks on prison officers as well as street demonstrations.

30 June Grundig announces the closure of its Belfast factory; a thousand jobs are lost.

2 July A government discussion paper, *The Government of Northern Ireland: Proposals for Further Discussion,* proposes either an Executive in which any party with a certain proportion of the vote would automatically have seats or a majority-rule Executive counterbalanced by a Council of the Assembly with a Catholic majority. Neither proposal arouses much enthusiasm, and on 27 November Atkins tells the House of Commons that there is not enough agreement to justify bringing forward proposals for a devolved administration.

6 August An ICTU delegation meets Margaret Thatcher in London to protest about unemployment in Northern Ireland (then 15 per cent of the work force). She tells them that public spending is 35 per cent higher per person in Northern Ireland than in the rest of the United Kingdom; despite this, an extra £48 million of public expenditure is later announced.

8 August Three people are killed and eighteen injured during violence on the ninth anniversary of the introduction of internment.

11 September Du Pont closes its Orlon plant in Derry; four hundred jobs are lost.

13 October ICI closes its fibre plant at Kilroot, Co. Antrim, with the loss of 1,100 jobs.

15 October Two leading members of the IRSP are killed by the Ulster Freedom Fighters (UFF). One is Ronnie Bunting, a son of the former loyalist leader Major Ronald Bunting.

23 October Republican prisoners in the H blocks reject an offer from the NIO to be allowed to wear 'civilian-style' clothes provided by the authorities instead of prison uniforms for at least part of the day.

24 October Republican prisoners issue a statement saying: 'The British are engaged in a cruel piece of teasing and political brinkmanship in an attempt to defuse the momentum of growing support for the "blanket men". They hope to deflect widespread criticism from concerned Irish people and give an erroneous impression that they are taking positive steps to solve the problem. They are more concerned with the loss of British face than the loss of Irish lives. We are not criminals and we are ready and willing to meet an agonising death on hunger strike to establish that we are political prisoners' (*Keesing's Contemporary Archives,* p. 30847).

27 October Seven H block prisoners begin a hunger strike, demanding the right to wear their own clothes. The hunger strikes are to have a deeply moving effect on many Catholics and lead to an upsurge of nationalist feeling with traditional Catholic religious overtones. By November the H block committees are able to turn out parades of supporters larger than any produced in the Catholic community since the early seventies. As one commentator later remarks, the hunger strikes 'articulated a tribal voice of martyrdom, deeply embedded in the Gaelic, Catholic nationalist tradition' (Kearney, *Myth and Motherland,* p. 12).

28 October Thatcher says there will be no concessions to those on hunger strike.

20 November In the House of Commons, Thatcher says: 'Let me make one point about the hunger strike in the Maze Prison. I want this to be utterly clear. There can be no political justification for murder or any other crime. The government will never concede political status to the hunger-strikers, or to any others convicted of criminal offences in the province' (*Hansard,* fifth series, vol. 994, col. 27).

8 December The first Anglo-Irish summit meeting between Haughey and Thatcher is held in Dublin. The Prime Minister acknowledges Britain's 'unique relationship' with Ireland and agrees to the establishment of joint studies groups on a range of subjects to find ways of expressing this uniqueness in 'new institutional structures'. The two leaders agree to devote the next of their twice-yearly meetings to 'special consideration of the totality of relationships within these islands.' The summit is described as a 'historic breakthrough' in Anglo-Irish relations and produces a certain euphoria in Dublin government circles. It is not until March 1981 that the Minister for Foreign Affairs, Brian Lenihan, finally concedes that the constitutional position of the North had not been discussed at the meeting.

10 December During the House of Commons debate on the extension of the Emergency Provisions Act, Atkins says: 'The protest movement within the prisons, from which the hunger strike stems, is one important arm in the strategy of the Provisional IRA. Its struggle to destroy law and order and overthrow democratic institutions in Northern Ireland does not stop at the prison gates; it is continued through other means inside. The protest is designed to contribute to its objective of securing political legitimacy for a movement whose only weapon is violence. It is also part of a wider attempt to discredit the measures that the government have been compelled to introduce to protect society from terrorism' (*Hansard,* fifth series, vol. 995, col. 1028).

Ian Paisley reveals that a senior official has negotiated with the hunger-strikers on the issue of prison conditions. Republican protest marches in support of the prisoners have already resulted in riots in Belfast, Derry, and Armagh.

12 December In a written answer in the House of Commons, Atkins announces that three women prisoners at Armagh Prison who have been taking part in the 'dirty protest' had joined the hunger strike on 1 December. One of them is Mairéad Farrell, jailed in December 1976 and serving three consecutive sentences of fourteen years for causing explosions, twelve years for possessing explosive substances, ten years for possessing firearms and ammunition, and five years for membership of the IRA (*Hansard,* fifth series, vol. 995, col. 490).

Six UDA prisoners in the Maze Prison begin a hunger strike, demanding segregation from republicans. The strike lasts only until 17 December, when it is called off.

15 December As twenty-three more republican prisoners join the hunger strike, one of the original seven, Seán McKenna, appears close to death.

16 December An IRA bomber, Gerard Tuite, and two others escape from Brixton Prison, London. He had been arrested in connection with the bombing of central London in 1978 and of Greenwich gas works and Canvey Island oil terminal in Essex.

Another seven republican prisoners join the hunger strike.

17 December Cardinal Ó Fiaich appeals to Thatcher to intervene personally in the hunger strike and calls on the prisoners, 'in the name of God,' to end their protest.

18 December The hunger strike is called off after fifty-three days following an appeal from Cardinal Ó Fiaich and with hints that there might be movement towards political status. One of the hunger-strikers, Seán McKenna, is critically ill and has been moved to Musgrave Park Hospital, Belfast. In the statement announcing the ending of the protest the prisoners say: 'In ending our hunger strike, we make it clear that failure by the British government to act in a responsible manner towards ending the conditions which forced us to a hunger strike will lead to inevitable and continual strife within H Blocks' (quoted by O'Clery, *Phrases Make History Here,* p. 187). The prisoners claim they have received a document from the government clarifying earlier proposals and in effect conceding all their demands. The Secretary of State denies this and says the document merely summarises the changes proposed since 4 December. The ending of the hunger strike brings a sense of relief throughout the North but leaves the seeds for further conflict.

30 December A prison officer is shot dead in east Belfast by a group calling itself the Loyalist Prisoners' Action Force.

By the end of 1980 the deteriorating state of the economy is as great a concern as political problems. Unemployment has risen to 94,000, with an average of eighty jobs lost each day during the year; 8,000 jobs had gone in the building industry alone. At the same time Thatcherite economics are being introduced throughout the United Kingdom, restricting vital public expenditure in Northern Ireland.

DEATHS ARISING FROM THE TROUBLES: 76. SHOOTINGS: 642. BOMBS PLANTED: 400 (280 explosions). INCENDIARIES: 2. FIREARMS FOUND: 203. EXPLOSIVES FOUND: 821 kg (1,810 lb). PERSONS CHARGED WITH TERRORIST AND SERIOUS PUBLIC ORDER OFFENCES: 550.

1981

5 January Rossi, Goodhart and Shaw are replaced at the NIO by Adam Butler (Minister of State), David Mitchell, and John Patten.

16 January Bernadette (Devlin) McAliskey and her husband are wounded when three masked loyalist gunmen smash their way into their home near Coalisland and begin shooting. She is shot seven times while dressing two of her children; though critically ill, she later recovers.

A part-time major in the UDR is shot dead at Warrenpoint Harbour, where he worked as a customs officer.

21 January Sir Norman Stronge (86), former Speaker of the Stormont Parliament, and his son James are murdered by the IRA at their home, Tynan Abbey, near the border. An IRA statement later says: 'This deliberate attack on the symbols of hated unionism was a direct reprisal for a whole series of loyalist assassinations and murder attacks on nationalist people and nationalist activities.'

5 February Republican prisoners warn of fresh hunger strikes if there is no change in prison policy. The republicans demand that they be treated as prisoners of war, which would involve segregation from loyalist prisoners.

6 February As a protest against the Thatcher-Haughey dialogue, Ian Paisley leads five hundred men up a hillside in Co. Antrim at midnight, where they display firearms certificates. On 9 February Paisley and other DUP leaders sign a covenant at Belfast City Hall modelled on the Ulster Covenant of 1912. Paisley also announces a series of rallies as part of a 'Carson Trail' campaign.

1 March On the fifth anniversary of the ending of special-category status for offences committed after March 1976, the IRA leader in the Maze Prison, Bobby Sands (serving a fourteen-year sentence for firearms offences), begins a new hunger strike, aimed at regaining political status. The Catholic Bishop of Derry, Dr Edward Daly, criticises the action and says it is not morally justified in the circumstances. With the hunger-strike tactic raising the stakes in their campaign for political status, republican prisoners call off the 'dirty protest' the following day to focus attention on the hunger strike.

5 March Frank Maguire, MP for Fermanagh-South Tyrone, dies. In the ensuing weeks there is considerable argument over whether there can be an agreed nationalist candidate to contest the by-election. Sinn Féin is slow to see the opportunity the election provides and at first is happy to see Maguire's brother, Noel Maguire, stand. Bernadette McAliskey undermines this arrangement by declaring her own interest in the seat. After the Catholic Bishop of Clogher speaks in favour of Maguire's candidacy, McAliskey makes it clear that she will stand down only in favour of a H block prisoners' candidate. The idea is picked up by a Belfast Sinn Féin member, Jim Gibney, who convinces the Sinn Féin leadership (who are concerned about the political repercussions of not winning the by-election) to put forward a candidate.

15 March A second IRA prisoner, Francis Hughes, joins the hunger strike.

22 March Sands and Hughes are joined on hunger strike by Raymond McCreesh and Patsy O'Hara, leader of the INLA prisoners in the Maze.

26 March Bobby Sands is nominated for the Fermanagh-South Tyrone by-election.

29 March The SDLP withdraws its nomination of Austin Currie in the by-election, leaving two nationalist candidates, Maguire and Sands. Maguire, yielding to 'moral pressure', withdraws the following day, leaving voters to choose between Sands and the Unionist candidate.

5 April The census is held, but the results when announced will be highly inaccurate, as many census forms in nationalist areas are not completed, as a demonstration of support for the hunger strike. The results will show the population of Northern Ireland to be 1,481,959, with 414,532 Catholics (28.0 per cent), 339,818 Presbyterians (22.9 per cent), 281,472 Church of Ireland (19.0 per cent), 58,731 Methodists (4.0 per cent), and 112,822 other denominations (7.6 per cent). 274,584 (18.5 per cent) do not state any religion. Besides the substantial under-representation in the number of Catholics, the census also shows a significant increase in the number of adherents of smaller religious groups and also in the number of people not stating any religion. It also shows that over 130,000 people have emigrated from Northern Ireland since 1971, twice the rate for the previous ten years.

7 April A woman collecting census forms is shot dead in Derry.

9 April The by-election for the vacant seat of Fermanagh-South Tyrone is held. The election resolves into a straight contest between the leader of the H block hunger-strikers, Bobby Sands (now forty days into his hunger strike and reported to have lost two stone in weight), and the Ulster Unionist Harry West, who held the seat between the two general elections of 1974. With the failure of the SDLP to put forward a candidate, nationalists in the constituency face the choice of abstaining, voting for a Unionist, and voting for the H block candidate. On a turn-out of 86.9 per cent, Sands receives 30,492 votes to West's 29,046 (there are 3,280 spoiled votes), giving a boost to the hunger strike, causing dissension within the SDLP, and increasing the bitterness between Protestants and Catholics throughout Northern Ireland. When the result is formally declared on 11 April there are parades celebrating the republican victory in many areas, which deteriorate into riots in Belfast, Lurgan, and Cookstown.

The British government makes it clear that the result will not change its policy on refusing political status to republican prisoners.

20 April Three TDs, accompanied by Bobby Sands's election agent, Owen Carron, visit Sands in the Maze Prison and later seek urgent talks with the British government.

21 April At a press conference in Saudi Arabia, Thatcher refuses the Irish TD's request for talks saying: 'It is not my habit or custom to meet MPs of a foreign country about a citizen of the United Kingdom.' Asked about the hunger strike she says: 'We are not prepared to consider special category status for certain groups of people serving sentences for crime. Crime is crime, it is not political.'

23 April In the wake of rioting in nationalist areas over much of the previous week, loyalist paramilitaries reactivate their co-ordinating organisation, the Ulster Army Council.

Sands's sister Marcella announces that she has made an application on behalf of her brother to the European Commission on Human Rights, on the grounds that the British government has broken three articles of the European Convention on Human Rights. On 25 April two European Commissioners visit the Maze Prison but fail to meet Sands when he demands that Brendan McFarlane (the IRA leader in the prison), Gerry Adams (vice-president of Provisional Sinn Féin) and Danny Morrison (editor of *An Phoblacht*) be present. On 4 May the European Human Rights Commission decides that it has no power to proceed with Sands's case.

28 April Humphrey Atkins states: 'If Mr Sands persists in his wish to commit suicide, that is his choice. The government will not force medical treatment upon him.' The Pope's private secretary, Father John Magee, visits Sands but fails to persuade him to end his hunger strike; on the following day he meets the Secretary of State before returning to the Maze Prison to meet the three other hunger-strikers.

30 April After a Cabinet meeting, Atkins issues a statement saying: 'The Provisional IRA have deliberately planned and created a climate of tension and fear in a number of areas throughout Northern Ireland. They have brought about considerable concern by cynically playing upon and fostering inter-sectarian fears with the object of establishing conditions in which violence can be wilfully launched and subsequently justified ... All these activities have one clear objective, that is to provide an environment of fear within which the Provisional IRA can stir up sectarian conflict, and to enable them to exercise control of Catholic areas and present themselves as alone capable of protecting threatened people' (quoted in *Keesing's Contemporary Archives*, p. 31191).

4 May The *Irish Times* describes the mixture of nationalism and Catholicism that the hunger strikes have brought to the fore, reporting on one meeting in support of the hunger-strikers at which a speaker urged the crowd: '"Now when you all kneel down to say your Rosary tonight, as I know you will do, you'll be praying for Bobby Sands, so we'll say a decade now." And the young man who a minute earlier led the H-Block chant reverently dealt out a decade of the Rosary. A moment before they had been shouting, "One, two, three, four, open up the H-Block door." Now on the steps of the Enniskillen Town Hall, the Rosary was said, rhythmic, flowing, automatic and passing Catholic housewives joined in. Prayer and protest are easy companions in Fermanagh.' The Catholic nature of the protest would also become evident in the obituary notices for hunger-strikers appearing in the *Irish News,* often calling for 'God's curse on you, England,' or invoking 'Mary, Queen of Ireland'. Murals in nationalist areas of Belfast also display elements of Catholic religious sentiment, the hunger-striker portrayed as Christ, with rosary beads being frequently used.

5 May Bobby Sands dies on the sixty-sixth day of his hunger strike, sparking rioting in Northern Ireland and in the Republic. The IRA also launches a series of attacks on members of the army and RUC, which continue throughout the month. In the face of widespread international criticism of how the British government has handled the situation, Thatcher says in the House of Commons: 'Mr Sands was a convicted criminal. He chose to take his own life. It was a choice that his organisation did not allow to many of its victims' (*Hansard,* sixth series, vol. 4, col. 17).

7 May Almost 100,000 people attend Sands's funeral in Belfast.

8 May Another Provisional IRA prisoner, Joe McDonnell, begins a hunger strike in place of Sands.

9 May The IRA explodes a bomb at Sullom Voe oil terminal in the Shetland Islands, a quarter of a mile from where the Queen is officially opening the complex.

10 May In an interview with RTE the Catholic Bishop of Derry, Dr Edward Daly, says: 'I would not describe Bobby Sands's death as suicide. I could not accept that. I don't think he intended to bring about his own death' (quoted by O'Clery, *Phrases Make History Here,* p.189).

12 May Francis Hughes, who has been on hunger strike since 15 March, dies on the fifty-ninth day of his protest. He was serving a life sentence for murder, fourteen years for attempted murder, and two terms of twenty years for other offences; it was alleged that he had been a republican activist since the age of sixteen and had been involved in more than thirty killings. The news of Hughes's death increases the wave of rioting in republican areas of Belfast and Derry that have persisted since the death of Bobby Sands on 5 May. In Dublin a mob of two thousand people attempts to break into the British embassy.

14 May Brendan McLaughlin, a member of the IRA, replaces Hughes on hunger strike. In a deteriorating security situation, the English and Welsh soccer teams cancel their matches against Northern Ireland in Belfast.

19 May Five soldiers are killed by an IRA land mine near Bessbrook. In west Belfast an eleven-year-old girl is killed when she is hit in the head by a plastic bullet.

20 May District council elections are held in an atmosphere dominated by the hunger strikes; as a result, more extreme parties benefit, while the centre is squeezed. On the unionist side the DUP as a party outvotes the Ulster Unionists for the first time (as opposed to European Parliament elections, where the DUP outvotes Ulster Unionists on Paisley's personal vote). It more than doubles its share of first-preference votes to 26.6 per cent (142 seats), while the Ulster Unionists take 26.5 per cent (152 seats, a loss of 26). Alliance loses a quarter of its first-preference votes and falls to 8.9 per cent (down to 38 seats from 70). On the nationalist side the SDLP increases its vote slightly, but its proportion of the poll falls to 17.5 per cent (103 seats) from 20.6 per cent in 1977. The only other significant grouping is the Irish Independence Party, which takes 3.9 per cent of first-preference votes and wins 21 seats. The turn-out is 66.2 per cent.

21 May Raymond McCreesh (serving fourteen years for the attempted murder of soldiers) and Patsy O'Hara (serving eight years for possessing a grenade) both die on the sixty-first day of their hunger strike. The Catholic Primate, Cardinal Ó Fiaich, condemns the government's 'rigid stance' and warns that it will face 'the wrath of the whole nationalist population' if it continues. On 22 May, Kieran Doherty joins the hunger strike.

26 May Brendan McLaughlin, who has been on hunger strike since 14 May, receives medical attention for a perforated ulcer and internal bleeding, and the following day he is taken off the hunger strike. On 28 May he is replaced by Martin Hurson.

28 May Two IRA men are killed in a gun battle with the army in Derry. Margaret Thatcher visits Northern Ireland and says the hunger strike campaign may be the IRA's last card. 'Suffering is being inflicted on all parts of the population. The security forces are the targets of Provisional IRA terrorism, the Protestant community of their threats, the Catholic community of their intimidation ... neither I nor any of my colleagues wish to see a single person die of violence in Northern Ireland—policeman, soldier, civilian or prisoner on hunger strike' (quoted in *Keesing's Contemporary Archives,* p. 31192).

29 May Nine republican prisoners, four of them on hunger strike, are nominated for the approaching general election in the Republic.

2 June The UDA launches a new political party, the Ulster Loyalist Democratic Party, later renamed the Ulster Democratic Party.

3 June The Irish Commission for Justice and Peace, a body set up by the Catholic Bishops' Conference, issues proposals for improvements in conditions in the Maze Prison that support the hunger-strikers' demands on free association, work and clothing but oppose political status. The proposals are at first welcomed both by the NIO and the prisoners, but by 28 June the prisoners are describing the proposals as a 'major dilution' of the five demands. Discussions between the NIO and ICJP continue into the next month, but on 8 July the commission accuses the NIO of 'clawing back' on earlier offers, and by 12 July it is clear that the attempt by the ICJP at mediation has failed.

8 June Tom McElwee joins the hunger strike.

10 June Eight IRA prisoners on remand for murder and illegal possession of firearms shoot their way out of Crumlin Road Prison in Belfast using three hand-guns that have been smuggled in to them. Two of those who escape wear prison officers' uniforms taken from officers whom they had held hostage.

11 June A minority coalition government of Fine Gael and the Labour Party is elected in the Republic. On 30 June, Garret FitzGerald succeeds Charles Haughey as Taoiseach. The election also returns two H block prisoners, Kieran Doherty and Paddy Agnew. While the hunger strikes continue, relations between Britain and the Republic remain cool.

12 June The British government publishes an amendment to the

Representation of the People Act that prohibits prisoners standing for Parliament.

13 June The IRA attempts to blow up a car being used by Lord Gardiner on a visit to Belfast, but the bomb falls off the car and fails to explode. An IRA statement issued after the incident claims that Gardiner is 'the political architect of the criminalisation policy and the H-Blocks.'

15 June In a change of tactics, Provisional Sinn Féin announces that a prisoner will join the hunger strike every week. Paddy Quinn joins the protest.

22 June Michael Devine, a member of the INLA, joins the hunger strike.

29 June Laurence McKeown begins his hunger strike.

30 June In a policy statement on prisons, the government says its two major principles in the dispute are that political status will not be granted and that the authorities should retain control of prisons. Humphrey Atkins says that changes in the areas of work, clothing and association have been suggested in the hope of ending the hunger strike but that 'the great difficulty about such a move is that it would encourage the hope that political status based on the so-called "five demands" could still be achieved.'

2 July Atkins suggests the setting up of an advisory committee made up of fifty elected representatives to help govern Northern Ireland. The idea is eventually dropped through lack of support.

3 July A federal court in the United States orders Noraid to register as an agent of the IRA.

4 July In an apparent easing of their position, the hunger-strikers say they will be happy to see any changes in prison conditions being applied to all prisoners, thus weakening the demand for the British government to concede political status to republican inmates.

8 July Joe McDonnell (serving a fourteen-year sentence for fire-bombing a Belfast furniture shop) dies after sixty-one days on hunger strike.

McDonnell, who replaced Bobby Sands, is the fifth prisoner to die; he is to be replaced by Patrick McGeown.

10 July There is rioting after McDonnell's funeral when soldiers chase members of an IRA firing-party, seizing guns and making several arrests.

13 July Martin Hurson (serving twenty years for conspiracy to murder, possessing firearms, and membership of the IRA) is the sixth hunger-striker to die. He had been on hunger strike for forty-five days.

14 July Matt Devlin joins the hunger strike.

15 July Atkins announces that members of the International Committee of the Red Cross have been invited to investigate prison conditions. On 16 July members of the International Red Cross visit prisoners on hunger strike in the Maze. The following day they hold discussions with Atkins. In the following weeks the Red Cross representatives meet over two thousand prisoners in four prisons, but on 23 July the leader of the delegation announces that they can find no role to play in the dispute, because it is completely deadlocked.

18 July Over 120 gardaí and 80 protesters are injured in Dublin during a demonstration outside the British embassy in support of the hunger strike.

19 July Republican prisoners on hunger strike reject attempts by the Swiss Red Cross to mediate with the British government. Neither the prisoners nor the government appear willing to compromise on the question of 'political status'.

29 July Provisional Sinn Féin and IRSP members visit the hunger-strikers and suggest that the protest be suspended for three months so that prison reforms can be monitored, but the prisoners refuse to accept this proposal.

31 July At the request of his family, Paddy Quinn receives medical treatment to save his life after forty-seven days on hunger strike.

1 August Kevin Lynch, a member of the INLA (serving four years for firearms offences), is the seventh prisoner to die. He had been on hunger strike for seventy-one days.

2 August Kieran Doherty (serving twenty-two years for firearms and explosives offences), one of the prisoners elected to the Dáil in June, dies after seventy-three days on hunger strike. He is the eighth prisoner to die during the protest. On 3 August, Liam McCloskey, a member of the INLA, joins the protest.

8 August Thomas McElwee (serving twenty-two years for the manslaughter of a woman during a series of fire-bomb attacks) is the ninth prisoner to die; he had been on hunger strike for sixty-two days. Two days later Patrick Sheehan joins the protest. During the weekend of 8 and 9 August (also the anniversary of the introduction of internment) over a thousand petrol bombs are thrown at the army and RUC. On 17 August another IRA man, Jackie McMullan, begins a hunger strike.

20 August Michael Devine (serving twelve years for firearms offences), leader of the INLA in the Maze Prison, is the tenth hunger-striker to die. He had been on hunger strike for sixty days. The family of Patrick McGeown, forty-two days into his hunger strike, agree to his receiving medical attention in order to save his life.

Against the background of the continuing hunger strikes, the second by-election of the year takes place in Fermanagh-South Tyrone as a result of the death of Bobby Sands. Owen Carron of Provisional Sinn Féin stands as an 'Anti-H-Block Proxy Political Prisoner', his main opposition coming from an Ulster Unionist member of Dungannon District Council, Ken Maginnis, a teacher and former part-time major in the UDR. Candidates also stand for Alliance, the Workers' Party (Republican Clubs), 'General Amnesty', and 'Peace'. The SDLP again decides not to contest the election. With an increased turn-out (88.6 per cent), Carron not only wins the seat (with 31,278 votes) but takes 786 votes more than Sands. Maginnis's vote (29,048) is almost exactly the same as West's had been in April. Close (Alliance) receives 1,930 votes, Moore (Workers' Party) 1,132, Green (General Amnesty) 249, and Hall-Raleigh (Peace) 90. The number of spoiled votes falls to 804.

On 23 August, in the wake of this electoral triumph, Provisional Sinn Féin announces that it will contest future Northern Ireland elections as well as the Westminster seat of West Belfast held by Gerry Fitt, who has come out against the hunger strike.

24 August Bernard Fox joins the hunger strike.

27 August The boundary commission recommends that Northern Ireland should in future have seventeen seats at Westminster.

31 August Hugh Carville joins the hunger strike.

1 September Lagan College, Northern Ireland's first integrated secondary school, opens, with the aim of encouraging greater contact between Protestant and Catholic children. By 1993, one per cent of pupils in Northern Ireland are being educated in integrated schools.

4 September The family of Matt Devlin allow him to receive medical attention to save his life after he has been on hunger strike for fifty-two days.

6 September The INLA says it will not replace prisoners on hunger strike at the same rate as before. There are 28 INLA prisoners in the Maze, compared with 380 IRA men. Laurence McKeown is the fourth hunger-striker to receive medical attention at the request of his family, having been on hunger strike for seventy days. The following day John Pickering joins the protest.

The Catholic Bishop of Down and Connor, Dr Cahal Daly, appeals to republican prisoners to end their hunger strike, saying: 'Your capacity for endurance, however misguided, is not so common in this materialistic age that Ireland can afford to be deprived of it' (quoted by O'Clery, *Phrases Make History Here,* p. 190).

13 September James Prior becomes Secretary of State for Northern Ireland, in succession to Humphrey Atkins. Lord Gowrie (Minister of State) and Nick Scott replace Alison and Lord Elton at the NIO. In September 1985 Prior is to say that 'the Northern Ireland Office is always regarded as the dustbin.'

14 September Gerard Hodgkins joins the hunger strike.

17 September On his first visit as Secretary of State, Prior goes to the Maze Prison. With four prisoners' lives having been saved through the intervention of their families, the hunger strike appears to be collapsing. Despite this, James Devine joins the protest on 21 September. The SDLP openly attacks the hunger strike.

24 September Bernard Fox ends his hunger strike after thirty-two days. Provisional Sinn Féin says he was 'dying too quickly.'

26 September Liam McCloskey ends his hunger strike after fifty-five days after being told that his family would intervene to save his life if he became unconscious. He is the last member of the INLA on hunger strike.

27 September In an interview with RTE, Garret FitzGerald sets out his ideas for what becomes known as his 'constitutional crusade'. He says: 'What I want to do is lead a crusade, a republican crusade, to make this a genuine republic on the principles of Tone and Davis ... I believe we could have the basis then on which many Protestants in Northern Ireland would be willing to consider a relationship with us ... If I were a Northern Protestant today, I can't see how I could be attracted to getting involved with a state that is itself sectarian—not in the acutely sectarian way Northern Ireland was, in which Catholics were repressed, [but] the fact is our laws and our constitution, our practices, our attitudes reflect those of a majority ethos and are not acceptable to Protestants in Northern Ireland ... If the people of this state want to remain fundamentally a 26-county state, based on a majority ethos, and are not prepared to work with the people of Northern Ireland towards unity ... well, then, I will accept defeat and leave politics at that stage if necessary.'

29 September The British Labour Party conference votes to 'campaign actively' for a united Ireland by consent.

3 October The remaining hunger-strikers—Pat Sheehan (fifty-five days), Jackie McMullan (forty-eight days), Hugh Carville (thirty-four days), John Pickering (twenty-seven days), Gerard Hodgkins (twenty days), and James Devine (thirteen days)—end their protest after their families say they will intervene to save their lives. The following day a statement by republican prisoners says: 'Mounting pressure and cleric-inspired demoralisation led to interventions and five strikers have been taken off their fast. We accept that it is a physical and psychological impossibility to recommence a hunger strike after intervention ... a considerable majority of the present hunger strikers' families have indicated that they will intervene and under these circumstances, we feel that the hunger strike must, for tactical reasons, be suspended' (quoted by O'Clery, *Phrases Make History Here,* p. 191).

Despite the ending of the hunger strike, republican prisoners in the Maze Prison continue with their 'blanket protest'. While the Provisional IRA has been forced to accept that Thatcher will not concede 'political status', they are nevertheless to win substantial concessions on several issues. More importantly, the Fermanagh-South Tyrone by-elections have given Sinn Féin a taste for political power, which will have repercussions in the following years.

6 October Prior concedes one of the republican prisoners' five demands by announcing that they will be allowed to wear their own clothes at all times. He also makes partial concessions on other demands by saying that half of lost remission will be restored, association will be permitted in adjacent wings of the H blocks in recreation rooms and exercise areas, and a greater number of visits will be allowed. By 25 October all but 10 of the 399 prisoners involved in the 'blanket protest' are wearing their own clothes. Though the issue of prison work is still a matter of disagreement, Prior says that 'the possibility of widening the scope of work in prisons can be examined.'

The Hunger Strikes

The hunger strikes transformed the political character of the Northern Ireland problem. Now republican prisoners appeared in the unwonted role of being prepared to accept suffering for their cause rather than simply inflicting suffering on its behalf. The mass turn-out at the prisoners' funerals revealed that the standing of the prisoners in Catholic areas had risen dramatically, and this was soon reflected in a novel development: an impressive Sinn Féin electoral intervention. By June 1983 Sinn Féin had obtained some 13.4 per cent of the vote in the North, which compared well with the SDLP's 17.9 per cent.

The British government, meanwhile, faced the real possibility that the political wing of the Provisional IRA would take over from the SDLP as the principal representative of Northern Catholics. In fact Sinn Féin's support had already reached its peak in the 1980s, and the SDLP its nadir. Observers failed to note that the SDLP's share of the vote had in fact remained fairly steady. After all, in the 1979 general election it had also been 18.3 per cent.

There were increasingly two Catholic Northern Irelands: one that was in work and one that was not; one that lived in urban ghettos or traditional republican heartlands and one that did not. Sinn Féin's success was due more to the mobilisation of previously untapped support in these deprived and alienated areas than any collapse in SDLP support. In 1985 the majority of SDLP supporters gave their second preference to the moderate pro-Union Alliance Party, while only a third did the same for Sinn Féin. But these subtleties were lost on frightened policy-makers. Instead the perception grew that in resisting the demands of the hunger-strikers, Thatcher had won the battle and lost the war. The fear of Sinn Féin superseding the SDLP, carefully cultivated and even exaggerated by the Irish government (Garret FitzGerald's memoirs are explicit on this point), was the decisive impulse behind the process that led to the signing of the Anglo-Irish Agreement.

The hunger strikes, not in themselves but through later political developments, had therefore been one of the turning-points of the Troubles, a turning-point that eventually had deep implications for the local Protestant community—ironically in many respects, because they had not been directly involved in the original dispute between the British government and the hunger-strikers. As slightly mystified onlookers few unionists realised that these events would have such serious implications for themselves.

10 October Chelsea Barracks in London is bombed by the IRA; a woman and a man are killed, and forty people, including twenty-three soldiers, are injured. It is the first time that a remote-control detonator has been used by the IRA outside Northern Ireland.

17 October Major-General Sir Stewart Pringle, Commandant-General of the Royal Marines, is badly injured when an IRA bomb explodes under his car in London.

22 October The European Court rules that the British government has broken the European Convention of Human Rights by treating homosexuality as a crime in Northern Ireland. In July 1982 the government introduces new legislation to bring the law into line with that in England and Wales.

26 October A bomb explodes in Oxford Street, London, killing a police explosives expert who had tried to defuse it.

31 October At the Sinn Féin ardfheis Danny Morrison confirms the party's intention of contesting elections by stating: 'Who here really believes we can win the war through the ballot box? But will anyone here object if, with a ballot paper in one hand and the Armalite in the other, we take power in Ireland?' (*An Phoblacht/Republican News,* 5 November 1981).

6 November After talks in London, Thatcher and FitzGerald decide to set up an Anglo-Irish Inter-Governmental Council, which will provide for regular meetings between the two governments.

10 November In the House of Commons, Thatcher says that 'Northern Ireland is part of the United Kingdom—as much as my constituency is' (*Hansard,* sixth series, vol. 12, col. 427). This later leads commentators to misquote her as saying that Northern Ireland is 'as British as Finchley.'

13 November The twenty-eight INLA prisoners decide to end their protest over prison work from 1 December.

An IRA bomb explodes at the London home of the British Attorney-General, Sir Michael Havers.

14 November Rev. Robert Bradford, the Ulster Unionist MP for South Belfast and a Methodist minister, is murdered by the IRA at a community centre at Finaghy in Belfast. A caretaker is also killed. After the murder the IRA issues a statement claiming that Bradford was 'one of the key people responsible for winding up the loyalist paramilitary sectarian machine in the North.' Ian Paisley comments that 'the blood of the murdered not only lies on the skirts of those who did this evil deed, but on the British government who by political and security policies created the circumstances in which such a crime can be done with impunity' (quoted in *Keesing's Contemporary Archives,* p. 31576). On 17 November Prior receives a hostile reception from members of the congregation when he attends the funeral service for Robert Bradford.

16 November In the wake of Bradford's murder the DUP MPs Ian Paisley, Peter Robinson and John McQuade are suspended from Parliament for five days after protests about security. Six hundred people take part in a loyalist 'Third Force' march in Enniskillen; Paisley threatens that unionists will make Northern Ireland ungovernable.

23 November A loyalist 'day of action' to protest against the security situation is marked by stoppages and rallies in Protestant areas. A Third Force rally in Newtownards is attended by up to fifteen thousand men.

December Three members of the staff of Kincora Boys' Home, Belfast, and two others are jailed for sexual offences against youths in their care. One of those jailed is William McGrath, house father at Kincora, who is allegedly involved in a loyalist paramilitary group called 'Tara'.

21 December Following pressure from a hundred American Congressmen, including 'Tip' O'Neill, Edward Kennedy, and Daniel Moynihan, the State Department revokes Ian Paisley's visa because of statements he has made in Northern Ireland.

December is the first month since June 1971 with no deaths due to the Troubles.

DEATHS ARISING FROM THE TROUBLES: 101. SHOOTINGS: 1,142. BOMBS PLANTED: 529 (explosions: 398). INCENDIARIES: 49. FIREARMS FOUND: 357. EXPLOSIVES FOUND: 3,419 kg (7,540 lb). PERSONS CHARGED WITH TERRORIST AND SERIOUS PUBLIC ORDER OFFENCES: 918.

1982

January Unemployment reaches 113,000, or 20 per cent of the work force (24 per cent for men and 14 per cent for women).

13 January In an interview with the *Belfast Telegraph* the NIO minister Lord Gowrie says that direct rule is 'very un-British. It is an absurdity that one has almost absolute power … I suppose that if I had my way I would have dual citizenship. Why not have people living in the North who regard themselves as Irish administered by Ireland and Britain?'

15 January The Secretary of State, Jim Prior, announces that a committee of inquiry will investigate the Kincora Boys' Home scandal. However, this will be a private inquiry.

21 January Prior meets John De Lorean, who allegedly demands £40 million in grants for his car company or says the government will face the prospect of massive sackings.

Two members of Sinn Féin, Owen Carron and Danny Morrison, are arrested after trying to enter the United States illegally from Canada. They are later deported to Canada.

27 January The Fine Gael and Labour Party coalition government in the Republic collapses over the issue of tax increases on petrol, beer and cigarettes when an independent TD votes against the budget.

28 January Prior says De Lorean was not offered any more money; Sir Kenneth Cork is appointed to look into the company's affairs.

29 January The loyalist leader John McKeague is shot dead by the INLA.

12 February Three of the five members of the committee of inquiry into the Kincora Boys' Home scandal resign, saying the RUC had not dealt with all the criminal aspects of the case.

1,100 of the 2,600 De Lorean workers are sacked.

15 February The chairman of Harland and Wolff announces that 1,000 of the remaining 7,000 jobs are to go.

18 February A Fianna Fáil minority government is returned in the Irish general election. None of the seven Sinn Féin candidates is elected.

Prior announces a full public inquiry into the Kincora Boys' Home affair.

19 February The De Lorean Motor Company goes into receivership. In May it is announced that the plant is to cease production, with a loss of 1,500 jobs. By 19 October, when Prior announces the closure of the company, 8,500 cars have been completed. De Lorean had hoped to sell 20,000 cars a year (at $25,000 each) in the American market, but receivers say that a target of 8,500 cars would have been more realistic. On the same day John De Lorean is arrested in Los Angeles and charged with possessing cocaine.

1 March British Enkalon announces that it is to close its plant at Antrim, with a loss of 850 jobs.

2 March Several shots are fired by the IRA at the Northern Ireland Lord Chief Justice, Lord Lowry, while he is visiting Queen's University in Belfast. Lord Lowry is not injured, though a lecturer standing nearby is wounded.

4 March The Ulster Unionist candidate, Rev. Martin Smyth (Grand Master of the Orange Order), wins the South Belfast by-election brought about by the murder of Rev. Robert Bradford in November 1981. The most significant factor in the election is the antagonism between the Ulster Unionists and the DUP, which results in both parties putting forward a candidate. Smyth receives 17,123 votes, David Cook (Alliance) 11,726, Rev. William McCrea (DUP) 9,818, and Dr Alasdair McDonnell (SDLP) 3,839 votes. One of the other candidates is the UDA political spokesman, John McMichael, standing for the Ulster Loyalist Democratic Party, who receives 576 votes. The turn-out is 66.2 per cent.

Gerard Tuite, who escaped from Brixton Prison in London in December 1980, is arrested in the Republic. On 6 March he is charged in Dublin with causing explosions in London, the first person to be charged in the Republic for a crime committed in Britain. In July he is sentenced to ten years' imprisonment.

25 March Three soldiers are killed and five other people injured in an IRA ambush on the Springfield Road in west Belfast.

5 April The White Paper *Northern Ireland: A Framework for Devolution* is published. It proposes the election of a 78-member Assembly with the task of reaching agreement on how devolved powers should be exercised. If 70 per cent of Assembly members could reach agreement, then powers would be devolved at the discretion of the Secretary of State. Control of local functions could also be devolved, one department at a time, again provided there was agreement within the Assembly. The scheme thus acquired the name 'rolling devolution'.

From the outset, however, there is limited support for the plan. In February an Ulster Unionist delegation had told the Secretary of State that it opposed the scheme, and on 12 March the party's executive had rejected it in favour of the 1976 Convention report. On 14 March the SDLP also voices its opposition when John Hume says the plan for rolling devolution is 'largely unworkable'. The DUP meanwhile supports devolution but not at the cost of enforced power-sharing. Only Alliance shows any great enthusiasm for the plan.

Despite this the British Cabinet approves the plan for 'rolling devolution' on 25 March. The scheme also had few enthusiastic supporters in the Cabinet beyond the former Secretaries of State Whitelaw, Pym, and Atkins. With Anglo-Irish relations cooling since the return of Haughey to power in the Republic, Thatcher also insists that a separate chapter on Anglo-Irish relations be removed from the White Paper (O'Leary et al., *The Northern Ireland Assembly,* p. 69).

Northern Ireland is once again pushed into the background of British politics when Argentina invades the Falkland Islands on 2 April. As a result, the bill for the new Assembly is introduced in the House of Commons on 20 April in far from auspicious circumstances.

19 April Eleven-year-old Stephen McConomy dies three days after being hit in the head by a plastic bullet in Derry. His death leads to rioting and demands for the banning of plastic bullets. The incident also leads to a debate in the European Parliament, which on 13 May calls on member-states to end the use of plastic bullets.

20 April Two people are killed and twelve injured in a series of co-ordinated IRA attacks throughout the North.

3 May After the sinking of the Argentine ship *Belgrano* by a British submarine, the Irish Minister for Defence, Paddy Power, says: 'We felt that

Argentina were the first aggressors. Obviously Britain themselves are very much the aggressors now' (quoted by O'Clery, *Phrases Make History Here,* p. 194).

8 May Nicholas Budgen resigns as an assistant government whip because of his opposition to the Northern Ireland Bill.

10 May The Taoiseach, Charles Haughey, appoints the SDLP deputy leader, Séamus Mallon, to the Seanad.

During the debate on the Northern Ireland Bill, Prior says: 'A policy of continuing with direct rule does not offer a long-term answer. We either move to a position of total integration ... or we seek a gradual devolution of power, which is the course that the government believe should be followed' (*Hansard,* sixth series, vol. 23, col. 469). The Northern Ireland Act (1982), which establishes the rules for the new Assembly, becomes law on 23 July.

1 June Lieutenant-General Sir Robert Richardson succeeds Sir Richard Lawson as army commander in Northern Ireland.

4 June In Dublin the INLA shoot dead Jim Flynn, the man believed to be responsible for the murder of Séamus Costello in 1977.

18 June Speaking in London, Lord Gowrie, Minister of State at the NIO, says: 'Northern Ireland is extremely expensive on the British taxpayer ... if the people of Northern Ireland wished to join with the south of Ireland, no British Government would resist it for twenty minutes' (quoted by O'Clery, *Phrases Make History Here,* p. 194).

20 July Eight soldiers are killed by two IRA bombs at Knightsbridge and Regent's Park, London. The first explodes as a mounted detachment travels through Hyde Park on its way to change the guard at Horse Guards Parade; two guardsmen are killed and seventeen onlookers injured; seven army horses are also killed. Two hours later the second bomb detonates under the bandstand in Regent's Park, killing six bandsmen and injuring twenty-four. The body of one bandsman is hurled fifty yards and impaled on park railings. Three other people die later as a result of the explosions.

29 July With Anglo-Irish relations soured by Ireland's neutral attitude during the Falklands War, Thatcher says that 'no commitment exists for

Her Majesty's Government to consult the Irish government on matters affecting Northern Ireland.'

20 August Harland and Wolff announces the loss of 1,280 more jobs, out of a total of 6,600.

25 August The SDLP decides to contest the Assembly elections but not to take its seats.

September Male unemployment climbs above 25 per cent; overall unemployment is now 22 per cent.

1 September The INLA wounds a DUP member of Belfast City Council.

15 September Two children and a soldier are killed in an INLA explosion at Divis Flats in Belfast.

1 October The British Labour Party conference calls for a ban on plastic bullets throughout the United Kingdom.

6 October Des O'Malley, Minister for Trade, Commerce and Tourism, resigns from the Irish government over disagreements with Haughey on Northern Ireland and the economy. He later forms the Progressive Democrats.

19 October An INLA bomb explodes at the Ulster Unionist Party's offices in Belfast, causing extensive damage.

20 October The election for the new Northern Ireland Assembly is held. It is most notable for being the first to be contested by Provisional Sinn Féin, which receives 64,191 first-preference votes (10.1 per cent of the valid poll) and takes five of the seventy-eight seats. Two of those elected are Gerry Adams and Martin McGuinness. The SDLP, by contrast, does comparatively poorly, with 118,891 votes (18.8 per cent of the poll) and fourteen seats. On the unionist side, with tensions arising from the hunger strike receding, the Ulster Unionists re-establish their lead over the DUP. The UUP receives 188,277 votes (29.7 per cent of first-preference votes) and twenty-six seats to the DUP's 145,528 votes (23.0 per cent) and twenty-one seats.

The idiosyncrasies of proportional representation with the single transferable vote are demonstrated by the fact that Alliance, with fewer first-preference votes (58,851 or 9.3 per cent) takes twice as many seats as Sinn Féin. The two remaining seats are won by Frank Millar (independent Unionist) and Jim Kilfedder (UPUP). In South Antrim, where twenty-six candidates stand for ten seats, the count lasts more than thirty hours, the longest for any count in Britain or Ireland. Three candidates are elected on the twenty-third and final count, including an Ulster Unionist candidate who received only 979 first-preference votes (Flackes and Elliott, *Northern Ireland: A Political Directory,* p. 341). The turn-out is 63.5 per cent. The SDLP and Sinn Féin, both standing on an abstentionist platform, refuse to take their seats.

The performance of Sinn Féin causes panic in the British establishment, which blames Prior for giving Sinn Féin the opportunity to demonstrate its electoral support. Many observers also become obsessed with the possibility of Sinn Féin displacing the SDLP as the main political representative of Northern nationalism.

27 October Three RUC men are killed by a 1,000 lb bomb planted outside Lurgan.

4 November The Irish government led by Charles Haughey collapses after losing a vote of confidence in the Dáil.

5 November An American court acquits five men of plotting to send arms to the IRA the previous year. Their defence claimed that their actions had been approved by the CIA, though this was denied by the prosecution. One of the defendants, Michael Flannery, a director of Noraid, is later elected grand marshal of the New York St Patrick's Day parade.

11 November Three unarmed IRA men—Gervaise McKerr, Seán Burns, and Eugene Toman—are killed by the RUC at a check-point near Lurgan. The deaths of the three men spark the first of a rash of claims that the police and army are pursuing a 'shoot to kill' policy; the incident, with others, eventually leads to the Stalker-Sampson inquiry. The inquests into the deaths of the men have not been completely resolved ten years later.

The first sitting of the Northern Ireland Assembly takes place. James Kilfedder is elected presiding officer.

16 November Lenny Murphy, the leader of the 'Shankill Butchers', is shot dead by the IRA. He had recently been released from prison. It is believed that loyalist paramilitaries colluded with the IRA in the murder of Murphy because they could no longer control him. Two RUC reservists shot at a check-point in Markethill, Co. Armagh, and a Catholic shopkeeper shot in Belfast die on the same day.

18 November Patrick Gilmour, father of the IRA informer Raymond Gilmour, is kidnapped by the IRA. Relatives claim that the IRA say he will not be released until Gilmour retracts his evidence.

24 November Michael Tighe is killed and Martin McCauley wounded by an RUC patrol observing a farm near Craigavon. The incident encourages nationalist fears that the police and army are operating a 'shoot to kill' policy.

A general election in the Republic leads to the return of a Fine Gael and Labour Party coalition government headed by Garret FitzGerald.

30 November Prior addresses the Northern Ireland Assembly and announces that the strength of the RUC is to be increased by 500 and the RUC Reserve by 300.

6 December Eleven soldiers and six other people are killed by an INLA bomb at the Droppin' Well disco at Ballykelly, Co. Londonderry. Cardinal Ó Fiaich describes the bombing as a 'gruesome slaughter'. In the House of Commons the following day Thatcher says: 'This is one of the most horrifying crimes in Ulster's tragic history. The slaughter of innocent people is the product of evil and depraved minds and the act of callous and brutal men' (*Hansard,* sixth series, vol. 33, col. 708). She also denounces a proposed visit by Sinn Féin leaders at the invitation of the Greater London Council.

7 December In the Supreme Court in Dublin the Chief Justice, Mr Justice Thomas O'Higgins, rejects the idea that 'any charge associated with terrorist activity should be regarded as a charge in respect of a political offence.' The decision permits the extradition of Dominic McGlinchey to face charges in the North.

12 December Two INLA men, Séamus Grew and Roddy Carroll, are shot dead by the RUC at a check-point near Armagh, yet another event in a growing string of alleged 'shoot to kill' incidents. In April 1984 an RUC man is found not guilty of Grew's murder.

Two Sinn Féin leaders, Gerry Adams and Danny Morrison, take part in a phone-in programme on the London radio station LBC. The event follows a week of antagonism between the government and the Labour-controlled Greater London Council, which had invited the Sinn Féin members to London on the day before the Ballykelly bombing. With the council refusing to withdraw its invitation, the Home Secretary, William Whitelaw, bans Adams and Morrison from entering Britain under the Prevention of Terrorism Act on 8 December. The following day the leader of the council, Ken Livingstone, accepts an invitation from Sinn Féin to visit Northern Ireland instead.

14 December The Ulster Unionist Party decides not to take its seats on Assembly scrutiny committees until Prior clarifies the power of the Speaker to appoint and rotate chairmanships and vice-chairmanships. The Ulster Unionists do not end their boycott until February 1983.

16 December An Election Petition Court deprives Séamus Mallon of his Assembly seat because he is a member of the Seanad.

17 December Michelin announces that its their factory at Mallusk, Co. Antrim, will close in the new year, leading to the loss of over two thousand jobs.

20 December Parliament approves an increase in the number of Northern Ireland seats in the House of Commons from twelve to seventeen. It also decides that any future Northern Ireland Assembly will return five members per constituency, a total of eighty-five.

DEATHS ARISING FROM THE TROUBLES: 97. SHOOTINGS: 547. BOMBS PLANTED: 332 (explosions: 219). INCENDIARIES: 36. FIREARMS FOUND: 288. EXPLOSIVES FOUND: 2,298 kg (5,070 lb). PERSONS CHARGED WITH TERRORIST AND SERIOUS PUBLIC ORDER OFFENCES: 686.

1983

16 January A County Court judge, William Doyle, is shot dead by the IRA while leaving a Catholic church in Belfast.

1 February The Irish Minister for Foreign Affairs, Peter Barry, meets the Secretary of State for Northern Ireland, Jim Prior, in London and expresses doubt that the Northern Ireland Assembly has a useful future.

17 February The Labour Party in the House of Commons decides to oppose the Prevention of Terrorism Act in its existing form.

23 February Despite British opposition, the Political Committee of the European Parliament decides to investigate whether the EEC can help solve Northern Ireland's economic and political problems. A Danish Liberal member, Nils Haagerup, is appointed to prepare the report.

2 March The Assembly votes unanimously for a motion urging the government to stop the proposed inquiry by the European Parliament. It sets up a Security and Home Affairs Committee.

11 March The Irish government announces that it is setting up an all-Ireland forum, as proposed by the SDLP. The decision clearly results from the threat that Sinn Féin poses to the SDLP as the largest nationalist party in the North. The Forum is designed to represent the Irish constitutional parties (excluding primarily Sinn Féin) and to deliver a joint statement on the principles involved.

Prior says that the British government will not co-operate with the European Parliament's inquiry into Northern Ireland.

21 March Margaret Thatcher meets Garret FitzGerald at an EEC summit meeting, her first meeting with a Taoiseach in over fifteen months.

22 March A Sinn Féin candidate wins a district council by-election in Omagh in the first council election contested by that party for almost half a century.

24 March The Ulster Unionists, DUP and Alliance reject invitations to take part in the New Ireland Forum.

11 April In the first of many trials based on evidence by informers continuing into 1984 and 1985, fourteen UVF men are jailed for a total of 200 years on the evidence of Joseph Bennett. Bennett has been granted immunity from prosecution for his own involvement in crimes (including the killing of a postmistress in 1982, for which two of his accomplices were later convicted for twelve years, partly as a result of his evidence) in return for his evidence. It later emerges that up to £70,000 has been offered to informers in return for their evidence.

Harland and Wolff announce 700 further redundancies.

20 April There is a Northern Ireland Assembly by-election in Armagh, brought about by the unseating of Séamus Mallon on the grounds that he is also an Irish senator at the time of the election in October 1982. The SDLP calls on voters to ignore the election and refuses to put up a candidate. As a result the Ulster Unionist Jim Speers (26,907 votes) easily defeats his only challenger, Tom French of the Workers' Party (4,920 votes). The turn-out is a mere 34.1 per cent.

27 April An anti-abortion amendment to the Constitution of Ireland proposed by Fianna Fáil is carried in the Dáil by 87 votes to 13 and will be put to the people in a referendum later in the year.

16 May The INLA claims to have kidnapped the wife of the informer Harry Kirkpatrick. On 3 August, Kirkpatrick's stepfather and daughter are also kidnapped in the Republic but are freed by the Gardaí two weeks later. On 3 June Harry Kirkpatrick is sentenced to life imprisonment for crimes including five murders.

30 May The first meeting of the New Ireland Forum is held in Dublin.

6 June Bernadette McAliskey is refused a visa by the US State Department.

9 June The United Kingdom general election returns the Conservative Party with a large majority. In Northern Ireland seventeen seats are contested for the first time as a result of changes introduced by the boundary commission.

Most results produce clear majorities, though in the new seat of East Antrim, Roy Beggs (UUP) defeats Jim Allister (DUP) by only 367 votes, and in Mid-Ulster a split in both the unionist and the nationalist vote leads to Rev. William McCrea (DUP) defeating Danny Morrison (Sinn Féin) by only 78 votes. Enoch Powell retains South Down for the Ulster Unionists from Eddie McGrady of the SDLP by 548, votes and Jim Nicholson (UUP) wins the new seat of Newry and Armagh from Séamus Mallon by 1,554 votes. In Fermanagh-South Tyrone the entry of an SDLP candidate leads to a split in the nationalist vote and the defeat of Owen Carron (Sinn Féin). The seat is won by Ken Maginnis (UUP).

All these results are overshadowed by events in West Belfast, a safe nationalist seat, where the sitting MP, Gerry Fitt, now an independent, is challenged by Gerry Adams (Sinn Féin) and Dr Joe Hendron (SDLP). In a bitterly fought contest the constitutional nationalist vote is split and Adams (16,379 votes) wins the seat with a majority of 5,445 over Hendron (10,934 votes), with Fitt third (10,326 votes). Though defeated, Fitt remains proud of the fact that half his votes come from Protestant areas of the constituency. This is to prove significant once again in the 1992 general election in the same constituency.

The result gives the Ulster Unionists eleven seats (with 34.0 per cent of valid votes) and the DUP three seats (20.0 per cent), with Jim Kilfedder, John Hume and Gerry Adams winning the other seats. The SDLP receives 137,012 votes (17.9 per cent of the poll) to Sinn Féin's 102,701 (13.4 per cent), further raising fears that Sinn Féin may be about to replace the SDLP as the main nationalist party. Alliance, the only significant centre party, manages to stabilise its support, receiving 61,275 votes (8.0 per cent). The turn-out is 73.3 per cent.

While much emphasis is again placed on the showing of Sinn Féin in relation to the SDLP, few commentators observe that the greatest decline in SDLP support has taken place in the period between 1975 and 1979—before the Sinn Féin challenge emerged. Instead most attention is focused on Gerry Adams, presented as the symbol of the alleged modernisation and radicalism of Sinn Féin. Adams's victory misleads some observers into assuming that Sinn Féin's overtaking of the SDLP is inevitable: one journalist goes as far as to say that 'all Gerry Adams has to do is not get killed and he can't lose' (Alan Murdoch, *Marxism Today,* March 1984, p. 3). On 10 June, Whitelaw lifts the ban on Adams entering Britain.

13 June In the wake of the general election, Lord Gowrie, Mitchell and John Patten are replaced at the NIO by the Earl of Mansfield (Minister of State) and Chris Patten.

15 June In an interview with the *Irish Times,* Prior sardonically comments on local public spending by saying: 'In Northern Ireland we're all Keynesians.'

3 July Gerry Fitt's unoccupied home in Belfast is set on fire by republican supporters.

13 July Four UDR soldiers are killed by an IRA land mine in Tyrone, the heaviest UDR casualties in a single incident.

17 July Merlyn Rees, the former Secretary of State for Northern Ireland, says that a Cabinet sub-committee had considered withdrawal from Northern Ireland between 1974 and 1976 but no minister had favoured it.

21 July Following his defeat in the general election, Gerry Fitt is made a life peer.

25 July Goodyear announces the closure of its plant in Craigavon, with the loss of 800 jobs.

5 August After four months the trial based on the evidence of the IRA informer Christopher Black ends with twenty-two people being jailed for a total of more than four thousand years. The alleged leader of the Provisional IRA group is sentenced to 963 years' imprisonment for crimes including conspiracy to murder and attempted murder.

9 August On the anniversary of the introduction of internment there is rioting in nationalist areas of Belfast and an unarmed youth is shot dead. The following day a soldier is charged with his murder. Two members of Noraid, part of an eighty-strong party visiting Northern Ireland supposedly to investigate cases of discrimination against Catholics, are later fined for their involvement in rioting. At the same time the Irish National Caucus is putting pressure on the US government to cancel a $150 million order for eighteen 'Sherpa' aircraft made by Short Brothers of Belfast, claiming that the company discriminates against Catholics.

14 August French police seize a consignment of weapons bound for the IRA on a ferry from Le Havre to Rosslare.

25 August The INLA releases Elizabeth Kirkpatrick, wife of the informer Harry Kirkpatrick.

28 August Ken Livingstone, leader of the Greater London Council, says that Britain's treatment of the Irish over eight hundred years has been worse than Hitler's treatment of the Jews.

7 September In a referendum on abortion in the Republic two-thirds vote for a 'pro-life' amendment being added to the Constitution. With the strong line in support of the amendment taken by the Catholic Church, one anti-amendment campaigner commented that the referendum had been won 'with a Carmelite in one hand and a ballot box in the other' (quoted by O'Clery, *Phrases Make History Here,* p. 200).

25 September Thirty-eight IRA inmates of the Maze Prison, using guns and knives, seize a lorry in the prison compound and break out. One prison warder is killed and another seriously wounded. Nineteen of the prisoners are soon recaptured but the rest get away, despite a massive search. By August 1992 five had been recaptured, three had been killed in ambushes or shoot-outs with the SAS, while eleven were still on the run. Nothing is known of the whereabouts of six of the eleven; of the others, Kevin Barry Artt and James Smyth are in custody in the United States on passport violation charges, Patrick John McIntyre was freed in 1987 when a Dublin court quashed an extradition order, and Dermot Finucane and James Pius Clarke were freed by judges of the Supreme Court in Dublin in 1990 when their extradition was rejected. In June 1991 the High Court in Belfast awarded £47,500 to twelve prisoners assaulted by warders after their recapture.

26 September Prior sets up an inquiry into the Maze escape under Sir James Hennessy.

Patrick Gilmour, father of the informer Raymond Gilmour, is released by the IRA after ten months in captivity.

11 October After meeting the Northern Ireland Assembly's Security Committee, Prior says he will resign if the Hennessy Inquiry finds that his policies were responsible for the Maze Prison escape.

28 October Sir George Terry's report into the Kincora Boys' Home scandal finds no evidence that the RUC, army or civil servants were involved in the events or had tried to cover them up. The report criticises the media, social services and politicians and recommends that there be no further inquiries into the affair. Despite several investigations, much local opinion of all political shades remains unconvinced by the official explanation.

7 November The first formal meeting of British and Irish heads of government for two years takes place at Chequers between Thatcher and FitzGerald. The meeting is indicative of improving relations after a period of coolness during and after the Falklands War. FitzGerald later claims that by March the following year 'the British cabinet now accepted our analysis of the situation and had come to the view that it might now be more dangerous to do nothing than to attempt an initiative aimed at stabilising the situation. Accordingly, following the publication of the Forum report a set of proposals for the future government of Northern Ireland would be brought to the government for approval and then presented to the British' (FitzGerald, *All In a Life,* p. 497).

8 November Adrian Carroll, brother of an INLA member killed by the RUC in December 1982, is shot dead in Armagh. Four members of the UDR are later convicted of the murder. Three of the 'UDR Four' are released in July 1992 when their convictions are overturned.

13 November Gerry Adams, MP for West Belfast, is elected President of Sinn Féin at its annual ardfheis. The replacement of Ruairí Ó Brádaigh by Adams is indicative of the swing in power from Southern republicans to the North.

14 November The Ulster Unionist chairman of Armagh District Council, a part-time member of the UDR, is killed when two IRA bombs explode under his car as he leaves a council meeting.

20 November Three men, all church elders, are killed and seven other people wounded when republican terrorists burst into a Pentecostal church in Darkley, Co. Armagh, during a Sunday service and begin firing at random with automatic weapons. The shooting is claimed by the 'Catholic Reaction Force'. On 22 November the Ulster Unionist Party withdraws from the Northern Ireland Assembly in protest after the government refuses to change its security policy. The RUC later says that one of the weapons used in the attack had previously been used by the INLA. On 27 November, Dominic McGlinchey, reputed to be chief of staff of the INLA, admits that the organisation was indirectly involved in the Darkley massacre.

23 November Lord Justice Gibson throws out the uncorroborated evidence of the INLA informer Jackie Grimley.

24 November An American supermarket executive, Don Tidey, is kidnapped by the IRA close to his home in Rathfarnham, Co. Dublin.

4 December An SAS undercover team shoots dead two IRA members near Coalisland.

7 December An Ulster Unionist member of the Assembly, Edgar Graham, is murdered by the IRA at Queen's University, Belfast, where he was a lecturer in the Faculty of Law.

8 December An FEA report on the Northern Ireland Civil Service says that Catholics are under-represented in senior positions.

12 December The report on Northern Ireland by the European Parliament prepared by Nils Haagerup calls for power-sharing and an EEC plan for the economic development of Northern Ireland.

16 December Don Tidey is rescued; in the ensuing gun battle a soldier and a Garda cadet are killed.

17 December An IRA bomb explodes outside Harrod's department store in London. Six people are killed, including three police officers; more than ninety are injured. The IRA later says that its Army Council had not authorised the attack and that it regretted the deaths.

DEATHS ARISING FROM THE TROUBLES: 77. SHOOTINGS: 424. BOMBS PLANTED: 367 (explosions: 226). INCENDIARIES: 43. FIREARMS FOUND: 166. EXPLOSIVES FOUND: 1,706 kg (3,760 lb). PERSONS CHARGED WITH TERRORIST AND SERIOUS PUBLIC ORDER OFFENCES: 613.

1984

15 January In an RTE interview Cardinal Ó Fiaich says: 'If a person is convinced that he is joining [Sinn Féin] for these reasons [community activities] and that his positive reasons outweigh any interpretation that may be given his membership as condoning support for violence and crime, he may be morally justified' (quoted by O'Clery, *Phrases Make History Here,* p. 201).

18 January The Secretary of State, Jim Prior, announces a public inquiry under the Health and Social Services Order (1972) into the Kincora Boys' Home scandal.

24 January The NIO agrees to the request by Londonderry District Council to officially change its name to Derry City Council. The SDLP-controlled council also refuses to allow the Union Jack to fly on council property. In March, Chris Patten, the minister responsible for allowing the name change, has a home-made Tricolour thrown at him by Gregory Campbell of the DUP while he is giving evidence to the Environment Committee of the Northern Ireland Assembly. After the incident Patten caustically notes that, in the absence of the Ulster Unionist Party, Campbell was acting chairman of the Assembly's Security Committee (*Northern Ireland Assembly Reports,* no. 133 and 144).

26 January The Hennessy Report on the Maze Prison escape is published. It lays most of the blame on the prison staff. The governor resigns, but Jim Prior says there will be no ministerial resignations, since the report shows 'no policy failures.' Unionists renew calls for Prior to resign.

30 January The Prison Officers' Association supports the Northern Ireland Prison Governors' Association in stating that political restraints imposed by the NIO after the 1982 hunger strike were responsible for the Maze escape. The Minister for Prisons, Nick Scott, rejects this criticism.

1 March Frank Millar (Ulster Unionist), son of the veteran independent unionist of the same name, is returned unopposed in a South Belfast by-election for the Assembly brought about by the murder of Edgar Graham in December.

6 March A deputy governor at the Maze Prison is shot dead at his home in Belfast by the IRA.

14 March Gerry Adams and three other Sinn Féin members are wounded in a UFF gun attack while driving back from a court appearance in Belfast city centre. In March 1985 three men are sentenced to between twelve and eighteen years' imprisonment for the attempted murder.

17 March Dominic McGlinchey, who had absconded during the court case to extradite him to the North, is captured after a shoot-out with the Gardaí. Within hours of his capture he is handed over to the RUC, becoming the first republican to be extradited from the Republic to Northern Ireland to face terrorist charges.

22 March A new Prevention of Terrorism Act, which provides for the arrest and detention of those suspected of terrorism, becomes law. The new act modifies the existing law in the light of suggestions contained in a report prepared by Lord Jellicoe. The act expires after five years, at which time a new bill must be introduced. Under the Prevention of Terrorism Act the Secretary of State can proscribe organisations connected with terrorism and issue exclusion orders from Northern Ireland, and the police can arrest suspects without warrant and detain them for forty-eight hours, or up to seven days with the authority of the Secretary of State. The new act also makes it illegal to collect money for proscribed organisations and to withhold information from the police relating to terrorist offences.

29 March The Haagerup Report is adopted by the European Parliament by a vote of 124 to 3; only Ian Paisley, John Taylor and a member from the Republic, Neil Blaney, vote against. The report rejects the idea of a British withdrawal from Northern Ireland and says there is no prospect of a united Ireland in the foreseeable future but also claims that Northern Ireland is not entirely an internal United Kingdom problem. It calls for a power-sharing administration and an integrated economic plan for Northern Ireland.

8 April Mary Travers, daughter of a magistrate, is shot dead by the IRA as she walks home from church in Belfast. Her father, Tom Travers, is wounded in the attack. He had been trying a case in which Gerry Adams was charged with obstruction, which had been adjourned following the attempt on Adams's life.

12 April Lord Mansfield retires from the NIO because of ill health. Lord Lyell replaces him as government spokesman in the House of Lords.

1 May The Robert Quigley informer trial ends; ten people are jailed.

2 May The report of the New Ireland Forum is published. It restates traditional nationalist arguments that Ireland is one nation and that Britain is ultimately responsible for partition by 'refusing to accept the democratically expressed wishes of the Irish people' (section 3.3) and by establishing an 'artificial political majority in the North' (section 4.1). At the same time the report is unambiguous on the question of political violence as a means of effecting change: 'Attempts from any quarter to impose a particular solution through violence must be rejected along with the proponents of such methods. It must be recognised that the New Ireland which the Forum seeks can come about only through agreement and must have a democratic basis' (section 5.2).

The report concludes that 'the desire of nationalists is for a united Ireland in the form of a sovereign, independent Irish state.' Two other structural arrangements for a united Ireland are examined in detail, a federal or confederal state and joint authority. While Garret FitzGerald says that a unitary state is 'the ideal we would aspire to,' Charles Haughey counters that a unitary state is 'not an option, it is the wish of the parties of the Forum ... Neither of these other two arrangements, federation or joint sovereignty, would bring peace and stability to the North.' The Minister for Foreign Affairs, Peter Barry, later describes the report as 'a new nationalist political agenda, which to a remarkable degree is realistic, generous and flexible' (*Irish Times,* 24 September 1984).

18 May Two off-duty soldiers are killed by a car bomb after they have competed in a fishing competition near Enniskillen; a third soldier dies later. Ten other people are injured in the explosion. Two RUC men are killed in a 1,000 lb land mine explosion at Camlough, Co. Armagh. Both attacks were carried out by the IRA.

23 May The Ulster Unionists announce that they are ending their boycott of the Assembly.

29 May At a meeting of Belfast Education and Library Board, Councillor George Seawright launches a tirade against Catholics who object to the British national anthem being played at concerts. 'Taxpayers' money would be better spent on an incinerator and burning the whole lot of them. The priests should be thrown in and burned as well' (quoted by O'Clery, *Phrases Make History Here,* p. 203).

31 May The Lear Fan aircraft company in Belfast announces that it is sacking all but approximately thirty employees, with the loss of 350 jobs. The government has invested £45 million in the company since 1980. In May 1985 the company decides to cease trading.

1 June The President of the United States, Ronald Reagan, arrives in Ireland for a four-day visit.

5 June Three RUC men are acquitted of murdering an unarmed IRA man, Eugene Toman, in 1982. Delivering his judgment, Lord Justice Gibson says the RUC men should be commended 'for their courage and determination in bringing the three deceased men to justice, in this case to the final courts of justice.'

14 June Elections for the European Parliament are held. In Northern Ireland there are eight candidates for the three seats. With 230,251 first-preference votes (33.6 per cent), Ian Paisley is elected on the first count. John Taylor, the Ulster Unionists' sole candidate, receives 147,169 votes (21.5 per cent) and is elected on the second count as a result of transfers from Paisley; the Workers' Party and Ecology candidates are also eliminated. On the third count David Cook of Alliance (34,046 first-preference votes, 5.0 per cent) and Jim Kilfedder (20,092 votes, 2.9 per cent) are eliminated; and on the fourth count John Hume (151,399 first-preference votes, 22.1 per cent) is elected on transferred votes, ahead of Danny Morrison of Sinn Féin (91,476 first-preference votes, 13.3 per cent). With a turn-out of 64.3 per cent (valid votes) the election shows a significant increase over its 1979 equivalent. Over 110,000 more votes are cast; Paisley increases his vote by almost 60,000, the Unionist candidate (John Taylor) by 20,000, and John

Hume by over 10,000. Jim Kilfedder's vote drops by almost 20,000 and the Alliance vote by 5,000.

Danny Morrison increases the Sinn Féin vote by approximately 50,000 on the previous European election but is still heavily outvoted by John Hume, who has conceded much nationalist territory to the Provisionals and instead concentrates on, and wins, moderate Catholic support away from other parties. It is the first real setback for Sinn Féin in its latest excursion into politics and leads to a series of conflicting rationalisations within the party about the reasons for the defeat. At first Adams argues that the Sinn Féin defeat is due to an overestimation of Catholic toleration of violence, for although violence has declined generally, the republican share of violence has increased substantially under the new leadership. In July, however, Adams suggests that it might be a bad thing to take over from the SDLP as the catch-all party for Catholics, as this would lead to a diminution in social radicalism ('Brass Tacks', BBC2, July 1984). Morrison also attempts to play down the significance of the electoral reverse by saying, 'Electoral politics will not remove the British from Ireland. Only armed struggle will do that ... I think there's very little reason for the IRA to lower its range, so to speak' (*Magill,* September 1984).

July The unemployment figure reaches 121,636, or 21 per cent of the working population.

18 July The House of Commons Public Accounts Committee calls the loss of £77 million on the De Lorean Motor Company 'one of the gravest cases of the misuse of public resources in many years.'

25 July Jim Prior says of the report of the New Ireland Forum: 'The British government's response was measured and realistic. We did set our realities and I personally think that our realities were more real than some of the suggested solutions put forward in the Forum Report. They seemed to beg a question the whole time saying that nothing can be done without consent. That is the weakness of the Report ... I don't think parliament or Westminster or Great Britain is particularly concerned about the Forum Report' (*Irish News,* 26 July 1984). Prior also confirms that he will be leaving Northern Ireland in the autumn.

28 July The Noraid leader Martin Galvin is banned from entering the United Kingdom.

31 July A suspected IRA man, Séamus Shannon, is extradited from the Republic to Northern Ireland. He is wanted in connection with the murders of Sir Norman and James Stronge in January 1981. In December 1985 he is acquitted of the murders by Belfast Crown Court.

12 August Seán Downes is killed by a plastic bullet when the RUC attempts to arrest Martin Galvin at an internment anniversary rally in west Belfast. On 11 October the European Parliament votes in favour of a motion calling on the British government to ban the use of plastic bullets. British Conservative members of the European Parliament and Ian Paisley vote against the motion.

15 August Rioting breaks out in Protestant areas in protest against the trial based on evidence by the informer William 'Budgie' Allen and continues for the next three nights.

17 August The Labour Party spokesman on Northern Ireland, Clive Soley, calls for the 'harmonisation' of Northern Ireland with the Republic as a prelude to reunification. He tells the *Irish Times* that 'pensions and other social welfare entitlements for the whole of the island would be paid through Dublin, but those for Northern Ireland would be financed by the British exchequer.' It is not clear whether Soley intended benefits to be paid at the British or the Irish levels. In October, Soley holds talks with members of Sinn Féin. However, this does not lead to any change in the Labour Party's policy of 'unity by consent', and in a television interview on 12 October the leader of the party, Neil Kinnock, says that Irish unity will not be achieved for 'many, many decades' ('Newsnight', BBC2, 12 October 1984).

22 August The Co. Armagh coroner resigns after reviewing files on two INLA men killed by the RUC in 1982. He says there are 'grave irregularities' in the RUC documents.

3 September The inquest into the deaths of the two INLA men shot by the RUC is postponed pending the results of an investigation by the Greater Manchester Police into the RUC's investigation of the shootings.

6 September The government announces that the project to bring natural gas to Northern Ireland from Kinsale, Co. Cork, has been abandoned and that subsidies to the gas industry will end, meaning the loss of 1,000 jobs.

11 September Douglas Hurd becomes Secretary of State for Northern Ireland. Rhodes Boyson replaces Adam Butler as Minister of State.

20 September In the *Irish Press,* Gerry Adams suggests that it might be a bad idea for Sinn Féin to take over from the SDLP as the main nationalist party, as this might lead to a British constitutional initiative that would delude many northern nationalists.

24 September John Cushnahan becomes leader of the Alliance Party in succession to Oliver Napier.

26 September The leader of Fianna Fáil, Charles Haughey, rejects the idea of joint authority over Northern Ireland, saying: 'All you would have would be the Irish government helping the British government to rule the Six County area, over which the British would retain sovereignty ... the advocates of joint authority are looking for it in the security area. That, in my mind, would be a recipe for civil war in the North, with spill-over effects in the South' (*Belfast Telegraph,* 26 September 1984).

29 September Gardaí seize the trawler *Marita Ann* off the coast of Co. Kerry and find seven tons of arms and ammunition on board. In June 1987 an American court sentences four American citizens to between four and ten years' imprisonment for attempting to smuggle weapons to the IRA. In August the same year two Americans and two Irishmen are jailed by a French court for three to four years for their involvement in the incident.

2 October An article in the *Irish Times* shows that in the first nine months of 1984 the Provisional IRA has killed twenty-two local Protestant members of the security forces, six British soldiers, one Catholic ex-UDR man, a magistrate's daughter, an assistant prison governor, two alleged informers, and an alleged criminal. In the same period the army and police have killed five people and loyalist paramilitaries four (*Irish Times,* 2 October 1984).

11 October An opinion poll conducted by the *Belfast Telegraph* says that 58 per cent of Protestants and 50 per cent of Catholics are 'basically satisfied' with direct rule.

12 October The Grand Hotel, Brighton, being used by many senior Conservative Party members during the party conference, is bombed by the IRA in an attempt to assassinate most of the British Cabinet. The 20 lb bomb explodes at 2:54 a.m., slicing four floors out of the middle of the building and killing five people, including Sir Anthony Berry MP and Roberta Wakeham, wife of the government chief whip. The Secretary of State for Trade and Industry, Norman Tebbitt, is one of more than thirty people injured in the blast. Margaret Thatcher narrowly escapes injury: a bathroom she had been in two minutes earlier is wrecked. In a statement aimed at the Prime Minister the IRA later says: 'Today, we were unlucky, but remember, we only have to be lucky once—you will have to be lucky always.'

13 October In his speech to the Conservative Party conference, Douglas Hurd rejects all three of the New Ireland Forum's proposals, including that of joint authority.

14 October In the *Observer* a leading member of Sinn Féin, Danny Morrison, says: 'If that bomb had killed the British Cabinet, examine then what would have happened. There would have been a rethink within British political circles and it probably would have led to a British withdrawal in a much shorter period. It would have been unique in British constitutional history, apart maybe from Guy Fawkes.'

1 November The unofficial Kilbrandon Report by a committee of British politicians and academics gives its response to that of the New Ireland Forum. The majority call for a five-member Executive made up of three Northern Ireland politicians (possibly members of the European Parliament), the Irish Minister for Foreign Affairs, and the Secretary of State for Northern Ireland: this would be the unlikely combination of Douglas Hurd, Peter Barry, Ian Paisley, John Taylor, and John Hume. It is not clear how this proposal is intended to reduce the alienation of Sinn Féin voters.

4 November The *Sunday Press* claims that Margaret Thatcher has twice asked civil servants to draw up documents on repartition since the report of the New Ireland Forum was published, that they were horrified at the prospect and had refused to do so.

19 November A joint communiqué after a two-day Anglo-Irish summit meeting at Chequers between Margaret Thatcher and Garret FitzGerald states: 'The identities of both the majority and the minority communities in Northern Ireland should be recognised and respected and reflected in the structures and processes of Northern Ireland in ways acceptable to both communities.' After the summit Thatcher comments on the main proposals of the New Ireland Forum by saying: 'A united Ireland was one solution. That is out. A second solution was confederation of the two states. That is out. A third solution was joint authority. That is out. That is a derogation from sovereignty.' FitzGerald is later reported to have described Thatcher's behaviour at the press conference as 'gratuitously offensive'.

14 December Private Ian Thain is the first soldier to be convicted of murdering a civilian while on duty in Northern Ireland. In January 1987 he is released and resumes service with his unit.

18 December The Northern Ireland Lord Chief Justice, Lord Lowry, throws out the evidence of the informer Raymond Gilmour and acquits the thirty-five defendants. Many of those involved had been held on remand for over two years.

24 December In the Appeal Court in Belfast, Lord Lowry overturns the convictions of fourteen loyalists on evidence given by the informer Joseph Bennett.

DEATHS ARISING FROM THE TROUBLES: 64. SHOOTINGS: 334. BOMBS PLANTED: 248 (explosions: 193). INCENDIARIES: 10. FIREARMS FOUND: 187. EXPLOSIVES FOUND: 3,871 kg (8,535 lb). PERSONS CHARGED WITH TERRORIST AND SERIOUS PUBLIC ORDER OFFENCES: 528.

1985

20 January In an RTE interview the Secretary of State, Douglas Hurd, suggests that political machinery could be created to improve Anglo-Irish relations.

19 February The Irish government passes legislation to freeze £1$ million in a bank account believed to be controlled by the IRA.

23 February John Hume meets members of the IRA but no discussions take place, because Hume objects to the meeting being videotaped.

25 February Des O'Malley is expelled from Fianna Fáil for refusing to vote against a bill to liberalise contraceptive legislation in the Republic.

28 February Nine members of the RUC are killed and thirty injured in an IRA mortar attack on a police station in Newry. An IRA statement says: 'This was a major and well-planned operation indicating our ability to strike where and when we decide.'

7 March Two men are sentenced to thirty-five years' imprisonment for planning the 1981 bombings in London.

22 March Sir Robert Pascoe is named to succeed Sir Robert Richardson as army commander in June.

15 May District council elections are held. With a turn-out of 60.1 per cent, the Ulster Unionists take 29.5 per cent of first-preference votes (winning 190 seats) and re-establish their lead over the DUP (24.3 per cent, 142 seats). In a highly polarised situation, the Alliance vote falls to 7.1 per cent and it wins only 34 seats, despite the fact that the number of council seats available has increased by 40 to 566. The SDLP improves its share of the first-preference vote to 17.8 per cent but loses two seats (down to 101). Contesting council elections for the first time, Sinn Féin takes 11.8 per cent of first preferences, winning 59 seats.

20 May Four RUC men are killed by a 1,000 lb IRA bomb at the Killeen border post near Newry.

4 June A Sinn Féin member is elected chairman of Fermanagh District Council with the support of the SDLP, which holds the post of vice-chairman. In Magherafelt District Council a similar allocation leads to an SDLP chairman and Sinn Féin deputy chairman.

14 June A 1,000 lb IRA bomb causes widespread damage in Belfast. It is the first large bomb in the city centre for two years.

24 June A raid on a Glasgow tenement building by detectives of the Anti-Terrorist Branch uncovers a list of places where bombs with delayed-action firing devices were to be planted, to be set to detonate at the height of the summer holiday season. A bomb is found at one of the listed targets, the Rubens Hotel near Buckingham Palace.

25 June A bilateral treaty is signed in Washington that prevents fugitives in either the United States or the United Kingdom accused or convicted of certain terrorist offences escaping extradition by claiming a political motive for their actions.

27 June Hurd announces that in future no government funds will be provided to some local community groups, because of their 'close links with paramilitary organisations.'

29 June Patrick Magee is charged in London with the murder of those killed in the Brighton bombing in October 1984.

3 July Loyalists demonstrate in Portadown against suggestions that a traditional Orange parade should be rerouted away from a Catholic area. Four days later there are clashes between the RUC and nationalists when an Orange church parade is permitted to pass through a Catholic area. On 12 July, however, another Orange march is prevented from following the same route by the RUC, resulting in serious rioting for two days.

15 July In a speech to the American Bar Association in London, Margaret Thatcher says it is necessary to starve terrorists of 'the oxygen of publicity.'

21 July In Portadown a United Ulster Loyalist Front is formed to oppose the rerouting of traditional Orange parades by the RUC.

30 July After pressure from the Home Secretary, Leon Brittan, the Governors of the BBC prevent the transmission of 'Edge of the Union', which features an interview with Martin McGuinness of Sinn Féin. It is later shown in an amended form after protests from journalists and the threat of resignation by the Controller of BBC Northern Ireland.

7 August Journalists go on strike over the decision not to show 'Edge of the Union'. The BBC World Service goes off the air for the first time.

20 August Séamus McAvoy, a Co. Tyrone builder, is shot dead by the IRA in his flat in Dublin. McAvoy, who supplied prefabricated huts to the RUC, is the first person to be murdered by the IRA for working or providing materials for the police or army in Northern Ireland.

3 September Tom King becomes Secretary of State for Northern Ireland (Hurd becomes Home Secretary). Richard Needham subsequently replaces Chris Patten as Parliamentary Under-Secretary.

4 September An IRA mortar attack seriously damages the RUC training depot in Enniskillen.

18 September John Stalker submits to the Chief Constable, Sir John Hermon, an initial report of his inquiry into accusations of a cover-up of a 'shoot to kill' policy by members of the RUC.

8 October The conviction of the former INLA leader Dominic McGlinchey is overturned by the Northern Ireland Court of Appeal. He is re-extradited to the Republic on 11 October to face further charges.

17 October In the South Down by-election an Ulster Unionist, Jeffrey Donaldson, is elected to the Assembly. The election is most notable for having a turn-out of 21.3 per cent, one of the lowest ever.

2 November After a march by 5,000 members of the United Ulster Loyalist Front through Belfast, a campaign is launched to establish 'Ulster Clubs' throughout Northern Ireland to oppose any Anglo-Irish agreement.

9 November Speaking of his aspiration for a united Ireland, the SDLP deputy leader, Séamus Mallon, says: 'We cannot, will not and must not put this aspiration on the back boiler. We cannot make liars of ourselves, we cannot leave it in suspended animation for any length of time, or, like in County Armagh, the boys in the balaclavas will come along and say, "We are the only people pursuing this course"' (quoted by O'Clery, *Phrases Make History Here,* p. 211).

15 November The Anglo-Irish Agreement is signed by Margaret Thatcher and Garret FitzGerald at Hillsborough Castle, Co. Down, ending months of negotiations and speculation. Article 1 (*a*) states that the two governments 'affirm that any change in the status of Northern Ireland would only come about with the consent of a majority of the people of Northern Ireland.' At the same time it fails to say exactly what the current status of Northern Ireland is, a point quickly latched on to by unionist critics of the agreement.

The agreement establishes an Inter-Governmental Conference to deal regularly with political matters, security and related matters, legal matters (including the administration of justice), and the promotion of cross-border co-operation. The issue of 'political matters' is particularly sensitive. Article 5 (*a*) says that the conference will look at measures to 'recognise and accommodate the rights and identities of the two traditions in Northern Ireland, to protect human rights and to prevent discrimination. Matters to be considered in this area include measures to foster the cultural heritage of both traditions, changes in electoral arrangements, the use of flags and emblems [and] the avoidance of economic and social discrimination.'

Article 5 (*c*) states that 'if it should prove impossible to achieve and sustain devolution on a basis which secures widespread acceptance in Northern Ireland, the conference shall be a framework within which the Irish government may, where the interests of the minority community are significantly or especially affected, put forward views on proposals for major legislation and on major policy issues, which are within the purview of the Northern Ireland departments.' The Irish government interprets this as covering an extremely wide range of issues in Northern Ireland. Under article 2 (*b*) the British government is also committed 'in the interests of promoting peace and stability' to make 'determined efforts' to resolve any differences which arise within the conference with the Irish government.' The FitzGerald government and the Irish media interpret this as giving them more than consultation but less than joint authority.

After signing the agreement, Thatcher declares: 'I went into this agreement because I was not prepared to tolerate a situation of continuing violence.' The Treasury Minister, Ian Gow, a personal and political friend of Thatcher, resigns in protest, saying that 'the involvement of a foreign power in a consultative role in the administration of the province will prolong, and not diminish, Ulster's agony.' The UFF immediately declares members of the Anglo-Irish Conference and Secretariat to be 'legitimate targets'.

After the signing of the agreement FitzGerald approaches Thatcher on the issue of seeking money from EEC countries for the International Fund for Ireland associated with the agreement. He is 'taken aback by her reaction. "More money for these people?" she said, waving her hand in the general direction of Northern Ireland. "Look at these schools; look at these roads. Why should they have more money? I need that money for my people in England, who don't have anything like this." I was frankly quite nonplussed at this singular declaration of English nationalism on an occasion when I had expected rather to have to cope with what had so often been described to me as her "unionism"' (FitzGerald, *All In a Life,* p. 568).

Something of the degree of secrecy in which the agreement was drawn up is later revealed by the then Chancellor of the Exchequer, Nigel Lawson. He noted that the agreement had largely been negotiated by the Cabinet secretary, Robert Armstrong, because Thatcher considered the Cabinet 'far too leaky to be taken into her confidence.' He believed that the only members fully aware of the details of the negotiations were Tom King, Douglas Hurd, and possibly the Defence Secretary, Michael Heseltine. Lawson himself had considerable doubts about the agreement but did not oppose it openly in the Cabinet; nor did any of his colleagues. Lawson believed that 'over the years there had been a succession of well-intentioned political initiatives launched to deal with the Irish problem, and each of them had ended in tears, if not in bloodshed. It had made me highly sceptical of the wisdom of any Northern Ireland initiative' (Lawson, *The View from No. 11,* p. 699).

The Anglo-Irish Agreement

The Anglo-Irish Agreement sent a shudder of horror through the unionist community. It accentuated fears of British betrayal, and Margaret Thatcher, who only shortly before had appeared as a reassuring figure, became the focus of much rage. Ian Paisley told his congregation at the Martyrs' Memorial Church: 'We pray this night that thou wouldst deal with the Prime Minister of our country. We remember that the apostle Paul handed over the enemies of truth to the Devil that they might learn not to blaspheme. O God, in wrath take vengeance upon this wicked, treacherous, lying woman; take vengeance upon her, O Lord, and grant that we shall see a demonstration of thy power.' Much anger was also focused locally on the NIO, though in fact the Foreign Office and the Cabinet Office had taken the decisive role in committing Britain to the agreement, while the NIO had been rather more sceptical. In the midst of much heated rhetoric—especially about the failure to consult unionists—it was difficult to detect the real significance of the agreement.

Above all, the Anglo-Irish Agreement ushered in an era of direct rule with a green tinge, symbolised by the permanent presence of Irish Government officials at Maryfield, Co. Down. The agreement was novel in its explicit acceptance of a role for the Irish government in the affairs of the North as a defender of the interests of the nationalist community. This role was much less than the joint authority proposed by the New Ireland Forum—shared responsibility for all aspects of the administration of government—but it was more than purely consultative. Much of the confusion in unionist politics arose from the difficulties involved in coping with this fact. The agreement also acknowledged that the British government would support a united Ireland if majority consent existed for it in the North. Here it was less novel: the same point was enunciated in 1973 at the time of the Sunningdale agreement.

The Anglo-Irish Agreement explicitly attempted to encourage devolution on a cross-community basis, but, despite a later inaccurate claim by Thatcher to this effect, it was not possible to 'knock out' its institutions by agreeing to power-sharing. In the absence of any agreement on devolution the Anglo-Irish Agreement gave a paradoxical shape to the governmental institutions of the North. In substance the system was, administratively and economically, increasingly integrated with the United Kingdom. This was intensified by the growing reliance of the entire community on the British subvention. Nevertheless, the new role of the Irish government in Northern Ireland affairs appeared to be irreversible, and for many this implied the eventual evolution of a formalised system of joint authority.

16 November In the Assembly the DUP deputy leader, Peter Robinson, attacks the Anglo-Irish agreement and says: 'The Prime Minister signed away the Union at Hillsborough Castle yesterday. We are on the window-ledge of the Union. But I can tell you that that does not mean we will jump off' (*Northern Ireland Assembly Debates,* vol. 18, p. 127–8). A Unionist resolution calling for a referendum on the agreement is approved by 44 votes to 10. Unionists also announce that they will withdraw from all advisory boards in Northern Ireland in protest at the agreement.

The political correspondent of the *Irish Times,* John Cooney, writes that the agreement has given the Republic 'a foothold in decisions governing Northern Ireland.' This view is reiterated by the Minister for Justice, Michael Noonan, the following day when he says: 'In effect we have been given a major and substantial role in the day-to-day running of Northern Ireland.'

An editorial in the *Irish News* that welcomes the signing of the agreement says: 'The new Treaty marks an historic step in the involvement of Britain in the affairs of this country. For the first time since December 6, 1921, the representatives of the Irish and British governments have entered into a binding international agreement designed, as the preamble states, "to reconcile and to acknowledge the rights of the two major traditions that exist in Ireland."

'No one would claim that the document is in itself a solution, but it is a brave and commendable attempt to begin the healing process. Its historic significance can be gauged by the fact that from the establishment of the Northern State in 1921 until the late 1960s, it was not even possible for British MPs to raise discussion of Northern Ireland matters at Westminster. And as recently as 1971 the then British Prime Minister, Edward Heath, delivered a stern rebuff to the Irish government for daring to interfere in "the internal affairs of the United Kingdom" ...

'A number of articles in the Agreement are of immediate interest to Northern nationalists. Article 1, it is true, reiterates the British "guarantee" to unionism but in an important rider, the British government makes a written commitment to implement Irish unity *on its own initiative* in the event of a majority emerging in favour of that proposal. This is significant for two reasons: firstly, it legitimises for the first time in a solemn international agreement the objective of Irish unity, and secondly, it removes any possible justification for violence by its implicit assertion by Britain that she has no ulterior motive, strategic or otherwise, for remaining in Ireland. This must go for some way towards removing suspicion about "perfidious Albion".

'Moreover, for the first time the Irish government has been given a direct say in the internal administration of the North and, specifically, a role as the advocate of the minority at the highest levels. Through the Intergovernmental Council and the Secretariat, Dublin will be involved in a very extensive range of issues here ...'

18 November Harold McCusker comes closest to expressing the general unionist reaction to the agreement when he says in the House of Commons: 'I never knew what desolation felt like until I read this agreement last Friday afternoon. Does the Prime Minister realise that, when she carries the agreement through the house, she will have ensured that I shall carry to my grave with ignominy the sense of the injustice that I have done to my constituents down the years—when, in their darkest hours, I exhorted them to put their trust in this British House of Commons, which one day would honour its fundamental obligation to them to treat them as equal British citizens? Is it not the reality of this agreement that they will now be Irish-British hybrids and that every aspect—not just some aspects—of their lives will be open to the influence of those who have coveted their land?' (*Hansard,* sixth series, vol. 87, col. 29).

Senator Mary Robinson, the future President of Ireland, resigns from the Labour Party in protest at the Anglo-Irish Agreement, because it is 'unacceptable to all sections of unionist opinion.' She says: 'I do not believe it can achieve its objective of securing peace and stability within Northern Ireland or on the island as a whole.'

19 November The eighteen unionist-controlled district councils adopt an adjournment policy against the agreement and threaten to refuse to adopt rates.

20 November Tom King is attacked by a crowd of loyalists when he visits Belfast City Hall. In October 1986 the loyalist councillor George Seawright is sentenced to nine months' imprisonment for his part in the attack.

21 November The Dáil approves the Anglo-Irish Agreement by 88 votes to 75. Unionists lose a legal challenge to the Anglo-Irish Agreement.

23 November Over 100,000 (some estimates say over 200,000) unionists attend a massive demonstration against the Anglo-Irish Agreement at Belfast City Hall attended by fourteen of the fifteen Unionist MPs.

25 November A Unionist application for a judicial review of certain aspects of the agreement is turned down by the High Court in London.

26 November A two-day debate on the Anglo-Irish Agreement begins in the House of Commons. James Molyneaux, says: 'The agreement will bring not peace but a sword ... I have to say honestly and truthfully that in forty years in public life I have never known what I can only describe as a universal cold fury, which some of us have thus far managed to contain' (*Hansard,* sixth series, vol. 87, col. 764, 767).

Speaking in the same debate in support of the agreement, John Hume says: 'This is the first time that we have had a real framework within which to address the problem. The problem is not just about relationships within Northern Ireland. One need only listen to the speeches of Northern Ireland members to know that it is about relationships in Ireland and between Britain and Ireland. Those interlocking relationships should be addressed within the framework of the problem. The framework of the problem can only be the framework of the solution, and that is the British-Irish framework. There is no road towards a solution to this problem that does not contain risks. The road that has been chosen by both governments is the road of maximum consensus and is, therefore, the road of minimum risk. We should welcome that ...

'The agreement gives us no more than an opportunity to begin the process of reconciliation. The choices offered to the people of Northern Ireland are the choices offered by honourable members here present. The unionist parties have consistently sought to protect the integrity of their heritage in Ireland—the Protestant heritage—and no-one should quarrel with that. A society is richer for its diversity. My quarrel with the unionist parties has been that they have sought to protect their heritage by holding all the power in their own hands, and by basing that on sectarian solidarity. That is an exclusive use of power which is inherently violent because it permanently excludes a substantial section of the community from any say in its affairs' (*Hansard,* sixth series, vol. 87, col. 780–1).

28 November The House of Commons votes in favour of the Anglo-Irish Agreement by 473 votes to 47.

29 November It is revealed that three hundred building workers have been sacked after their employers refuse to undertake further work for the police or army as a result of IRA threats against themselves and their families.

3 December Speaking in Brussels, Tom King says: 'We have signed an agreement in which the Prime Minister of the Republic of Ireland ... has in fact accepted for all practical purposes and into perpetuity that there will never be a united Ireland.' The comment sparks a row between the British and Irish governments.

5 December Unionists set up a Grand Committee of the Northern Ireland Assembly to examine the effects of the Anglo-Irish Agreement on Northern Ireland government departments. On the following day the Alliance Party withdraws from the Assembly.

11 December The first session of the Anglo-Irish Conference at Stormont is marked by protests and clashes between the RUC and loyalists. Workers at Harland and Wolff, Shorts and Ballylumford power station hold a lunchtime protest meeting against the agreement, and two thousand later march to the site of the Anglo-Irish Secretariat at Maryfield, near Belfast. Thirty-eight members of the RUC are injured in the clashes.

At the conclusion of the Conference meeting it is announced that a code of conduct is to be introduced for the RUC in 1986 and that all army patrols coming into contact with the public will be accompanied by members of the RUC. The Irish government agrees to move more gardaí to the border.

17 December All fifteen Unionist MPs resign their seats in order to fight by-election campaigns on the grounds of their opposition to the Anglo-Irish Agreement.

18 December The conviction of twenty-five people on the evidence of the INLA informer Harry Kirkpatrick marks the beginning of the end of the system. By the end of the Kirkpatrick trial the confessions of almost thirty informers from paramilitary groups of all shades have resulted in over six hundred arrests, and nearly three hundred people have been charged, mostly in 1982 and 1983. The chief cause for concern in these trials is the significant number of people charged and convicted exclusively on evidence provided by informers, who often receive immunity from prosecution for their own offences in return. By the end of the Kirkpatrick case the fourteen people convicted in the Joe Bennett UVF case (1983) have already had their convictions overturned on appeal. Other convictions based on the evidence of informers are overturned in the following years.

DEATHS ARISING FROM THE TROUBLES: 55. SHOOTINGS: 238. BOMBS PLANTED: 215 (explosions: 163). INCENDIARIES: 36. FIREARMS FOUND: 173. EXPLOSIVES FOUND: 3,344 kg (7,370 lb). PERSONS CHARGED WITH TERRORIST AND SERIOUS PUBLIC ORDER OFFENCES: 522.

1986

3 January An Assembly member, Pascal O'Hare, resigns from the SDLP because he believes the Anglo-Irish Agreement has 'copperfastened' the Union.

16 January Two members of the IRA who escaped from the Maze Prison in 1983, Brendan McFarlane and Gerard Kelly, are arrested in the Netherlands.

23 January Brian Mawhinney, MP for Peterborough (a native of Northern Ireland), is appointed a junior minister in the NIO.

24 January By-elections are held for the fifteen House of Commons seats held by Unionists, under the slogan *Ulster says no.* West Belfast and Foyle are not contested. The Unionists' intention is to use the by-elections as a referendum on the Anglo-Irish Agreement. Not wishing to help this strategy, the SDLP contests only four marginal seats. In four safe seats the Unionists are forced to run a 'dummy' candidate to provide opposition. A unionist supporter who adopts the name 'Peter Barry' (the name of the Irish Minister for Foreign Affairs involved in implementing the Anglo-Irish Agreement) stands in the two Co. Antrim seats, Strangford and East Londonderry and receives a total of 6,777 votes. There are 418,230 votes against the Anglo-Irish Agreement; but with the Ulster Unionists losing the Newry and Armagh seat to the SDLP deputy leader, Séamus Mallon, the by-elections appear to be something of a pyrrhic victory. Nevertheless the overwhelming Protestant opposition to the agreement is evidenced by the slump in support for the Alliance Party, which receives only 32,095 votes, as Protestants vote for parties clearly opposed to it.

5 February As pressure on the RUC continues, the Chief Constable, Sir John Hermon, orders leaders of the RUC union, the Northern Ireland Police Federation, not to talk to the media without receiving clearance from RUC headquarters. The chairman of the federation later calls a news conference without seeking official approval and says that the federation's freedom of speech is protected by the Police Act (1970).

7 February As a result of a case brought by the Alliance Party, the High Court orders Belfast City Council to take down the BELFAST SAYS NO banner erected on the front of the City Hall in protest at the Anglo-Irish Agreement. The court also orders the council to resume normal business.

24 February The Republic signs the European Convention on the Suppression of Terrorism (1976).

25 February James Molyneaux and Ian Paisley meet Margaret Thatcher for talks on the Anglo-Irish Agreement and seem satisfied that she has agreed to consider their idea for round-table talks on devolution. On their return to Belfast, however, talks with local unionist representatives show them to be out of touch with grass-roots feeling and they later declare there will be no more discussions with Thatcher until the Anglo-Irish Agreement has been dropped.

Belfast City Council refuses to set a rate. Other unionist-controlled councils followed their lead.

26 February The two Unionist leaders announce a general strike for 3 March in protest at the Anglo-Irish Agreement. They call for a peaceful protest.

3 March The Unionist 'Day of Action' shuts down much of commerce and industry. Rioting occurs in loyalist areas of Belfast. Snipers later fire on the RUC during rioting in Protestant areas. The RUC later say that there have been 237 reports of intimidation and fifty-seven arrests; forty-seven members of the RUC are injured during the protests.

11 March The US House of Representatives unanimously approves a $250 million aid package to Northern Ireland over the next five years in support of the Anglo-Irish Agreement.

12 March Evelyn Glenholmes, top of Scotland Yard's wanted list, is arrested in Ireland on suspicion of involvement in the 1984 Brighton bombing. On 24 March, however, administrative errors in the extradition warrant allow her to walk free, to the fury of the British and Irish governments. Alan Dukes, the Irish Minister for Justice, later lays the blame for the fiasco on the British Attorney-General, Sir Michael Havers.

13 March As a result of unionist protests against the Anglo-Irish Agreement it is announced that an extra battalion of troops is to be brought to Northern Ireland to support the RUC.

Two men are sentenced to eight years' imprisonment by the High Court in Glasgow for attempting to acquire arms for the UVF.

19 March The NIO minister Richard Needham announces that the Northern Ireland Department of the Environment will set the rates for the eighteen Unionist-controlled district councils that are refusing to do so in protest at the Anglo-Irish Agreement.

31 March The banning of an Apprentice Boys' parade in Portadown leads to furious clashes between the RUC and loyalists, which continue sporadically over the following weeks. In Lisburn eleven Catholic homes are attacked with stones and petrol bombs. On the following day, as rioting continues, twenty-year-old Keith White receives head injuries during disturbances in Portadown; he dies two weeks later, the first Protestant to be killed by a plastic bullet.

1 April Thirty-nine policemen and thirty-eight civilians are injured during rioting in Portadown, 147 plastic bullets are fired, there are eighty-eight cases of damage to property and thirty-three arrests.

10 April As attacks on the RUC by Protestants continue, the Chairman of the Northern Ireland Police Federation calls on the Chief Constable to withdraw from future meetings of the Anglo-Irish Intergovernmental Conference.

27 April In an interview with the *Observer,* John Hume comments that he had 'always expected a furious Unionist reaction to the agreement, but the Protestant boil had to be lanced. Mrs Thatcher is the right person in the right place in the right time, and they are recognising that she will not be broken.' He predicts that the crisis will be resolved by the end of the summer, when unionists will agree to talks with the SDLP.

1 May Rothman closes its cigarette factory in Carrickfergus, with the loss of 800 jobs. On 26 August, Gallaher announce the closure of its Belfast factory, with the loss of a further 700 jobs.

6 May Belfast City Council avoids a £25,000 fine by temporarily ending the suspension of business. However, it soon begins a policy of deferring business.

14 May The inaugural public meeting of the integrationist Campaign for Equal Citizenship is held in Belfast. The new pressure group, under the leadership of Robert McCartney QC, advocates the full administrative integration of Northern Ireland into the United Kingdom and also begins a campaign to get the main British political parties to organise in Northern Ireland, arguing that sectarianism can only be defeated by giving electors the opportunity to vote for parties based on class and economic interests. Though the Conservative Party later organises in Northern Ireland, the Labour Party refuses to do so.

20 May The NIO minister Nick Scott tells the House of Commons that there have been 368 cases of intimidation against RUC members during recent loyalist violence against the Anglo-Irish Agreement. Eventually over five hundred police homes are attacked and 150 families forced to move. The dilemma of RUC members is typified by the comment of one middle-ranking officer who says: 'We are being asked to enforce the will of Parliament against the will of the majority of the people … But whatever their own views too many men have mortgages and family commitments to rebel' (*Fortnight,* 24 February–9 March 1986). The Chief Constable, Sir John Hermon, later reveals that the RUC had plans to evacuate hundreds of police families to houses in Britain that had been made available through the Association of Chief Police Officers in England. The Anglo-Irish Agreement 'was a political initiative by two sovereign states and it was not my business. My business was to ensure that any political initiative was resolved within the democratic process and not by mob rule on the streets. I had a quite firm determination that there would not be a repeat of 1974 when the subversives and politically motivated strikes bring the whole state down around them. I was quietly determined … that the RUC could handle the situation but I also knew that if they couldn't do that then they were not the force for Northern Ireland. And I was quite prepared, if necessary, to see them sacrifice themselves' (*Sunday Life,* 29 March 1992).

5 June John Stalker is replaced as officer in charge of the investigation into the alleged RUC 'shoot to kill' policy begun in 1982, which is taken over by the Chief Constable of West Yorkshire, Colin Sampson. Stalker is suspended from duty on 30 June while an investigation is conducted into his association with so-called 'known criminals'; on 22 August, after an investigation, he is cleared and reinstated as Deputy Chief Constable of Greater Manchester. However, in December he resigns from the police.

11 June Patrick Magee and four others are found guilty of conspiring to cause explosions in Britain, including the Brighton bomb. Magee later receives eight life sentences.

23 June The Northern Ireland Assembly is dissolved. Ian Paisley and twenty-one other members are forcibly ejected by the RUC the next morning after refusing to leave the building. James Molyneaux says the Anglo-Irish Agreement had made the achievement of any sort of democracy in Northern Ireland virtually impossible.

26 June A referendum in the Republic rejects the introduction of a restricted form of divorce by 935,842 votes to 538,729, a vote of 63.5 per cent in favour of retaining the constitutional ban. On 3 July Garret FitzGerald criticises the 40 per cent of voters who abstained and says the result is 'something of a setback to the long-term prospect of the two parts of Ireland coming closer together politically ... It cannot reasonably be denied that we have a long way to go before we create in this part of Ireland a society that would seem welcoming to, open to and attractive to people of the Northern Unionist tradition.'

2 July Four members of the UDR are sentenced to life imprisonment for the murder of Adrian Carroll, a Catholic man murdered while returning from work in November 1983. They are to become known as the 'UDR Four'.

6 July There are clashes between members of the Orange Order and the RUC in Portadown when the police attempt to prevent the Orangemen from passing through the (Catholic) Obin Street area of the town.

10 July Ian Paisley, Peter Robinson and about four thousand loyalists occupy Hillsborough, Co. Down, in protest at the Anglo-Irish Agreement.

11 July There is rioting in Protestant areas of Belfast and Portadown, which continues through most of the following week. On 14 July, Catholic homes are attacked in Rasharkin, Co. Antrim, by a group of about fifty loyalists. Over the 12 July period more than a hundred people are injured in sectarian confiicts.

17 July The convictions of eighteen men named by the IRA informer Christopher Black in August 1983 are overturned by the Appeal Court.

22 July The UVF informer Joe Bennett is sentenced to ten years' imprisonment for armed robbery by Nottingham Crown Court. The crime was committed after Bennett had been resettled in England under the name John Graham.

26 July Three RUC men are shot dead by the IRA as they sit in a parked car in the centre of Newry.

28 July The IRA issues a warning to civilians working for the army or police. Two days later the IRA murders a Protestant businessman who has provided supplies to the security forces. A week later the IRA issues a further statement listing people who they consider to be 'part of the war machine' and who will be 'treated as collaborators' and 'must expect to suffer the consequences.' The list includes civil servants, building contractors, anyone supplying fuel, food or cleaning services to the security forces, British Telecom, Standard Telephones, companies that transport members of the police or army, and firms supplying vending machines to them. Sinn Féin gives its full backing to the statement.

5 August The IRA threatens to murder civilians involved in administration, maintenance or building work for the police or army. In the previous year the IRA have already killed four businessmen involved in building work. On 7 August the UFF announces that it is expanding its own list of 'legitimate targets' in response to the IRA's threat to civilians.

7 August The deputy leader of the DUP, Peter Robinson, is arrested in Clontibret, Co. Monaghan, two miles inside the Republic, after five hundred loyalists temporarily take over the village and assault two gardaí. On 15 August, when Robinson is remanded in Dundalk, his supporters are stoned and petrol-bombed. At his trial in January 1987 the judge, Mr Justice Barr, describes Robinson as 'a senior extremist politician' and fines him £15,000.

13 August Yet another error in an extradition warrant leads to an IRA suspect, Gerard O'Reilly, being freed by a Dublin court.

22 August Short Brothers announce that all loyalist flags and posters must be removed from their Belfast aircraft factories. The decision leads to a walk-out of 1,000 employees on 27 August; the issue is at least partly resolved two days later when the chairman of the company issues a letter to all workers saying that the Union Jack will fly from the company flagstaff at all times and asks workers to remove loyalist emblems voluntarily.

27 August The IRA tells car dealers to warn customers of the danger of buying a car that had belonged to a member of the police or army and 'advises' doctors, solicitors and clergymen who need to visit RUC stations to display 'appropriate signs' on their cars. The nature of the threats are clarified the following day when the IRA shoots dead a Protestant electrician because he had worked at a local UDR base.

3 September The Ulster Unionist MP Harold McCusker says that with the Anglo-Irish Agreement the Union with Britain is not worth fighting for, much less dying for.

5 September A joint working party of Unionist politicians advises district councillors to resign on 15 November in order to force the NIO to appoint commissioners.

11 September Nick Scott is promoted to Minister of State at the NIO on the departure of Rhodes Boyson. Peter Viggers is appointed as an Under-Secretary.

14 September One of the UVF's commanders, John Bingham, is murdered by the IRA, which claims he was behind a recent spate of murders of Catholics.

18 September The British and Irish governments formally establish an international aid fund of £35 million to promote social and economic development in Northern Ireland and in the border areas of the Republic.

October Unemployment reaches a peak of 135,000, or 23 per cent of those available for work.

15 October The Provisional IRA announces that it will support Sinn Féin members taking their seats in the Dáil.

28 October In an interview with RTE, President Gaddafi of Libya calls on 'all Irish youth in the North and South to participate in the struggle for the liberation of Ulster' (quoted in *Keesing's Contemporary Archives,* p. 35222).

2 November A Sinn Féin conference votes by a two-thirds majority to end its policy of abstention from the Dáil. Ruairí Ó Brádaigh and Dáithí Ó Conaill, with about a hundred others, walk out in protest and subsequently form Republican Sinn Féin.

7 November The Lord Mayor of Belfast, Sammy Wilson of the DUP, bans NIO ministers from attending the Remembrance Day ceremony at City Hall.

10 November Ian Paisley launches a new organisation, Ulster Resistance, aimed at destroying the Anglo-Irish Agreement.

15 November On the first anniversary of the signing of the Anglo-Irish Agreement up to 200,000 unionists attend a rally at Belfast City Hall. Later 150 youths attack and loot shops in the city centre. Rioting in Protestant areas lasts for two days; two people are killed and seventy-five injured, and there are 110 arrests.

3 December Two escapers from the Maze Prison, Brendan McFarlane and Gerard Kelly, are extradited from the Netherlands and appear in court in Lisburn on charges relating to their escape.

23 December The convictions of twenty-four men jailed on the evidence of the informer Harry Kirkpatrick are quashed by the Court of Appeal, and the men are freed.

DEATHS ARISING FROM THE TROUBLES: 61. SHOOTINGS: 392. BOMBS PLANTED: 254 (explosions: 172). INCENDIARIES: 21. FIREARMS FOUND: 174. EXPLOSIVES FOUND: 2,443 kg (5,385 lb). PERSONS CHARGED WITH TERRORIST AND SERIOUS PUBLIC ORDER OFFENCES: 655.

1987

3 January At Belfast City Hall, as part of the campaign against the Anglo-Irish Agreement, UUP and DUP leaders launch a petition to the Queen calling for a referendum on the agreement. The petition, containing over 400,000 signatures, is handed in to Buckingham Palace on 12 February but apparently has no impact on government policy.

8 January A DUP councillor, David Calvert, is wounded by an INLA gunman at a shopping centre in Craigavon.

20 January In the Republic, Garret FitzGerald's coalition government collapses after the Labour Party withdraws its support.

The Home Secretary, Douglas Hurd, refers the case of the Birmingham Six back to the Court of Appeal.

A feud breaks out between the INLA and a breakaway faction calling itself the Irish People's Liberation Organisation when two leading members are shot dead in a bar in Drogheda. The feud lasts until March and results in thirteen murders, including that of the wife of Dominic McGlinchey on 1 February.

26 January The Unionist MP Harold McCusker is sentenced to seven days' imprisonment for failing to pay a fine imposed for his refusal to pay road tax in protest at the Anglo-Irish Agreement.

29 January The UDA's political think tank, the New Ulster Political Research Group, publishes *Common Sense.* It calls for a written constitution for Northern Ireland and a devolved government based on consensus and shared responsibility.

7 February The UFF plants a number of incendiary devices in Dublin and in Co. Donegal.

13 February Castlereagh District Council is fined £10,000 for contempt of court after defying a court order to resume normal business. By now most district councils are undertaking some business to avoid court orders.

19 February A general election in the Republic leads to the formation of a Fianna Fáil minority government led by Charles Haughey on 10 March.

23 February The High Court in Belfast fines Belfast City Council £25,000 for failing to resume normal business; the council also has to pay £11,000 in legal costs. The Northern Ireland Department of the Environment later appoints a commissioner to set council rates in areas where unionist-controlled councils have refused to do so in protest at the Anglo-Irish Agreement.

24 February The two main Unionist parties announce the setting up of a task force to produce possible alternatives to the Anglo-Irish Agreement.

11 March Garret FitzGerald resigns as leader of Fine Gael and is succeeded by Alan Dukes.

17 March President Ronald Reagan authorises the first grant of $50 million to the International Fund for Ireland, established in conjunction with the Anglo-Irish Agreement.

23 March Colin Sampson hands his report on the alleged 'shoot to kill' policy to the RUC Chief Constable, Sir John Hermon.

The IRA kills a civilian prison worker as he sits in his car at Magee College in Derry. Two RUC detectives are later killed when the car explodes as they approach it to investigate the murder. An IRA bomb at a British army base at Rheindalen in Germany injures thirty-one people.

1 April An RUC spokesman says that under new public order legislation the flying of the Union Jack could be illegal in areas where it is considered provocative. On 10 April ten unionist MPs take part in a march through Belfast that has been made illegal by the new public order legislation.

8 April There is a confrontation between mourners and police at the funeral of an IRA man, Lawrence Marley (reportedly the man who planned the 1983 Maze Prison escape), killed by the UVF six days earlier. The funeral has already been postponed twice as a result of earlier confrontations between the RUC and mourners. On 22 April a statement issued after a meeting of the Intergovernmental Conference at Stormont says there is a need for more sensitive policing by the RUC of paramilitary funerals.

23 April Peter Archer, the Labour Party spokesman on Northern Ireland, expresses his support for the controversial MacBride fair employment principles. The nine-point MacBride code (named after the IRA chief of staff and later Irish Minister for Foreign Affairs Seán MacBride and based on the 1977 Sullivan Principles relating to American investment in South Africa), launched in November 1984, has the declared aim of using the influence of investors in American companies operating in Northern Ireland to encourage fair employment. Given the heavy involvement of the strongly republican Irish National Caucus, however, many observers are sceptical about whether the aim of the campaign is to achieve a higher level of Catholic employment or rather to encourage American companies to leave Northern Ireland, thus increasing political instability.

25 April Lord Justice Maurice Gibson, the second most senior judge in Northern Ireland, and his wife are killed by a 500 lb IRA bomb planted in a parked car on the border at Killeen, Co. Armagh, as they drive home from Dublin after a holiday. The explosives used in the attack are believed to have been supplied by Libya.

6 May The Secretary of State, Tom King, announces that the RUC is to recruit 500 more full-time reservists.

8 May Eight IRA men are shot dead during an attack on Loughgall RUC station in Co. Armagh. A civilian caught in the firing is also killed. In the period leading up to the incident, intelligence agents discover that the IRA is planning a bomb attack on the station, and an operation involving forty members of the SAS is set up to ambush the IRA unit. SAS men are positioned inside the police station and in a wood close by, with a further sixteen men assigned to cut off the IRA unit if it tries to escape from. At 7:15 p.m. a van (to be used as the getaway vehicle) and a mechanical digger with a 200 lb bomb in the front head towards the station. The van stops in front of the police station and two IRA men get out. The SAS open fire, shooting over a hundred rounds into the digger and the van. During the fight the IRA men detonate the bomb, destroying part of the police station. Though they are wearing body armour, they are killed by the heavy fire from the SAS. None of the SAS soldiers is seriously injured.

The ambush in effect wipes out the IRA's East Tyrone unit. The civilian is killed when he is shot as he drives through one of the SAS groups. After the ambush the area is sealed off and the SAS are removed from the scene by helicopter. The ambush inflicts the IRA's highest death toll in any one incident (*Sunday Life*, 18 October 1992).

19 May Robert McCartney is expelled from the UUP because he is president of the integrationist Campaign for Equal Citizenship and for his criticism of Ulster Unionist leaders.

2 June In the run-up to the general election Lord Fitt, former leader of the SDLP, says: 'I would not vote for the SDLP, because it is not a socialist party ... Both they and the Dublin government want to see Mrs Thatcher re-elected' (*News Letter*). Fitt's view is affirmed by Austin Currie, a senior figure in the SDLP, who comments that 'in terms of Northern Ireland, and the nationalist position in Ireland generally, the Labour Party has always been a disappointment. Going back to 1949 when they copperfastened partition, and 1974 when Wilson and Rees were spineless—I have serious reservations about the Labour Party in that connection. I'm sorry to have to say it but—from the point of view of nationalist Ireland—a continuation of Maggie Thatcher in power, for a limited period of time, would be to our advantage' (*Fortnight*, June 1987). On the eve of the election Fitt continues his attack on the SDLP by writing: 'I wish to point out that the SDLP were only admitted to the Socialist International by my credentials. Now their support for a reactionary government brands them as class traitors' (*Irish Times*, 10 June 1987).

11 June The Conservative Party wins the general election. In Northern Ireland the UUP loses South Down to the SDLP, leading to the retirement of Enoch Powell from politics. The chief beneficiary of the election is the SDLP, which increases its vote (to 154,087) and its share of the poll (by 3.2 per cent) compared with the 1983 election. As a result of the continuing unionist electoral pact the UUP vote increases to 276,230 (37.8 per cent) but the unionist vote in general slumps as the DUP vote declines to 85,642 (11.7 per cent). Another significant development on the unionist side is the candidacy of the integrationist Robert McCartney in North Down, where, standing as a 'Real Unionist', he takes 14,467 votes. The Sinn Féin vote declines to 83,389 (11.4 per cent), while Alliance improves its performance, receiving 72,671 votes (10.0 per cent).

In the subsequent government reshuffle Nick Scott is replaced as Minister of State at the NIO by John Stanley.

2 July The report of the Unionist Task Force led by the general secretary of the UUP, Frank Millar, and the deputy leader of the DUP, Peter Robinson, proposes an alternative to the Anglo-Irish Agreement that would involve the opening of discussions with the government and lead to some form of devolved power-sharing administration. The party leaders, James Molyneaux and Ian Paisley, fail to respond to the report, and as a result Millar (permanently) and Robinson (temporarily) resign from their positions. Debate also continues, particularly within the UUP, between those who favour greater integration with Britain (increasingly the majority) and a declining number favouring some form of devolved government.

3 July Edward Campbell, found shot dead at a quarry on the Upper Crumlin Road, is the first taxi driver to be killed as a result of the Troubles.

Shorts aircraft factory closes three of its production areas as a result of a dispute with workers over the display of loyalist emblems. Production is resumed several days later, and the dispute is eventually resolved when the company agrees to permanently fly the Union Jack outside its factory. In return the workers voluntarily remove loyalist emblems.

26 August The IRA shoots dead two off-duty RUC detectives and injure several other bystanders in an attack on a Belfast bar.

14 September James Molyneaux and Ian Paisley meet Tom King at Stormont for 'talks about talks'. It is the first meeting between unionist political leaders and government ministers in nineteen months.

15 September In the wake of mounting pressure on the issue of fair employment from supporters of the MacBride principles in the United States, the NIO launches *Religious Equality of Opportunity in Employment: An Employers' Guide to Fair Employment.*

3 October Dr John Alderdice is elected leader of the Alliance Party in succession to John Cushnahan.

18 October The army defuses a 3,000 lb bomb in Omagh.

1 November 150 tons of arms and ammunition, including twenty Soviet-made surface-to-air missiles, are seized on the *Eksund* off the French coast. It later emerges that the IRA has already received three deliveries of weapons from Libya. In the trial of the captain of the *Eksund* in the High Court in Dublin in 1990 a Garda superintendent claims that the ship had brought 242 tons of arms and explosives from Libya in the two years before its seizure, while the prosecution claims that the weapons were to have been used in large-scale IRA attacks in Co. Armagh and on the Maze Prison.

8 November As marchers assemble for the annual Remembrance Day ceremony in Enniskillen, a bomb planted by the IRA in a disused school explodes, bringing part of the building down on those standing nearby, killing eleven people and injuring another sixty-three. Among those killed are three married couples. Local headmaster, Ronnie Hill, is left in a coma. The IRA later claims that the army set off the explosion by using a high-frequency scanning device.

The revulsion that the atrocity arouses does much to improve community relations in the area and loses the IRA support throughout the world. Pressure from the local Catholic community leads the SDLP to change its policy of supporting Sinn Féin for the posts of chairman and deputy chairman of Fermanagh District Council and to support Ulster Unionists instead. The move helps improve relations in the area. An important figure in the attempt to improve local relations is Gordon Wilson, father of Marie Wilson, a nurse killed in the blast. He says that he forgives his daughter's killers, and says, 'I shall pray for those people tonight and every night.'

19 November Loyalist politician George Seawright is shot in the head by a gunman as he sits in his car on the Shankill Road. The shooting is carried out by the IPLO, the breakaway group from the INLA. Seawright dies from his injuries two weeks later.

22 November Margaret Thatcher attends a rearranged Remembrance Day service at Enniskillen in which seven thousand people take part.

23 November Searches for IRA weapons north and south of the border lead to forty people being arrested.

18 December A County Court judge, Andrew Donaldson, resigns in protest at inadequate arrangements for his safety.

22 December The deputy leader of the UDA, John McMichael, is killed by an IRA booby-trap bomb planted under his car at his home in Lisburn. The Chief Constable of the RUC, John Hermon, later implies that McMichael may have been set up by others within the organisation, because he was investigating racketeering by members of the UDA. Among those suspected of collusion is another senior UDA man, Jim Craig, believed to have been heavily involved in racketeering. Craig is murdered in an east Belfast bar in October 1988.

By the end of the year the seasonally adjusted unemployment figure has fallen by over 8,000 on the previous year but still stands at 120,600, 17 per cent of the working population.

DEATHS ARISING FROM THE TROUBLES: 95. SHOOTINGS: 674. BOMBS PLANTED: 384 (explosions: 236). INCENDIARIES: 9. FIREARMS FOUND: 206. EXPLOSIVES FOUND: 5,885 kg (12,975 lb). PERSONS CHARGED WITH TERRORIST AND SERIOUS PUBLIC ORDER OFFENCES: 471. CASUALTIES ARISING FROM PARAMILITARY ATTACKS: 184.

1988

8 January A hundred guns with ammunition are seized when the RUC stop three cars near Portadown, the biggest seizure of loyalist arms up to this time; three UDA men are arrested. On 1 November a senior UDA figure, Davy Payne, is jailed for nineteen years after being convicted of possession of arms in connection with the incident.

9 January In the fourth such attack since June 1985, an IRA bomb explodes at the law courts in Belfast, causing extensive damage.

11 January John Hume begins a series of discussions with the President of Sinn Féin, Gerry Adams, in an attempt to find common ground on the conditions for an all-Ireland settlement. The SDLP lays much emphasis on the view that since the Anglo-Irish Agreement, Britain has assumed a neutral stance in Irish affairs. He claims that 'Britain is now saying that she has no interest of her own in being here and that her only interest is to see agreement among the people who share the island of Ireland' (quoted by Alexander and O'Day, *The Irish Terrorism Experience,* p. 140).

25 January The Attorney-General, Sir Patrick Mayhew, announces that there will be no prosecutions arising from the Stalker-Sampson inquiry into the alleged 'shoot to kill' policy of the RUC, which resulted in the deaths of six men in 1982.

27 January Gardaí make their biggest IRA arms find on a beach near Malin Head, Co. Donegal, when they uncover two oil storage tanks containing grenades, explosives, and ammunition.

28 January After a seven-week hearing, the Court of Appeal in London rejects the appeal of the six men convicted of the 1974 Birmingham pub bombings. It rejects the idea that there has been a large-scale conspiracy by the police and that confessions had only been obtained by the police beating the six men. New scientific evidence suggesting that positive tests for nitroglycerine on the men's hands could have been caused by their handling playing-cards is also rejected. Summing up, Lord Chief Justice Lane says:

'The longer this trial has gone on the more convinced this court has been that the verdict was correct.' The Labour Party MP Chris Mullin, who leads the campaign for a retrial, says it is 'a black day for British justice.' The outcome of the appeal also sours Anglo-Irish relations and leads the Irish Minister for Justice to say that he is 'amazed and saddened' by the decision.

3 February The RUC makes a further find of loyalist weapons, including rocket-launchers, rifles, revolvers, a sub-machine gun, and 12,000 rounds of ammunition.

5 February John Stalker claims that he was taken off the 'shoot to kill' inquiry because his investigation was about to cause a political dispute that would have resulted in several resignations. He says that his investigation showed that trained RUC squads had shot dead the six unarmed republicans and then made up stories to cover the truth. He adds, however, that there was no official policy to kill suspects rather than arrest them. He also says that it is now too late to prosecute those involved. The issue is still far from over, however, and on 12 February the Irish government temporarily stops meetings between the Gardaí and the RUC in protest.

16 February William Quinn, extradited from the United States in October 1986, is sentenced to life imprisonment for the murder of a London policeman in February 1975. He is the first person to be extradited from the United States under the extradition treaty that came into force in July 1986.

22 February As Anglo-Irish relations grow cooler, the Irish government orders its own inquiry into the killing of Aidan McAnespie by machine-gun fire from a British army post on the border the previous day. British authorities claim the killing was the result of an accidental ricochet, a point that is borne out when the body is later exhumed for a second post-mortem examination in the South. This concludes that McAnespie was indeed killed by a ricochet. Nationalists query the necessity for any gunfire, however, and allege that the dead man had been persistently harassed by the RUC.

6 March In Gibraltar three unarmed IRA members on 'active service' are shot dead by the SAS at point-blank range. Seán Savage, Daniel McCann and Mairéad Farrell were all known as republican activists. Farrell had served a ten-year jail sentence and McCann two years for terrorist activities.

The IRA members had been followed around Gibraltar by the Security Service (MI5), but SAS soldiers dressed in civilian clothes later took over the surveillance, supposedly with the intention of arresting them. The SAS claimed that they were spotted and, fearing that a bomb was about to be detonated, shot all three IRA members dead.

Spokesmen for the Ministry of Defence at first suggest that a bomb had been found in a car belonging to the three and that this could have been detonated by remote control. A statement in the House of Commons the following day by the Foreign Secretary, Geoffrey Howe, rejects the view that the bomb had been planted. Howe outlined the government's view of the events by saying that another IRA member had recently crossed into Gibraltar to carry out reconnaissance for a plan to plant a bomb at a guard-mounting ceremony that involved fifty soldiers. The Gibraltar police were alerted and the police commissioner then asked for military assistance. Just before 1 p.m. on 6 March one of the three IRA members brought a car from Spain into Gibraltar and parked it in the area where the army band assembled. An hour and a half later the other two IRA members entered Gibraltar on foot and joined the third member just before 3 p.m. By now the security forces believed the car bomb had been set. 'About 3:30 p.m. all three left the scene and started to walk back towards the border. They were challenged by the security forces. When challenged, they made movements which made the military personnel operating in support of the Gibraltar police to conclude that their own lives and the lives of others were under threat. In the light of this response, they were shot. Those killed were later found not to have been carrying arms.' No explosives were found in the car, but keys found on one of the bodies led to another car, which contained three false passports and electrical equipment used for making bombs (*Hansard,* sixth series, vol. 129, col. 21–2). On 8 March a third car belonging to the IRA members, containing 140 lb of plastic explosive, was found in Marbella.

Controversy surrounds the circumstances in which the three were killed. Several witnesses who saw Savage and Farrell being shot claim that they were given no warning before being killed, and at the inquest in September it is revealed that at least twenty-seven shots had been fired and that one of the IRA members had been shot sixteen times. The affair is complicated further in March the following year when Spanish police say that British intelligence were aware that the three IRA members were not carrying weapons when they were shot.

11 March Andy Tyrie resigns as chairman of the UDA after narrowly losing a vote of confidence in its Inner Council. Four days earlier a bomb, believed to have been planted by loyalists, was found under his car.

16 March Three mourners are killed at Milltown Cemetery in Belfast at the funeral of the three IRA members killed in Gibraltar. A loyalist, Michael Stone, throws grenades and shoots indiscriminately at mourners, killing three and injuring more than fifty others. The RUC had stayed away from the funeral in an attempt to keep tension to a minimum. As the bodies are being lowered into the graves, Stone begins shooting and throwing grenades at mourners. Holding the crowd back with an automatic pistol, he throws more grenades before running towards the nearby motorway. He is caught and beaten by the crowd before the RUC arrive and intervene to save his life. Gerry Adams claims that the incident had occurred as a result of collusion between the security forces and loyalists. The UDA and the UFF both deny any involvement, claiming that Stone is a maverick acting on his own.

19 March During the funeral procession of IRA man Kevin Brady, one of three people killed by Michael Stone at Milltown three days earlier, army corporals Derek Wood and David Howes (who had arrived in NI the previous week) of the Signals Regiment are beaten by a mob then driven away to be killed by the IRA. The two corporals drove toward the IRA cortege at high speed then tried to reverse their car but had their exit blocked by a black taxi. The windows of the car were smashed and they were dragged out. One of the soldiers fired a warning shot before they were overpowered, beaten and stripped and then dragged to waste ground where they were shot.

The presence of Wood and Howes in the area, dressed in civilian clothes, is never satisfactorily explained. It is later suggested that the mob thought they were being attacked by loyalist gunmen, though Gerry Adams later claims that the corporals were part of an SAS operation. Father Alec Reid, who administered the last rites to the two men after the murders, says, 'Our parish is seen as dripping in the blood of the murders.' As a result of the incident the RUC decides to change its policy of maintaining a low profile during terrorist funerals.

22 March Relations between the government and television companies again come under strain when the companies refuse to hand over untransmitted film showing the attack on Wood and Howes. After taking legal advice, they later hand over the film to the RUC.

31 March Amnesty International decides to investigate the deaths of the three IRA members in Gibraltar.

15 April For the first time the RUC code of conduct is published.

28 April The Foreign Secretary, Sir Geoffrey Howe, fails in an attempt to ban a Thames Television documentary on the circumstances surrounding the Gibraltar killings. The government describes the programme as 'trial by television' and accuses it of containing 'damaging inaccuracies.'

1 May Three off-duty British servicemen are killed by the IRA in the Netherlands. An aircraftman is killed and two colleagues injured when their car is machine-gunned in Roermond; a car bomb kills two other servicemen and injures a third at Nieuw-Bergen.

4 May Margaret Thatcher makes an unsuccessful attempt to prevent the showing of a BBC Northern Ireland documentary on the Gibraltar inquests; the programme is shown the following evening.

15 May Three Catholics are killed and nine others injured in a UVF machine-gun attack on the Avenue Bar in central Belfast.

25 May The government produces a new White Paper on fair employment in an attempt to strengthen the existing (1976) legislation. Proposals include the compulsory monitoring of the religious make-up of companies' employees and the creation of a new Fair Employment Commission, to replace the Fair Employment Agency.

1 June Lieutenant-General John Waters replaces Sir Robert Pascoe as army commander in Northern Ireland.

10 June In Bangor a 'model Conservative association' is launched as part of a campaign to get the main British political parties to organise in Northern Ireland.

13 June A Dublin judge refuses to extradite an IRA suspect, Patrick McVeigh, to Northern Ireland on the grounds that it has not been proved that the man named in the warrant is the same man who is in court. The decision has no legal precedent.

15 June Six soldiers are killed in Lisburn by an IRA bomb after taking part in a 'fun run'. A bomb explodes under their unmarked van when they stop at traffic lights on the way back to their barracks. It is believed that the IRA attached the bomb under the van while the soldiers took part in the run.

23 June An army helicopter is forced to land after it is hit by gunfire from the IRA near Crossmaglen.

1 July In the House of Commons the Labour Party spokesman on Northern Ireland, Kevin McNamara, says: 'Inequality of opportunity in employment because of religion is the last of the great issues still unresolved from the civil rights marches of 1969 and before. Housing remains imperfect, but the greatest disparities have disappeared. Political gerrymandering has been brought under control and great progress has been made there' (*Hansard,* sixth series, vol. 136, col. 640).

4 July The Chief Constable, John Hermon, says that more than twenty members of the RUC, including two superintendents, will face disciplinary proceedings following the investigations into the alleged 'shoot to kill' policy in 1982. The Northern Ireland Police Authority had earlier voted not to pursue disciplinary action against Hermon and two other senior RUC officers by a majority of one.

5 July Patrick Ryan, an Irish priest, is arrested in Brussels for alleged involvement with the IRA.

21 July Following earlier announcements that Harland and Wolff and Northern Ireland Electricity are to be privatised, the government states that Northern Ireland's largest industrial employer, the aircraft manufacturers Short Brothers, is also to be sold off.

23 July A 1,000 lb IRA bomb kills a married couple and their six-year-old son as they drive along a border road. The bomb was intended to kill a judge, Justice Ian Higgins. The IRA admits its mistake and offers its 'deepest sympathy' to the victims. IRA 'mistakes' have been responsible for seventeen deaths since the Enniskillen bombing.

27 July Ian Stewart replaces John Stanley as Minister of State at the NIO.

1 August One soldier is killed and nine injured in an IRA bomb attack on Inglis Barracks in north London. It is the first IRA bomb to explode in Britain since the Brighton bombing four years earlier.

4 August In Belleek, Co. Fermanagh, the IRA murders two Protestant building workers who had worked on repairs at the RUC station.

8 August In the run-up to the anniversary of internment, three people are killed in sectarian conflicts in Belfast, two of them Catholics murdered by the 'Protestant Action Force'.

Sir Brian Hutton succeeds Lord Lowry as Lord Chief Justice for Northern Ireland.

20 August Eight soldiers are killed and twenty-eight injured when their bus is blown up by a 200 lb IRA land mine hidden in a drainage culvert outside Ballygawley, Co. Tyrone. The soldiers were returning to barracks in Omagh, having been home on leave.

23 August Gerard Harte is the first person to be extradited under the Republic's new arrangements for extradition. On 27 August one of the Maze Prison escapers, Robert Russell, is also extradited from the Republic and handed over to the RUC.

30 August Three IRA men are shot dead by the SAS outside Drumnakilly, Co. Tyrone.

31 August Another IRA 'mistake' leads to the deaths of two pensioners in Derry. Seán Dalton and Sheila Lewis went to a neighbour's flat because they had not seen him for several days. Dalton climbed through a window and set off a booby-trap bomb. The missing man is believed to be held by the IRA, and the intention was to kill RUC personnel who came to investigate.

3 September In a reversal of the low-key policy pursued earlier in the year, 500 RUC men and a hundred soldiers guard an IRA funeral.

6 September The RUC discovers a loyalist gun factory near Ballynahinch, Co. Down. In March a former UDR member is jailed for fourteen years for running the gun factory.

30 September At the end of a nineteen-day inquest into the deaths of the three IRA members shot in Gibraltar, the jury decides, by nine to two, that the SAS soldiers who shot them had acted lawfully, supporting the view put forward by the government that the soldiers believed the IRA members were armed and had already planted a bomb, even though this proved to be incorrect. During the inquest the SAS soldiers involved, who gave evidence behind screens in order to protect their identity, said they believed that a bomb was about to be exploded by remote control. The question whether or not the three had been warned before being shot remained unresolved, as there was conflicting evidence.

5 October Brian Mawhinney, the minister responsible for education in Northern Ireland, says that his department has a duty to promote integrated schools. On 11 October the director of the Council for Maintained (Catholic) Schools, Monsignor Colm McCaughan, says that Catholic parents who send their children to integrated schools are breaking canon law.

10 October At Winchester, three people suspected of being an IRA murder squad are charged with plotting to murder the Secretary of State, Tom King, at his home.

11 October Ian Paisley interrupts a speech by the Pope in the European Parliament. Holding up a message saying JOHN PAUL II ANTICHRIST, he shouts: 'I renounce you as the Antichrist' several times, before being removed from the chamber.

14 October Representatives of the UUP, DUP, SDLP and Alliance meet for two days in Duisburg, Germany, to find a formula for inter-party talks. Differences over the Anglo-Irish Agreement mean that they make no real progress.

15 October A leading UDA man, Jim Craig, and a bystander are killed and four other people injured when the UFF attack a bar in east Belfast. The killing is part of a feud within the UDA involving the misuse of funds.

19 October In the House of Commons the Home Secretary, Douglas Hurd, announces a ban on the broadcasting of direct statements by representatives of Sinn Féin, Republican Sinn Féin, and the UDA. He says: 'For some time, broadcast coverage of events in Northern Ireland has included the occasional appearance of representatives of paramilitary organisations and their political wings, who have used these opportunities as an attempt to justify their criminal activities. Such appearances have caused widespread offence to viewers and listeners throughout the United Kingdom, particularly just after a terrorist outrage. The terrorists themselves draw support and sustenance from access to radio and television—from addressing their views more directly to the population at large than is possible through the press. The government have decided that the time has come to deny this easy platform to those who use it to propagate terrorism. Accordingly, I have today issued to the chairmen of the BBC and the IBA a notice ... requiring them to refrain from broadcasting direct statements by representatives of organisations proscribed in Northern Ireland and Great Britain and by representatives of Sinn Féin, Republican Sinn Féin and the Ulster Defence Association' (*Hansard,* sixth series, vol. 138, col. 893). The order also forbids the broadcasting of statements by anyone inviting support for the organisations named, but it excludes statements made in Parliament. It would also be lifted in periods leading up to an election. Hurd notes that the ban follows similar provisions that already operate in the Republic, and says: 'This is not a restriction on reporting. It is a restriction on direct appearances by those who use or support violence.'

Television news and documentary producers manage to circumvent the ban to some extent by showing film of the banned person and reporting what they said, or by using an actor to dub their words. The ban also leads to a speech by Éamon de Valera being removed from a school history programme.

Nevertheless, the ban has some impact. Sinn Féin's director of publicity, Danny Morrison, later claims that in the four months before the ban they had 471 inquiries but only 110 in the four months immediately following it (Elliott and Smith, *Northern Ireland: The District Council Elections of 1989,* p. 8).

20 October One day after the placing of broadcasting restrictions on television and radio, Tom King announces that he has laid a draft order in council before Parliament that will permit courts 'to allow whatever weight they think proper to the fact that someone remained silent when questioned—for example, where circumstances were such that an innocent person might reasonably have been expected to protest his innocence and draw attention to facts which served to establish it' (*Hansard,* sixth series, vol. 138, col. 994). This curtailment of the right to silence brings bitter condemnation from civil liberties groups and opposition MPs, on the grounds that it undermines part of the foundations of the legal system, the fact that a person is presumed innocent until proved guilty.

27 October After nearly fifteen hours of deliberation a jury in Winchester, by a majority verdict, finds Finbarr Cullen, John McCann and Martina Shanahan guilty of conspiracy to murder Tom King. The three people had been spotted in August by the Secretary of State's daughter sitting on the wall of his house. When the suspects were arrested the police found the registration number of King's car and what were believed to be the names and car registration numbers of several other potential IRA targets.

15 November There are only minor protests by unionists on the third anniversary of the Anglo-Irish Agreement.

22 November Margaret Thatcher announces that remission for prisoners in Northern Ireland jails is to be reduced from half to a third of their sentence, as in Britain, reversing a change made by Merlyn Rees in 1976.

25 November The Belgian government turns down a request from Britain for the extradition of Patrick Ryan to face charges of conspiracy to murder and cause explosions, saying that the extradition application is 'vague and flawed,' a fact later admitted by the Crown Prosecution Service. Ryan is instead deported to the Republic. The incident again mars Anglo-Irish relations, with Margaret Thatcher saying: 'It is no use governments adopting great declarations and commitments about fighting terrorism if they then lack the resolve to put them into practice.' The extradition row continues on 3 December at an EEC summit meeting in Rhodes when Thatcher lambastes the Belgian Prime Minister for his country's failure to extradite Ryan and then proceeds to attack Charles Haughey over the same issue. The

Taoiseach in return feels slighted by what he sees as Thatcher's attempt to dictate to another sovereign state.

29 November The European Court of Human Rights rules that Britain has breached the European Convention of Human Rights by detaining suspects for more than four days without charging them. On 22 December the government announces its decision to derogate from the convention and to retain a seven-day detention period.

13 December The Irish Attorney-General, John Murray, rejects Britain's request for the extradition of Patrick Ryan, on the grounds that he would not receive a fair trial. Margaret Thatcher describes the decision as a 'great insult' to the British people.

15 December The government introduces a new Fair Employment Bill for Northern Ireland in an attempt to resolve arguably the last major 'civil rights' issue from the 1960s. The bill makes compulsory the monitoring of the 'perceived religion' of the work force for companies with twenty-five or more (later eleven or more) employees. It also gives greater leeway to schemes for countering imbalances in the work force and replaces the FEA with a new and stronger Fair Employment Commission. The bill also insists that appointments be made only on merit.

The primary reason for the new bill is based on government figures that show that male Catholic unemployment is still more than double male Protestant unemployment (Catholic female unemployment is only slightly higher than Protestant female unemployment) and that Catholics are over-represented in semi-skilled and unskilled jobs and under-represented in skilled posts, despite twelve years of the existing (1976) fair employment legislation. The campaign in the United States organised by those supporting the MacBride principles and the lobbying of the Irish government through the Intergovernmental Conference are also factors in pressuring the British into introducing new legislation.

The reasons for the religious differences in employment and unemployment and the perceived failure of the FEA become a source of heated argument. While critics claim that the FEA has continually bowed to pressure from the government not to undertake certain investigations or to water down its conclusions, unionists and others claim that religious discrimination in itself is not an important factor in explaining the different economic positions of the two communities and that the FEA has had to exaggerate the extent of discrimination to justify its own existence. An integrationist pressure group, the Institute for Representative Government, in *Fair Employment or Social Engineering,* calculates that if Catholics were to take up jobs in security occupations to the extent that their numbers warranted, male Catholic unemployment would fall by 7 per cent and male Protestant unemployment rise by 4 per cent, narrowing the gap by half.

The deterioration of the economy also made it difficult for the FEA to operate effectively. The average rate of unemployment rose from 5.7 per cent in 1975 to 18.3 per cent in 1986; the number of unemployed men alone rose from 26,700 (6.5 per cent) to 91,400 (22.0 per cent). In 1986, with an annual average of 125,300 unemployed, the number of vacancies notified to the employment services that were unfilled at the end of the year was just under 2,300.

20 December Three RUC men are ordered by the Northern Ireland Appeal Court to give evidence to a fresh inquest into the deaths of the three men killed by the RUC in 1982 that led to the Stalker-Sampson inquiry into an alleged 'shoot to kill' policy by the police.

21 December A bomb-making factory is accidentally found in London. Scotland Yard later admits to finding a list at the scene with the names of more than a hundred prominent people on it.

DEATHS ARISING FROM THE TROUBLES: 94. SHOOTINGS: 538. BOMBS PLANTED: 458 (explosions: 253). INCENDIARIES: 8. FIREARMS FOUND: 489. EXPLOSIVES FOUND: 4,728 kg (10,420 lb). PERSONS CHARGED WITH TERRORIST AND SERIOUS PUBLIC ORDER OFFENCES: 440. CASUALTIES ARISING FROM PARAMILITARY ATTACKS: 122.

1989

23 January The Provisional IRA says it has 'stood down and disarmed' its west Fermanagh unit after it killed a man it claimed was working under cover for the RUC on 15 January. The statement said it had been unhappy with the unit for some time.

26 January The report of an independent inquiry into the Thames Television documentary that investigated the shooting by the SAS of three IRA members in Gibraltar in March 1988 largely vindicates the programme-makers. Margaret Thatcher rejects the report and says that the original criticisms of the programme still stand.

12 February Patrick Finucane, a solicitor, is shot dead by loyalists at his home in north Belfast. The murder follows a comment by the Home Office minister Douglas Hogg on 17 January criticising 'a number of solicitors in Northern Ireland who are unduly sympathetic to the cause of the IRA.'

14 February A Sinn Féin councillor, John Davey, is shot dead by loyalists near his home in Co. Londonderry.

20 February Three IRA bombs destroy army barracks being used by the Parachute Regiment at Tern Hill in Shropshire.

22 February An FEA press statement reveals that in 1988, while the proportion of the agency's junior staff was roughly in line with the religious make-up of the catchment area, only 35 per cent of its senior staff were Protestants, an under-representation by some 30 per cent. The FEA explains these figures by stating that 'all anti-discrimination bodies are more attractive as places of employment for members of the group whose under-representation has led to the establishment of the bodies.' In November 1992 Protestants are still under-represented in the FEA's replacement, the FEC, accounting for 51 per cent of its staff (*News Letter,* 26 November 1992).

3 March Michael Stone is jailed for thirty years for the murders committed at Milltown Cemetery in March 1988.

7 March Three Protestant men are shot dead by the IRA in Coagh, Co. Tyrone. The IRA claims they were members of the UVF, but this is denied by their families and the RUC. The following day two soldiers are killed and six injured in an IRA land mine explosion in Co. Londonderry.

14 March Eighteen RUC members connected with the 1982 Armagh shootings that sparked claims of a 'shoot to kill' policy are reprimanded.

15 March The Elected Authorities (Northern Ireland) Act becomes law. The act requires a signed declaration from candidates standing for district councils that they will not express support for proscribed organisations or acts of terrorism. It also disqualifies for five years anyone who has served a jail sentence of three months or more.

21 March The IRA ambush and kill Chief Superintendent Harry Breen and Superintendent Ken Buchanan as they cross the border in Co. Armagh after a meeting with members of the Gardaí. They are believed to have been followed by the IRA, even though they wore plain clothes and were in an unmarked car. Breen, who was the RUC divisional commander in south Armagh, is the most senior policeman to be killed in the Troubles.

21 April Three loyalists are arrested in a Paris hotel as they give what are believed to be parts of an anti-aircraft missile made by Shorts factory in Belfast to a South African embassy official. An arms dealer is also present. It later emerges that the parts belong to a display model stolen from Shorts earlier in the year. The Foreign Office later summons the South African ambassador to give an explanation of the affair. In October 1991 the three loyalists are given suspended sentences and fined.

27 April It is announced that the Chairman of the FEA, Bob Cooper, is to head the new Fair Employment Commission.

5 May Britain gives three South African diplomats a week to leave the country after it is discovered that South Africa has been willing to exchange British defence secrets for arms with loyalists. It is suggested that the South Africans have already sent arms to loyalists in 1987 in the hope of acquiring defence technology from Shorts.

17 May In district council elections the UUP takes 31.3 per cent of valid first-preference votes (up 1.8 per cent on 1985) and win 194 seats. By contrast, the DUP vote falls to 18 per cent (from 24.3 per cent) and 110 seats. Other loyalists and unionists take 4.8 per cent of the poll (up from 3.1 per cent in 1985) and twenty-five seats. The SDLP strengthens its position among nationalist voters, taking 21.0 per cent of first-preference votes (17.8 per cent in 1985) and 121 seats, a gain of twenty. Sinn Féin takes 11.2 per cent (11.8 per cent in 1985) and forty-three seats (down sixteen). In the political 'centre' the Alliance vote declines slightly to 6.9 per cent, though it gains four seats (up to thirty-eight) as a result of transfers on lower preferences from other parties. The Workers' Party increases its share to 2.1 per cent (from 1.6 per cent) and keeps its four seats.

One of the most significant developments is the emergence of the Conservatives in North Down, where they head the poll with 24.9 per cent of the vote (in the lowest turn-out for any district council election, 40.5 per cent) and become the largest group on the council, with six seats; a Conservative is also returned in Lisburn. In general, however, the Conservative vote represents less than 1 per cent of the total vote. Newtown Abbey returns the only Labour councillor. The turn-out is a modest 56.1 per cent, the lowest since district councils were formed in 1973.

31 May Sir John Hermon retires as Chief Constable of the RUC and is succeeded by Dublin-born Hugh Annesley of the London Metropolitan Police.

1 June Two men from Andersonstown in west Belfast are sentenced to life imprisonment for the murder of Corporal Derek Wood and Corporal David Howes in March 1988 in the first in a number of trials connected with the killings.

7 June Tom King announces that Northern Ireland's largest industrial employer, Shorts, is to be sold to the Canadian company Bombardier.

15 June The Northern Ireland election for the European Parliament is held; the turn-out is a mere 48.3 per cent. Ian Paisley, with 160,110 votes, again tops the poll, and though this is 70,000 less than in 1984 his share of the vote declines only to 29.9 per cent (from 33.6 per cent). John Hume's support holds up better and he receives 136,335 votes, down 15,000 but an increase in the share of the vote to 25.5 per cent (from 22.1 per cent). The

UUP candidate, Jim Nicholson (replacing John Taylor), receives 118,785 votes (22.2 per cent), down 30,000 from 1984 but slightly increasing the party's share of the vote. For Sinn Féin, Danny Morrison receives 48,914 votes (9.2 per cent, down from 13.3 per cent in 1984), a drop of over 40,000. John Alderdice of Alliance receives 27,905 votes (5.2 per cent), 6,000 less than David Cook in 1984 but a slight increase in the share of the poll. Laurence Kennedy, standing as a Conservative, takes 25,789 votes, 4.8 per cent of first-preference votes. An Ecology Party candidate receives 6,568 votes, just ahead of Séamus Lynch of the Workers' Party (5,590 votes) and two Labour candidates, who receive a combined vote of less than 1 per cent. Paisley is elected on the first count, Hume on the second, and Nicholson on the third.

In the Republic a general election leaves Fianna Fáil, with seventy-eight seats, as the largest party but without an overall majority. The eventual outcome is a coalition government of Fianna Fáil and the Progressive Democrats led by Charles Haughey, with Des O'Malley as Minister for Industry and Commerce.

2 July A British soldier is killed in Hannover, Germany, and his wife and children injured when an IRA bomb explodes in their car.

17 July A businessman from Warrenpoint, John McAnulty, is kidnapped and murdered by the IRA.

24 July In a government reshuffle Tom King, Ian Stewart, Lord Lyell and Peter Viggers leave the NIO. Peter Brooke becomes Secretary of State and John Cope Minister of State, with Lord Skelmersdale and Peter Bottomley Under-Secretaries.

31 July A 1,000 lb IRA bomb packed into a laundry van explodes at the High Court in Belfast, causing extensive damage.

9 August As tension increases in the run-up to the twentieth anniversary of the arrival of troops on the streets of Northern Ireland, fifteen-year-old Séamus Duffy dies from injuries caused by a plastic bullet during rioting in Belfast. On 15 August the publicity director of Noraid, Martin Galvin, is arrested in Derry for breaking an exclusion order. Though there is rioting and several bombs explode, the RUC manages to contain the threat of widespread violence.

30 August The UFF hands leaked official documents to a BBC reporter and claims that the army, UDR and RUC all leak information to it, because no official action is taken against republican suspects. In the wake of allegations that a recent UFF murder victim, Loughlin Maginn, had been killed as a result of such information, nationalists call for a full investigation. The Irish government calls for the matter to be the first issue for discussion at the next meeting of the Anglo-Irish Conference. On 14 September the Deputy Chief Constable of Cambridgeshire, John Stevens, is appointed by Hugh Annesley to investigate the theft and leaking of intelligence documents.

7 September The IRA murders the German wife of a British soldier in Dortmund.

22 September An IRA bomb planted in the barracks of the Royal Marines School of Music in Deal, Kent, kills ten bandsmen and injures twenty-two. Security for the barracks was provided by a private firm and was criticised for being too lax.

8 October Twenty-eight members of the UDR are arrested in connection with the Stevens inquiry into the leaking of official documents to loyalist paramilitaries.

17 October It is announced that corruption proceedings will be taken against the police involved in the conviction of the 'Guildford Four'.

19 October After fourteen years in jail, three of the Guildford Four—Gerard Conlon, Carole Richardson, and Patrick Armstrong—are released. Paul Hill is still in custody because he is implicated in another case that has not been resolved; his conviction is quashed in April 1994. The Court of Appeal decides that the 1975 convictions were based on confessions fabricated by the police. It is claimed that the Director of Public Prosecutions at the time also suppressed scientific evidence that conflicted with the 'confessions'. The collapse of the case against the Guildford Four also cast doubts on the convictions of the Maguire family, whom Conlon had reputedly named as the bomb-makers for those wrongly convicted of the Guildford bombings. On the same day Sir John May is appointed to inquire into the circumstances leading to, and deriving from, the trial of the Maguire family and their co-defendants as well as that of the Guildford Four.

28 October An RAF corporal and his six-month-old daughter are shot dead by the IRA at a petrol station in Wildenrath, Germany.

3 November Peter Brooke arouses controversy by suggesting that the government might talk to Sinn Féin, provided the IRA first renounces the use of violence. In the interview, given to mark his first hundred days as Secretary of State, Brooke says that military means could contain but not defeat the IRA and that the government would be 'flexible and imaginative' if the IRA renounced violence. His comments bring criticism from Unionists, the Labour Party, and some Conservatives, who say that his statements encourage terrorism.

18 November Three paratroopers are killed by an IRA land mine at Mayobridge, Co. Down. A British army staff sergeant and his wife are injured by an IRA car bomb in Colchester, Essex.

27 November Two IRA bombs destroy a light aircraft at Shorts factory in east Belfast.

29 November Two men, one of whom had been convicted of running guns for the IRA in New York in 1985, are shot dead by the UVF in Ardboe, Co. Tyrone.

13 December Two soldiers die in an IRA attack on a border post at Rosslea, Co. Fermanagh.

21 December Two men are arrested on anti-terrorist charges after they go to check an arms cache in Dyfed, Wales. It had been found seven weeks earlier but had been left intact in an attempt to catch those who put it there. The haul includes firearms, detonators, and 100 lb of plastic explosive.

DEATHS ARISING FROM THE TROUBLES: 62. SHOOTINGS: 566. BOMBS PLANTED: 420. INCENDIARIES: 7. FIREARMS FOUND: 246. EXPLOSIVES FOUND: 1,377 kg (3,035 lb). PERSONS CHARGED WITH TERRORIST AND SERIOUS PUBLIC ORDER OFFENCES: 433. CASUALTIES ARISING FROM PARAMILITARY ATTACKS: 212.

1990

2 January A taxi driver who is a member of the Ulster Democratic Party is killed by an IRA booby-trap bomb.

The Fair Employment Commission replaces the Fair Employment Agency.

4 January The government launches the Community Relations Council, to promote contact between Protestants and Catholics and the acceptance of cultural differences.

7 January A Catholic taxi driver is murdered by the 'Protestant Action Force', believed to be a cover name for the UVF. Attacks on taxi drivers continue throughout the year.

The Sinn Féin director of publicity, Danny Morrison, is arrested with eight other men after the RUC raid a house in west Belfast where a man is being held captive.

9 January In a speech to businessmen in Bangor, Peter Brooke launches a bid for inter-party talks and devolution. He claims he has found enough common ground to make talks worth while and he appeals to Unionists to end their 'internal exile'. He offers to operate the Anglo-Irish Agreement sensitively but does not suggest the suspension or 'natural break' in Anglo-Irish Conferences that would enable Unionists to participate in talks.

Ards Borough Council becomes the first Unionist-controlled council to end the boycott of NIO ministers.

13 January Three men robbing a betting shop in west Belfast are shot dead by an army undercover unit. The robbers were wearing masks and two carried replica guns, while the third waited in a car. In September the *Independent* reports that the driver had been shot in the head from a distance of less than two feet; the other men had been shot ten and thirteen times. The incident provokes renewed claims that the army is following a 'shoot to kill' policy, as eyewitnesses claim that the plain-clothes soldiers fired at two of the men while they were on the ground.

16 January The Unionist MP John Taylor calls for an end to the boycott on talks with NIO ministers.

20 January Brian Nelson, arrested at the request of the Stevens inquiry team, appears in court accused of possessing details on republicans that would be of use to terrorists. On 26 January he is isolated from other prisoners, and on 28 January the *Sunday Tribune* leaks the news that Nelson has worked for army intelligence.

22 January An RUC inspector, Derek Monteith, is shot dead by the IRA in the kitchen of his home near Armagh.

9 February At Belfast Magistrates' Court a UDA leader, Tommy Lyttle (arrested in January at the request of the Stevens inquiry team), is accused of having ordered that a threatening letter and bag of bullets be sent to the sister of Brian Nelson. UDA resentment at the pressure being exerted by the Stevens inquiry is shown the following night when shots are fired at an RUC patrol on the Shankill Road.

12 February Harold McCusker, MP for Upper Bann and deputy leader of the UUP, dies from cancer at the age of fifty.

18 February On BBC radio Peter Brooke says that while he will not rule out a gap in Anglo-Irish Conference meetings to enable talks to take place, there could be no full-scale suspension.

19 February A BBC television programme on the UDR says that nearly two hundred members or ex-members have been convicted of serious offences. The Irish Minister for Foreign Affairs later says that the UDR 'now has no role to play' in Northern Ireland. On 21 February the Labour Party's spokesman on Northern Ireland, Kevin McNamara, says there is a 'crisis of confidence' in the regiment; on 1 March, however, the General Board of the Presbyterian Church says that disbanding the UDR would be 'totally irresponsible'.

24 February The Unionist Party ends the boycott of NIO ministers by district councils and allows discussions with ministers on issues of 'specific importance to any council area or relevant board.'

26 February The first meeting of the British-Irish Interparliamentary Body in London is boycotted by unionists.

27 February What purport to be the January 1988 proposals of the unionist leaders to Tom King are published in the *Irish Times.* They include a consular office for the Republic in Northern Ireland, an interparliamentary body, contacts between British and Irish ministers, and ad hoc meetings between Northern and Southern representatives. A devolved assembly would use committees with membership proportionate to party strength. There would also be safeguards for minorities. The UUP leader, James Molyneaux, says the report is not completely authentic, and in any event the proposals would only be open to discussion when the workings of the Anglo-Irish Agreement had been suspended.

1 March The Supreme Court in Dublin rejects the appeal by Chris and Michael McGimpsey against the High Court decision in July 1988 that article 1 of the Anglo-Irish Agreement contradicts articles 2 and 3 of the Constitution of Ireland. Instead the court rules that articles 2 and 3 are a 'claim of legal right' over the 'national territory'; they are not merely 'aspirational' but rather a 'constitutional imperative'. Consequently article 1 of the Anglo-Irish Agreement does not recognise the position of Northern Ireland within the United Kingdom, as had been claimed by the former Secretary of State for Northern Ireland, Tom King.

A statement by the NIO minister Richard Needham at a private meeting in the House of Commons that under the Helsinki Final Accord the border has been made permanent is made public in the *Belfast Telegraph.*

13 March The Supreme Court in Dublin refuses to extradite two men who had escaped from the Maze Prison during the mass break-out in 1983. The court says there would be a risk to the lives of Dermot Finucane and James Pius Clarke if they were returned to a prison in the North, a claim strongly denied by Britain. Margaret Thatcher describes the decision as 'grossly offensive' and says the decision encourages terrorists to think of the Republic as a safe haven. The following day Peter Brooke says the decision is 'an unacceptable slur' on the reputation of the prison service. The *Irish Press,* however, says the reaction is 'highly predictable'. The combined effect of the Supreme Court and extradition decisions is a deterioration in relations between London and Dublin.

14 March In an attempt to reassure unionists in the wake of the Supreme Court decision, the NIO minister Brian Mawhinney tells the House of Commons: 'The people of Northern Ireland and the United Kingdom have lived with this territorial claim for over fifty years. The United Kingdom government have never accepted it, do not accept it and have said so, as I do again tonight. We regard it as having no validity in international law. It has never had any practical effect on Northern Ireland's position as part of the United Kingdom' (*Hansard,* sixth series, vol. 169, col. 648). Two weeks later (27 March 1990) Sir Geoffrey Howe, leader of the house, repeats this assurance by stating that 'the status of Northern Ireland in international law is clear: it is part of the United Kingdom' (*Hansard,* sixth series, vol. 170, col. 286).

Seven prison officers and several prisoners are injured in fighting at Crumlin Road Prison, where republican and loyalist prisoners are not segregated. The trouble in the prison continues throughout the year.

18 March In the wake of the extradition and McGimpsey decisions there are calls for change in the Republic. The *Sunday Tribune* says that 'any hesitation on the extradition front represents a scandal' and calls for articles 2 and 3 of the Constitution to be amended. On 21 March a motion in the Seanad introduced by independent members calling for articles 2 and 3 to be changed is easily defeated.

20 March Five people are injured when two bombs planted by the IRA explode at Shorts factory in Castlereagh.

24 March The Labour MP Chris Mullin claims that the real perpetrators of the 1974 Birmingham pub bombings had all been questioned by West Midlands Police within a year of the event but had been released. He says that two of the men who carried out the bombings are at present in prison for other offences, two live in Ireland and one in England.

25 March A 1,000 lb IRA bomb severely damages an RUC station in Ballymena.

6 April The Supreme Court in Dublin refuses to hand over the former Fermanagh-South Tyrone MP Owen Carron, wanted for a firearms offence in the North, on the grounds that the offence is linked with the 'political' offences of another suspect. A passenger in Carron's car was found to be carrying weapons when it was stopped by the RUC in Fermanagh in 1985. Both were charged with possession of firearms, and the passenger was later convicted. Carron, however, absconded before his trial. Following in the wake of the Finucane and Clarke decisions, this development further worsens relations between London and Dublin. The Irish Minister for Foreign Affairs, Gerry Collins, says he is 'greatly disturbed' by the decision but that the government has to respect and accept the verdict and that any strain it created could be dealt with through the Intergovernmental Conference.

9 April Four UDR soldiers are killed when a 1,000 lb IRA bomb explodes under their vehicle outside Downpatrick. Linking the killings to the extradition decisions in Dublin, Margaret Thatcher says: 'We need all the help we can get to fight people who attempt these murders and those who succeed.'

11 April Despite the strain in Anglo-Irish relations, Charles Haughey makes the first official visit by a Taoiseach since Seán Lemass in 1965 by attending a conference of the Institute of Directors in Belfast. Four hundred loyalists protest against Haughey's presence at the conference, which is opened by the UUP Lord Mayor, Reg Empey.

16 April Republican prisoners break up furniture at Crumlin Road Prison in protest at the absence of segregation. On 18 April the UFF threatens 'the strongest possible action' against warders as tension in the prison continues.

27 April The Court of Appeal overturns the convictions of those found guilty of plotting to kill the former Secretary of State Tom King in 1988. During the trial King had commented that the government was planning to allow juries to infer that defendants who remain silent may be guilty; the court rules that, as the three had refused to give evidence during their trial, the jury may have been influenced by King's remarks and that their conviction is therefore unsafe. The three are later rearrested and deported from Britain.

4 May Brooke concedes that political talks will consider an alternative to the Anglo-Irish Agreement.

8 May Cardinal Tomás Ó Fiaich (66) dies from a heart attack during a visit to Lourdes in France.

13 May There is further trouble over segregation at Crumlin Road Prison when loyalist prisoners climb onto the roof. The following day eight prison officers are injured in fights with loyalists.

15 May There is controversy at the funeral of Cardinal Ó Fiaich when Gerry Adams and Martin McGuinness attend the Mass. The Secretary of State, Peter Brooke, the Chief Constable of the RUC, Hugh Annesley, the Taoiseach, Charles Haughey, and the Irish President, Dr Patrick Hillery, are present at the same time.

16 May An army sergeant is killed and another soldier injured by an IRA bomb at a recruiting office in London.

17 May A summary of the Stevens Report says that there has been collusion between security forces and loyalist paramilitaries. Stevens (Chief Constable of Cambridgeshire) says that after an eight-month inquiry he has found that the leaking of information was 'restricted to a small number of members of the security forces and is neither widespread nor institutionalised'; any collusion could be minimised by the tighter control of documents. The report is critical of the fact that some members of the UDR have been recruited despite adverse vetting reports by the RUC.

During the course of the inquiry fifty-eight people were charged or had their files sent to the Department of Public Prosecutions; thirty-four of these cases involved the collection of information, ten were firearms offences, three involved intimidation, and one the possession of an RUC uniform. The accused include ten UDR members, twenty-six UDA men, and six members of the UVF.

18 May David Trimble (UUP) wins the Upper Bann by-election with a majority of almost fourteen thousand votes. The Conservatives field a candidate for the first time, Colette Jones, but despite a message of support from John Major and visits by several ministers, including the chairman of the Conservative Party, Kenneth Baker, she receives just over a thousand votes, finishing sixth, and loses her deposit.

22 May After a lengthy meeting with Brooke in London, Unionist leaders say they are 'well satisfied with the results.'

24 May There is more trouble at Crumlin Road Prison on the issue of segregation; twenty-five cells are damaged by republican prisoners. On 29 May the IRA say it will take 'offensive action' against prison staff. Loyalists also react against the lack of segregation by burning a train travelling between Lisburn and Bangor, firing shots at a prison officer's home in Newtownards on 31 May, and firing on a prison officer's car in the Shankill Road area on 1 June. On 2 June prison officers' homes in Lisburn are petrol-bombed.

27 May The IRA kills two Australian lawyers on holiday in Roermond in the Netherlands, Nick Spanos and Stephen Melrose, after mistaking them for off-duty British servicemen. The murders help undermine support for the IRA in Australia and lead to a major fall in financial support from republican sympathisers there.

1 June An army recruit is killed and two others are wounded by two IRA gunmen as they wait for a train to take them on leave at Lichfield station, Staffordshire. The following day a British army major is shot dead by the IRA in Germany.

6 June A 65-year-old retired RUC reservist and his 66-year-old wife are killed by an IRA bomb planted under their car in north Belfast. Gerry Adams later says that the killing of the couple cannot be condoned but maintains that Sinn Féin's relationship with the IRA is one of 'critical support'.

13 June Terence O'Neill, the former Prime Minister of Northern Ireland, dies in Hampshire.

14 June In London the Home Office announces that the convictions of the Maguire Seven cannot be upheld, because of the irregularities in the scientific evidence. On 12 July the Maguire family case is referred to the Court of Appeal by the Home Secretary.

16 June Two alleged IRA members believed to be part of the cell responsible for attacks on British servicemen are arrested on the border between the Netherlands and Belgium; a third escapes into the Netherlands, despite being handcuffed, but is rearrested by Dutch police on 18 June, as is a fourth man the following day. A local farmer had called the police after he heard weapons being fired in a nearby wood, and two men and a woman were arrested. The men escaped by running off but one was later rearrested. The woman is named as Donna Maguire, acquitted earlier in the year by the Special Criminal Court in Dublin on a charge of carrying explosives.

23 June Asked about the IRA during a press conference in New York, Nelson Mandela, Vice-President of the African National Congress, says that 'every community is entitled to fight for its right to self-determination.' At another press conference in Dublin on 2 July Mandela says that there should be talks between the British government and the IRA. The statement is denounced by all sections of political opinion except Sinn Féin.

26 June In London an IRA bomb explodes at the Carlton Club, to which many Conservative Party members belong. The IRA says it has 'struck at the heart of Tory rule.'

30 June Two RUC men are shot dead by the IRA in the centre of Belfast.

5 July In the House of Commons, Peter Brooke says that he is unable to report agreement on a schedule for talks because of the problem concerning the timing of when the Irish government will formally enter the talks. He adds that the controversy over articles 2 and 3 of the Irish Constitution has not helped. A six-hour meeting between Brooke and Gerry Collins on 13 July and another five-hour meeting of the Anglo-Irish Conference on 17 July make no further progress. In October the *Irish Times* reveals that a speech Brooke had intended to make to the House of Commons had been stymied by opposition from the SDLP and Dublin. The draft had said that substantial progress on talks on the internal government of Northern Ireland was required before moving on to North-South dialogue. On 23 July the *Times* reveals that unionist leaders would hold discussions with the Republic only as part of the United Kingdom delegation but that the SDLP objected to the use of the term 'United Kingdom' and wanted 'Britain' and 'Ireland' instead.

20 July An IRA bomb explodes at the London Stock Exchange, causing extensive damage. Several warnings were given, and there are no casualties.

23 July Peter Bottomley leaves the NIO without being replaced by another minister.

24 July Three policemen and a nun are killed by a 1,000 lb IRA bomb near Armagh. The device is detonated as the RUC men drive past, and the nun, Sister Catherine Dunne, driving in the opposite direction, is caught in the blast.

26 July Parliament goes into recess for the summer, but Brooke promises to renew moves on the talks process in September. There is a widely held belief among unionists that the talks have been spiked by the SDLP, working through the Irish government. Consequently the Ulster Unionists appear to take a tougher line on the talks throughout the summer, placing much emphasis on the Republic's territorial claim to Northern Ireland.

30 July The Conservative MP for Eastbourne, Ian Gow, a long-time critic of the IRA, is killed outside his home by an IRA bomb planted under the front seat of his car. The murder is also seen as an indirect attack by the IRA on Margaret Thatcher by killing one of her closest friends.

The High Court in Dublin rejects the appeal against the extradition to Britain of Desmond Ellis.

6 August The IRA attaches plastic explosives to a car outside a house where the former Cabinet Secretary, Lord Armstrong, once lived. On 13 August another IRA bomb is found in the garden of General Sir Anthony Farrar-Hockley, Commander of Land Forces in Northern Ireland between 1970 and 1972.

21 August It is announced that Lieutenant-General Sir John Wilsey will replace Sir John Waters as army commander in Northern Ireland.

24 August After almost 1,600 days of being held hostage in Beirut, the Belfast-born schoolteacher Brian Keenan is released. He is handed over by the 'Islamic Dawn' group to Syrian officers in Damascus and later flown to Dublin, where he receives a rapturous reception. A proposal by the SDLP that Keenan be made a freeman of the city of Belfast leads the independent unionist councillor Frank Millar to say that Keenan should 'stay with your friend Charlie Haughey, we don't want you.' A civic reception for Keenan given by the Lord Mayor of Belfast is held on 17 September.

29 August The Home Secretary, David Waddington, announces that the case of the Birmingham Six is to be sent back to the Court of Appeal, on the grounds that fresh scientific evidence suggests that a crucial part of the evidence leading to the conviction of two of the men may have been fabricated.

5 September The IRA continues to attack those undertaking work for the army or police when it wounds two brothers in Magherafelt. The IRA has already killed a worker at Castlederg on 18 August. In response to the latest action the UFF says it will consider Catholics working in Protestant areas to be 'legitimate targets'.

A 1,000 lb IRA bomb damages the RUC station at Loughgall, Co. Armagh.

6 September The Security Minister, John Cope, claims that there is collusion between loyalists and republicans to bring about segregation at Crumlin Road Prison in Belfast.

7 September In a speech in Ballymena, Peter Brooke attempts to relaunch the talks process. He states that he might have to 'set the pace and show the way.' The media widely interpret this as an ultimatum, but in the end nothing concrete comes from the statement.

It is revealed that an Ulster Television history programme for schools could not use the voices of Éamon de Valcra or Seán MacBride because of the 1988 restrictions on broadcasting.

18 September Air Chief Marshal Sir Peter Terry is shot and wounded in an IRA attack at his home in Stafford. As Governor of Gibraltar, Terry had authorised the use of the SAS that led to the death of three IRA members in 1988.

27 September A 4 lb plastic explosive planted by the IRA is discovered at a conference on terrorism in London. The IRA later says that the target had been the Foreign Office minister William Waldegrave.

30 September Martin Peake (17) and Karen Reilly (18) are shot dead by the army after they drive a stolen car through a check-point in west Belfast. Peake had been in court on three previous occasions, and the IRA had broken his arm and ankle earlier in the year to stop him stealing cars. Gerry Adams later accuses the army of carrying out a 'shoot to kill' policy. In June

1993 Private Lee Clegg is found guilty of murdering Karen Reilly and is sentenced to life imprisonment. A second member of the Parachute Regiment is sentenced to twelve years' imprisonment for the attempted murder of Martin Peake, perverting the course of justice, and conspiring to pervert the course of justice.

1 October At a fringe meeting of the Labour Party conference the SDLP deputy leader, Séamus Mallon, calls for Brooke to tear up the documents he had produced in July for his talks process. He also says that there is no such thing as the 'internal affairs of Northern Ireland.' On 7 October, John Hume supports the view that the present form of the talks should be abandoned and stresses that, as previous attempts at devolution have failed, the emphasis should be on 'transcending' the agreement.

2 October Addressing North Down Conservatives, the former Conservative minister Edwina Currie says that Northern Ireland MPs are 'rickety old knights in rusting armour', not taken seriously by other MPs. By the end of the year Conservative associations have been formed in eleven of the seventeen Northern Ireland constituencies.

6 October A fresh cycle of 'tit-for-tat' killings begins to gather pace. A Catholic man is shot by the 'Protestant Action Force' while in a car with his girl-friend at the same Lough Neagh beauty spot where the IRA killed a UDR soldier two weeks earlier.

9 October A leading IRA man, Desmond Grew, and a Sinn Féin councillor, Martin McCaughey, are shot dead by an army under-cover team after they are spotted carrying automatic rifles at a farm near Loughgall, Co. Armagh. Grew is believed to have been involved in the murder of an RAF corporal and his six-month-old daughter in Germany in 1989. McCaughey had been wounded in a gun battle with the RUC in March.

13 October Two RUC dog handlers are murdered by the IRA in Belfast city centre.

With support for Fine Gael's candidate for the Irish presidency, Austin Currie, lagging at 20 per cent, a party spokesman admits that the 'northern factor' is their candidate's main problem.

16 October A Catholic is shot dead in north Belfast by the UFF, who claim he was a member of the IPLO. Shortly afterwards a former RUC reservist is shot dead by the IRA in the same area.

23 October A Protestant taxi driver is killed by the IRA in Belfast. The body of a Catholic taxi driver murdered by the UVF in retaliation is found in Co. Tyrone the following day.

24 October Six soldiers and a civilian are killed when the IRA force two 'human bombs' to drive to army check-points. Three Catholic men, who the IRA claim worked for the security forces, are strapped into cars loaded with explosives and told to drive to their targets while their families are held hostage. Though the men are told they will be given time to get out of the cars, the IRA detonates the bombs by remote control as soon as they are in place. At a check-point near Derry, Patsy Gillespie and five soldiers are blown to bits. At Killeen, near Newry, a member of the Royal Irish Rangers is killed when another attempted 'human bomb' explodes; the driver escapes with a broken leg. The third bomb, at Omagh, fails to detonate.

28 October An ounce of plastic explosive is found during a search of Maghaberry Prison. On 31 October the NIO say that another ounce has been found at the prison.

31 October Charles Haughey saves his government by sacking his deputy, Brian Lenihan, an hour before a vote of confidence forced by opposition parties. In the wake of the revelation that Lenihan attempted to use party political influence on the President in 1982, Fianna Fáil's coalition partners, the Progressive Democrats, threaten to withdraw their support if Lenihan is not removed. The government wins the vote of confidence by 83 to 80.

6 November It is announced that Cahal Daly is to be the new Catholic Primate of All Ireland. He is installed on 16 December.

9 November Mary Robinson, a 46-year-old lawyer with liberal and feminist opinions, is elected President of Ireland, defeating the Fianna Fáil candidate, Brian Lenihan, on the second count. On the first count Robinson receives 38.9 per cent of the vote to Lenihan's 44.1 per cent and Austin Currie's 17 per cent. On the second count, transfers from Currie go overwhelmingly to

Robinson. Her victory is interpreted by liberals as symptomatic of a radical transformation in Irish politics, centring on a 'rainbow coalition' of interests.

In a speech in his constituency, Peter Brooke says that Britain has no 'strategic or economic interest' in Northern Ireland and would accept the unification of Ireland if consent existed for it.

10 November Two RUC men and two civilians are ambushed and killed by the IRA in Co. Armagh while out wildfowling.

11 November At Kilburn in London 70 lb of plastic explosive, weapons, ammunition and documents are discovered. Seven people are held under the Prevention of Terrorism Act.

13 November In the wake of the poor showing of the Fine Gael candidate in the presidential election, Alan Dukes resigns as leader of Fine Gael. A week later John Bruton becomes leader of the party and announces that he wants articles 2 and 3 amended to state that unification can only come by consent.

14 November Desmond Ellis is extradited to Britain from the Republic.

23 November A 3,500 lb IRA proxy bomb is driven to an army check-point at Rosslea, Co. Fermanagh, but fails to explode.

24 November The Apprentice Boys of Derry reject the offer of £277,500 from the International Fund for Ireland to cover half the cost of a heritage centre.

27 November Following Margaret Thatcher's failure to win outright victory in the Conservative Party leadership contest and her subsequent withdrawal from the race, John Major becomes party leader and Prime Minister. Though he is two votes short of outright victory, his opponents, Michael Heseltine and the former Secretary of State for Northern Ireland, Douglas Hurd, withdraw from the contest.

29 November In a government reshuffle spread over several days, John Cope and Lord Skelmersdale are replaced at the NIO by Lord Belstead and Jeremy Hanley. Brian Mawhinney is promoted to Minister of State. Lord

Belstead becomes the first minister to serve at the NIO on two separate occasions.

30 November Five hundred extra soldiers are brought in to Northern Ireland in an attempt to foil an expected IRA bombing campaign in the period before Christmas.

1 December A former UDR soldier is shot dead at Kilrea. The following day a Catholic man is shot dead by the UVF in retaliation.

12 December In the Dáil a bill introduced by the Workers' Party to amend articles 2 and 3 of the Constitution is defeated by 74 votes to 66. Fine Gael and Labour support the bill, but Fianna Fáil, the Progressive Democrats and independents oppose it.

20 December A record number of prisoners in Northern Ireland are released on parole for seven days over Christmas, including 144 serving life sentences.

23 December The IRA announces a three-day truce over Christmas for the first time in fifteen years.

28 December In an interview with the *Belfast Telegraph,* Peter Brooke says that while the talks that had taken place throughout the year had not produced an answer, there had been 'real advances,' 'new thinking about difficult issues, re-analysis of positions and goals, and re-evaluation of the validity of traditional aims in the context of the nineteen-nineties.'

30 December A member of Sinn Féin, Fergal Caraher, is killed and his brother wounded when soldiers open fire at a check-point at Cullyhanna, Co. Armagh. The RUC claims that their car had failed to stop at the check-point and had knocked down two soldiers.

DEATHS ARISING FROM THE TROUBLES: 76. SHOOTINGS: 557. BOMBS PLANTED: 286. INCENDIARIES: 33. FIREARMS FOUND: 179. EXPLOSIVES FOUND: 1,969 kg (4,340 lb). PERSONS CHARGED WITH TERRORIST AND SERIOUS PUBLIC ORDER OFFENCES: 383. CASUALTIES ARISING FROM PARAMILITARY ATTACKS: 174.

1991

5 January The planting of incendiary devices by the IRA leads to the destruction of a factory and six shops in the Belfast area. The NIO minister responsible for the economy, Richard Needham, reacts angrily by asking whether jobs created in west Belfast as a result of the investment demanded by Sinn Féin will also be fire-bombed. Gerry Adams later accuses Needham of 'theatrical hysterics'.

24 January In the middle of an upsurge in violence, the army confirms that it has withdrawn 600 extra soldiers brought to Northern Ireland before Christmas.

27 January After IRA fire-bombs damage two more furniture shops in Belfast, Richard Needham announces that £25 million intended for social and economic schemes will instead go to pay for the damage caused by the IRA incendiary devices.

2 February In an interview with the *Irish Independent,* Garret FitzGerald says that he had considered a referendum on articles 2 and 3 of the Constitution at the time of the signing of the Anglo-Irish Agreement but eventually decided not to take the risk.

3 February The IRA uses the 'human bomb' tactic again, forcing a man to drive his van with a 500 lb bomb into a UDR base in Magherafelt by making his wife travel with them in another vehicle. The driver shouts a warning and escapes before the explosion, but part of the base and fifty surrounding houses are badly damaged. Three employees from the same firm have already been murdered, because the company undertook work for the security forces.

7 February The IRA fires a mortar bomb into the garden of number 10 Downing Street, which lands less than fifteen yards from a room where John Major is chairing a meeting of the Cabinet. Two other mortars overshoot the area and land harmlessly. No-one is injured, and the meeting resumes in the basement.

At the renewed appeal of the Birmingham Six against their convictions, the Department of Public Prosecutions announces that scientific evidence against the men has been dropped.

14 February A new extradition dispute breaks out between Britain and Ireland when the charges under which Desmond Ellis was originally extradited from the Republic are dropped and new charges introduced by a British court, contrary to Irish laws on extradition. On 4 June, after protests from the Irish government, the original charges against Ellis are lodged against him at the Central Criminal Court in London.

18 February One person is killed and forty-three injured when an IRA bomb explodes at Victoria Station in London during the morning rush hour.

3 March Four Catholic men are shot dead in a UVF gun attack on a public house in Cappagh, Co. Tyrone. Two of the men are later identified as members of the IRA.

4 March Belfast City Council votes by 21 to 19 to end its ban on visits by ministers. On 25 March the final remnants of the boycott of government ministers by unionist politicians is removed when the NIO minister Richard Needham visits Belfast City Hall. Unionist politicians continue to refuse to participate in the British-Irish interparliamentary body, which meets in London in June and in Dublin in December.

6 March In Paris five crew members of the *Eksund* are sentenced to between five and seven years' imprisonment for the plot to smuggle guns from Libya to the IRA in 1987.

14 March After sixteen years in jail, the 'Birmingham Six' are freed. Hugh Callaghan, Paddy Hill, Gerry Hunter, Richard McIlkenny, Billy Power and Johnny Walker had been convicted in 1975 for the worst incident of mass murder in British peacetime history. They had been found guilty on the basis of scientific evidence and confessions, which it is claimed were beaten out of them by the police. The six are released after their second appeal in three years. The Home Secretary, Kenneth Baker, acknowledges that this is the third case in eighteen months involving Irish people where there has been a miscarriage of justice. The decision to release the Birmingham Six comes after new tests on West Midlands Police documents suggest that members of the police may have forged notes and given false evidence. Scientific tests purporting to show that two of the men had handled explosives are also shown to be unreliable.

After the Irish government agrees that Peter Brooke could decide when they should enter the talks process, a new formula for the talks is presented to the parties involved. By 25 March all those involved in the talks process have agreed to these arrangements.

18 March A House of Commons motion supported by 100 MPs urges the Queen to dismiss the Lord Chief Justice, Lord Lane, over the Birmingham Six affair.

26 March In the House of Commons, Brooke makes a statement on the talks, saying: 'It is accepted that discussions must focus on the three main relationships: those within Northern Ireland, including the relationship between any new institutions there and the Westminster parliament; among the people of the island of Ireland; and between the two governments' (*Hansard*, sixth series, vol. 188, col. 765). The aim is to produce a new and more broadly based agreement. The process will begin with discussions between the Northern Ireland parties aimed at achieving devolved government ('strand 1' of the talks) with North-South discussions ('strand 2') and Irish-British discussions ('strand 3') to begin when the Secretary of State feels it appropriate. It is also decided that the results of the talks will form part of a complete package. As a result, those engaged in the discussions repeatedly comment that 'nothing is agreed until everything is agreed.'

28 March A 29-year-old man and two teenage girls, all Catholics, are shot dead in a UVF attack on a mobile shop in Craigavon.

4 April A 1,000 lb IRA bomb explodes in Banbridge, causing widespread damage.

9 April After a meeting of the Intergovernmental Conference, the Irish Minister for Foreign Affairs, Gerry Collins, announces that a ten-week gap will follow the next meeting on 26 April to allow discussions to take place.

16 April An explosion at Shorts aircraft factory in east Belfast is the sixth IRA bomb to hit the company in two years.

17 April The UVF, UFF and Red Hand Commando announce a cease-fire under the name of the Combined Loyalist Military Command, to begin on 30 April and to coincide with the talks process. Before that date, however, both the UVF and UFF, as well as the IRA, continue sectarian attacks.

21 April The United Kingdom census is held. The results will show the population of Northern Ireland to be 1,577,836; there are 605,639 Catholics (38.4 per cent of the population), 336,891 Presbyterians (21.3 per cent), 279,280 members of the Church of Ireland (17.7 per cent), and 59,517 Methodists (3.8 per cent). There are numerous other Protestant groups, of which the largest are the Baptists (19,484), Brethren (12,446), and Ian Paisley's Free Presbyterian Church of Ulster (12,363), with 12,386 describing themselves merely as 'Protestant' and 10,556 as 'Christian'; all other groups have fewer than 10,000 adherents. 7.3 per cent do not state any denomination, while 3.8 per cent have no religion. 15 per cent of the population are of pensionable age (5.2 per cent are aged seventy-five or over), while 25 per cent are under the age of sixteen.

The 1981 census showed 414,532 Catholics, 339,818 Presbyterians, 281,472 Church of Ireland, and 58,731 Methodists. However, these figures were badly distorted by the fact that 274,000 (18.5 per cent) refused to answer the question on religion. The 1981 census was also carried out during the hunger strikes, with republicans organising a campaign against the completing of census forms.

22 April The Fair Employment Commission publishes a report based on the first annual monitoring returns of the 'perceived religion' of companies with more than twenty-five employees. This suggests that approximately 65 per cent of those employed are Protestant and 35 per cent Catholic.

25 April GEC announces the closure of its plant at Larne, with the loss of five hundred jobs.

26 April A meeting of the Anglo-Irish Conference agrees to a gap of ten weeks before the next meeting, creating the opportunity for the talks process to begin on 30 April. The initial meetings of the strand 1 talks are postponed, however, because there is confusion over the details of where the talks will take place and who will chair the later stages. At the end of May the British government proposes Lord Carrington as an independent chairman for strand 2 talks, but he is immediately rejected by unionists because of comments about the 'bigotry and insobriety' of Northern Ireland politicians in his memoirs.

9 May Sinn Féin's former publicity director, Danny Morrison, is convicted, with seven others, of falsely imprisoning an RUC informer and is sentenced to eight years in jail.

25 May The UFF sidesteps its own cease-fire commitment by killing a Sinn Féin councillor, Eddie Fullerton, in Co. Donegal. The UDA says the cease-fire does not apply to the Republic.

26 May A large IRA bomb explodes, damaging more than a hundred houses and injuring thirteen people in a Protestant housing estate in Cookstown.

30 May Three UDR soldiers are killed and thirteen injured when a lorry containing a 2,000 lb IRA bomb explodes after it is rolled down a hill into the perimeter fence of a base at Glenanne, Co. Armagh.

3 June The SAS shoot dead three IRA men on 'active service' in Coagh, Co. Tyrone. Nearly two hundred shots are fired at the car in which they were travelling. Two rifles are found near the burnt-out car; one of the weapons had been used in the murder of three Protestants in the same village two years earlier.

9 June An IRA bomb containing up to 600 lb of explosives detonates in a Protestant housing estate in Donacloney, Co. Down. The IRA offers the explanation that many members of the security forces live in the estate, but the attack is widely seen as part of a campaign of increasingly openly sectarian attacks on the Protestant community.

12 June As part of the campaign in the United States in support of the MacBride principles, the Mayor of New York, David Dinkins, signs a law denying contracts to companies in Northern Ireland that do not comply with the principles.

14 June An Australian diplomat, Sir Ninian Stephen, is named as the agreed independent chairman for strand 2 of the talks process. By 17 June, when the talks finally get under way, there are only three weeks until the next meeting of the Anglo-Irish Conference. With the unionists saying they will talk only until 9 July, when preparations for the next Anglo-Irish meeting will begin, Brooke pre-empts the complete breakdown of the process by ending the talks on 3 July.

18 June A further five hundred soldiers are brought to Northern Ireland. The total number is said to be 11,000.

26 June The Maguire Seven are finally cleared by the Court of Appeal in London after serving sentences ranging from four to fourteen years and after one of them has died in jail. The quashing of the convictions comes as a result of an interim report from an inquiry headed by Sir John May, which concludes that the prosecution failed to prove there were traces of nitroglycerine on the Maguires' hands and gloves, casting doubt on the reliability of the evidence of prosecution scientists. Counsel for the defence had argued that the Maguires could have been contaminated with nitroglycerine from a dirty hand-towel they had used. When the May report is finally published in September 1992, however, its conclusions about how the contamination occurred are inconclusive and so fail to completely vindicate the Maguires, causing fresh anger.

29 June Cecil McKnight, a former senior UDA member, is killed by the IRA in Derry.

3 July Five men charged as a result of the Stevens inquiry into intelligence leaks to loyalists are jailed for between four and seven years. One of those imprisoned is the senior UDA man Tommy Lyttle, who is sentenced to seven years' imprisonment for making threats to kill.

4 July With the ending of the talks process by Brooke the previous day, loyalist paramilitaries announce that they have called off their cease-fire.

5 July A Dutch court acquits four IRA suspects of the murder of two Australian tourists in Roermond in May 1990. Three of those acquitted are held in custody pending requests for extradition to Germany, while the fourth is returned to Ireland.

7 July Two IRA suspects, Nessan Quinlivan and Pearse McAuley, break out of Brixton Prison and shoot a motorist and steal his car to make their getaway.

9 July Proposed defence cuts include plans to merge the UDR with the Royal Irish Rangers and to reduce the size of the Territorial Army (which plays no role in local security arrangements) by 36 per cent, proportionately double the reduction proposed for the rest of the United Kingdom.

19 July A Dundalk man, Thomas Oliver, is shot dead by the IRA, who claim he was a Garda informer. The claim is denied by his family and the Gardaí; the murder loses the IRA a great deal of support in the area and leads to several anti-IRA rallies on the southern side of the border.

28 July Seven incendiary devices planted by the UFF explode in shops in the Republic. The following day a DUP councillor, Rhonda Paisley (daughter of Rev. Ian Paisley), says the attacks are 'perfectly understandable' in view of the British government's 'betrayal' of Northern Ireland.

29 July In Dublin the captain of the IRA gun-running ship *Eksund,* Adrian Hopkins, is jailed for three years, with a further eight-year sentence suspended because of time already spent in custody. On 24 July the prosecution withdraws eleven of the twelve charges against Hopkins.

12 August It is announced that the case of Judith Ward, jailed for the Bradford coach bombing in 1974, is to be reviewed.

17 August The murder of two republicans by loyalist gunmen in separate incidents brings to seven the death toll for one week. On 12 August the UFF kills a member of Sinn Féin in Co. Tyrone, and on 16 August they kill another Sinn Féin election worker in Co. Londonderry as he arrives for work. On the same day the UVF murders an IPLO activist in Belfast. The ending of the loyalist truce with the termination of the talks process sees an upsurge in loyalist terrorist incidents, which include an attack on a bus carrying the families of republicans near Markethill, Co. Armagh, on 14 August. Two women are injured in the attack. The reintroduction of internment is again raised, without any result.

21 August A 500 lb IRA bomb explodes near a police station in Kilrea, severely damaging nearby homes and churches.

28 August Liam Kearns and David Madigan, who sought sanctuary in Newry Cathedral ten days earlier after being ordered to leave Ireland by the IRA following an attack on two members of Sinn Féin, leave the cathedral.

29 August Sinn Féin wins a council by-election in Belfast, making it the second-largest party in the city council, with nine seats.

August The number of unemployed rises by 5,000 on the previous month to reach 103,612 (14 per cent).

3 September At the Young Unionist conference a senior UUP member, John Taylor, says that one in three Catholics is 'either a supporter of murder or worse still a murderer' (*Fortnight,* October 1991).

4 September An IRA plan to blow up an army check-point at Annaghmartin, Co. Fermanagh, using a massive 8,000 lb of explosives fails when the trailer carrying the bomb becomes bogged down in a field.

13 September The army defuses two UFF bombs planted in Catholic areas, one in Belfast and one in Portaferry. The UFF says it would retaliate for IRA attacks on Protestant lives, jobs, and homes.

16 September In a series of talks lasting until 20 September, Brooke meets party leaders in an attempt to restart the talks process. With the possibility of a Westminster general election in November, however, this proves to be mainly a sounding-out exercise.

A Sinn Féin councillor, Bernard O'Hagan, is shot dead by the UVF at a technical college in Magherafelt. On the same day the IRA attempts to kill three men in Belfast who it claims are loyalists.

21 September There is trouble in Crumlin Road Jail in Belfast when a fire, apparently started by loyalist prisoners, breaks out in the dining-hall. On the following day fifty republican prisoners wreck furniture and attempt to set up barricades in the prison. The NIO says the incidents are part of a concerted campaign to force it to introduce segregation in the prison.

7 October An IRA suspect, Donna Maguire, is extradited from the Netherlands to Germany to be tried for the murder of a British soldier in July 1989. In October 1992 Maguire, with Seán Hick and Paul Hughes, also stands trial in Germany for the murder of Major Michael Dillon-Lee, who was shot dead in front of his wife in Dortmund in June 1990.

8 October The UFF declares that in future members of the GAA will be considered 'legitimate targets'. The UFF had earlier set fire to a GAA hall in Kircubbin, Co. Down, claiming that the association supports the 'republican war machine'. The threat is widely condemned by unionist politicians, including Ian Paisley, and by Protestant church leaders. The following day the UFF issues another statement saying that only those GAA members with strong republican links will be attacked. The controversy draws attention to the GAA ban against members of the RUC and British army, which is defended by its president.

10 October In Belfast the murder of a Protestant in a Shankill Road bar by the IPLO leads to the killing of a Catholic taxi driver by the UFF several hours later. Further loyalist murders continue throughout the month.

15 October The Governor of California vetoes a bill that endorses the MacBride principles.

20 October Republican gunmen make an unsuccessful attempt on the life of the former UUP Lord Mayor of Belfast Fred Cobain.

23 October A spokesman for the West Belfast branch of the Irish-language organisation Glór na nGael is jailed for fourteen years for keeping weapons at his home. The question of the government's reluctance to provide funds for the organisation remains a source of controversy throughout the year.

25 October In the first case of its kind, the FEC announces that a south Belfast company has been disqualified from receiving government contracts because it failed to return forms giving the religious make-up of its work force.

30 October Desmond Ellis, who was at the centre of an extradition dispute earlier in the year, is acquitted of conspiring to cause explosions. He is expelled from Britain by an exclusion order signed by the Home Secretary the following day.

2 November Two soldiers are killed and eighteen other people injured when an IRA bomb explodes in the military wing of Musgrave Park Hospital in Belfast. The IRA says it has struck at a 'military base'. It is the first attack on a hospital during the Troubles.

5 November The UFF throws a grenade at (mainly Catholic) supporters of Cliftonville football team at Windsor Park football ground in Belfast; no-one is injured. The UFF says the attack is in retaliation for the IRA bombing of Musgrave Park Hospital three days earlier.

8 November A report from the Equal Opportunities Unit of the Northern Ireland Civil Service says that 57 per cent of civil servants are Protestants, 36 per cent Catholics, and the rest from outside Northern Ireland. However, Catholics still make up only 21 per cent of senior personnel.

9 November A Catholic woman and her son are killed in a fire caused by a loyalist petrol-bomb attack on their home at Glengormley, Co. Antrim.

11 November Dublin City Council votes to stop Sinn Féin having the use of the Mansion House for its ardfheis, because of Sinn Féin's support for the IRA.

13 November Four Protestants are killed in a series of IRA attacks in Belfast; in one of them a five-week-old girl is wounded twice. The following day loyalists retaliate by killing a Catholic taxi driver in Belfast and three workers near Lurgan. The UVF apologises for killing John Lavery, a Protestant, who was one of the three men killed at Lurgan. The government announces that the RUC will be allowed to recruit another 440 members and that five hundred more soldiers will be sent to Northern Ireland.

15 November With twenty people having been killed in the previous five weeks and seven in the last two days alone, soldiers are drafted into Belfast from other areas. More than 1,200 part-time UDR members are also temporarily put on full-time duty. The reintroduction of internment is mentioned more seriously than at any time in recent years, but again the idea is dropped when the security situation eases.

Two IRA members are killed in St Albans, Hertfordshire, when a bomb they are planting explodes prematurely. Visiting the scene of the explosion two days later, the Home Secretary, Kenneth Baker, says, 'Those who live by terror will die by terror.'

22 November The FEC rules that religious or political symbols at places of work might be interpreted as intimidatory. The chairman of the commission, Bob Cooper, later says that pictures of the Pope or the Queen might be considered offensive. A DUP MP, William McCrea, describes the decision as 'treasonable'.

24 November A loyalist prisoner on remand in Crumlin Road Jail, Belfast, is killed and eight others injured by an explosion caused by the IRA in the prison's dining-hall. A second prisoner dies four days later.

27 November Four men are arrested at the home of the leader of the Northern Ireland Conservative Party, Laurence Kennedy, after his wife raises the alarm.

29 November The magazine of the Northern Ireland Police Federation calls for the reintroduction of internment.

4 December John Major visits Charles Haughey in Dublin. They agree to meet for talks twice a year. Brooke later meets party leaders again and puts a new proposal for talks to them on 20 December.

A 1,200 lb IRA car bomb explodes in Glengall Street, Belfast, causing severe damage to the Grand Opera House, next to the Ulster Unionist Party head office.

8 December A series of IRA incendiaries explodes in England, causing damage to shops in Blackpool and Manchester. Further fire-bombs explode in the same cities the following day.

9 December After the upsurge in violence throughout the year Brooke announces a freeze on public spending in several areas to meet the increased cost of IRA bomb damage. Brian Mawhinney assumes responsibility for law and order in Northern Ireland in place of Lord Belstead. The year has also been characterised by an increase in the number of murders committed by loyalists. By the end of the year the UVF will have killed nineteen people and the UDA or UFF a further fifteen. The IRA has also returned to a bombing campaign. The cost of damage to homes for the year exceeds £2 million, more than the cost for the previous five years.

12 December Over seventy people are injured by a 2,000 lb IRA bomb planted at a police station in Craigavon. A nearby church, school and houses are also damaged.

14 December Fire-bombs cause damage to a London shopping centre; the following day an IRA incendiary device explodes at the National Gallery, and on 16 December a bomb explodes on a railway line in south London. Further IRA incendiary devices disrupt trains in London on 23 December.

18 December A 500 lb bomb damages the Belfast law courts.

21 December Two Protestants are killed when an IPLO gunman fires at random into a bar in the Donegall Road area of Belfast. Hours later a Catholic man is killed in retaliation by the UFF, and a further UFF attack on a bar the following day kills another Catholic man.

23 December For the second year in a row the IRA calls a three-day cease-fire.

DEATHS ARISING FROM THE TROUBLES: 94. SHOOTINGS: 499. BOMBS PLANTED: 368. INCENDIARIES: 237. FIREARMS FOUND: 164. EXPLOSIVES FOUND: 4,167 kg (9,185 lb). PERSONS CHARGED WITH TERRORIST AND SERIOUS PUBLIC ORDER OFFENCES: 404. CASUALTIES ARISING FROM PARAMILITARY ATTACKS: 138.

1992

5 January An 800 lb bomb explodes in Bedford Street, Belfast, causing widespread damage. The following day a 500 lb bomb causes extensive damage to High Street.

10 January A 5 lb bomb left in a briefcase by the IRA in London explodes three hundred yards from Downing Street.

17 January Seven Protestant building workers who had worked at a military base in Co. Tyrone are killed as they drive home when a massive IRA bomb blows up their minibus at Teebane Crossroads, near Cookstown. The eighth victim, the driver, dies four days later. Gerry Adams describes the mass murder as 'a horrific reminder of the failure of British policy in Ireland' (*Fortnight,* March 1992).

The Secretary of State, Peter Brooke, shocks the community by singing 'My Darling Clementine' while appearing on 'The Late Late Show' in Dublin just after the Teebane massacre has been announced. He later reveals that he has offered his resignation over the affair.

22 January The former UDA intelligence officer and army agent Brian Nelson pleads guilty to five charges of conspiracy to murder and fourteen charges of possessing information useful to terrorists. Two charges of murder are withdrawn. Nelson is sentenced to ten years' imprisonment. The outcome seems designed to protect the security forces from justifying their actions in court.

4 February An off-duty RUC constable, Allen Moore, enters the Sinn Féin office on the Falls Road in Belfast and shoots dead three people before driving away and later killing himself.

5 February Five Catholics, including a sixteen-year-old boy, are murdered by loyalist gunmen at Seán Graham's bookmaker's shop on the Ormeau Road, Belfast. Seven other people are wounded. The statement by the UFF admitting responsibility concludes, 'Remember Teebane.'

6 February Albert Reynolds is elected leader of Fianna Fáil in succession to Charles Haughey and is later ratified as Taoiseach by the Dáil.

16 February Four IRA members are shot dead by under-cover soldiers in Co. Tyrone after they open fire on the RUC station in Coalisland with a heavy-calibre machine-gun mounted on the back of a lorry.

22 February The leader of the Workers' Party, Proinsias de Rossa, and five other TDs walk out of a meeting in Dublin and announce that they are forming a new organisation, at first called New Agenda and, from 28 March, Democratic Left. The split comes after de Rossa fails to get the Workers' Party to repudiate its links with the Official IRA.

28 February An IRA bomb at London Bridge station injures twenty-eight people.

2 March The Libyan leader, Muammar Gaddafi, says he is severing ties with the IRA.

Two UDR soldiers are convicted with a third man of aiding and abetting the UFF murder of Loughlin Maginn in August 1989. The murder led to the setting up of the Stevens inquiry.

5 March The commercial centre of Lurgan is destroyed when a 1,000 lb bomb planted by the IRA explodes; another bomb causes extensive damage in Belfast city centre.

9 March Figures published by the FEC based on returns from over 1,700 employers show that Catholics make up 35 per cent of those employed but 38 per cent of those available for work. Of the RUC's 11,233 employees, 93 per cent are Protestant. The publication of the information is opposed by the Confederation of British Industry and Northern Ireland Chamber of Commerce.

10 March 3,500 lb of explosives, four mortars and other weapons are found by gardaí at Drumkeen, Co. Donegal. Three people are arrested. There are further weapons finds in Co. Donegal on 15 March.

24 March A 500 lb IRA bomb explodes near Donegall Pass RUC station in Belfast, causing extensive damage to the surrounding area.

4 April With experts predicting no overall majority after the general election, Unionist MPs believe they may hold the balance of power in the new Parliament. James Molyneaux says the main British parties know what the Unionists want: a new British-Irish Agreement, the replacement of the Order in Council system of legislation for Northern Ireland, and the formation of a House of Commons select committee for Northern Ireland. The Labour Party's spokesman on Northern Ireland, Kevin McNamara, says there is 'no way' his party will do a deal with the Unionists in the House of Commons.

9 April The Conservative Party wins the general election with a majority of twenty-one seats. In Northern Ireland the SDLP vote increases to 23.5 per cent (21.1 per cent in 1987), while Sinn Féin declines only slightly to 10 per cent (from 11.4 per cent). The DUP vote rises to 13 per cent (from 11.7 per cent) as a result of its decision to stand against the UUP in safe 'unionist' seats for the first time since 1986. The UUP vote declines to 34.5 per cent (from 37.8 per cent), mainly as a result of competition from the Conservatives. The combined vote of the two avowedly modernising and non-sectarian pro-Union parties, Alliance (8.7 per cent) and Conservative (5.7 per cent), is greater than that of the DUP. Joe Hendron of the SDLP displaces Gerry Adams in West Belfast, while all other sitting MPs are returned. Sinn Féin claims Hendron is elected because the UDA told Protestants in the area to vote for Hendron to get Adams out.

10 April Two IRA bombs explode in the centre of London, killing three people. The IRA warning creates confusion by saying that the bomb is at the Stock Exchange rather than at its actual location, the Baltic Exchange. In August the *Belfast Telegraph* reports that £800 million has been paid out in insurance claims as a result of the City of London explosion. This compares with £615 million paid since 1969 for damage resulting from the Troubles in Northern Ireland.

11 April In the post-election government reshuffle the former Attorney-General Sir Patrick Mayhew replaces Peter Brooke as Secretary of State for Northern Ireland. Michael Mates (deputy secretary of state with responsibility for security) and Robert Atkins (responsible for the economy) become Ministers of State, while Lord Arran is appointed an Under-Secretary. Of the pre-election NIO ministerial team only Jeremy Hanley (now responsible for the political talks) remains.

14 April An off-duty army recruiting sergeant shot by the INLA in Derby the previous day dies. He is the first person to be killed by the INLA in Britain since Airey Neave in March 1979.

27 April A meeting of the Intergovernmental Conference in London agrees that there should be a three-month suspension of meetings to allow political talks in Northern Ireland to begin again. Sir Patrick Mayhew and the Irish Minister for Foreign Affairs, David Andrews, are at odds about whether the Government of Ireland Act is seriously open to discussion. The following day Albert Reynolds supports Andrews's view by stating in the Dáil that the Government of Ireland Act will have to be included in any talks.

28 April The murder of Philomena Hanna, a 26-year-old Catholic woman in a west Belfast pharmacy, by UFF gunmen causes a wave of revulsion at a particularly senseless murder.

29 April Political talks reconvene at Stormont with opening statements from the four parties.

1 May A 1,000 lb IRA bomb at a border post in Co. Armagh kills one soldier and wounds several others.

2 May A large number of arms, including fifty-one automatic rifles, two machine-guns and 20,000 rounds of ammunition, are found in a concealed bunker at a farm near Newmarket, Co. Cork. On 1 May three assault rifles are found in a small drum buried at Newcastle, Co. Limerick, the second arms find in the area in a month.

5 May The inquest into the deaths of Seán Burns, Gervaise McKerr and Eugene Toman, shot dead by the RUC near Lurgan in November 1982, reopens. Gregory Burns, the brother of one of those killed, walks out of the inquest and says he has no confidence in the system. In 1990 the House of Lords had ruled that the policemen involved could not be compelled to give evidence at the inquest.

In London the appeal of Judith Ward against her conviction for involvement in the Bradford coach bomb in November 1974 opens. Her counsel says she was mentally unstable when she confessed to being involved in the bombing. The conviction is quashed on 4 June, with judges accusing the forensic scientists involved in the case of having concealed evidence.

8 May Following a government review the Home Secretary, Kenneth Clarke, announces that the leading role in intelligence-gathering to counter IRA actions in Britain will be transferred from the Special Branch of the Metropolitan Police to the Security Service (MI5).

12 May It is alleged that soldiers from the Parachute Regiment wrecked two bars in Coalisland, following an incident in which a member of the regiment lost both legs in an IRA land mine explosion. The following day the commanding officer is removed from his post. On 17 May there is further trouble in Coalisland, during which it is alleged that soldiers from the King's Own Scottish Borderers put down their guns to become involved in a fist-fight with local people. Later, members of the Parachute Regiment arrive and open fire on a crowd outside a bar. Three civilians are shot in the leg and four others injured. On 24 May it is reported that Brigadier Tom Longland, commander of the Third Brigade, based in Armagh, has been transferred; the army denies that his removal has any connection with events in Coalisland. The Parachute Regiment is removed from its patrolling duties before the end of its tour of duty.

13 May A leaked SDLP submission to strand 1 of the talks suggests that Northern Ireland be governed by a six-member Northern Ireland Executive Commission, with three members elected (from a single constituency) and one member each nominated by the British and Irish governments and the EC. The chairmanship or presidency would be held by the elected member receiving the highest number of first-preference votes (*News Letter,* 14 May 1992). The document is regarded with some coolness by the Alliance and unionist parties and by the British government.

8 June A BBC television programme claims that Brian Nelson has been involved in ten murders, attempted murders or conspiracies to murder carried out by the UDA with the knowledge of his army controllers. He had also identified sixteen other people who were later killed or had attempts made on their lives. Army intelligence also failed to pass on to the RUC information about some planned attacks.

12 June At the end of twelve hours of talks, and despite the fact that negotiations on strand 1 (the internal government of Northern Ireland) are deadlocked, the parties agree tentative moves towards strands 2 and 3 of the talks process.

Paul 'Dingus' Magee, who escaped from Crumlin Road Prison in 1981 and was later convicted *in absentia* of being involved in the murder of an SAS captain in Belfast and who absconded from bail while the Supreme Court in Dublin was considering his extradition, is charged with the murder of a special constable in Yorkshire on 7 June. The special constable was killed and a colleague wounded when they stopped two men in a car. Michael O'Brien from Co. Dublin is also charged. In March 1993 Magee and O'Brien are sentenced to life and eighteen years' imprisonment, respectively.

19 June In London, representatives of the British and Irish governments and Northern Ireland parties discuss a provisional agenda for strand 2 of the talks process. Unionists seem to be in favour of pushing ahead with discussions as quickly as possible, and on 22 June, Ian Paisley accuses the Republic of 'time-wasting' over the holding of a meeting to set the terms for strand 3 of the talks (between Britain and Ireland).

21 June In a speech at the annual Wolfe Tone commemoration in Co. Kildare a leading Sinn Féin member, Jim Gibney, says: 'We know and accept that the British government's departure [from Ireland] must be preceded by a sustained period of peace and will arise out of negotiations [involving] the different shades of Irish nationalism and Irish unionism' (*Northern Star,* August 1992). The statement encourages the belief in some quarters that Sinn Féin and the IRA might be moving towards calling off the campaign of violence.

30 June Northern Ireland politicians meet British and Irish government representatives in London as part of a framework-setting meeting for strand 3 of the talks process (British-Irish relations). Those present include Sir Patrick Mayhew and David Andrews (joint chairmen), Ian Paisley, and John Alderdice (leader of Alliance). On 7 July the *Irish Times* claims that Paisley insisted at this meeting that articles 2 and 3 of the Constitution of Ireland must be changed without the *quid pro quo* of Southern involvement in Northern Ireland's internal affairs. On the following day it claims that Mayhew supported the Unionist and Alliance proposals for strand 1 in his opening statement. This plan would involve an Assembly with committee chairmen and vice-chairmen elected in proportion to party strength. Devolved powers would be equal to, or greater than, those given to the 1973 Assembly. Sensitive legislation would require a weighted majority; a panel of three people elected directly would also have 'significant consultative, monitoring, referral and representational functions.'

1 July After strand 1 discussions with Sir Patrick Mayhew at Stormont, political parties, including the DUP, agree to talks with politicians from the Republic under strand 2. This shift in the unionist line is encouraged by a 'private' letter from Mayhew to James Molyneaux on 1 July indicating that the British government is unenthusiastic about the SDLP proposals with its direct role for the EC in Northern Ireland. The Unionists feel they have to reciprocate, if only so that the possible creation of a Northern Ireland select committee in the House of Commons will not be endangered. On the other hand, they risk appearing to accept the view that Dublin has a legitimate role to play in the North, something the British government already conceded in 1985 and that unionists have been unable to reverse.

The Royal Irish Regiment comes into existence with the amalgamation of the Ulster Defence Regiment and the Royal Irish Rangers. The 6,000-strong UDR battalions will continue to operate in Northern Ireland, with the two former RIR battalions being reduced to one general service battalion of 900 soldiers, which would serve both in Northern Ireland and abroad.

2 July The bodies of three IRA men murdered by the IRA are found in separate areas of Co. Armagh. One of those killed is Gregory Burns, a brother of Seán Burns, killed by the RUC in November 1982. The IRA claim that two of the men had supplied information to the RUC and one to the Security Service (MI5). The body of a woman found in the Republic the previous day is that of the girl-friend of one of the three men, who, it is claimed, murdered her when they discovered she was about to expose their activities to the IRA.

6 July Three days of discussion between the Northern Ireland parties, the British government and the Republic (strand 2 of the talks process) begin in London. Three DUP members resign from the party in protest against discussions concerning Northern Ireland being held with representatives of the Republic. The London talks appear to indicate a move away from the inflexibility characteristic of the parties up to this time. The UUP leadership in particular seems to have had a change of heart, probably brought about by the attitude of the British government, which gives the impression that it wishes to reduce the unionist sense of isolation. The British may have been brought to this conclusion by the fact that the Anglo-Irish Agreement has not brought the hoped-for reduction in violence. Despite this, strand 2 talks adjourn on 24 July (until 2 September) without any real sign of a meeting of minds.

8 July There is antagonism between Orange marchers and protesters on the lower Ormeau Road, Belfast, at the bookmaker's shop where five Catholics were killed by loyalist gunmen on 5 February. Nationalists wave Tricolours while some Orange marchers shout 'Up the UFF' and give two-fingered salutes. Sir Patrick Mayhew says the actions of some of the marchers 'would have disgraced a tribe of cannibals.'

29 July Three of the 'UDR Four'—Winston Allen, Noel Bell, and James Hegan—are released after their conviction for the murder of Adrian Carroll in 1983 is quashed by the Appeal Court in Belfast. RUC notes of their confessions had been tampered with. Neil Latimer, convicted of actually committing the murder, is not released, because of other evidence against him.

31 July Channel 4 and Box Productions are fined £75,000 at the High Court in London in connection with the broadcasting of a programme that claimed there was an 'inner circle' in the RUC that colluded with loyalist paramilitaries in an organised manner. The programme-makers had refused to name the source of this information and were found guilty of contravening the Prevention of Terrorism Act. On 2 August the Chief Constable of the RUC, Sir Hugh Annesley, issues a statement saying there is no truth in the allegations and that the story had been invented to discredit the force.

2 August Two bombs, each over 200 lb, explode in Bedford Street, Belfast, causing extensive damage to an area completing repairs after another bomb earlier in the year.

10 August Sir Patrick Mayhew announces that the UDA will be banned from midnight. The decision is widely welcomed by British politicians and by nationalists. The principal controversy that surrounds the banning is why the government has chosen this particular time. The most obvious explanation for the banning is the upsurge in loyalist killings during the year, including those at the Ormeau Road bookmaker's shop, with the UFF claiming responsibility for thirteen killings so far in 1992—the first time it has murdered more people than the IRA since the early seventies. On the following day Ian Paisley claims that the move is part of a process organised by the Irish government to bring Sinn Féin to the negotiation table.

12 August Police in London seize three vans containing up to 12 tons of IRA explosives, the biggest explosives find in Britain. Five people from the Republic are arrested but are later released.

21 August 21-year-old Hugh McKibben is shot dead by the IPLO on a bus outside the Lámh Dhearg GAA social club in Hannahstown, Co. Antrim, on the outskirts of west Belfast; two other men are wounded. The killing follows the murder of a leading IPLO member, Jimmy Brown, on 18 August as part of an internal feud.

28 August John De Lorean pays back £5 million to the IDB by selling his house in New York. The receivers hoped to recover a further £2 million from other investigations, though more than £50 million is outstanding. The government had invested almost £80 million in the De Lorean project (*Belfast Telegraph,* 28 August 1992).

9 September Ian Paisley and Peter Robinson walk out of the strand 2 talks at Stormont because articles 2 and 3 of the Constitution of Ireland are not to be discussed first. Two DUP members remain behind as observers.

12 September A confidential discussion paper from the Stormont talks process proposing a range of structures and institutions purportedly aimed at 'overcoming lack of adequate channels of communication and co-operation between North and South,' said to have been prepared by Sir Patrick Mayhew, uses phrases such as 'an agreed Ireland' and 'powers to be exercised through North/South channels.' The document outrages Ulster Unionists and is shelved after James Molyneaux writes to Mayhew to demand that it be withdrawn or his party will leave the talks.

20 September The continuing flow of leaked papers from the talks process indicates that the talks are grinding to a halt. *Sunday Life* claims that a confidential Irish government paper says there will be no movement on articles 2 and 3 until concessions are made to nationalists. Unionists continue to insist that the Irish government sponsor changes to the articles first. The *Sunday News* meanwhile publishes details of a strand 1 sub-committee document of 10 June giving a 'possible outline framework' for devolved government. It suggests an 85-member Assembly (elected by PR) that would control existing government departments through committees. The chairmen (becoming in effect the responsible ministers) and deputy chairmen of the departmental committees would be appointed broadly in proportion to party numbers in the Assembly.

The parties are divided on the vote that would be required for a decision to be taken: the SDLP propose 75 per cent, the UUP and Alliance propose 70 per cent, and the DUP propose 65 per cent. The Secretary of State would retain control of powers not devolved (such as security) and ensure that the Assembly was run fairly but would not interfere in its day-to-day matters. The most novel feature of the plan is the creation of a three-member 'panel' to be elected on the same basis as the European Parliament elections and also likely to return one UUP, one DUP and one SDLP member. The panel would consult and advise the Secretary of State, inspect and review the Assembly and NIO decisions, approve some appointments to public bodies, and have some say in how public finances are spent. The document also suggests that 'any individuals or representatives of parties who condone the use of violence for political ends,' primarily Sinn Féin, might be excluded from executive power.

21 September An Ulster Unionist delegation led by James Molyneaux begins three days of strand 2 talks at Dublin Castle. The range of topics discussed includes constitutional matters, terrorism and security co-operation, identity and allegiance, and channels of communication. The DUP do not attend the talks.

23 September A 2,000 lb IRA bomb destroys the forensic science laboratories in south Belfast, injuring more than twenty people and causing damage to a thousand houses. Repairs to the damaged houses are estimated to cost over £6 million.

26 September John Hume says in a radio interview that Northern Ireland is 'not a natural political entity and therefore you cannot have a normal democracy.' He proposes a system of government with six commissioners, one appointed by Dublin, each running a Northern Ireland department, with an elected Assembly to question and make proposals to the commissioners.

30 September With the talks process resuming at Stormont and British-Irish relations (including articles 2 and 3) due for discussion, the DUP returns to the negotiations. The Irish government describes Ian Paisley as having an *à la carte* approach to the talks.

12 October One man is killed and four others injured by the eighth small IRA bomb to explode in London in a week.

16 October Sheena Campbell, a law student who had stood as a Sinn Féin candidate in the Upper Bann by-election in 1990, is shot dead by the UVF in Belfast.

20 October Robert Irvine, an off-duty sergeant in the Royal Irish Regiment, is shot dead by the IRA at Rasharkin, Co. Antrim. He is the first member of the new regiment to be murdered.

21 October A 200 lb IRA bomb destroys the main street of Bangor.

30 October A 250 lb IRA bomb explodes at Glengormley RUC station in Co. Antrim, injuring thirteen people and damaging almost two hundred houses.

In London the IRA force a taxi driver to take a bomb close to Downing Street, where it explodes.

3 November The Belfast unit of the IPLO announces that it is disbanding after one of its members has been killed and eight wounded by the IRA in a series of attacks three days earlier. On 7 November the Dublin-based Army Council faction of the IPLO also announces that it is disbanding.

6 November After the series of IRA bombs that have damaged Protestant homes, the UFF says it will retaliate by extending its campaign to 'the entire republican community'.

In Dublin the coalition government collapses after the Progressive Democrats refuse to support a vote of confidence. The Taoiseach, Albert Reynolds, had accused the PD leader, Des O'Malley, of not telling the truth to an investigation into the misuse of government funds in beef subsidies.

9 November The Ulster Unionists table a series of proposals in an attempt to stop the talks process collapsing. They include a Bill of Rights for

Northern Ireland to protect minorities. Nationalists would have a 'meaningful role' in the administration of Northern Ireland, and, given 'the reality that a significant proportion of the Roman Catholic community in Northern Ireland may aspire to a united Ireland,' there should be an 'Inter-Irish Relations Committee' formally linking members of the Assembly and the Dáil. In return, the Unionists want Dublin 'to define a means whereby the aggressive and irredentist Articles 2 and 3 in the Irish Constitution would be removed.' From the SDLP they seek 'a de facto commitment to a Northern Ireland where all constitutional parties would be able to play a meaningful role.'

10 November As the Maryfield secretariat begins work for the forthcoming meeting of the Anglo-Irish Conference, Unionists withdraw from the talks process. Sir Patrick Mayhew says that informal party contacts will continue. Sir Ninian Stephen, the independent chairman, reports in diplomatic fashion that 'the talks have not resulted in a comprehensive accommodation in relation to the deep-seated and long-standing problems they have been addressing.' After two years and at a cost of £5 million, the talks have served only to emphasise the seemingly irreconcilable differences between nationalism and unionism.

It is revealed that a loyalist terrorist group, the 'Red Branch Knights', have threatened to kill Mayhew, because of his involvement with the Anglo-Irish Agreement.

The Failure of the Brooke-Mayhew Talks

The failure of the talks process, though widely signalled in advance by many of its participants, was a deep disappointment for the British government. Ironically, British pressure on unionism since the Anglo-Irish Agreement appeared to have worked. The UUP had made the symbolic trip to Dublin at which the DUP had baulked. They had also moved significantly during the talks process itself, in effect conceding in principle both power-sharing and an Irish dimension—but this movement by the Unionists did not lead to a deal with the SDLP. The SDLP remained wedded throughout the process to its original 'European model', which suggested one EC, one Dublin and one London nominee on a six-member Northern Ireland executive commission. Moreover, the proposed parliamentary assembly was to be modelled on the European Parliament: that is to say, it was to be a largely advisory body, without a legislative role and with no effective control over the executive. These proposals, predictably, found no favour with the UUP and DUP; less predictably, they found no favour with the Alliance Party or the British government. Few observers in Brussels believed that the EC was keen to play such a role. The talks were also deadlocked on the issue of articles 2 and 3 of the Constitution of Ireland.

As the talks collapsed, press briefings by the NIO referred to the possibility of a change in the SDLP's attitude when the party's ordinary membership realised how much was on offer. Such a development was, however, rather unlikely. The Anglo-Irish Agreement had created a context in which it became logical—almost compellingly so—for constitutional nationalists and the British Labour Party to argue for a form of joint authority, perhaps with a European dimension. It has to be understood too that the collapse of the 1974 experiment made it very difficult for the SDLP to trust Unionists. There remained too the reality of the Provisional IRA's campaign. At the end of twenty-five years of the Troubles it can be seen that there was a new subtlety in political discourse. Mainstream unionists now conceded ground on power-sharing and the Irish dimension, while constitutional nationalists aimed for joint authority rather than a united Ireland. Nevertheless a widely acceptable solution was not yet in sight: indeed, the 'power-sharing plus Irish dimension' plan that had magnetised so many people of good will was, temporarily at least, losing its political relevance.

12 November The NIO announces that it is introducing 'goals and timetables' in an effort to promote the number of Catholics in higher civil service posts. At the same time it says that these are not quotas (which are illegal), and there will be no preferential treatment on grounds of religion, political opinion, or sex. On 11 December the NIO sets a target of 25 per cent of the 152 most senior civil service posts to be held by Catholics by the end of 1996. The government estimates that the present figure is 17 per cent.

13 November A 500 lb IRA bomb destroys the central shopping area of the mainly Protestant town of Coleraine.

14 November In an incident similar to that of February, three Catholic men are shot dead by the UFF at a bookmaker's shop on the Oldpark Road in north Belfast.

In London the Metropolitan Police stop an IRA attempt to plant a 1,000 lb bomb. A policeman is wounded and one man is captured during the incident. The following day an IRA attempt to plant another 1,000 lb bomb at Britain's tallest building at Canary Wharf, London, is foiled by security men.

16 November The first meeting of the Anglo-Irish Conference since April is held in Dublin and is dominated by the deteriorating security situation.

23 November With the IRA bombing campaign continuing, many towns begin closing security gates for the first time since the seventies. It is also announced that security barriers are being erected on the main roads leading into Lisburn.

25 November Voters in the Republic go to the polls in a general election. The election is a triumph for the Labour Party, which doubles its vote and its representation in the Dáil, though it remains only the third-largest party. Support for both Fianna Fáil and Fine Gael drops by approximately 5 per cent.

Controversy surrounds the killing of an unarmed IRA man by the RUC on the Falls Road in Belfast. The man had allegedly just left a bomb-making factory but was not carrying any explosives when he was shot dead.

1 December Two small IRA bombs injure twenty-five people in Belfast city centre. The following day there are forty-six bomb scares in the city and in Lisburn. An IRA attempt to explode a large van bomb in Tottenham Court Road in the centre of London is foiled when the bomb is defused by the police.

3 December Two bombs explode in Manchester, injuring more than sixty people.

4 December A report from Sir John May, a retired judge of the Court of Appeal, into the wrongful convictions of the Maguire family is published. It criticises the Home Office for being too 'reactive' in relation to calls for the Maguire case to be referred back to the Court of Appeal and calls for a new tribunal—independent of the Home Office—to review alleged miscarriages of justice.

7 December It is revealed that the Ulster Unionists on Belfast City Council have proposed a plan to involve all parties except Sinn Féin on its committees, with membership proportional to the total number of city councillors. Chairmanships and vice-chairmanships (but not the positions of Lord Mayor and Deputy Lord Mayor) will also be awarded on a proportional basis. Later, SDLP members leave a meeting with Unionists over their refusal to rotate the post of Lord Mayor.

10 December Despite increased security checks, violence increases in the period before Christmas. A Belfast City Council worker is wounded in an INLA murder attempt, IRA incendiaries damage three buildings in a Belfast industrial estate, and the UFF explodes seven incendiaries in shops in Dublin and in towns close to the border. A statement says: 'Sheer luck prevented our operation from bringing you a fiery Christmas. You will not be so lucky in 1993. We will bring 1993 in with a bang.'

In London two IRA bombs explode at a shopping complex at Wood Green, injuring eleven people, including five policemen.

13 December In Belfast, loyalists fire a rocket at an area of Crumlin Road Prison that they believe republican prisoners are using at the time. No-one is injured. They claim the attack is in retaliation for the deaths of two loyalists in a republican explosion in the prison in 1991.

16 December In a controversial speech at Coleraine, Sir Patrick Mayhew says that soldiers could be withdrawn from the streets and that Sinn Féin could be included in future talks if the IRA ends its campaign.

Two small bombs explode in London, injuring four people.

24 December The IRA calls a three-day cease-fire.

31 December The UDA issues a statement saying that it will intensify its campaign 'to a ferocity never imagined.'

DEATHS ARISING FROM THE TROUBLES: 85. SHOOTINGS: 506. BOMBS PLANTED: 371. INCENDIARIES: 126. FIREARMS FOUND: 194. EXPLOSIVES FOUND: 2,167 kg (4,775 lb). PERSONS CHARGED WITH TERRORIST AND SERIOUS PUBLIC ORDER OFFENCES: 418. CASUALTIES ARISING FROM PARAMILITARY ATTACKS: 207.

1993

3 January Patrick Shields and his son Diarmuid are murdered by the UVF in Pomeroy, Co. Tyrone. Several weeks later Diarmuid Shields's girl-friend commits suicide because she cannot come to terms with his death.

12 January The *Times* (London) reports that the UDA plans to attack a 'pan-nationalist front', regarded as including the SDLP, the GAA and members of the Irish government as well as Sinn Féin and the IRA.

In the Republic the Labour Party and Fianna Fáil agree to form a coalition government.

21 January In a letter to John Hume, John Major rejects a request for a new independent inquiry into Bloody Sunday but adds: 'The government made clear in 1974 that those who were killed on "Bloody Sunday" should be regarded as innocent of any allegation that they were shot whilst handling firearms or explosives' (*Irish Times*, 23 January 1993).

5 February Lieutenant-General Roger Wheeler replaces Sir John Wilsey as army commander in Northern Ireland.

24 February John Major meets President Clinton in Washington for discussions on a range of issues, including a proposed 'peace envoy' for Northern Ireland. Major opposes the idea of a peace envoy but is more tolerant of the idea of sending a representative on a 'fact-finding' mission to report to Clinton on Northern Ireland.

26 February Three IRA bombs planted at a gas works in Warrington, Cheshire, cause a massive explosion; a fourth bomb fails to explode. Earlier a policeman is wounded when he stops a car in the same area. Two men are later arrested.

2 March In a speech in Bangor the Secretary of State for Northern Ireland, Sir Patrick Mayhew, attempts to calm unionist fears aroused by a speech in Coleraine in December 1992 that suggested that Britain was 'neutral' on the issue of Northern Ireland's position within the United Kingdom by saying that this could only be changed by the will of a majority of its people.

7 March A 500 lb IRA bomb causes severe damage to the main street of Bangor, five months after a terrorist bomb destroyed the other half of the street. Four RUC men are injured, and the cost of the damage is estimated at £2 million.

10 March In the House of Commons the Labour Party votes against the continuation of the Prevention of Terrorism Act. It had previously abstained on the vote.

20 March Three-year-old Jonathan Ball is killed and fifty-six people injured when two IRA bombs explode in a shopping centre in Warrington, Cheshire. On 25 March twelve-year-old Timothy Parry dies as a result of injuries. The incident creates a wave of revulsion throughout Britain and Ireland against terrorist killings.

25 March Four Catholic building workers are shot dead by the UFF and a fifth wounded as they arrive for work in Castlerock, Co. Derry. The IRA later says that one of those killed was a member of their organisation. In the evening the UFF murder a Catholic teenager and injure another on the outskirts of Belfast.

26 March The RUC discovers five tons of fertiliser suitable for making bombs near the scene of one of the previous day's murders in west Belfast. On 30 March a further ton of fertiliser capable of being used to make bombs is found in the same area. This is believed to be the last of a large quantity of material stolen in the Republic.

1 April In a speech on Northern Ireland aimed at nationalist opinion, Albert Reynolds defends the Constitution of Ireland and says that it 'took the gun out of politics on this side of the Border.' He also says: 'All Irish people now want another framework that will take the bomb and bullet out of the politics of the entire island ... Any attempt in a political vacuum to walk away from constitutional republicanism would be a very dangerous exercise and would most certainly provide a new recruiting platform for terrorism' (*Dáil Debates,* vol. 429, col. 19–20) Unionists perceive the Taoiseach's speech as closing the door on any meaningful talks, while Gerry Adams says Reynolds needs to seek an agreement with London to end partition.

10 April John Hume and Gerry Adams meet for talks in Derry. It is the first time in two years that the parties have had official discussions.

23 April An IRA bomb damages a tank at an oil terminal in North Shields, Northumberland.

24 April An IRA bomb containing over a ton of fertiliser-based explosive detonates at the NatWest Tower in the centre of London, killing one person, injuring over thirty, and causing damage estimated at over £1,000 million.

After their second meeting in two weeks, John Hume and Gerry Adams issue a joint statement that says that 'the Irish people as a whole have a right to national self-determination. This is a view shared by a majority of the people of this island, though not by all its people. The exercise of self-determination is a matter for agreement between the people of Ireland. It is the search for that agreement and the means of achieving it on which we will be concentrating. We are mindful that not all the people of Ireland share that view or agree on how to give meaningful expression to it. Indeed we do not disguise the different views held by our own parties. As leaders of our respective parties, we have told each other that we see the task of reaching agreement on a peaceful and democratic accord for all on this island as our primary challenge' (*Irish News,* 26 April 1993).

30 April Five people are wounded in a sectarian attack by the UFF on a bookmaker's shop in Belfast. Only the fact that one of the gunmen's rifles jams prevents more injuries.

19 May District council elections return 197 Ulster Unionists, with 29.3 per cent of the first-preference vote (compared with 194 seats and 31.3 per cent in 1989), 103 DUP councillors with 17.3 per cent of the vote (110 and 17.7 per cent in 1989), 127 SDLP with 22.0 per cent (121 and 21.4 per cent), 51 Sinn Féin with 12.4 per cent (43 and 11.2 per cent in 1989), 44 Alliance with 7.6 per cent (38 seats and 6.9 per cent), six Conservatives with 1.5 per cent (seven and 1.0 per cent). The turn-out is 56.7 per cent.

Three former detectives are cleared of the charge of conspiracy to pervert the course of justice by manufacturing the interview notes of one of the Guildford Four.

20 May A 1,000 lb IRA bomb explodes outside the Grand Opera House beside the UUP head office in Belfast. Thirteen people are injured, including a woman and her three children, and an estimated £62 million worth of damage is caused to the surrounding area.

22 May A 1,000 lb IRA van bomb devastates the centre of Portadown, injuring six people and causing £8 million worth of damage. There are further explosions in Belfast and Magherafelt the following day.

27 May President Mary Robinson meets the Queen in Buckingham Palace. It is the first official contact between a British monarch and an Irish president.

Jeremy Hanley is replaced by Michael Ancram at the NIO as part of a government reshuffle.

18 June Mary Robinson faces a storm of protest from unionists after she shakes hands with Gerry Adams during a private reception for community leaders in west Belfast. The British government had advised against the visit.

25 June Sir John Wheeler is appointed to the NIO in succession to Michael Mates. Mates had resigned the previous day following the controversy surrounding his defence of the fugitive businessman Asil Nadir.

26 June On a two-day visit to Northern Ireland, John Major calls for the resumption of talks between constitutional parties.

A member of the UVF, Brian McCallum, is fatally wounded and eighteen others are injured when a grenade explodes during an Orange march that was being held back from the peace line on the Springfield Road, Belfast. On 2 July his funeral is followed by serious rioting in Protestant areas of Belfast, Bangor, and Lurgan.

28 June It emerges that a 1992 Labour Party discussion document, which had been supported by the party's spokesman on Northern Ireland, Kevin McNamara, suggested that local parties be given six months to agree a form of devolved administration; if the parties failed to reach agreement, the British and Irish governments would then begin talks aimed at bringing about joint British-Irish authority over the North. Options for a Labour Party government include joint sovereignty, which would last for twenty years and would be supported by a three-person panel elected from within Northern Ireland. The proposals are generally welcomed by nationalists but rejected outright by unionists.

A grenade attack on an Orange parade on the Shankill Road, Belfast, leaves thirty people injured.

4 July In an interview with the *Sunday Tribune,* Gerry Adams says republicans might be prepared to accept joint authority as 'part of the process towards an end to partition.'

5 July A 1,500 lb IRA bomb explodes in Newtownards.

15 July A UVF statement admits that the organisation carried out the Dublin and Monaghan bombings in May 1974, in which thirty-three people died.

22 July Ulster Unionists support the Conservative government in a vote of confidence over the 'social chapter' of the Maastricht Treaty. John Major says that no deal has been done with the UUP, but Rev. Martin Smyth MP says that he expects a House of Commons Select Committee on Northern Ireland to be established soon.

8 August The UFF murders the son of a Sinn Féin councillor, Bobby Lavery, at his home on the Antrim Road, Belfast.

13 August Six IRA incendiary devices explode in Bournemouth, England. The town's pier is also damaged by an IRA bomb.

22 August A *Sunday Times* report suggests that a sixty-point peace plan had been drawn up by the British army late in 1992 but that no action had been taken because the IRA had rejected pressure from Sinn Féin leaders for an extended Christmas cease-fire.

25 August The 'Red Hand Commando' states that it will attack bars or hotels holding folk music nights, saying that the music is part of the 'pan-nationalist front'. The organisation withdraws the threat the following day.

1 September The UVF murders a Catholic van driver in east Belfast and a prison officer at his home in the north of the city. On the following day the UVF threatens to kill more prison officers unless there are reforms in prison conditions. The threat is withdrawn on 10 September.

3 September The centre of Armagh is severely damaged by a 1,000 lb IRA bomb.

7 September An independent American delegation led by a former congressman, Bruce Morrison, arrives in Ireland for a fact-finding visit, which coincides with a week-long lull in IRA activity.

11 September In a speech to the British-Irish Association in Newnham College, Cambridge, Sir Patrick Mayhew attempts to relaunch inter-party talks, saying that the objectives of the talks process remain valid and that their success remains a possibility.

16 September After a meeting with John Major in London, John Hume says that he does not 'give two balls of roasted snow' for critics of his continuing talks with Gerry Adams.

25 September John Hume and Gerry Adams say they have agreed to forward a report on the position of their discussions to Dublin for consideration. As Hume flies to Boston the following day the Hume-Adams statement is greeted with scepticism by the British and Irish governments and hostility from unionists. Hume urges critics to suspend immediate judgment and in Boston creates some confusion by saying that no report has yet been sent to the Irish government.

27 September An *Irish Times* report claims that the Hume-Adams agreement calls on the British government to declare that it has no long-term interest in Ireland and that it will actively pursue unionist consent for a united Ireland. IRA violence would be ended if the government made a formal declaration that the Irish people as a whole had a right to national self-determination.

A 300 lb IRA car bomb explodes in Belfast city centre, causing widespread damage. Later in the day a 500 lb bomb causes extensive damage in south Belfast.

2 October Three IRA bombs explode in Hampstead, north London, damaging a number of shops and flats. On 4 October another five devices explode in north London, injuring four people.

6 October The UFF murders a Catholic man and wounds two others in a bar in west Belfast. The UFF claims the attack is in response to the Hume-Adams talks and the 'pan-nationalist' front. A bomb planted by the UVF explodes outside a Sinn Féin office on the Falls Road, Belfast.

7 October In London the trial of three former policemen accused of perjury and conspiracy to pervert the course of justice in the case of the Birmingham Six is terminated because of what the judge describes as the 'saturation' publicity surrounding the trial.

10 October A statement by the Ulster Unionist MP Martin Smyth that Sinn Féin could join political talks if it openly rejected violence leads to a dispute among members of the party.

16 October At the UUP annual conference, Molyneaux says that the Hume-Adams proposals seek 'to determine Ulster's future outside the United Kingdom.' He says: 'When fellow-travellers end their exploitation, intimidation and racketeering and all arms and explosives are surrendered then there will be a lengthy period of quarantine before access to the democratic processes can be even considered.'

22 October In the House of Commons, John Hume says his talks with Gerry Adams provide 'the most hopeful dialogue and the most hopeful chance of lasting peace that I have seen in twenty years.' He calls on the British and Irish governments to 'hurry up and deal with it' (*Hansard,* sixth series, vol. 230, col. 530).

23 October An IRA bomb explodes in a fish shop on the Shankill Road, Belfast, killing ten people and injuring fifty-seven. Those killed include the owner of the shop and his daughter, and one of the bombers, Thomas Begley. The Provisional IRA says the bomb was intended to kill members of the UFF, who, they claim, were meeting in a room in the former UDA office above the shop.

26 October Two Catholic workmen are shot dead and five others wounded in a UFF gun attack in west Belfast.

27 October In the Dáil, Dick Spring proposes a list of six 'democratic principles' that he believes will produce a sustainable peace. The Northern Ireland situation should not be changed by the use, or threat, of violence; any political settlement must depend on freely given consent; there can be no talks between the governments and those who use, threaten or support violence; there can be no secret agreements with organisations supporting violence as a price for its cessation; those claiming to advance peace should renounce the use or support of violence for good; if violence was renounced and sufficiently demonstrated 'new doors could open' and the governments would wish to respond 'imaginatively' (*Dáil Debates,* vol. 435, col. 257). On 29 October, Sir Patrick Mayhew describes the Spring principles as 'very reassuring'.

Gerry Adams is widely condemned after he helps carry the coffin of the Shankill bomber Thomas Begley.

28 October Two brothers, Gerard and Rory Cairns, are murdered by the UVF at their home near Lurgan.

29 October After a meeting in Brussels, John Major and Albert Reynolds present a six-point statement (similar to the Spring principles) containing details of what they see as the prerequisites for peace. They describe John Hume's efforts as 'courageous and imaginative' but say they will not adopt or endorse the Hume-Adams proposals.

30 October Two UFF gunmen enter the Rising Sun bar in Greysteel, Co. Londonderry, and fire at random at customers celebrating Halloween. Seven people are killed and thirteen wounded. The UFF claims it attacked the 'nationalist electorate', in revenge for the Shankill bombing.

Twenty-seven people die as a result of the Troubles during October, the greatest number in any month since October 1976.

1 November In the House of Commons the Labour Party MP Dennis Skinner remarks that 'people outside Parliament understand only too well that the government have dealt with terrorists over the decades.' John Major replies: 'If the implication of his remarks is that we should sit down and talk with Mr Adams and the Provisional IRA, I can only say that that would turn my stomach and those of most honourable members; we will not do it' (*Hansard,* sixth series, vol. 231, col. 35).

4 November After a meeting with John Major in London, John Hume says that there could be peace within a week if his proposals were accepted.

15 November At the Guildhall in London, John Major says that terrorists have to be persuaded to end violence unconditionally and choose the path of democratic political activity. 'Some would deny them that path on account of their past and present misdeeds. I understand that feeling, but I do not share it ... But if the IRA end violence for good, then—after a sufficient interval to ensure the permanence of their intent—Sinn Féin can enter the political arena as a democratic party and join the dialogue on the way ahead ... There can be no secret deals, no rewards for terrorism, no abandonment of the vital principle of majority consent.'

19 November The *Irish Press* leaks a secret plan for the future of Northern Ireland drawn up by officials of the Department of Foreign Affairs. It calls on the British government 'to acknowledge the full legitimacy and value of the goal of Irish unity by agreement.' In return the Irish government would accept that constitutional change in the North could only come about with the agreement of a majority within Northern Ireland. There should be joint North-South administrative bodies with executive powers. New executive and legislative structures should include measures to promote the acceptance by representatives of both communities of each other's rights. The Anglo-Irish Agreement would be expanded by having representatives of agreed political institutions in Northern Ireland formally associated with the Anglo-Irish Conference, which 'will be the forum for both governments to jointly guarantee and monitor the commitment ... that such institutions will provide for the equitable and effective participation in power of representatives of both communities.' If devolved institutions were to fail, the Conference would have powers to intervene.

Reacting to the proposals, the Ulster Unionist MP David Trimble says that Unionists 'will not be party to the marginalisation of the unionist community.'

22 November A press statement from the loyalist paramilitaries' co-ordinating body, the CLMC, says that they are earnestly seeking peace 'in accordance with the overwhelming desire of the population.' However, they also warn that they are preparing for war if peace is 'bought at any price.'

24 November Customs officers at Teesport, Yorkshire, discover 300 assault rifles, 4,400 lb of explosives with detonators and thousands of bullets aboard a Polish container ship. The weapons, valued at £250,000, were intended for the UVF.

After a meeting with the Prime Minister in London, Ian Paisley says that Major had told him that if he had received the Irish Foreign Affairs document he would have 'kicked it over the house-tops.' The DUP MP William McCrea, who attended the meeting, is believed to have already received documentary evidence of contacts between government officials and Sinn Féin.

28 November The *Observer* reveals that the British government has had a secret channel of communication with Sinn Féin and the IRA for three years and has been in regular contact since February. Sir Patrick Mayhew claims that contacts had developed as a result of an oral message from the IRA leadership received on 22 February that stated: 'The conflict is over but we need your advice on how to bring it to a close. We wish to have an unannounced cease-fire in order to hold dialogue leading to peace. We cannot announce such a move as it will lead to confusion for the volunteers, because the press will misinterpret it as a surrender. We cannot meet the Secretary of State's public renunciation of violence, but it would be given privately as long as we were sure we were not being tricked' (*Hansard,* sixth series, vol. 233, col. 785). Mayhew says that the government made a substantive response on 19 March, stating that 'any dialogue would follow an unannounced halt to violent activity. We confirm that if violence had genuinely been brought to an end, whether or not that fact had been announced, then dialogue could take place.' An IRA reply on 10 May did not provide the unequivocal assurance the British sought. Mayhew claims that an IRA message of 2 November stated: 'In plain language please tell us through the link as a matter of urgency when you will open dialogue in the event of a total end to hostilities. We believe that if all the documents involved are put on the table ... we have the basis of an understanding.' (*Hansard,* sixth series, vol. 233, col. 786). A British response on 5

November stated: 'If, as you have offered, you were to give us an unequivocal assurance that violence has indeed been brought to a permanent end, and that accordingly Sinn Féin is now committed to political progress by peaceful and democratic means alone, we will make clear publicly our commitment to enter exploratory dialogue with you. Our public statement will make clear that, provided your private assurance is promptly confirmed publicly after our public statement and that events on the ground are fully consistent with this, a first meeting for exploratory dialogue will take place within a week of Parliament's return in January' (*Hansard,* sixth series, vol. 233, col. 787).

Gerry Adams denies that republicans initiated contacts with the British government. On 28 June 1998 the *Observer* claims that a former Catholic priest, Denis Bradley, had acted as a contact between republicans and the British and Irish governments over a period of twenty years. It also says that Bradley was the author of the message received by the British government on 22 February 1993. Sinn Féin consistently denies that it sent the message.

Loyalists claim that there have been contacts between Protestant paramilitaries and the Irish government since the spring.

29 November Sir Patrick Mayhew faces only limited criticism of his policy of maintaining secret contacts with Sinn Féin when he defends his position in the House of Commons. Ian Paisley is ordered to leave the chamber after accusing Mayhew of telling a lie (*Hansard,* sixth series, vol. 233, col. 790).

Sinn Féin publishes a set of documents that it says have been exchanged with the British government over the previous months. Martin McGuinness says that the message of 22 February is a fake and that the British are 'counterfeiting their own documents to meet their current needs.' On 1 December, Mayhew admits that there are twenty-two inaccuracies in the British version of the documents covering contacts with republicans.

2 December Sinn Féin issues a further set of documents concerning contacts with the government. Martin McGuinness says that the British government initiated contact with Sinn Féin in 1990. In 1992 his party had been briefed on the state of inter-party talks by the British, and in 1993 the British had sought fuller discussions with Sinn Féin representatives. On 19 March 1993 Sinn Féin received a position paper from the British. On 10 May the British government was informed that the IRA would call a fourteen-day suspension of operations to enable talks to take place. According to Sinn

Féin, the British government was hesitant about deeper involvement, because it was 'under siege'. Later leaks also led the government to give a limited briefing on the talks to the UUP.

In July, Sinn Féin passed on its response (drawn up in April) to the British communication of 19 March, in which it outlined the conditions under which it would enter negotiations. After this, Sinn Féin says that exchanges became less frequent. On 5 November it received a document from the British government that purported to be a response to a message from Sinn Féin three days earlier. Sinn Féin immediately repudiated the authenticity of the communication of 2 November (*Setting the Record Straight*).

5 December Two Catholic men are shot dead by the UFF outside a taxi depot in north Belfast. On 7 December the UFF murder another Catholic man at his home in east Belfast.

12 December Two RUC men are shot dead by the IRA in Fivemiletown, Co. Tyrone.

15 December In London, John Major and Albert Reynolds issue a Joint Declaration on Northern Ireland. The governments commit themselves to work towards a new political framework founded on consent and encompassing arrangements within Northern Ireland, for the whole of Ireland, and between Britain and Ireland (para. 2). The British government says it has 'no selfish strategic or economic interest in Northern Ireland.' Its primary interest is to see peace, stability and reconciliation established by agreement among all the people of Ireland, and they will work together with the Irish government to achieve such an agreement, which will embrace the 'totality of relationships'.

The role of the British government will be to encourage, facilitate and enable the achievement of such agreement over a period through a process of dialogue and co-operation based on full respect for the rights and identities of both traditions in Ireland. It accepts that such agreement may, as of right, take the form of agreed structures for Ireland as a whole, including a united Ireland achieved by peaceful means on the following basis.

The British government agrees that it is for the people of Ireland alone, by agreement between the two parts, to exercise their right of self-determination on the basis of consent, freely and concurrently given, North and South, to bring about a united Ireland, if that is their wish. It reaffirms as a binding obligation that it will, for its part, introduce the necessary legislation to give effect to this, or equally to any measure of agreement on future relationships in Ireland that the people living in Ireland may themselves freely so determine without external impediment (para. 4).

For the Irish government, the Taoiseach accepts that 'the democratic right of self-determination by the people of Ireland as a whole must be achieved and exercised with and subject to the agreement and consent of a majority of the people of Northern Ireland' (para. 5). Recognising unionist fears, the Taoiseach agrees to examine 'elements in the democratic life and organisation of the Irish State that can be represented to the Irish Government in the course of political dialogue as a real and substantial threat to their way of life and ethos, or that can be represented as not being fully consistent with a modern democratic and pluralist society, and undertakes to examine any possible ways of removing such obstacles' (para. 6). He also confirms that if there is an overall settlement, his government will put forward proposals for change in the Constitution of Ireland that would reflect the principle of consent in Northern Ireland (para. 7).

There will be 'institutional recognition' of the links between the people of Britain and Ireland as part of the 'totality of relationships' (para. 9).

Both governments confirm that 'democratically mandated parties which establish a commitment to exclusively peaceful methods and which have shown that they abide by the democratic process, are free to participate fully in democratic politics and to join in dialogue in due course between the Governments and the political parties on the way ahead' (para. 10). The Taoiseach also suggests that democratic parties consult together about the political future in a Forum for Peace and Reconciliation, to be held in the Republic (para. 11).

In the House of Commons, Major attempts to reassure unionists by saying that the declaration 'reaffirms the constitutional guarantee in the clearest possible terms.' He also states: 'What is not in the declaration is any suggestion that the British Government should join the ranks of persuaders of the "value" or "legitimacy" of a united Ireland; that is not there. Nor is there any suggestion that the future status of Northern Ireland should be decided by a single act of self-determination by the people of Ireland as a whole; that is not there either. Nor is there any timetable for constitutional change, or any arrangement for joint authority over Northern Ireland. In sum, the declaration provides that it is, as it must be, for the people of Northern Ireland to determine their own future' (*Hansard,* sixth series, vol. 234 col. 1072–3).

In the Dáil, Dick Spring says that an end to violence would involve paramilitaries handing over their arms. 'Questions were raised on how to determine a permanent cessation of violence. We are talking about the handing up of arms and are insisting that it would not be simply a temporary cessation of violence to see what the political process offers' (*Dáil Debates,* vol. 437, col. 776). This point is later reiterated by Sir Patrick Mayhew when he states: 'If they hold on to arms, if you know they have got them, then quite patently they are not giving up for good.'

The Downing Street Declaration

It has to be conceded that there was no hint of the Downing Street Declaration in Sir Patrick Mayhew's strategy speech to the British-Irish Association in Cambridge on 11 September. His emphasis there was on the renewal of the talks process, involving the mainstream constitutional parties—not on the need to draw the 'men of violence' into the political process. Yet by December the Downing Street Declaration appeared, with precisely this objective.

To explain this shift of emphasis, it is helpful to turn to the words of Martin Mansergh, then the principal adviser to Albert Reynolds. 'In June 1993, not without much soul-searching on the republican side, the draft [of a 'formula for peace'] was handed over to the British government by the Taoiseach. To say they handled it with kid gloves would be something of an understatement. They were prepared to discuss, but not negotiate it, and on several occasions in the autumn of 1993 many of them would have preferred to set it aside. But an initiative that might bring peace was always going to be more important than attempts to restart inter-party talks or even early discussions of the Framework Document' ('The background to the peace process', *Irish Studies in International Affairs,* 1995, p. 154).

The Irish government clearly had a different agenda—based on the belief that the Adams leadership was sincerely interested in peace, in which both the Downing Street Declaration and the *Irish Press* leak of 19 November played a key part. It is a tribute, however, to British adroitness that they accommodated a highly persistent Irish strategy while retaining the support of the Molyneaux Unionists. In part this was achieved by allowing Molyneaux and other unionists a contribution to the text. Indeed, in concert with Albert Reynolds, Archbishop Robin Eames helped to draft paragraphs 6–8 of the declaration.

The Downing Street Declaration proved to be a document of considerable originality and sophistication. For unionists it formalised a distasteful message—albeit one already sent by Peter Brooke in 1990: 'the Prime Minister ... reiterates on behalf of the British government that they have no selfish strategic or economic interest in Northern Ireland.' In truth, though, only in the brief aftermath of the Second World War had the belief in a 'selfish strategic interest' really existed in London.

The real novelty of the Downing Street Declaration lay elsewhere. It is necessary at this point to consider the complex language of the declaration's fourth paragraph. After the declaration, the phraseology of the Hume-Adams agreement continued to dominate the political scene, but its content was dramatically altered. One of the most effective slogans of Irish nationalism had been given a new, decidedly softer, conceptual content; and this had been done by a Fianna Fáil government. The self-determination of the Irish people was conceded by Britain, but solely on the basis that the Irish Government only wished to operate that principle in favour of Irish unity with the support of a majority in the North.

Superficially, the rhetoric of the Hume-Adams process had been conceded but, in essence, the process had been stripped of its content in a quite dramatic way. The British, it is true, were now 'facilitators'—not for Irish unity but for an agreed Ireland; and an 'agreed' Ireland, by definition, could not be a united Ireland until there was majority consent in the North. 'The role of the British government will be to encourage, facilitate and enable the achievement of such agreement over a period through a process of dialogue and co-operation based on full respect for the rights and identities of both traditions in Ireland.'

As Martin Mansergh explained later, 'the British government wish to promote enough political agreement to prevent the two communities from fighting each other and harming British interests ... They had made it clear that they will not be persuaders for a united Ireland nor do they wish to see it come about' (*Irish Times,* 3 July 1995).

20 December In a radio interview, Molyneaux rejects the proposition that the Downing Street Declaration represents a 'sell out' of unionists.

21 December Gerry Adams calls for 'direct and unconditional dialogue' with the British and Irish governments and says that the Downing Street Declaration 'needs to be clarified.'

23 December The IRA announces a three-day cease-fire, to begin at midnight.

Two members of the Royal Marines are acquitted of the murder of the Sinn Féin member Fergal Caraher in Cullyhanna, Co. Armagh, in December 1990.

28 December About four hundred republican activists meet in Loughmacrory, Co. Tyrone, to discuss the Downing Street Declaration. None of those present is believed to have supported the Declaration.

30 December The UVF says that it will not support another 'publicity stunt' by Ian Paisley, and that it does not feel threatened by the Downing Street Declaration.

DEATHS ARISING FROM THE TROUBLES: 84. SHOOTINGS: 476. BOMBS PLANTED: 289. INCENDIARIES: 61. FIREARMS FOUND: 196. EXPLOSIVES FOUND: 3,944 kg (8,695 lb). PERSONS CHARGED WITH TERRORIST AND SERIOUS PUBLIC ORDER OFFENCES: 372. CASUALTIES ARISING FROM PARAMILITARY ATTACKS: 126.

1994

5 January The NIO Minister of State Robert Atkins is replaced by the Under-Secretary Tim Smith. On 11 January the Earl of Arran is replaced by Baroness Denton, the first woman to serve as a minister in the NIO.

7 January Gerry Adams writes to John Major seeking clarification of the Downing Street Declaration. On 20 January, Major's private secretary replies, saying 'there can be no question of renegotiation' of the Joint Declaration, which provides 'a balanced framework for peace and democracy.'

8 January In an *Irish News* interview, Gerry Adams criticises Sir Patrick Mayhew's post-declaration statement that talks between the government and Sinn Féin will concern decommissioning, commenting: 'This is what they want. They want the IRA to stop so that Sinn Féin can have the privilege twelve weeks later, having been properly sanitised and come out of quarantine, to have discussions with senior civil servants on how the IRA can hand over their weapons.'

11 January The Irish government announces that the order banning Sinn Féin from radio and television will not be renewed. The ban lapses at midnight on 19 January.

27 January In London, IRA incendiary devices detonate in three shops in Oxford Street. A further fire-bomb explodes in the same area the following day, while others are defused on 28 and 29 January.

29 January President Clinton authorises a 'limited-duration' visa for Gerry Adams. The decision, supported by the National Security Council and Irish-American politicians, is taken against the advice of the State Department and the British government.

10 February The former INLA leader Dominic McGlinchey is shot dead in Drogheda.

21 February In a BBC television programme Sir Patrick Mayhew confirms that two 'unauthorised' meetings with IRA representatives took place in 1993 but says no official was authorised to say that Britain intended to withdraw eventually from Northern Ireland.

26 February At the Sinn Féin ardfheis Gerry Adams says the Downing Street Declaration is a significant departure in attitude by the British towards Ireland, but, 'having declared that the Irish are entitled to exercise the right to self-determination without external influence, they then proceed, or so it seems to me, to interfere.' To loud applause he adds: 'One also has to ask, does anyone really expect the IRA to cease its activities so that British civil servants can discuss with Sinn Féin the surrender of IRA weapons after we have been "decontaminated"?' (*Irish News,* 28 February 1994).

1 March John Major ends a two-day visit to Washington that is viewed as an attempt to repair the damage caused to Anglo-American relations by the decision to grant a visa to Gerry Adams.

9 March The House of Commons votes to create a Select Committee on Northern Ireland Affairs. It is established on 28 March, with Sir James Kilfedder as chairman.

The IRA fire five mortars from cars parked near Heathrow Airport in London; none of them explodes. On 11 March four more mortars hit Heathrow but fail to explode. An RAF plane with the Queen on board lands while the police are searching the terminal. On 13 March, Heathrow shuts down for two hours after a third IRA mortar attack.

30 March The IRA announces a three-day cease-fire for 6–8 April to demonstrate its sincerity towards the peace process. On a visit to Northern Ireland, John Major says: 'What people in Northern Ireland want is not a cease-fire over two or three days but a permanent end to violence.' The following day Cardinal Cahal Daly says the forthcoming IRA cease-fire shows that republicans are sincere in the search for peace.

6 April Margaret Wright is beaten and shot dead in a loyalist band-hall in the Donegall Road area of Belfast. It is thought that her loyalist killers believed she was a Catholic. On 12 April a UVF member, Ian Hamilton, is shot dead by the organisation, which claims he admitted killing Wright. On 28 September 1995 another loyalist reputed to be connected with the killing is shot dead in Bangor.

21 April The Northern Ireland Lord Chief Justice, Sir Brian Hutton, quashes the conviction of Paul Hill for the murder of a former British soldier in 1974. He declares the conviction 'unsafe and unsatisfactory' and says that the 'inhuman treatment' Hill suffered at Guildford police station may have led him to confess to the murder.

24 April The IRA murders two Protestant men in Garvagh, Co. Londonderry, saying they were UFF members. The claim is denied by the UFF.

8 May Rose Ann Mallon, a 76-year-old Catholic from Co. Tyrone, is shot dead by the UVF at her home near Dungannon. On 27 July surveillance cameras are discovered near the house, leading the family to call for an inquiry.

12 May While he is cradling his one-year-old baby nephew on his shoulder, 23-year-old Martin Bradley is shot dead by a UFF gunman in Belfast. The RUC say he is the victim of mistaken identity.

17 May Two Catholic workmen are shot dead by the UVF at a building site in the Tiger Bay area of Belfast. The following day two more Catholic men are fatally wounded by loyalist gunmen at a taxi office in Armagh.

19 May The NIO issues a 21-page 'commentary' on the twenty questions submitted by Sinn Féin through the Irish government. It says the British government's primary interest is 'to see peace, stability and reconciliation established by agreement among all the people' of Ireland. It accepts the validity of all electoral mandates, including that of Sinn Féin. However, 'all who join in political dialogue should demonstrate a commitment to exclusively peaceful methods and to the democratic process.' Britain will 'encourage, facilitate and enable … a process of dialogue and co-operation based on full respect for the rights and identities of both traditions in Ireland.' It will also introduce legislation 'to give effect to any measure of agreement on future relationships which the people of Ireland may freely determine.' The commentary reiterates the view that 'any change in the constitutional status of Northern Ireland would be subject to the consent of a majority of its people.' Albert Reynolds describes the British response as 'comprehensive and positive.'

21 May An IRA member, Martin Doherty, is shot dead by the UVF during an attack on a bar in Dublin that is holding a republican function.

30 May At a Belfast press conference Rev. Ian Paisley describes James Molyneaux as 'a Judas Iscariot.' On 1 June the UUP leader says Paisley's remark is 'a shattering blow' to unionist unity.

1 June In the Dáil the Minister for Foreign Affairs, Dick Spring, says the key to Sinn Féin joining political discussions is a permanent cessation of violence, and that there will have to be a verification of the handing over of arms (*Dáil Debates,* vol. 443, col. 1021).

2 June A helicopter carrying twenty-five senior anti-terrorist experts crashes in fog on a hillside on the Mull of Kintyre, Argyll; all those aboard are killed. In June 1995 an RAF report states that pilot error was responsible for the crash, but in March 1996 an inquiry concludes that there is no evidence of pilot error. In May 1998 the report of a House of Commons Select Committee on Defence finds 'no compelling evidence' that design failure led to the crash.

9 June In Germany, Paul Hughes and Donna Maguire from Newry and Seán Hick from Dublin are acquitted of the murder of a British army officer in Dortmund in 1990. Hick and Hughes are released, while Maguire is held on further charges. On 28 June 1995 Maguire is sentenced to nine years' imprisonment for involvement in the bombing of a British army barracks in Osnabrück in 1989 but is later released because she had been held on remand for almost four years.

13 June Elections for the European Parliament, held on 9 June, return the three sitting members. Ian Paisley receives 163,246 first-preference votes (29.2 per cent) and John Hume 161,992 (28.9 per cent); both are elected on the first count. An Ulster Unionist, Jim Nicholson, receives 133,459 votes (23.8 per cent) and is elected on the second count. Three Sinn Féin candidates receive 55,215 votes (9.9 per cent), and Alliance receives 23,157 votes (4.1 per cent).

15 June Albert Reynolds sends a letter giving 'clarification' of the Downing Street Declaration to Gary McMichael of the UDP. It states: 'We do not seek to impose constitutional change by stealth or coercion, whether it be a united Ireland, or joint sovereignty or joint authority. What we seek is a new accommodation between the two traditions on this island ... The Irish Government have a strong moral duty towards the Nationalist community in Northern Ireland, because of experience in the past, to ensure that the principles of equal citizenship, equality of treatment and parity of esteem are translated into practice' (*Belfast Telegraph,* 24 June 1994).

16 June Two UVF members and another loyalist are killed and a fourth man wounded in an INLA gun attack on the Shankill Road, Belfast.

18 June UVF gunmen murder six men and wound five others when they open fire on a group of people watching a televised football match at the Heights bar in Loughinisland, Co. Down. Sir Patrick Mayhew says the 'moral squalor' of the killers is beyond description.

24 June John Major and Albert Reynolds hold a meeting during a European Union conference in Corfu. Reynolds says that 'executive boards' might be a better description for the type of North-South bodies he has in mind. A British official says: 'There is no question of imposing a joint authority on some aspects of the government of Northern Ireland.' In what later becomes known among the negotiators as the 'Corfu test', Major insists that the document must contain the removal of the Republic's territorial claim and that Dublin must recognise the 'legitimacy' of Northern Ireland. This 'test' is used by the negotiators on all proposals for changes to the Constitution of Ireland (*Sunday Tribune,* 5 March 1995).

30 June The government announces that nearly forty prisoners are to be transferred from jails in England to Northern Ireland.

10 July The IRA fire forty shots into the home of the DUP MP Rev. William McCrea in Magherafelt.

11 July The UDP spokesman, Ray Smallwoods, is shot dead by the IRA at his home in Lisburn.

12 July A lorry with over 4,000 lb of explosives hidden in false compartments is seized at the port of Heysham, Lancashire. It is believed that the IRA planned to use the explosives in London.

16 July Crumlin Road prison in Belfast is extensively damaged after nearly a hundred loyalist prisoners go on a rampage through the jail.

24 July At a special Sinn Féin ardfheis in Letterkenny, Co. Donegal, Gerry Adams says the Downing Street Declaration 'suggests a potentially significant change in the approach of the governments to resolving the conflict in Ireland, and we welcome this. But it does not deal adequately with some of the core issues, and this is crucial.'

31 July Two leading UDA men are shot dead by the IRA on the Ormeau Road in Belfast.

7 August Kathleen O'Hagan, who is pregnant at the time, is shot dead in front of her children by the UVF in Co. Tyrone.

8 August Trelford Withers, a part-time member of the RIR, is shot and killed by the IRA at his shop in Crossgar, Co. Down.

15 August The leader of Fine Gael, John Bruton, says Sinn Féin cannot be involved in political negotiations until the IRA calls a total cessation of violence. He says that the 'worst possible scenario' would be if the government set strict terms but was forced to relax them under threat of a resumption of violence.

28 August Gerry Adams and John Hume issue a joint statement that says: 'A just and lasting peace in Ireland will only be achieved if it is based on democratic principles. It is clear that an internal settlement is not a solution … If a lasting settlement is to be found there must be fundamental and thoroughgoing change, based on the right of the Irish people as a whole to national self-determination.'

29 August Gerry Adams says he has met the IRA Army Council and has told it that he believes the conditions now exist for moving the peace process forward.

31 August An IRA statement announces: 'Recognising the potential of the current situation and in order to enhance the democratic peace process and underline our definitive commitment to its success the leadership of Óglaigh na hÉireann have decided that as of midnight, Wednesday, 31 August, there will be a complete cessation of military operations. All our units have been instructed accordingly ... We note that the Downing Street Declaration is not a solution, nor was it presented as such by its authors. A solution will only be found as a result of inclusive negotiations. Others, not least the British government, have a duty to face up to their responsibilities. It is our desire to significantly contribute to the creation of a climate which will encourage this. We urge everyone to approach this new situation with energy, determination and patience.'

The announcement is greeted by triumphant celebrations in nationalist areas of Belfast and Derry. The British government, however, is sceptical of the IRA's intentions, as its statement does not refer to a 'permanent' cessation. Albert Reynolds accepts the IRA statement as implying a permanent cease-fire and comments: 'As far as we are concerned, the long nightmare is over.'

Unionists remain highly sceptical. A statement from the CLMC calls on James Molyneaux and Ian Paisley to meet John Major in order to find out 'if the constitution is being tampered with' and 'what deals have been done.' Paisley notes that the IRA has not declared a permanent cessation of violence: 'The only way that you could prove that there would be a permanent cessation is by the surrender of their killing machine, their Semtex [plastic explosive] stores, their guns, their mortars and their equipment.'

In Antrim a Catholic man is abducted and shot dead by the UVF.

Four IRA prisoners are transferred from Britain to jails in Northern Ireland.

The IRA Cease-fire

Was there a secret deal between the British government and the IRA—as so many loyalists alleged—to bring about the cease-fire? There is no doubt that the republican leadership was, rhetorically at least, principally motivated by the idea of a gesture to 'nationalist Ireland'—the Fianna Fáil government, the SDLP, and Irish America. Great emphasis was laid on the ability of this coalition to achieve results. There is also little doubt, however, that the republicans felt that a new agreement was about to be made; and it was one that might exclude them if they remained committed to violence. Albert Reynolds had encouraged this perception, especially in his discussions with them in early August. It seems likely that the republican leadership was aware of the broad contents of the Frameworks Document: central concepts were, after all, widely bruited in the media in mid-August. Ian Paisley pointed out: 'Mr Mallon ... said that the IRA had received a preview of the Framework Document. There we see something of the promises that were being made to the IRA' (*NI Brief,* October 1994)'.

On the other hand, if there was an understanding between the Provisionals and the British government it was inevitably an imperfect one. The British in their private communications had refused all talk of withdrawal. They had also made it absolutely clear publicly that the IRA would have to decommission its arms before the admittance of Sinn Féin to all-party talks—as Gerry Adams fully admitted in his interview with Tom Collins in the *Irish News* in January 1994. There was, therefore, no truth in the claim made later by Garret FitzGerald (*Irish Times,* 8 July 1995) and others that the British had slurred over this matter. Even in the Frameworks Document the understanding was imperfect, for the British withheld their internal government proposals for Northern Ireland from the Irish government—let alone the republican movement—until February 1995. It is doubtful too if they had shared with Adams their commitment to a referendum, as was announced by John Major in September. All in all, the caginess and even surprise that characterised British reaction to the cease-fire probably reflected genuine emotion.

In a way the cease-fire was above all a footnote to the Anglo-Irish Agreement, which was now working in a way no-one had intended. It had given the Irish government a prestigious role in the North, and this allowed it to act as a broker for a cease-fire in a way that was inconceivable a decade earlier. This allowed the republican movement to dilute its cardinal principle, which had been so forcefully articulated at the 1986 Sinn Féin ardfheis by Martin McGuinness: 'Our position is clear and it will never, never, never, change. The war against British rule must continue until freedom is achieved.' But still the question remained: what did the republican movement expect to get out of the peace process? Throughout the whole Hume-Adams process and the secret contacts with the government it had sought a commitment from the British government that it would act as a 'persuader' for Irish unity. Yet at no point does the British government appear to have given such a commitment; still less had it responded to Adams's support for joint authority.

1 September A Catholic man is killed by the UFF in north Belfast.

2 September An opinion poll in the *Belfast Telegraph* suggests that 56 per cent believe that the IRA cease-fire has come about as a result of a secret deal. Only 30 per cent believe the cease-fire is permanent.

Ian Paisley says he will invite other unionist organisations to join the DUP in a pan-unionist forum.

4 September Local people reopen several roads closed by the army along the Fermanagh and Tyrone border. The unofficial reopening of border roads continues in the following weeks.

A UVF car bomb explodes at a Sinn Féin office in west Belfast.

6 September After a meeting in Dublin, Albert Reynolds, John Hume and Gerry Adams issue a joint statement that says: 'We are at the beginning of a new era in which we are totally and absolutely committed to democratic and peaceful methods of resolving our political problems. We reiterate that our objective is an equitable and lasting agreement that can command the allegiance of all.' Andrew Hunter MP, Chairman of the Conservative Party's Committee on Northern Ireland, describes the meeting as a 'disastrous miscalculation' by Reynolds, with 'potentially the most damaging consequences.'

John Major throws Ian Paisley and other DUP members out of his office after the DUP leader refuses to accept his word that he had not made a secret deal with the IRA.

8 September The CLMC sets out a list of issues it requires assurances on before it is prepared to call a cease-fire, including ascertaining the *bona fides* of the permanence of the IRA cease-fire and being convinced that no secret deals have been concocted between the government and the IRA.

As security arrangements begin to be relaxed, British soldiers begin wearing berets instead of helmets while on patrol in Northern Ireland.

The Belfast coroner abandons the inquests into the deaths of the six men killed by the RUC in Armagh in 1982, because of the refusal of the Chief Constable to provide the inquest with the Stalker report.

9 September The Ulster Unionist MP John Taylor says he believes the IRA cease-fire is 'for real.'

10 September There is an attempted escape by six prisoners (including five IRA men) from Whitemoor jail in Cambridgeshire. On 22 September plastic explosive and detonators are found at the prison.

12 September Two people are injured when the detonator of a 3 lb UVF bomb explodes on a Belfast–Dublin train.

16 September During a visit to Belfast, John Major says that any political agreement will be subject to the approval of the people of Northern Ireland through a referendum. He also announces the end of the broadcasting ban on proscribed organisations. Albert Reynolds says that a referendum on the outcome of political talks will also be held in the Republic.

Sir Patrick Mayhew says that ten border roads will be reopened. On 22 September he announces the reopening of six more roads.

18 September In an interview with the *Observer,* Albert Reynolds says the unification of Ireland will not come about 'in this generation'. The statement is generally welcomed by unionists, but Martin McGuinness says nationalists expect that 'this problem can be solved an awful lot quicker than that.'

23 September The United States government grants a visa to Gerry Adams enabling him to make a second trip to America. The former NIO minister Michael Mates also flies to the United States in an attempt to counter the publicity surrounding Adams's visit.

3 October The American government ends its policy of prohibiting contact with Sinn Féin. The following day a Sinn Féin delegation led by Gerry Adams meets senior government officials in Washington. Adams later participates in a television debate with the Ulster Unionist MP Ken Maginnis.

10 October Loyalist leaders are given permission to enter the Maze Prison by the NIO to discuss a cease-fire with loyalist prisoners.

13 October A statement from the CLMC announces: 'After having received confirmation and guarantees in relation to Northern Ireland's constitutional position within the United Kingdom, as well as other assurances, and, in the belief that the democratically expressed wishes of the greater number of people in Northern Ireland will be respected and upheld, the CLMC will universally cease all operational hostilities as from 12 midnight on Thursday the 13th October 1994. The permanence of our cease-fire will be completely dependent upon the continued cessation of all nationalist/republican violence; the sole responsibility for a return to war lies with them. In the genuine hope that this peace will be permanent, we take the opportunity to pay homage to all our fighters, commandos and volunteers who have paid the supreme sacrifice. They did not die in vain. The Union is safe ... In all sincerity, we offer to the loved ones of all innocent victims over the past twenty-five years, abject and true remorse. No words of ours will compensate for the intolerable suffering they have undergone during this conflict. Let us firmly resolve to respect our differing views of freedom, culture and aspiration and never again permit our political circumstances to degenerate into bloody warfare.'

Reacting to the cease-fire, John Major says it is 'another very important part of the jigsaw falling into place.' In the Dáil, Albert Reynolds says: 'This decision effectively signifies the end of twenty-five years of violence, and the closure of a tragic chapter in our history' (*Dáil Debates,* vol. 445, col. 1807).

The Loyalist Cease-fire

The announcement of a cease-fire by the Combined Loyalist Military Command demonstrated a new confidence among loyalist paramilitaries. But while murders committed by the UVF, UFF, Red Hand Commando and others in the early nineties had shown that they could be as ruthless as their republican counterparts (in 1993, for the first time since 1975, loyalists murdered more people than republicans), a new generation of more politically astute spokesmen was beginning to emerge from the parties associated with the loyalist paramilitaries.

The cease-fire statement of October 1994 went beyond the IRA's in two significant aspects. Firstly, the CLMC stated that their cease-fire was dependent on the continued cessation of IRA violence—a position clarified and strengthened in August the following year when the CLMC said there would be no 'first strike' by loyalists. Secondly, they offered an apology 'to the loved ones of all innocent victims over the past twenty-five years.' How significant this apparently newly discovered open-mindedness and their 'abject and true remorse' was would, of course, be determined by the loyalists' future actions.

The reason the loyalists could afford to be magnanimous was clear: as self-appointed defenders of the constitutional status quo their aim was to oppose moves that might lead towards a united Ireland, unlike the IRA, whose objective was to continually exert pressure in order to erode the position of Northern Ireland within the United Kingdom. Thus it was that, in the wake of the IRA cease-fire, loyalists sought reassurances that no secret deal had been done by the two governments with the republicans that would weaken Northern Ireland's position within the United Kingdom. Having been reassured on this point, the CLMC statement could announce that 'the Union is safe.'

The new generation of loyalist political leaders—David Ervine, Billy Hutchinson, and Gary McMichael, as well as Ray Smallwoods (killed by the IRA in July)—had, however, gone some way in moving loyalist pronouncements away from the traditional 'not an inch, no surrender' stance towards a more sophisticated view of Northern Ireland's place within the Union. Crucially, the cease-fire statement noted that they had been assured that 'the democratically expressed wishes of the greater number of people in Northern Ireland will be respected and upheld.'

As with Gerry Adams in America, loyalist leaders would now achieve near-celebrity status in the Republic. PUP and UDP members entered the bastion of their traditional enemies for political discussions as well as for social events. But despite these beneficial developments, the underlying loyalist suspicion of the Republic remained. In June, Albert Reynolds, in his 'clarification' of the Downing Street Declaration to Gary McMichael, noted that the Irish government had 'a strong moral duty towards the Nationalist community in Northern Ireland, because of experience in the past, to ensure that the principles of equal citizenship, equality of treatment and parity of esteem are translated into practice.'

Reynolds, rather than taking the traditional nationalist view, might perhaps have shown the courage he had demonstrated in other areas of the peace process and proclaimed the Irish government to be the defenders of the civil rights of all the citizens of Northern Ireland. Though relations between loyalists and the South might be showing the first signs of a thaw, confidence-building between loyalists and the Irish government clearly still had some way to go.

20 October The NIO minister Tim Smith resigns in the midst of controversy surrounding the paying of MPs by political lobbyists. Smith is replaced by Malcolm Moss the same day.

Marjorie (Mo) Mowlam replaces Kevin McNamara as Labour Party spokesperson on Northern Ireland.

21 October On a two-day visit to Belfast, John Major announces the lifting of exclusion orders on Gerry Adams and Martin McGuinness and the removal of road-blocks on all unapproved roads between Northern Ireland and the Republic. He says he will make a 'working assumption' that the IRA cease-fire is permanent and that preliminary talks with Sinn Féin will begin before Christmas. During his visit he also promises to review the role of the army and to establish an Assembly in Northern Ireland and calls an investment conference for December.

23 October During a visit to London, Martin McGuinness states that IRA violence could return if a satisfactory outcome is not produced by the peace process.

24 October In the United States a six-member loyalist delegation led by Gary McMichael of the UDP and David Ervine of the PUP addresses the National Committee on American Foreign Policy.

28 October Albert Reynolds opens the Forum for Peace and Reconciliation in Dublin. The British ambassador does not attend the opening, because of the presence of Sinn Féin representatives.

A cease-fire is announced by the republican splinter group the 'Catholic Reaction Force'.

30 October In Dublin, Gerry Adams says there are 'clear efforts' by the British government to reduce the momentum of the peace process.

In Belfast, police and residents are involved in scuffles on the Ormeau Road during a protest against the passing of an Orange parade through the area.

1 November President Clinton announces that he intends to call a conference on trade and investment in Ireland in the spring of 1995. The American government also says that it will increase its contribution to the International Fund for Ireland from $20 million to $30 million a year over the next two years.

4 November The deputy leader of the SDLP, Séamus Mallon, calls for the RUC to be split into four local police forces. The Chief Constable, Sir Hugh Annesley, dismisses this suggestion on 10 November.

10 November Frank Kerr is murdered by the IRA during the robbery of a postal sorting office in Newry. The Irish government later suspends the release of nine republican prisoners due the following day. On 12 November an IRA statement says the 'cessation of military operations is a complete one and covers any use of arms. The IRA leadership has granted no one permission to use arms since August 31st.' The IRA admits killing Frank Kerr on 20 November but say the action 'was not sanctioned by the IRA leadership.'

14 November At the Lord Mayor's banquet in London, John Major says that talks with loyalist political representatives will begin before Christmas.

17 November Albert Reynolds resigns as Taoiseach following controversy surrounding the appointment of Harry Whelehan to the position of President of the Supreme Court. On 19 November, Fianna Fáil elects Bertie Ahern as the new party leader.

30 November John Hume and Gerry Adams issue a statement saying: 'The demilitarisation process should be accelerated and inclusive negotiations, aimed at securing agreement and an overall settlement, should begin without further delay. The British government has a key role to play in this. They can and should be persuaders for agreement between the Irish people.'

1 December President Clinton appoints the former Senate majority leader George Mitchell to be a special economic adviser on Ireland from January 1995.

9 December British civil servants meet Sinn Féin representatives at Stormont in the first formal meeting in more than two decades. One of the main issues for discussion on the British side is the question of the handing in of weapons, while Sinn Féin push for 'parity of esteem' for their party.

12 December The acting Taoiseach, Albert Reynolds, says it is not a 'sensible precondition' to require the IRA to hand in weapons before multilateral talks begin.

13 December A two-day investment conference, attended by three hundred delegates, begins in Belfast. It is addressed by John Major and the US Commerce Secretary, Ron Brown. The economic forum is picketed by republicans in protest at the exclusion of Sinn Féin representatives.

14 December In Belfast, John Major announces a £73 million investment package for Northern Ireland. He also says that 'huge progress' will have to be made towards the destruction of IRA arms before talks with Sinn Féin can be formalised.

15 December John Bruton, a strong critic of the IRA, is elected Taoiseach. He leads a coalition government that also includes the Labour Party and the Democratic Left. The Labour Party leader, Dick Spring, remains Tánaiste (deputy head of the government) and spokesman on Foreign Affairs.

British government officials hold exploratory talks with UDP and PUP representatives at Stormont.

18 December In a *Sunday Tribune* interview, John Bruton warns that the peace process should not get into a stalemate on decommissioning.

19 December A 2 lb plastic explosive bomb is defused at a shop in Enniskillen. The IRA denies responsibility.

21 December John Bruton meets Gerry Adams for talks in Dublin.

22 December The government releases ninety-seven paramilitary prisoners on Christmas parole. Thirty are granted parole in the Republic, while nine IRA prisoners are given early releases.

DEATHS ARISING FROM THE TROUBLES: 62. SHOOTINGS: 348. BOMBS PLANTED: 222. INCENDIARIES: 115. FIREARMS FOUND: 178. EXPLOSIVES FOUND: 1,285 kg (2,835 lb). PERSONS CHARGED WITH TERRORIST AND SERIOUS PUBLIC ORDER OFFENCES: 349. CASUALTIES ARISING FROM PARAMILITARY ATTACKS: 192.

1995

15 January The government announces that the ban on ministers having contacts with Sinn Féin, the UDP or the PUP is to end.

27 January John Bruton and Dick Spring hold their first formal meeting with Sinn Féin representatives.

Seán Kelly from Belfast is sentenced to nine terms of life imprisonment for his involvement in the Shankill Road bombing of October 1993.

1 February Extracts from the Frameworks Document are published in the *Times* (London). The paper claims that 'the British and Irish Governments have drawn up a document that brings the prospect of a united Ireland closer than it has been at any time since partition in 1920.' John Major later makes a television broadcast to appeal for support for his policies.

7 February The Dáil accepts John Bruton's proposal that the state of emergency declared in the Republic in June 1940 and renewed in 1976 be lifted.

A plastic explosive device is defused in Newry. The IRA denies it is responsible for planting the bomb.

9 February A meeting between Sinn Féin and NIO officials is called off after Sinn Féin representatives claim the room is bugged.

22 February The documents *Frameworks for the Future* are published. *A Framework for Accountable Government in Northern Ireland* proposes a single-chamber Assembly of about ninety members elected by PR, with all-party committees overseeing the work of Northern Ireland departments. The work of the Assembly would in turn be overseen by a directly elected Panel of three individuals.

A New Framework for Agreement, dealing with North-South relations, states (para. 10) that the guiding principles for achieving co-operation in the search for overall agreement are '(i) the principle of self-determination, as set out in the Joint Declaration; (ii) that the consent of the governed is an essential ingredient for stability in any political arrangement; (iii) that agreement must be pursued and established by exclusively democratic, peaceful means, without resort to violence or coercion; (iv) that any new political arrangements must be based on full respect for, and protection and expression of, the rights and identities of both traditions in Ireland and even-handedly afford both communities in Northern Ireland parity of esteem and treatment, including equality of opportunity and advantage.'

The function of North-South institutions will be to 'promote agreement among the people of the island of Ireland; to carry out on a democratically accountable basis delegated executive, harmonising and consultative functions over a range of designated matters to be agreed; and to serve to acknowledge and reconcile the rights, identities and aspirations of the two major traditions' (para. 13*b*). Membership will consist of department heads from the Northern Ireland Assembly and the Republic, and areas where harmonisation would take place include agriculture and fisheries, industrial development, consumer affairs, transport, energy, trade, health, social welfare, and education and economic policy. The objective of the North-South body will be to 'provide a forum for acknowledging the respective identities and requirements of the two major traditions ... and promote understanding and agreement among the people and institutions in both parts of the island. The remit of the body should be dynamic, enabling progressive extension by agreement of its functions to new areas. Its role should develop to keep pace with the growth of harmonisation and with greater integration between the two economies' (para. 38).

The Irish government will introduce and support proposals for change in the Constitution of Ireland. These changes 'will fully reflect the principle of consent in Northern Ireland and demonstrably be such that no territorial claim of right to jurisdiction over Northern Ireland contrary to the will of a majority of its people is asserted' (para. 21).

In the House of Commons, John Major attempts to reassure unionists by stating: 'There is a triple safeguard against any proposals being imposed on Northern Ireland: first, any proposals must command the support of the political parties in Northern Ireland; secondly, any proposals must then be approved by the people of Northern Ireland in a referendum; and thirdly, any necessary legislation must be passed by this Parliament. That provides a triple lock designed to ensure that nothing is implemented without consent' (*Hansard,* sixth series, vol. 255, col. 358). Unionists, nevertheless, remain opposed to the document.

2 March A former RUC constable, James Seymour, dies from injuries sustained in an IRA attack on Coalisland police station nearly twenty-two years earlier. He had been paralysed and partly comatose since the attack.

7 March In Washington, Sir Patrick Mayhew outlines a three-point plan for the decommissioning of IRA weapons that would allow Sinn Féin to join political negotiations. He says there must be a 'willingness in principle to disarm progressively,' agreement on the method of decommissioning, and a start to the process of decommissioning as a 'tangible confidence-building measure.' The proposal that only a beginning be made to decommissioning before talks begin is attacked by unionists as capitulating to the IRA.

10 March The UUP says it rejects the Frameworks Document proposals in their entirety.

14 March 150 UVF prisoners in the Maze Prison riot after warders carry out searches for 'illicit material'. The following week there are a number of loyalist attacks on the homes of prison officers.

15 March Following the American decision on 9 March to grant Gerry Adams a visa and permission to raise funds, relations between Britain and the United States appear to reach a new low point. John Major does not speak to President Clinton about the issue for several days, despite Clinton's efforts to contact him. On 4 April, Clinton and Major meet for discussions in Washington; at the end of three hours of talks they appear to have patched up their differences.

16 March In Newry an improvised explosive device partially detonates while being defused by army technical officers.

18 March The Ulster Unionist Council re-elects James Molyneaux leader of the UUP. A 21-year-old student, Lee Reynolds, challenges him for the leadership and receives 88 votes to Molyneaux's 521, with 10 votes spoiled. Molyneaux claims the 15 per cent who voted against him were 'taking a kick at John Major through me.'

22 March The NIO minister Michael Ancram participates in a meeting between civil servants and members of the UDP and PUP.

31 March Official statistics show that republicans have been responsible for fifty-one 'punishment beatings' since the cease-fires began. In the same period loyalists carried out thirty-nine attacks on individuals. After one such incident in north Belfast a twenty-year-old man was found impaled on railings, his fingers broken and his face battered.

Senior DUP and UUP members meet in Belfast. It is the highest level of contact between the two parties since the disputes that followed the Downing Street Declaration.

1 April Bomb disposal experts defuse an incendiary device in a Belfast grocery shop. It is the third such device to be found in Belfast in a week.

13 April Sir Patrick Mayhew invites local parties to bilateral talks.

16 April In Dublin, Gerry Adams says that 'if the British won't listen to reasoned and reasonable argument then let them listen to the sound of marching feet and angry voices. We cannot accept the exclusion of the Sinn Féin electorate from the dialogue and negotiations which will shape the future of Ireland and the Irish people.'

17 April The RUC reroutes an Apprentice Boys of Derry parade away from the lower Ormeau Road area of Belfast. Two hundred local people and Sinn Féin members protest against Orange parades passing through the area. On 23 April almost five hundred protesters demonstrate against a second Orange parade in the area. This parade is also rerouted by police.

23 April The *Sunday Tribune* publishes what it claims is an IRA document circulated on the eve of the cease-fire. It states that the initials TUAS contained in the document stand for 'total unarmed struggle', but they are later discovered to refer to 'tactical use of the armed struggle'. The document states: 'After prolonged discussion and assessment the leadership decided that if it could get agreement with the Dublin government, the SDLP and the IA [Irish-American] lobby on basic republican principles which would be enough to create the dynamic that would considerably advance the struggle then it would be prepared to use the TUAS option ... Nevertheless, differences aside, the leadership believes there is enough in common to create a substantial political momentum which will considerably advance the struggle at this time.' 'Substantial contributing factors' pointing towards this being the time for an initiative were John Hume being 'the only SDLP person on the horizon strong enough to face the challenge,' the Irish government being 'the strongest government in 25 years or more,' and President Clinton being 'the first US President in decades' to be substantially influenced by the Irish-American lobby. 'These combined circumstances are unlikely to gel again in the foreseeable future.'

24 April In a widely welcomed statement, the NIO announces that ministers will begin exploratory dialogue with Sinn Féin.

28 April An alleged drugs dealer, Mickey Mooney, is shot dead in a Belfast city centre bar. The murder is the first to be committed by 'Direct Action Against Drugs'.

3 May Approximately a hundred republicans are involved in a riot in Derry in protest at the visit of John Major to the city. Despite the disturbances, the first official talks between Sinn Féin and a government minister in recent years are set to continue.

10 May A Sinn Féin delegation led by Martin McGuinness meets the NIO minister Michael Ancram at Stormont. While the government seeks movement on the decommissioning of IRA weapons, the Sinn Féin delegation looks for the release of prisoners, the disbanding of the RUC, and access to the Secretary of State for talks.

15 May Bertie Ahern, leader of Fianna Fáil, meets members of the UDP and PUP for talks in Belfast.

18 May A joint UUP and SDLP delegation meets John Major in London to discuss economic and social matters. Shortly after the meeting the NIO issues a statement saying that Sir Patrick Mayhew will seek to meet Gerry Adams informally during the investment conference on Northern Ireland to be held in Washington. James Molyneaux decides not to attend the conference as a result of this decision.

24 May An investment conference on Northern Ireland, attended by nearly 1,300 delegates, opens in Washington. Sir Patrick Mayhew and Gerry Adams meet privately for thirty-five minutes.

1 June An SDLP councillor, Alasdair McDonnell, is elected Deputy Lord Mayor of Belfast, the first nationalist councillor to hold the position.

14 June In an interview with the *Irish Times,* Gerry Adams says that the surrender of IRA weapons as a precondition to negotiations was never mentioned by the British government before 31 August 1994. 'In my view, had a surrender of IRA weapons been imposed as a precondition to peace negotiations prior to the cessation, it is possible [that] there would have been no IRA cessation on September 1 last year.'

15 June In the lowest turn-out for parliamentary by-elections in Northern Ireland (39 per cent), Robert McCartney of the UKUP (10,124 votes) wins the North Down by-election brought about by the death of Sir James Kilfedder in March.

20 June After Sir Patrick Mayhew says that Sinn Féin cannot become involved in full talks until decommissioning begins, Martin McGuinness says that 'in reality there is not a snowball's chance in hell of any weapons being decommissioned this side of a negotiated settlement.'

22 June In a letter to the *Times,* Sir Patrick Mayhew praises the Prime Minister's 'commitment to a just settlement in Northern Ireland' and warns that internal Conservative Party opposition to John Major's leadership could put the peace process at risk. Later in the day, in a bid to see off opposition to his leadership, Major resigns as leader of the Conservative Party but says he will enter the resulting leadership contest.

3 July The release of Private Lee Clegg after four years in custody leads to widespread rioting in nationalist areas of the North. Breidge Gadd, chief probation officer for Northern Ireland, resigns from the Life Sentence Review Board in protest at the decision. John Bruton says he expects British authorities to apply the same rules 'to all other similar prisoner cases,' while Sinn Féin and loyalist paramilitary representatives demand the immediate release of all political prisoners. Rioting continues in nationalist areas the following night.

4 July John Major retains the leadership of the Conservative Party. Sir Patrick Mayhew rejects as 'outrageous' claims that Lee Clegg's release was linked to the party leadership contest.

5 July Confrontations between loyalists and the RUC occur in the Ormeau Road area of Belfast and with nationalists in Bellaghy, Co. Londonderry, as a result of protests involving Orange marches. There are also scuffles between Sinn Féin protesters and loyalists outside the Maze Prison.

9 July The RUC and Orange marchers become involved in a confrontation (later referred to as the 'siege of Drumcree') after police prevent Orangemen from marching along the (nationalist) Garvaghy Road in Portadown on their return from a church service. Ian Paisley and the Ulster Unionist MP David Trimble later attempt, but fail, to negotiate a compromise, and the RUC and Orangemen confront each other overnight.

10 July The Garvaghy Road confrontation continues in Portadown, with 1,000 members of the RUC confronting up to 10,000 Orange supporters. Intermittent clashes occur, with the protesters throwing bricks, stones and bottles and the police firing plastic bullets. Early the following morning, however, a compromise is reached between the RUC and Orangemen, and later in the day five hundred Orangemen march along the road, despite protests from residents but without any loyalist bands.

During the confrontation trouble occurs in loyalist areas throughout Northern Ireland. Larne Harbour is also brought to a standstill by loyalists supporting the Portadown Orangemen.

12 July Orange marches take place throughout Northern Ireland. In Portadown a confrontation is avoided when Orangemen agree not to march along the Garvaghy Road. In the lower Ormeau Road area of Belfast, however, a heavy RUC presence prevents nationalist protesters from stopping an Orange march. The Irish government later accuses the RUC of bias in favour of the marchers and lodges a complaint with the Anglo-Irish Secretariat at Maryfield. The homes of several Protestant and Catholic families are attacked, and there are arson attacks on five Orange Halls.

14 July After a meeting in Dublin, John Bruton, Dick Spring, John Hume and Gerry Adams issue a joint statement calling for all-party talks as soon as possible.

16 July Orangemen picket a Catholic church in north Belfast during Mass, following a series of sectarian attacks on Protestant homes, businesses and

Orange halls in the area. The following morning a fire is started in a Catholic primary school on the Shore Road, Belfast. Sectarian attacks on both Protestant and Catholic premises continue in the following weeks.

18 July Sir Patrick Mayhew and Michael Ancram meet Gerry Adams and Martin McGuinness secretly in Derry for talks on the peace process. John Major had personally authorised the British ministers to take part in the meeting. The talks are severely criticised by the UUP and DUP. It later emerges that another meeting between the two sides had taken place earlier. Official negotiations between the government and Sinn Féin begin again on 27 July.

28 July The Irish government gives early releases to twelve republican prisoners; thirty-three prisoners have been released since the IRA cease-fire. Three republican prisoners involved in a 'dirty' protest at Whitemoor Jail in Cambridgeshire are transferred to Northern Ireland prisons. Twenty-one prisoners convicted of terrorist offences have now been moved from Britain to Northern Ireland jails since the IRA cease-fire began.

Sir Patrick Mayhew lifts a ban, imposed ten years earlier, on fund-raising for organisations that were suspected of having paramilitary links.

30 July The RUC halts a 500-strong Sinn Féin march into Lurgan town centre to prevent a clash with up to 1,500 loyalists in a counter-demonstration. The loyalist protesters are addressed by Peter Robinson and David Trimble, who call on the crowd to hold their ground in order to halt the Sinn Féin march. Three RUC men and one civilian are injured in a subsequent confrontation between the police and loyalists.

8 August Members of the Apprentice Boys of Derry threaten to blockade Catholic churches if Orange marches in Belfast and Derry are rerouted. The Secretary of the Co. Down Committee of the Apprentice Boys states: 'Our parading is part of our religious worship. If people of other religions say we cannot practise our faith, then we will say that we will do the same thing to you.'

12 August A confrontation between the RUC and republicans protesting against an Apprentice Boys march in the lower Ormeau Road area of Belfast leads to twenty-two people being injured. In Derry the Apprentice Boys march around the city walls for the first time in twenty-five years.

Republicans conducting a sit-down protest against the march are removed by the RUC. Rioting later breaks out in Derry city centre. Sectarian clashes also occur at Dunloy and Rasharkin in Co. Antrim.

13 August Gerry Adams is widely criticised after he tells a demonstration at Belfast City Hall that the IRA 'haven't gone away.' The government and unionists say the statement underlines the need for IRA weapons to be decommissioned.

25 August Sir Patrick Mayhew announces that the government will produce a White Paper on the reform of RUC structures and an independent review of emergency legislation and that remission on the sentences of those convicted of terrorist crimes will be returned to 50 per cent.

A statement from the CLMC says that, provided the rights of the people of Northern Ireland are upheld, they 'will not initiate a return to war. There will be no first strike.' The statement notes: 'It is inconceivable for the Combined Loyalist Military Command to decommission weapons with a fully operational, heavily armed Republican war machine intact and refusing to relinquish their arsenals.'

28 August James Molyneaux announces his resignation from the leadership of the Ulster Unionist Party.

31 August On the first anniversary of the IRA cease-fire, Gerry Adams says his party will look constructively at any proposal addressing the issue of decommissioning of arms. The anniversary is marked by a number of republican pickets and vigils calling for all-party talks.

Gary McMichael of the UDP says loyalists are ready to decommission their arms if the IRA will do the same. The following day an IRA spokesman says 'there is absolutely no question of any IRA decommissioning at all, either through the back door or the front door.'

5 September British officials react angrily after the Irish government calls off the summit meeting between John Bruton and John Major scheduled for the following day after officials fail to reach agreement on the concept of a commission to oversee the decommissioning of arms. On 10 September newspaper reports claim that Irish officials were told by Sinn Féin representatives in early September that there would be 'bodies in the streets' if plans for an international body to oversee decommissioning went ahead and that this led to cancellation of the meeting by the Irish side.

8 September David Trimble is elected leader of the Ulster Unionist Party, defeating the previous favourite, John Taylor, on the third count. The following day Trimble says there is no evidence that the IRA is committed to exclusively peaceful methods.

12 September Sir Patrick Mayhew holds his first formal talks with representatives of the UDP and PUP.

The RUC confirms that certificates have been issued blaming an 'unlawful association' for causing damage to Orange halls in Newcastle and Banbridge. The decision leads unionists to claim that the IRA has breached its cease-fire.

14 September A fourteen-member 'Unionist Commission' holds its inaugural meeting in Belfast. While the DUP-inspired commission involves a range of unionist opinion, the UUP is represented only by two councillors sitting on the commission in a personal capacity.

16 September Gerry Adams ends a week-long visit to the United States, during which he met Vice-President Gore and the National Security Adviser, Anthony Lake.

18 September Sinn Féin and UDP spokesmen share a platform for the first time when Mitchel McLaughlin and Gary McMichael take part in a debate during the Liberal Democrats' conference in Glasgow.

19 September A four-member UDP delegation meets John Bruton and Dick Spring for talks in Dublin. The following day Bruton meets a delegation from the PUP.

27 September The European Court of Human Rights in Strasbourg rules that the shooting of three unarmed IRA members in Gibraltar in March 1988 breached the Human Rights Convention. The British government is ordered to pay the legal costs of the case, but no damages are awarded. On 24 December the government pays £38,700 to cover the legal costs of the families of the three IRA members.

30 September At the end of a one-day conference on the peace process attended by nearly eight hundred Sinn Féin activists, Gerry Adams says: 'Nearly all the speakers expressed both concern and some anger at the British government's response.' While some speakers were unhappy with the party's strategy, he says there was no personal criticism.

2 October In an interview with the *Irish Times,* David Trimble says that Dick Spring is 'wobbling out on a limb' on the issue of decommissioning paramilitary weapons before talks begin. He calls for the establishment of a new Northern Ireland Assembly and says they would debate with Sinn Féin if they took their seats in this assembly.

9 October Gerry Adams says that statements by his party have shown it is committed to 'the democratic and peaceful process.' 'It is self-evident that threats of any description from any quarter have no role in any such process. They are certainly no part of any talks process in which we will engage.' On 11 October, John Bruton says he believes Sinn Féin has satisfied the conditions of paragraph 10 of the Joint Declaration (a commitment to exclusively peaceful methods) and that all-party talks should begin as soon as possible.

12 October At the Conservative Party conference, Sir Patrick Mayhew says both governments are willing to invite an international commission to examine the question of illegally held arms and to advise how weapons might be decommissioned. At the same time preliminary talks would take place leading to all-party negotiations.

23 October Dick Spring meets David Trimble for talks in Belfast. Though they fail to agree on the decommissioning issue, the meeting is described as 'useful'. Spring also meets a PUP delegation led by the former UVF leader Gusty Spence.

25 October In London the Queen and President Mary Robinson share their first public engagement, celebrating the 150th anniversary of the foundation of Queen's University, Belfast, University College, Cork, and University College, Galway.

In the Dáil, John Bruton says he will meet John Hume and Gerry Adams whenever they wish. He was criticised by the Fianna Fáil leader,

Bertie Ahern, for having refused to meet the SDLP and Sinn Féin leaders together to discuss their proposals for the peace process earlier in the month.

31 October Michael Ancram meets Sinn Féin representatives for discussions. On 3 November the talks again break down on the issue of decommissioning. On 5 November, Gerry Adams says the British government has subverted the peace process to the point that it no longer exists. 'What we have now are two cessations of violence: one by the IRA, which is a complete military cessation which is now totally unanchored, and we have a conditional, qualified loyalist cessation.'

1 November David Trimble meets President Clinton for talks in Washington. The following day he calls on loyalist paramilitaries to 'take the courageous first step and the moral high ground by beginning the process of disarmament as quickly as possible.'

3 November The NIO publishes a document it had circulated to all political parties and the American and Irish governments the previous week. The 'Building Blocks' paper aims to 'facilitate a shared understanding among all those involved of the building blocks for a twin-track approach to the way forward.' It suggests that 'all-party preparatory talks and an independent international body to consider the decommissioning issue will be convened in parallel by the two governments.' A date for all-party negotiations might be announced, but achieving this target 'would depend on success in creating the necessary conditions to enable all parties to join in such negotiations constructively.' The international body would be asked to advise on how illegal arms could be removed from the political equation. The deputy leader of the DUP, Peter Robinson, attacks the proposals for jointly managed preparatory talks, saying this means 'that from now on there is effectively joint authority.'

8 November The act increasing the remission on the sentences of paramilitary prisoners from 33 per cent to 55 per cent becomes law; as a result, eighty-three prisoners are released from jails in Northern Ireland on 17 November. The new rules do not, however, apply to prisoners serving life sentences, while those convicted before 1989 and those serving five years or less already receive 50 per cent remission.

The SDLP issues a 'proposed statement to be made by both

governments,' which it had submitted to John Major in mid-October. The same proposals were also given to Michael Ancram by Martin McGuinness. The suggestions include launching the preparatory phase of all-party talks no later than 30 November, and asking the former American senator George Mitchell to head an international body that would advise the governments on the arms question. This body would report on 'whether it has been established that a clear commitment exists on the part of the respective political parties to an agreed political settlement, achieved through democratic negotiations, and to the satisfactory resolution of the question of arms.' The proposals are rejected by both the UUP and DUP. David Trimble says the government's twin-track proposals are 'not acceptable in their current form ... In any event, there is no question of any negotiations without decommissioning.'

10 November Gardaí arrest two men after seizing 2,000 lb of explosives a mile from the Co. Armagh border. The following week a further 14 lb of explosives, two mortar bomb launchers, a bag of detonators and ammunition are found at a farm near Castleblayney, Co. Monaghan.

14 November An Orange rally in the Ulster Hall, Belfast, organised by the recently formed 'Spirit of Drumcree' group, passes motions calling for radical change within the order, the resignation of the Grand Master, Martin Smyth, and the severing of links with the UUP.

17 November Four men from Castlederg are charged with four arson attacks, including a fire at a Free Presbyterian Church. Two of the men are also charged with membership of the IRA.

21 November A small explosion caused by a 'crude device' occurs outside Omagh Courthouse.

28 November After a week of intense diplomatic activity, a joint communiqué marks the formal launch in London of the twin-track approach. The governments note their 'firm aim' of achieving all-party talks by the end of February 1996. Invitations are sent to all parties to participate in intensive preparatory talks. At the same time an advisory 'international body' is to be established to provide an independent assessment of the decommissioning issue. The former American senator George Mitchell is asked to chair the body—later referred to as the Mitchell Commission. Harri Holkeri, a former Prime Minister of Finland, and General John de Chastelain, the Canadian Chief of Staff and former ambassador to the United States, are also asked to serve on the international body.

30 November Bill Clinton becomes the first serving President of the United States to visit Northern Ireland. He receives an almost universally warm welcome as he visits west Belfast, east Belfast, and Derry, before returning to Belfast city centre and switching on the Christmas lights. In a speech at Mackie's engineering factory in west Belfast he says: 'Here in Northern Ireland, you are making a miracle ... In the land of the harp and the fiddle, the fife and the Lambeg drum, two proud traditions are coming together in the harmonies of peace ... This twin-track initiative gives the parties a chance to begin preliminary talks in ways in which all views will be represented and all voices will be heard. It also establishes an international body to address the issue of arms decommissioning. I hope the parties will seize this opportunity.'

After condemning continuing paramilitary punishment beatings, Clinton continues: 'There will always be those who define the worth of their lives not by who they are, but by who they aren't; not by what they're for, but by what they are against. They will never escape the dead-end street of violence. But you, the vast majority, Protestant and Catholic alike, must not allow the ship of peace to sink on the rocks of old habits and hard grudges. You must stand firm against terror. You must say to those who would still use violence for political objectives—you are the past; your day is over.'

Clinton later holds separate private talks with the leaders of the five main political parties.

The European Court of Justice rules that the operation of the Prevention of Terrorism Act contravenes European Union law by breaching the freedom of movement guaranteed by the Treaty of Rome.

5 December Replying to the Irish government's invitation to talks, David Trimble writes: 'We are not prepared to negotiate the internal affairs of Northern Ireland with a foreign government.' He calls on the Irish government to revoke the Anglo-Irish Agreement and to remove its territorial claim to Northern Ireland. In a letter to John Major, Trimble refuses to endorse the twin-track approach but says he will keep lines of communication open.

7 December An IRA statement says the British government 'has sought only to frustrate movement into inclusive negotiations ... there is no question of the IRA meeting the ludicrous demand for a surrender of IRA weapons.' The following day John Major criticises the statement as 'a slap in the face for hundreds of thousands of people in Northern Ireland and the Republic, who last week demonstrated their massive desire for peace.'

19 December Chris Johnston, on bail in connection with a seizure of drugs in 1994, is shot dead in the Lower Ormeau Road area of Belfast. Responsibility for the murder is claimed by 'Direct Action Against Drugs'. The following day a senior RUC officer says they believe the killing of five alleged drugs dealers has been carried out by, or on behalf of, the IRA.

20 December The Irish government decides not to give permanent release to a further ten republican prisoners, because of the recent murders in Belfast. Irish security sources also claim that the Gardaí have foiled an attempt by IRA units to carry out a series of raids on cash shipments.

DEATHS ARISING FROM THE TROUBLES: 9. SHOOTINGS: 50. BOMBS PLANTED: 2. INCENDIARIES: 10. FIREARMS FOUND: 118. EXPLOSIVES FOUND: 5 kg (11 lb). PERSONS CHARGED WITH TERRORIST AND SERIOUS PUBLIC ORDER OFFENCES: 440. CASUALTIES ARISING FROM PARAMILITARY ATTACKS: 220.

1996

5 January The Chief Constable of the RUC, Sir Hugh Annesley, says the IRA is responsible for six murders claimed by 'Direct Action Against Drugs'.

10 January Sinn Féin publishes its submission to the international arms body, *Building a Permanent Peace.* It states that the IRA might agree to dispose of its weapons with independent verification but that this would not be considered until after a political settlement had been negotiated and only in the context of overall 'demilitarisation'.

24 January Ken Maginnis of the UUP and Pat McGeown of Sinn Féin take part in a radio discussion in Belfast.

The Mitchell report accepts that there is a commitment by those in possession of illegal arms to decommission but that paramilitary organisations will not decommission any arms before all-party talks. The report also suggests (para. 34) that the parties consider some decommissioning during the process of all-party negotiations, rather than before or after. It suggests that those involved in all-party negotiations affirm their commitment to democratic and exclusively peaceful means of resolving political issues and to the total disarmament of all paramilitary organisations; that such disarmament must be verifiable to the satisfaction of an independent commission; that the parties renounce for themselves and oppose any efforts by others to use force, or threaten to use force, to influence the course or the outcome of all-party negotiations; that they agree to abide by the terms of any agreement reached in all-party negotiations and to resort to democratic and exclusively peaceful methods in trying to alter any aspect of that outcome with which they may disagree; and that they urge that punishment killings and beatings stop and take effective steps to prevent such actions. Among a number of possible confidence-building measures, the report notes (para. 56) that an elected body with an appropriate mandate might be established.

In the House of Commons, John Major says the government is ready to introduce legislation to allow an elective process to go ahead as soon as practicable. He says there are two ways in which all-party negotiations can be taken forward: 'the first is for the paramilitaries to make a start to decommissioning before all-party negotiations. They can—if they will. If not, the second is to secure a democratic mandate for all-party negotiations through elections specially for that purpose' (*Hansard,* sixth series, vol. 270, col. 355).

John Hume attacks the proposal, saying, 'It would be particularly irresponsible for a government to try to buy votes to keep themselves in power' (*Hansard,* sixth series, vol. 270, col. 359). David Trimble welcomes Major's proposal and calls for elections in April or May. Gerry Adams says that Major has in effect dumped the twin-track process and is swapping one precondition to all-party talks for another. In Strasbourg, John Bruton warns that elections in Northern Ireland could be divisive and points out that the end of February remains the target date for the beginning of all-party talks.

25 January As arguments between the British and Irish governments continue over the proposal for elections, British government sources claim that John Major had informed John Bruton of his plan to push the idea for a new Northern Ireland body in a telephone call two days earlier. Irish government sources later say that they were unaware of the election proposal.

Sir Patrick Mayhew announces that the government intends to create a Northern Ireland Grand Committee to improve the accountability of the NIO and Northern Ireland departments. Nationalists interpret the announcement as part of a government move towards a unionist agenda.

26 January Gerry Adams says that Sinn Féin is implacable in its opposition to elections at this time and accuses John Major of having 'binned' the Mitchell report.

30 January The murder of the reputed INLA leader Frank 'Gino' Gallagher in a social security office on the Falls Road, Belfast, sparks an internal INLA feud.

Sir Patrick Mayhew and Gerry Adams meet at Stormont. Adams calls for the plans for an elected body to be dropped; Mayhew rejects this suggestion.

1 February Sir Patrick Mayhew and Dick Spring meet in London and attempt to repair some of the damage done to Anglo-Irish relations by recent developments. John Major later holds talks with David Trimble in the House of Commons. Trimble says that after elections his party will engage in 'dialogue' with Sinn Féin, though the need for decommissioning remains.

At the start of a four-day visit to the United States, Gerry Adams meets President Clinton, who calls for 'rapid progress to all-party talks.'

2 February In a paramilitary-style attack, fifty-seven shots are fired at the home of an RUC man near Moy, Co. Tyrone. In Dublin the Forum for Peace and Reconciliation publishes its report, *Paths to a Political Settlement in Ireland: Realities, Principles and Requirements.* Sinn Féin does not subscribe to the clauses of the report that say that the consent of a majority in Northern Ireland is required for any new agreement, describing this as providing a 'unionist veto'.

Mitchel McLaughlin of Sinn Féin and David Trimble share a platform during a debate on Northern Ireland at the World Economic Forum in Davos, Switzerland.

5 February In an *Irish Times* interview, John Taylor describes Dick Spring as 'the most detested politician in Northern Ireland' and 'a mouthpiece for Sinn Féin' and says that in the previous few weeks he could see 'no difference between Dick Spring and Gerry Adams.'

6 February As bilateral talks continue, a PUP delegation meets John Bruton and Dick Spring in Dublin. The loyalists say that the Irish government cannot expect to play a role in the internal affairs of Northern Ireland.

7 February Following a two-hour meeting with Sir Patrick Mayhew in Dublin, Dick Spring suggests that the peace process be carried forward by calling a conference similar to that held in Dayton, Ohio, on the Bosnian crisis. All political parties would be invited to the same building for two days of 'intensive multilateral discussions.' The proposal is generally accepted by nationalist parties in Northern Ireland but rejected by unionists.

9 February Ken Maginnis MP of the UUP and the chairman of Sinn Féin, Mitchel McLaughlin, take part in a debate for BBC television; the programme is not broadcast, because of later developments. Senior UUP members are said to be outraged by Maginnis's decision to take part in a debate with a member of Sinn Féin. A republican source describes the debate as 'ground-breaking'.

Shortly before 7 p.m. a statement from the IRA ending its cease-fire is authenticated. It says: 'It is with great reluctance that the leadership of Óglaigh na hÉireann announces that the complete cessation of military operations will end at 6 p.m. on February 9th, this evening. As we stated on August 31st, 1994, the basis for the cessation was to enhance the democratic peace process and to underline our definitive commitment to its success. We also made it clear that we believed that an opportunity to create a just and lasting settlement had been created. The cessation presented an historic challenge for everyone, and Óglaigh na hÉireann commends the leaderships of nationalist Ireland at home and abroad. They rose to the challenge. The British Prime Minister did not. Instead of embracing the peace process, the British government acted in bad faith, with Mr Major and the Unionist leaders squandering this unprecedented opportunity to resolve the conflict.'

At 7 p.m. a bomb in the underground car park of a six-floor office building near Canary Wharf Tower, London, explodes, killing two men, injuring more than a hundred others, and causing approximately £100 million worth of damage. The blast leaves a crater 14 feet wide and more than 20 feet deep.

John Major calls the explosion 'an appalling outrage' and says that the atrocity 'confirms again the urgent need to remove illegal arms from the equation.' John Bruton says the bombing is entirely unjustified and condemns it without reservation.

A senior American official says that Gerry Adams telephoned the White House shortly before the explosion. 'He said he was hearing some very disturbing news and he would call us back.' Adams blames the British government and unionist leaders for the breakdown in the cease-fire and says that Sinn Féin's 'peace strategy' remains the main function of his party.

In the Shankill Road area of Belfast shots are fired when loyalists attempt to hijack a car; a probable attack on a nationalist area is thwarted when the car's owner refuses to surrender it.

The police again begin wearing flak jackets while on patrol. The RUC says that patrols by armoured police vehicles will also be increased. Security around Belfast International Airport is also tightened.

The End of the IRA Cease-fire

When the cease-fire was announced, Gerry Adams declared his conviction that a purely political way forward existed for the republican movement. The new relationship that had been forged with Irish America, the SDLP under John Hume and the Irish government was the key. Nationalists spoke of the highly successful 'new departure' forged by Parnell in 1879 as the model for this altered strategy. Privately also some leading republicans said they had received a signal that the British would withdraw within ten years and that a deal had been struck to this end between the then Taoiseach, Albert Reynolds, and John Major.

Given these assumptions, the previous eighteen months had seemed like one disappointment after another; in essence, the British government refused to pressure the unionists into all-party talks while an atmosphere of threat and undiminished republican armament remained.

When the Mitchell Commission finally forced the British government to drop its precondition on arms, John Major then embraced David Trimble's proposal for an elected assembly to negotiate a settlement. Nationalist Ireland was stunned: a unionist leader had shown the ability to set the agenda in a way that was not conceivable in the era of his predecessor, James Molyneaux.

Mitchel McLaughlin, the National Chairman of Sinn Féin, an apparent 'dove', seemed to acknowledge that an electoral process was worthy of consideration. For others it appears to have been the *casus belli*; the reality was that there was a return to violence not because senior republicans realistically thought it could bring about a united Ireland but because they thought it could bring about a 'peace process' on more favourable terms, without problematical events such as elections.

The belief was that the British would drop their points of principle and exert pressure on the unionists to go to the negotiating table. But even if the British government were to do so, which was unlikely, the unionists would claim that all their previous reservations had been vindicated.

The choice of day for the return of violence could hardly have been more surprising. At midday Gerry Adams had been at his most peace-making on a local radio programme, speaking of his Protestant brothers and sisters. Mitchel McLaughlin had taken part in a ground-breaking television debate with Ken Maginnis, the Ulster Unionist MP for Fermanagh and South Tyrone, who had carried the coffins of many of his constituents killed by the IRA. It was yet another indication of the new era of dialogue that slowly appeared to be opening up. Conservative MPs in Dublin spoke in a surprisingly kindly way of the Irish government's Dayton-style talks proposal. Most amazingly of all, it was announced that two Sinn Féin councillors were scheduled to visit 10 Downing Street as part of a delegation seeking economic aid.

In the wake of the Canary Wharf attack, John Major called on Sinn Féin to condemn the bombing. Gerry Adams's statements contained no hint of condemnation. This may have indicated that the leadership of the republican movement was thinking of a new approach.

For some time, Sinn Féin had been trying to create clear water between itself and the IRA. Even a favoured reverential phrase fell into disrepute: 'What is the republican movement?' Martin McGuinness had earlier asked a surprised Spanish journalist. His point was that there was no unified movement of Sinn Féin and the IRA. This was a view John Major pointedly rejected on 21 December 1995 during a visit to Ballymena.

The purpose of such a manoeuvre was clear enough: Gerry Adams would hope to retain his image as a peace-maker and, as he made clear in an RTE interview on 9 February, continue to meet prime ministers and presidents. This could prove to be an illusion, but the republican movement was, arguably, no stranger to the politics of illusion. In the first instance it was the reaction of the Irish government that would be most telling: it would be unfortunate if London and Dublin were to drift apart at this time, though the nationalist view of British and unionist intransigence could prove a dangerous ideological battleground.

The irony was that senior Ulster Unionists had been preparing themselves for talks in the summer: a speech by John Taylor in his Strangford constituency had offered a rough blueprint. At the same time the British government offered much, not least a very soft negotiation of the Frameworks Document, to keep the truce alive. For the time being the only good news appeared to be the restrained reaction of the loyalist paramilitaries.

10 February The Irish Government rescinds a decision to release nine republican prisoners due to be freed that day.

David Trimble calls on John Hume and the Irish government to break off all contacts with Sinn Féin. Hume says he is doing everything in his power to ensure a total and absolute cessation of violence.

John Bruton says the IRA must resume its cease-fire immediately, otherwise Sinn Féin will be isolated in the political process. He says that this time the IRA will not only have to end violence but make it clear that it is doing so permanently.

Gerry Adams says that he learned of the breakdown in the cease-fire from the media. 'The IRA have never consulted Sinn Féin about operational matters and have never at any time involved us, and I would never at any time wish to be involved or see our party involved in those matters.'

Security in Northern Ireland is stepped up in the wake of the London bomb. The RUC mount permanent check-points outside a number of police stations, while army vehicles take part in joint patrols with the RUC in west Belfast. Police patrols are also increased on both sides of the border in an attempt to prevent IRA bombs being moved from the South to the North.

12 February David Trimble meets President Clinton and Anthony Lake for talks in Washington. Clinton rejects Trimble's call for a ban on visas for members of Sinn Féin and an end to Sinn Féin fund-raising.

In the House of Commons, John Major says: 'No-one, no-one took more risks for peace than the government over the past two years, but we never lost sight of the fact that the IRA commitment had not been made for good ... I regret to say that the events of last Friday showed that our caution about the IRA was only too justified. The timing of the return to violence may have been surprising: the fact that violence could resume was not ... In the absence of a genuine end to this renewed violence, meetings between British Ministers and Sinn Féin are not acceptable and cannot take place. That is also the position of the Irish Government' (*Hansard,* sixth series, vol. 271, col. 656).

The Labour Party leader, Tony Blair, says that whatever his differences with the Prime Minister, 'on this matter we shall stand four-square together in the cause of peace' (*Hansard,* sixth series, vol. 271, col. 659).

John Hume calls for referendums to be held in Northern Ireland and the Republic to ask whether people oppose the use of violence and if they want all parties brought to the table to begin the process of dialogue. In a television broadcast, John Major says he will continue working for a lasting peace in Northern Ireland. He states that it is the government's aim to bring together all democratic parties for talks, and that discussions have not taken place because Sinn Féin and the IRA did not give a commitment to put away their arms.

Ian Paisley Junior claims that the tax disc on the lorry used in the Docklands bomb was stolen from an English-registered lorry in Co. Armagh three weeks earlier. He notes that this event occurred before the completion of the Mitchell report on decommissioning.

13 February In Washington, David Trimble says that if Sinn Féin took its seats in the proposed 'peace convention' there would be decommissioning running alongside the operation of a convention in which there would be substantive negotiations. Unionists would, however, need to be reassured that any new IRA cease-fire was permanent and that they had accepted the Mitchell Principles.

In the Dáil John Bruton says: 'The British government made a mistake in its response to the Mitchell report. The Unionist parties made a mistake in not sitting down with Sinn Féin and asking them the hard questions face to face, but a comparison cannot be drawn between political mistakes and the response to those mistakes that took human life. Killing is never justified as part of the political process.' He says that the Irish government has 'not shut any door on Sinn Féin' and that he is willing to authorise direct contact between Sinn Féin leaders and government officials (*Dáil Debates,* vol. 461, col. 1090–1).

15 February An 11 lb IRA plastic explosive bomb planted in Charing Cross Road, London, is defused. The incident leads to a further tightening of security in the city.

16 February About four thousand people attend a trade union peace rally at Belfast City Hall. There are minor scuffles between those attending and Sinn Féin supporters carrying placards calling for all-party talks. A peace group collects more than half a million signatures calling for the cease-fire to be reinstated.

Irish officials meet Gerry Adams to consider ways in which the IRA cease-fire can be restored.

17 February John Hume and Gerry Adams meet for talks. A joint statement says they have recommitted themselves to do their utmost to restore the peace process. A further meeting takes place on 28 February.

18 February The premature detonation of a 5 lb IRA bomb on a bus in Aldwych, near Covent Garden, London, leaves an IRA man, Edward O'Brien, dead and six injured. A new IRA list of targets, bomb-making materials and 40 lb of plastic explosives are later found at O'Brien's flat.

28 February The British and Irish governments launch a package aimed at restarting the peace process. A firm date for all-party talks, 10 June, is announced. Political parties would be asked to attend 'proximity talks' to consider the structure, format and agenda for the all-party talks and to consider whether there should be a referendum in both Northern Ireland and the Republic to demonstrate support for a political settlement. Discussions would seek to reach agreement on the form of election used to lead to all-party negotiations, with elections to the negotiating forum to be held in May. Sinn Féin could take part in the negotiations provided it persuaded the IRA to renew its cease-fire. All participants would need to make clear their total and absolute commitment to the principles of democracy and non-violence set out in the Mitchell report. If IRA violence resumed during the talks, Sinn Féin would be excluded. John Major also warns that if there is no agreement at these talks, the government will impose its own proposals.

3 March Splinter elements of the UVF and UFF say they have ended their cease-fire and that they will 'execute' members of the IRA and Sinn Féin.

4 March Intensive political talks begin at Stormont. They are boycotted by the UUP, DUP, and PUP, while Sinn Féin is barred from entering the building. The sensitivities of the parties are such that discussions take place in ten different venues.

7 March An IRA spokesman tells *An Phoblacht* that the British and Irish governments have set unacceptable conditions for the all-party talks and that 'there is not the necessary dynamic to move us all away from conflict and towards a lasting peace.'

9 March A 2 lb IRA bomb explodes in Fulham, west London, but there are no casualties.

12 March The CLMC says it will maintain its cease-fire but warns that any further attacks by the IRA in Britain will lead to retaliation.

15 March Relations between the UUP and the Irish government are again soured when a British government document, 'Ground Rules for Substantive All-Party Negotiations', is sent to the Northern Ireland parties while Unionist leaders are in America. The proposals, suggesting that the Irish government be joint co-ordinator of the negotiations, are perceived by unionists as a further concession to nationalists.

Nine-year-old Barbara McAlorum is killed when INLA gunmen fire on her parents' home.

21 March The government announces that in the Northern Ireland elections, to be held on 30 May, voters will be asked to vote for a party rather than an individual candidate. The election will be held using the new boundaries for eighteen constituencies, with each constituency returning five representatives. Two extra seats will be allocated to each of the ten most successful parties throughout Northern Ireland as a whole.

The representatives elected could assume membership of a Forum that would meet regularly in Belfast when negotiations were not in session; however, the Forum would cease to exist if negotiations ended. The Forum would not be part of the negotiating process, but negotiators could commission discussions, studies or reports from it. The lifetime of the Forum is limited to twelve months, with a possible extension of a further twelve months.

22 March The INLA states that it is ending its tactical cease-fire from midday and will be operating from a position of defence and retaliation. The IRA meanwhile says that the latest proposals are not enough to carry all parties into meaningful negotiations.

27 March In an attempt to ease nationalist fears that the proposed Forum will become another unionist-dominated Stormont, John Bruton says he will do everything possible to 'insulate' the role of the Forum in the negotiating process. 'The priority being given to the Mitchell Report at the beginning of the discussions must not be construed to mean that this issue can be used to block discussions of other issues.'

2 April The government introduces the Prevention of Terrorism (Additional Powers) Bill to amend the Prevention of Terrorism (Temporary Provisions) Act and give the police increased powers to search individuals and premises. The Labour Party abstains on the bill, which becomes law the following day.

8 April Rioting occurs in Belfast after the RUC prevents an Apprentice Boys of Derry march passing along the (nationalist) Lower Ormeau Road.

17 April The IRA continues its London bombing campaign by exploding a small device in the Earl's Court area.

The White Paper *Northern Ireland: Ground Rules for Substantive All-Party Negotiations* is published. It sets out the British and Irish governments' view of the most suitable rules for all-party negotiations. The same day the Northern Ireland (Entry to Negotiations) Bill, aimed at providing delegates for the talks and establishing a Forum, is introduced in the House of Commons. It becomes law on 29 April.

24 April Two IRA bombs containing more than 30 lb of plastic explosive planted under Hammersmith Bridge in London partially detonate, causing minor damage.

Fergus Finlay, an adviser to Dick Spring, causes controversy by saying on a Channel 4 television programme that talks without Sinn Féin are 'not worth a penny candle.'

Both the SDLP and Sinn Féin say they will participate in the forthcoming elections. Sinn Féin says it will boycott the Forum.

30 April The PUP spokesman, David Ervine, says the stability of the loyalist cease-fire is the worst he has known it. The following day the UDP spokesman, David Adams, denies that the loyalist cease-fire is under threat.

5 May The mid-Ulster UVF claims to have planted three bombs at Dublin Airport. Though nothing is found, several fiights are delayed while the airport is searched. The unilateral action by the mid-Ulster UVF leads to a dispute between the UDA and UVF within the CLMC.

16 May John Major tells the *Irish Times* that he wants Sinn Féin to be part of the negotiations but that it cannot make a contribution without an IRA cease-fire. On the question of arms, he states that decommissioning will 'need to be addressed at the beginning of the talks and agreement reached on how the Mitchell recommendations on decommissioning can be taken forward, without blocking the negotiations.' The statement is perceived as another attempt by the government to involve Sinn Féin in talks by encouraging a renewal of the cease-fire.

20 May Gerry Adams says that Sinn Féin will agree to the Mitchell Principles. There is, however, no sign of a renewed IRA cease-fire, which all parties (Sinn Féin excepted) believe is a prerequisite for all-party negotiations.

24 May The UUP appears to harden its position on decommissioning when David Trimble says that his party wants to see 'equipment of some sort' appearing in the opening session of talks, a period that he says might last for days or weeks.

30 May The elections to all-party negotiations are held. The UUP remains the largest party, with 24.2 per cent of the vote and thirty seats in the forum; the DUP, with 18.8 per cent, wins twenty-four seats; the SDLP, with 21.4 per cent, wins twenty-one seats. Sinn Féin achieves its best result up to this time: 116,377 votes, 15.5 per cent, and seventeen seats. The strong Sinn Féin performance is interpreted in completely opposing ways—either as a vote to reinstate the cease-fire or, alternatively, as showing support for the hard line taken by republican militarists. More predictably, and at least partly as a result of the electoral system used, Alliance takes only 6.5 per cent of the vote and seven seats. Robert McCartney's recently formed United Kingdom Unionist Party wins 3.7 per cent of the vote and three seats. Four other parties—the PUP (3.5 per cent), UDP (2.2 per cent), Northern Ireland Women's Coalition (1.0 per cent), and a Labour coalition (0.9 per cent)—fail to win any of the constituency seats but, by finishing among the ten most successful parties, each win two seats in the Forum. The turn-out is 64.5 per cent.

4 June President Mary Robinson begins a four-day official visit to Britain, the first by an Irish head of state.

6 June A joint British-Irish paper gives George Mitchell the role of chairing plenary sessions of the talks as well as chairing a sub-committee dealing with decommissioning. Mitchell's colleagues on the International Body are also asked to participate: John de Chastelain to chair strand 2 (North-South) talks, with Harri Holkeri acting as an alternative in any area requiring an independent chairman. The plan is generally welcomed by nationalists but greeted with suspicion or hostility by unionists, who object to Mitchell's role.

7 **June** The murder of Detective-Garda Jerry McCabe during the robbery of a mail van in Adare, Co. Limerick, sours relations between the Irish government and Sinn Féin. John Bruton is further angered by statements from Sinn Féin members that they will not condemn the incident, because, they say, they will not indulge in 'the politics of condemnation'. It is not until 15 June that the IRA admits that members of its organisation were responsible for killing McCabe.

10 June Multi-party talks begin at Stormont, with John Major and John Bruton opening the proceedings. Sinn Féin is barred from participation because of the continuing IRA campaign. Unionists, meanwhile, continue to object to the role allocated to Mitchell, who does not assume the chair until 12 June.

14 June The Northern Ireland Forum holds its first meeting. John Gorman, a Catholic member of the UUP, is appointed interim chairman.

15 June A 3,500 lb IRA lorry bomb injures 200 people and causes damage estimated to cost between £100 and £300 million to the centre of Manchester. In the wake of the bomb, British and Irish public and political opinion noticeably hardens against republicans. John Bruton states that the IRA will have to declare an 'unconditional and irrevocable cease-fire' before Sinn Féin can be admitted to talks.

20 June In the Republic a substantial and active IRA bomb-making factory is discovered by Gardaí at Clonaslee, Co. Laois. Four men are arrested in connection with the discovery.

28 June The IRA fires two mortar bombs at a British army barracks in Osnabrück, Germany.

7 **July** A confrontation between the police and marchers develops after the RUC bans an Orange march along the Garvaghy Road to Drumcree parish

church in Portadown. Up to two thousand members of the RUC face thousands of loyalists, who attack them with bottles and stones. The police in turn use plastic bullets and tear gas.

8 July A Catholic taxi driver, Michael McGoldrick, is shot dead by Portadown members of the UVF near Lurgan.

9 July John Major meets David Trimble, Ian Paisley and Robert McCartney to discuss the Drumcree confrontation. The unionist politicians had said they would not take part in all-party talks until the RUC left Drumcree. A thousand extra soldiers are sent to Northern Ireland.

10 July Several towns, including Colcraine and Cookstown, are cut off by loyalist blockades.

11 July After a decision by the RUC to allow the Orange march to proceed at Drumcree, there is widespread rioting in nationalist areas, lasting for several days. In the wake of the decision some nationalists boycott Protestant-owned shops, increasing sectarian tensions still further.

12 July An Orange parade passes along the Lower Ormeau Road in Belfast, against the protests of local residents. A republican, Dermot McShane, is killed by an army personnel carrier during rioting in Derry.

In a BBC interview, John Bruton accuses the British government of having yielded to force, being inconsistent, and being partial in the application of the law. Sir Patrick Mayhew describes the comments as offensive.

13 July In a highly polarised political atmosphere, the SDLP announces that it is withdrawing from the Northern Ireland Forum.

14 July A 1,200 lb car bomb destroys the Killyhevlin Hotel near Enniskillen. The bomb is later claimed by a group referred to as the Continuity IRA.

15 July In the House of Commons, Sir Patrick Mayhew announces the setting up of a review to make recommendations to improve the management of controversial parades. On 31 July an Oxford University academic, Dr Peter North, is named to head the Independent Commission on Parades.

A BBC television programme reveals that David Trimble had discussions with the loyalist leader Billy Wright on 10 July during the Drumcree confrontation.

17 July SDLP and Sinn Féin members of Derry City Council vote to remove council facilities from the UUP mayor, Richard Dallas, because of his involvement in an Orange blockade of Craigavon Bridge.

18 July O'Connell Street in Dublin is sealed off after a hoax bomb warning from the UFF.

22 July Amid fears that the loyalist cease-fire is on the verge of collapse, John Major meets representatives of the PUP and UDP for talks in London.

2 August The UVF says that its Portadown unit is to be disbanded.

11 August Members of the Black Preceptory and local nationalists are involved in a fifteen-hour confrontation over a march in Bellaghy, Co. Derry. The parade eventually proceeds along part of its intended route.

20 August The Alliance leader, Dr John Alderdice, receives a life peerage.

28 August The CLMC (which includes the UDA and UVF) orders the loyalist hard-liners Billy Wright and Alex Kerr to leave Northern Ireland or face 'summary justice'. The following day Peter Robinson of the DUP calls for the UDP and PUP to be excluded from the talks. On 1 September a bomb explodes at the home of Alex Kerr's parents.

30 August Ronnie Flanagan is named to succeed Sir Hugh Annesley as Chief Constable of the RUC from 4 November.

3 September Hugh Torney, reputedly the former chief of staff of the INLA, is shot dead in Lurgan. On 9 September the 'GHQ' faction of the INLA announces that it is disbanding.

4 September The DUP MP Rev. William McCrea appears on a platform with Billy Wright at a loyalist rally in Portadown.

8 September Nationalist protesters in the mainly Catholic village of Dunloy, Co. Antrim, block an Orange march to a church service. A demonstration by Orangemen blocking the Ballymena–Ballymoney road in response is broken up by the RUC. On 14 September loyalists begin picketing Masses at a number of Catholic churches, including that in Harryville, Ballymena, in retaliation.

9 September As all-party talks resume, Ian Paisley calls for the exclusion of the PUP and UDP because of UVF and UDA threats against Billy Wright and Alex Kerr. On 11 September, after the governments state that the two parties will not be excluded, the DUP says this provides Sinn Féin with an invitation to enter talks without any change in the IRA's position.

23 September An IRA member, Diarmuid O'Neill, is shot dead during a police raid on a guesthouse in London. In another raid, an arms cache that includes over 20,000 lb of home-made explosive is discovered in a London warehouse.

30 September Army experts carry out a controlled explosion on a 250 lb bomb at College Square, Belfast. The bomb is claimed by the Continuity IRA.

David Trimble rejects proposals from the British and Irish governments on decommissioning and insists that decommissioning begin before substantive talks.

UDA and UFF prisoners in the Maze Prison say they are withdrawing support from the peace process because of IRA activity and the 'inactivity' of politicians.

7 October Two IRA car bombs explode inside Lisburn army barracks, injuring more than thirty people. PUP members were meeting UVF prisoners at the time; it is later reported that only the fact that there were no immediate casualties led loyalist paramilitaries to maintain their cease-fire. On 11 October, James Bradwell, a soldier seriously injured in the bombing, dies in hospital.

14 October Dr Marjorie (Mo) Mowlam, the Labour Party spokesperson on Northern Ireland, meets loyalist prisoners in the Maze Prison.

15 October The UUP and SDLP reach agreement on an agenda for the talks after decommissioning is in effect downgraded on the agenda.

18 October David Trimble meets loyalist prisoners in the Maze Prison.

3 November Seán Brady is installed as Archbishop of Armagh and succeeds Cahal Daly as head of the Catholic Church in Ireland.

25 November German police request the extradition of Róisín McAliskey, daughter of the former MP Bernadette McAliskey, in connection with the attack on Osnabrück army barracks in June. McAliskey, who is five months pregnant, is remanded in custody on 27 December and detained in Belmarsh Prison near London.

28 November In the House of Commons, John Major replies to recent IRA proposals suggesting Sinn Féin's immediate admission to talks after a renewed cease-fire is called but without decommissioning. He says the government is publishing a paper outlining the conditions that would allow Sinn Féin entry to all-party talks. 'We need to see an unequivocal restoration of the cease-fire, we need to be able to make a credible judgment that it is lasting, and we need to know that Sinn Féin will sign up to the Mitchell Principles. These matters are in Sinn Féin's hands' (*Hansard,* sixth series, vol. 286, col. 461).

29 November Sir Robert Carswell is named to succeed Sir Brian Hutton as Lord Chief Justice for Northern Ireland from January 1997.

30 November An estimated five hundred loyalists picketing a Catholic church in Harryville, Ballymena, clash with the RUC.

10 December Sir Patrick Mayhew announces cuts of £120 million in public service finances to meet increased security costs.

11 December Robert Salters is elected Grand Master of the Orange Order in succession to Rev. Martin Smyth.

13 December The Labour Party leader, Tony Blair, visits Northern Ireland and calls for an 'unequivocal cease-fire, backed up by actions which show it is genuine.'

20 December An RUC man guarding Councillor Nigel Dodds of the DUP is wounded by the IRA inside the Royal Belfast Hospital for Sick Children. The attack takes place while Dodds is visiting his son in hospital.

22 December A prominent republican, Eddie Copeland, is injured by a loyalist booby-trap bomb planted under his car.

DEATHS ARISING FROM THE TROUBLES: 15. SHOOTINGS: 125. BOMBS PLANTED: 25. INCENDIARIES: 4. FIREARMS FOUND: 98. EXPLOSIVES FOUND: 1,677 kg (3,700 lb). PERSONS CHARGED WITH TERRORIST AND SERIOUS PUBLIC ORDER OFFENCES: 595. CASUALTIES ARISING FROM PARAMILITARY ATTACKS: 326.

1997

1 January Two 500 lb bombs are left in dustbins in the grounds of Belfast Castle.

5 January A 250 lb bomb is defused near Cullyhanna, Co. Armagh.

13 January As talks resume, the DUP and UKUP call for the UDP and PUP to be expelled because of a series of punishment attacks and two bomb attacks on republicans at the turn of the year. Sir Patrick Mayhew says he believes the loyalist cease-fire is still intact.

16 January In London the trial of six men charged with escaping from Whitemoor Prison in September 1994 is stopped because of prejudicial publicity printed by the *Evening Standard.*

17 January Channel 4 News reports that three of those killed on Bloody Sunday in 1972 were shot by members of the Royal Anglian Regiment, contradicting the findings of the Widgery Tribunal. Demands for a fresh inquiry grow with the publication of Don Mullan's book *Eyewitness: Bloody Sunday* the following week. On 15 February, Sir Patrick Mayhew rules out a new inquiry.

27 January The NIO minister Michael Ancram rejects DUP and UKUP calls for the loyalist parties to be removed from the talks.

30 January The report of the Independent Review of Parades and Marches (the North Committee) is published. It recommends the establishment of a new independent body, the Parades Commission, to play the main role in the resolution of disputes and to consider whether legal restrictions should be imposed on contentious parades or protests.

10 February A 1,000 lb IRA bomb is defused near Strabane.

12 February A soldier, Stephen Restorick, is killed by an IRA sniper while manning a check-point at Bessbrook.

19 February The Irish Minister for Foreign Affairs, Dick Spring, warns the British ambassador that the continued detention of Róisín McAliskey could damage the peace process.

20 February In an *Irish News* interview the leader of the SDLP, John Hume, says that without a cease-fire by republicans he will 'look elsewhere' for political progress. He rejects the idea of a political pact with Sinn Féin, saying that such a pact without a cease-fire 'would be the equivalent of asking our voters to support the killing of innocent human beings by the IRA.'

The same paper reports that a Catholic civil servant who was awarded damages for sectarian harassment had been moved from her post, while the person responsible for the harassment remained as Lady Denton's private secretary.

22 February In an *Irish Times* article the President of Sinn Féin, Gerry Adams, says that any restoration of the IRA cease-fire will be 'genuinely unequivocal'. The following night John Bruton responds by saying that the republican movement must accept the principle of consent. 'Once it does that, the problem of decommissioning will cease to be a roadblock because by accepting consent republicans will change the nature of their assumptions about the peace process and decommissioning will be a natural concomitant of the new approach, not an imposed precondition' (*Irish News,* 24 February 1997).

27 February The Northern Ireland Arms Decommissioning Act is enacted.

3 March A 25 lb loyalist bomb is discovered outside a Sinn Féin office in Monaghan. The PUP denies any UVF involvement.

4 March An RTE television programme quotes Gerry Adams as telling Sinn Féin members at Athboy: 'Ask any activist in the North did Drumcree happen by accident, and they will tell you, "no" … three years of work on the Lower Ormeau Road, Portadown, and parts of Fermanagh and Newry, Armagh and Bellaghy and up in Derry … Three years of work went into creating that situation, and fair play to those people who put the work in' (*Irish Times,* 5 March 1997).

5 March The deadlocked multi-party talks are adjourned. The chairman, George Mitchell, says he will return when talks resume on 3 June.

7 March An IRA bomb is defused near Dungannon. The Portadown loyalist Billy Wright is sentenced to eight years' imprisonment for issuing death threats.

9 March The newly formed Loyalist Volunteer Force admits planting fire-bombs at two tourist centres in Banbridge and Newcastle, Co. Down. The LVF is believed to centre on disaffected loyalists in the Portadown area and to be led by Billy Wright.

13 March A soldier is injured in a grenade attack in north Belfast. Later in the day a soldier and an RUC man are injured in an IRA bomb attack in the Short Strand area of east Belfast.

In a speech in Washington, Mitchell attacks 'the twin demons of Northern Ireland,' violence and intransigence. The DUP view the speech as an attack on their party and call on Mitchell to resign as chairman of the talks.

14 March John Slane is shot and killed by UFF members in west Belfast. The sectarian murder casts doubts on the integrity of the loyalist cease-fire. The RUC later foil an INLA plan to murder a PUP member, Billy Hutchinson, in retaliation.

19 March An Apprentice Boys of Derry club announces that it is voluntarily rerouting its parade away from the Lower Ormeau Road, Belfast.

23 March Prison officers at the Maze Prison discover an escape tunnel running from a cell in a block holding IRA prisoners towards the perimeter wall. The incident again raises concerns about a lax security regime at the prison.

24 March A Presbyterian minister, David Templeton, dies of a heart attack six weeks after a loyalist 'punishment beating'. His private life had been the subject of a newspaper report eighteen months earlier, leading him to resign from his ministry.

26 March The members of the Parades Commission, which has the power to ban or reroute marches, are named. The chairman is the former trade unionist Alistair Graham; other members are Rev. Roy Magee (who played a role in brokering the loyalist cease-fire) and the SDLP member Bernadette McIvor.

The explosion of two IRA bombs at Wilmslow, Cheshire, and a false bomb alert at Doncaster railway station disrupt the rail network in England.

There is a confrontation between local nationalists and an under-cover army unit at Coalisland after the soldiers wound a man near the local RUC station.

29 March A 1,000 lb IRA bomb is discovered near an army base in Ballykinler, Co. Down. An RUC man is shot in the leg at Forkhill, Co. Armagh.

The shadow Secretary of State for Northern Ireland, Dr Mo Mowlam, says that an immediate IRA cease-fire would allow Sinn Féin to enter talks on 3 June. John Taylor, deputy leader of the UUP, says that if Sinn Féin is brought into the talks process the UUP will not be there.

30 March A 90 lb loyalist car bomb is defused at Sinn Féin offices in north Belfast. The loyalists claim that this is a 'measured' response to recent IRA attacks.

3 April Two IRA bombs near Birmingham close the busiest stretch of motorway in Britain.

5 April The Grand National horse race at Aintree, near Liverpool, is postponed for two days after an IRA bomb scare forces officials to abandon the race. The incident is part of a wave of IRA bomb explosions and scares that also disrupt rail and road services throughout England in the lead-up to the general election.

10 April An RUC woman is shot and wounded in Derry.

25 April The LVF leader Billy Wright is transferred from Maghaberry to the Maze Prison. After UVF prisoners refuse to accept him into their block, he is moved to block 6, part of which is already occupied by INLA prisoners.

28 April Up to ten prison officers are threatened at gunpoint by two INLA inmates at Maghaberry Prison. On 18 May, *Sunday Life* claims that the gun was originally intended to be used in an attempt to murder Billy Wright.

29 April UVF and UFF prisoners riot in protest against new security arrangements in the Maze Prison introduced after an IRA attempt to tunnel out of the prison. They say the new arrangements should apply only to IRA prisoners. The DUP spokesman on justice, Ian Paisley Junior, says the Maze Prison is out of control and run by the prisoners.

1 May The British general election sees a landslide victory for the Labour Party. In Northern Ireland, where a record 125 candidates stand, the UUP wins 32.7 per cent of the vote and ten seats (including a narrow win by William Thompson in the new constituency of West Tyrone); the SDLP, with 24.1 per cent, takes three seats (Foyle, Newry and Armagh, and South Down); the DUP, with 13.6 per cent, takes two seats (North Antrim and East Belfast). Sinn Féin receives a record 16.1 per cent of the poll and gains two seats (West Belfast from the SDLP and Mid-Ulster from the DUP), while Robert McCartney of the UKUP wins North Down. The Alliance Party receives 8.0 per cent of the poll but wins no seats. The turn-out is 67.3 per cent.

In the wake of the Labour Party's victory, Mo Mowlam is appointed Secretary of State for Northern Ireland; Adam Ingram becomes Minister of State with responsibility for security and economic development; Paul Murphy is Minister of State responsible for political development and finance and personnel, information service, European Union affairs and liaison on Scottish and Welsh devolution; Tony Worthington is Parliamentary Under-Secretary responsible for education, health and social services, and community relations; and Lord Dubs is Parliamentary Under-Secretary in charge of environment and agriculture and spokesman on Northern Ireland in the House of Lords.

7 May David Trimble becomes the first Northern Ireland politician to meet the Labour Party leader, Tony Blair, for talks after he becomes Prime Minister. Blair meets John Bruton in London the following day.

8 May A Catholic man, Robert Hamill, dies from injuries received on 27 April when he was kicked and beaten by a loyalist mob in Portadown. The

Hamill family accuse the RUC of failing to intervene to stop the attack while it was taking place.

9 May On a visit to Derry, Mo Mowlam says decommissioning will not be a stumbling block to all-party talks. 'What we want to see first is a cease-fire which is definite in words and deeds so that people know that it is serious. When we get that we will be very keen to see Sinn Féin in the talks process.'

An off-duty RUC man is shot dead by the INLA in a Belfast bar.

10 May A car bomb is abandoned by the Continuity IRA after the detonator explodes while it is being transported to a target in Belfast. The main bomb fails to explode, and the bombers abandon their car.

12 May Seán Brown, a prominent GAA official, is murdered, supposedly by the LVF, and his body left near Randalstown, Co. Antrim.

14 May The Speaker of the House of Commons, Betty Boothroyd, denies the Sinn Féin MPs, Gerry Adams and Martin McGuinness, access to House of Commons facilities because they have refused to take the oath of allegiance and failed to take their seats.

16 May In a speech in Belfast, Tony Blair says his 'agenda is not a united Ireland ... None of us in this hall today, even the youngest, is likely to see Northern Ireland as anything but a part of the UK. That is the reality, because the consent principle is now almost universally accepted.' He offers immediate talks between government officials and Sinn Féin but says the 'settlement train' is leaving with or without them.

The Chief Constable of the RUC, Ronnie Flanagan, says that 'constituent parts' of the CLMC have broken the cease-fire.

20 May John Hume tables a motion in the House of Commons calling on the government to reopen the inquiry into the events of Bloody Sunday in 1972.

21 May After Mo Mowlam meets members of residents' groups on the day of district council elections, the UUP MP Ken Maginnis accuses her of 'electioneering for Sinn Féin.'

The elections see further gains by Sinn Féin, which takes 16.9 per cent of first-preference votes and wins seventy-four seats. The UUP, with 27.9 per cent of first-preference votes, wins 185 seats; the SDLP, with 20.6 per cent, wins 120 seats; the DUP, with 15.6 per cent, wins ninety-one seats; and Alliance, with 6.6 per cent, wins forty-one seats. The PUP, with 2.2 per cent, wins six seats, while the UDP, with 1.0 per cent, wins four seats. For the first time, unionist councillors fail to win an overall majority on Belfast City Council. The turn-out is 53.6 per cent.

Martin McGuinness of Sinn Féin meets senior Stormont civil servants for the first time in more than a year.

24 May Loyalist protesters picketing a Catholic church in Harryville, Ballymena, again clash with the RUC. On 8 June loyalists break into the church and attempt to set it on fire.

The LVF claims responsibility for a crude bomb found in Dundalk.

29 May In London, President Clinton says Sinn Féin should participate in multi-party talks but calls for an IRA cease-fire first. He condemns those who take the attitude of 'we'll talk when we're happy and shoot when we're not.'

31 May A 1,000 lb IRA bomb is abandoned in west Belfast.

1 June An off-duty RUC man is beaten to death by a loyalist mob outside a pub in Ballymoney.

2 June Alban Maginness of the SDLP becomes the first nationalist to be elected Lord Mayor of Belfast. In the election Maginness is supported by Sinn Féin, Alliance and an Independent Unionist councillor and defeats a DUP nominee by 26 votes to 22.

3 June Multi-party talks resume at Stormont. The LVF and Continuity Army Council are proscribed.

4 June An INLA member is shot dead by gardaí during an armed robbery in Dublin.

Portadown District of the Orange Order sends 1,500 letters to Garvaghy Road residents explaining its position regarding its annual march. The Garvaghy Road Residents' Association calls for direct discussions with the

Orange Order. The Orangemen refuse, saying the association is directed by republicans and is insincere in saying it is seeking a compromise; the association in turn claims the Orangemen are not sincere.

6 June A general election in the Republic leads to a coalition government of Fianna Fáil and the Progressive Democrats, headed by Bertie Ahern. A successful Sinn Féin candidate later takes a seat in the Dáil for the first time.

11 June Robert Bates, a former member of the Shankill Butchers gang, is shot dead in Belfast. The murder is believed to be in revenge for the murder of a UDA member, allegedly killed by Bates, in 1977.

16 June Two RUC men on foot patrol are murdered by the IRA in Lurgan. Tony Blair bans further contact between senior civil servants and Sinn Féin.

21 June Two men are injured when a loyalist bomb explodes under their car in south Belfast.

24 June British and Irish government proposals on arms decommissioning are presented to the plenary talks and suggest a plan of parallel talks and decommissioning. Decommissioning would be supervised by an international commission, while two new sub-committees would deal with decommissioning and confidence-building measures. The proposals are accepted by the SDLP, welcomed with reservations by the UUP, but rejected by the DUP. Gerry Adams says the IRA will not hand over any guns.

25 June Tony Blair outlines the latest proposals in the House of Commons, saying that he expects to see substantive talks under way by September, with a settlement being reached by the following May. He says that an NIO document passed to Sinn Féin on 13 June suggested that an immediate and unequivocal IRA cease-fire could have led to the party being invited to talks by the end of July. He adds: 'There can be no question of trading guns for political concessions in all this' (*Hansard,* sixth series, vol. 296, col. 849).

26 June The IRA launch a rocket attack on an RUC vehicle in north Belfast.

27 June 'Proximity talks' between Orangemen and Garvaghy Road residents' representatives organised by Mo Mowlam fail to reach a compromise over the Drumcree march.

1 July The Taoiseach, Bertie Ahern, visits nationalist residents' groups in Belfast and Portadown and says he cannot guarantee his support if the Secretary of State decides to permit the Garvaghy Road march to go ahead.

2 July The LVF threatens to kill civilians in the Republic if the Drumcree march is banned.

3 July Tony Blair and Bertie Ahern hold their first meeting in London.

4 July Mo Mowlam meets Orangemen and residents of the Garvaghy Road separately in an attempt to resolve the Drumcree problem.

6 July Widespread rioting occurs in nationalist areas after protesters are cleared off the road by police while Orangemen are permitted to march down the Garvaghy Road in Portadown. A policewoman is shot in the face by the IRA in Coalisland, and a blast-bomb is thrown at a police station in west Belfast. Rioting continues over the next five days.

7 July A UDA man is killed in Dunmurry when an explosive device he is handling detonates.

8 July A leaked government document, dated 20 June, outlines its policy for dealing with the Drumcree crisis. The paper states that a 'controlled march' is the 'least worst option.'

10 July Orange leaders announce that they will reroute four marches on 12 July to avoid Catholic areas. The move is widely viewed as an important step towards maintaining peace in the coming days.

12 July Two Protestant teenagers are wounded by an IRA sniper while standing at a bonfire near the peace line in north Belfast.

14 July The NIO reveals that contacts between officials and Sinn Féin had continued since 16 June, despite assurances from Tony Blair and Mo

Mowlam that there would be no further contact after the IRA murder of two members of the RUC in Lurgan.

15 July In Aghalee, Co. Antrim, eighteen-year-old Bernadette Martin is shot dead by the LVF while sleeping at the home of her Protestant boyfriend.

16 July The text of the decommissioning document is pushed through by the British and Irish governments, with only one question being permitted. The DUP and UKUP withdraw temporarily from the talks. The UUP, though unhappy, decides to remain in the talks process though rejecting the paper on 23 July.

17 July A joint statement from John Hume and Gerry Adams welcomes the 'considerable progress' made in restoring the peace process.

18 July The government publishes the text of a letter sent to Martin McGuinness on 9 July, which states that Sinn Féin can participate in talks without any decommissioning of IRA weapons provided the Mitchell Principles are adhered to. The British climb-down on the arms question is attacked by unionists, who claim the government is prepared to buy a cease-fire at any cost.

19 July The IRA announces a restoration of its 1994 cease-fire, with a 'complete cessation of military operations' from midday on 20 July. The IRA maintains that it is 'committed to ending British rule in Ireland. It is the root cause of divisions and conflict in our country.' But it adds: 'We want a permanent peace and therefore we are prepared to enhance the search for a democratic peace settlement through real and inclusive negotiations.' The renewed cease-fire, received with a much more subdued public response than that of 1994, permits Sinn Féin to join the talks process two days later.

21 July In a radio interview, David Trimble accuses the government of duplicity and of giving 'secret assurances' to Sinn Féin. Later, after meeting Tony Blair in London, he tells a press conference that London and Dublin must keep their word to seek decommissioning during talks but adds that 'there are some possibilities for progress.' Trimble says he is not abandoning the talks but broadening them by initiating consultations between his party and Northern Ireland citizens.

After Sinn Féin representatives are admitted to Castle Buildings to prepare their offices, the DUP and UKUP withdraw permanently from the process in protest.

22 July The Prime Minister meets a DUP delegation, which proposes a new talks format, but this is rejected by Blair.

23 July The UUP votes against government proposals on decommissioning. However, the British and Irish governments insist that substantive negotiations will begin on 15 September.

25 July Bertie Ahern meets John Hume and Gerry Adams and welcomes the admittance of Sinn Féin to talks. A joint statement says that a settlement is possible 'only with the participation and agreement of the unionist people.'

31 July A 1,000 lb Continuity IRA bomb planted at a hotel near Lisbellaw, Co. Fermanagh, is made safe by bomb disposal experts.

6 August Mo Mowlam meets a Sinn Féin delegation at Stormont.

10 August An INLA statement criticises the IRA's cease-fire as 'bogus'.

11 August As a sign of relaxing security, army patrols again begin wearing berets instead of helmets.

12 August Martin McGuinness of Sinn Féin and Ken Maginnis of the UUP participate in a debate on a BBC television programme.

13 August Rioting by LVF prisoners in the Maze Prison causes severe damage. INLA prisoners in the same block are temporarily moved.

16 August A republican bomb factory is discovered by Gardaí at Crosskeys, Co. Cavan.

20 August A Portadown bar, believed to be used by supporters of the LVF, is smashed by a gang of approximately thirty men claiming to represent the UVF. The attack emphasises continuing tensions between loyalist groups.

26 August The British and Irish governments sign an agreement establishing an International Commission on Decommissioning.

28 August Relations between unionists and Mo Mowlam reach a new low point after she tells the *Belfast Telegraph* that she doesn't necessarily define consent in terms of numbers or 'in a functional, geographical sense.' The Alliance leader, John Alderdice, describes the remarks as confused and inaccurate. A meeting later in the day between UUP MPs and Mo Mowlam is described as 'hostile'. On 31 August the UDP threatens to withdraw from the talks unless Mo Mowlam gives a satisfactory definition of consent.

29 August In the House of Commons, Mo Mowlam says she accepts the IRA cease-fire as genuine and invites Sinn Féin to take part in negotiations from September.

30 August Up to fifty republicans attack New Barnsley RUC station in west Belfast with petrol bombs. The police fire plastic bullets in return.

William Ross MP of the UUP says unionists need 'very considerable confidence-building measures,' including the handing over of paramilitary weapons, before his party sits down with Sinn Féin. William Thompson MP had stated several days earlier that it would be a betrayal of unionists to sit at 'this squalid negotiation table'.

1 September David Trimble meets Catholic Church leaders as part of the UUP's consultation process in the run-up to the resumption of the Stormont talks.

8 September An LVF spokesman tells the *Irish Times* that it may attack foreign businessmen working in the Republic. 'The Republic has a territorial claim over my country. That is not a peaceful environment. The unionists of Ulster are the only people in the European Union who live under this threat. This threat has to be removed. Otherwise, Dublin will reap what it sows.'

9 September Sinn Féin signs the Mitchell Principles and joins all-party talks. The UUP, PUP and UDP withdraw from the talks for the day.

The US Attorney-General halts the extradition of six IRA members at the request of the Secretary of State, Madeleine Albright, who claims the suspension of the extraditions could help the peace process.

11 September A senior IRA spokesperson tells *An Phoblacht* that the IRA 'would have problems with sections of the Mitchell Principles' but that 'the IRA is not a participant in these talks.' On 13 September, in an article for the *News Letter,* Tony Blair warns Sinn Féin that it will be locked out of the talks if the IRA dishonours the Mitchell Principles. 'The two organisations are inextricably linked. One cannot claim to be acting independently of the other.'

15 September A joint statement by the Prime Minister and the Taoiseach attempts to deal with unionist concerns on consent and decommissioning and states that they view 'the resolution of the decommissioning issue as an indispensable part of the process of negotiation.'

All-party talks formally begin, under the chairmanship of George Mitchell. The UUP, PUP and UDP join the talks on 17 September. A UUP demand that Sinn Féin be expelled because of the IRA interview in *An Phoblacht* is rejected by the two governments on 24 September.

16 September A 350 lb van bomb planted by the Continuity IRA explodes at an RUC station in Markethill, Co. Armagh, causing extensive damage.

23 September The UUP and Sinn Féin sit down at the same conference table for the first time during the all-party talks.

24 September The International Commission on Decommissioning, headed by John de Chastelain, is officially launched. The other members of the commission are Brigadier Tauno Nieminen of Finland and Donal Johnson of the United States.

Agreement between the SDLP, UUP and fringe loyalists on a detailed procedural motion, including agreement to establish sub-committees on arms decommissioning and confidence-building measures, leads to the launch of substantive political talks. Though the motion states that decommissioning is 'an indispensable part' of the negotiations, the issue is in effect sidelined to allow negotiations to continue.

26 September Mo Mowlam is widely criticised after approving the transfer of Jason Campbell from Scotland to the Maze Prison at the request of the PUP. Campbell was convicted of the sectarian murder of a sixteen-year-old in Glasgow in 1995. The PUP later withdraws the request for Campbell's transfer.

30 September At the Labour Party conference, Mo Mowlam announces that internment is to be removed from the statute book.

5 October Martin McGuinness tells a Sinn Féin rally at Coalisland that the party is going to the negotiating table to 'smash the Union.'

7 October The Irish Minister for Foreign Affairs, Ray Burke, resigns following controversy over political donations and is replaced by David Andrews, who causes controversy among nationalists by stating in a television interview on 10 October that a united Ireland will not be achievable in his lifetime.

8 October The US State Department removes the Provisional IRA from its list of terrorist organisations, allowing fund-raising to be conducted on its behalf.

9 October David Trimble tells a fringe meeting at the Conservative Party conference that he has 'no expectation' of an agreement between unionists of any shape and Sinn Féin.

13 October During a visit to the talks at Castle Buildings, Tony Blair meets Sinn Féin leaders in Belfast and shakes hands privately with Gerry Adams. He is later visibly shaken after being barracked by loyalists during a tour of a shopping centre in a Protestant area of east Belfast.

The failure of PUP representatives to appear at a UDA rally marking the third anniversary of the loyalist cease-fire further emphasises tensions between the loyalist groups. The CLMC is formally disbanded later in the month.

16 October A republican group claims responsibility for a letter-bomb sent to David Trimble's constituency office. Similar devices had earlier been sent to other unionist politicians. A hoax bomb warning from the Continuity IRA disrupts a UKUP rally at Carryduff, Co. Down.

17 October Mo Mowlam announces details of the Parades Bill. Aspects of the bill are criticised by most local parties.

20 October UUP delegates leave the Stormont talks for the day in protest after the Irish government says it will not change articles 2 and 3 of the Constitution of Ireland.

25 October A man is killed by a car bomb in Bangor in what is believed to be part of a loyalist feud.

30 October The Continuity IRA plants a 12 lb plastic explosive bomb at a motor tax office in Derry.

In a *New Statesman* interview, Mo Mowlam says that civil servants leaking information to the press and political parties are undermining the peace process.

31 October A Belfast-born academic, Professor Mary McAleese, is elected President of Ireland with 59 per cent of the vote. Sinn Féin had expressed the view that McAleese was its preferred candidate.

6 November The *Irish Independent* reports that the IRA in Co. Louth has split over the peace process. On 12 November the *Irish Times* reports that thirty-five members of the South Armagh unit have split from the IRA, in opposition to the developing process. *An Phoblacht* denies that splits have occurred.

7 November Two men are arrested by Gardaí after 40 lb of plastic explosives and other weapons are found in Swords, Co. Dublin.

15 November Francie Molloy, a member of the Sinn Féin talks team, tells a meeting at Cullyhanna, Co. Armagh, that if the talks fail they will 'simply go back to what we know best.' He later says this is a reference to Sinn Féin's peace process.

17 November Loyalists create a spate of bomb scares in the Republic. A loyalist bomb is found by children in a shopping centre in Dundalk.

18 November The Emergency Provisions Act is renewed in the House of Commons, though the provision for internment is removed.

20 November Bertie Ahern and a UUP delegation led by David Trimble hold talks in London. Both parties describe the talks as positive.

The Continuity IRA plants a bomb outside the PUP office at Belfast City Hall.

25 November A report from the Decommissioning Commission says it has detailed estimates of the weapons held by paramilitary organisations.

27 November A former PUP negotiator, Jackie Mahood, is wounded in a gun attack in north Belfast. The attack is attributed to the UVF. Three other men are admitted to hospital in separate paramilitary attacks.

29 November The Irish Minister for Foreign Affairs, David Andrews, faces a storm of criticism from unionists of all shades after saying that a secretariat that would implement the decisions of a future North-South body would have 'strong executive functions not unlike a government.'

2 December In an attempt to make progress in the talks, George Mitchell proposes that a working group with two members per party be established. The task of the group would be to create a list of the main issues to be resolved and to devise structures for resolving these matters.

5 December In Dublin the Forum for Peace and Reconciliation meets for the first time since February 1996.

A Catholic man, Gerry Devlin, is shot and killed by the LVF at a GAA club in Glengormley, Co. Antrim.

7 December In Dublin, republicans opposed to the peace process launch the 32-County Sovereignty Committee. The fifteen-member committee is chaired by Michael Ahern from Co. Carlow; the vice-chairperson is Bernadette Sands-McKevitt, a sister of the hunger-striker Bobby Sands.

8 December Bertie Ahern meets Ulster Unionists at Stormont. Later in the day he also meets Gerry Adams.

10 December A republican prisoner, Liam Averill, convicted of two murders in 1994, escapes from the Maze Prison disguised as a woman after a prison Christmas party. Before a meeting with Tony Blair later in the day, part of the first Sinn Féin delegation to enter Downing Street since 1921, Gerry Adams says he wishes Averill good luck.

13 December Rioting by republicans in Derry following an Apprentice Boys march causes an estimated £5 million of damage.

22 December Four UUP MPs—William Ross, William Thompson, Roy Beggs, and Clifford Forsythe—write to David Trimble saying they are opposed to the direction the talks are taking and call for the party's withdrawal from the talks.

23 December UDA and UFF prisoners say they will review their support for the talks after Christmas, because they believe the government is 'working to a republican agenda.'

27 December The leader of the LVF, Billy Wright, is shot dead by INLA prisoners in the Maze Prison. Hours later loyalists murder a former republican prisoner, Séamus Dillon, who was working as a doorman at a hotel near Dungannon. The UUP calls for the resignation of the Secretary of State and her prisons advisers.

31 December The LVF admits responsibility for the murder of a Catholic man, Eddie Treanor, at a bar in Belfast.

DEATHS ARISING FROM THE TROUBLES: 22. SHOOTINGS: 225. BOMBS PLANTED: 93. INCENDIARIES: 9. FIREARMS FOUND: 105. EXPLOSIVES FOUND: 1,258 kg (2,775 lb). PERSONS CHARGED WITH TERRORIST AND SERIOUS PUBLIC ORDER OFFENCES: 405. CASUALTIES ARISING FROM PARAMILITARY ATTACKS: 228.

1998

6 January A 500 lb Continuity IRA bomb is defused in Banbridge.

10 January A cross-community social worker, Terry Enright, is murdered by loyalists outside a Belfast night club.

12 January Talks resume at Stormont. Following a weekend of telephone calls between the two heads of government and David Trimble, the British and Irish governments present the parties with the 'heads of agreement', which suggest balanced constitutional change to articles 2 and 3 of the Constitution of Ireland and the (British) Government of Ireland Act; a Northern Ireland Assembly with responsibility for local departments; a new British-Irish Agreement to replace the Anglo-Irish Agreement; an Intergovernmental Council consisting of representatives of assemblies throughout Britain and Ireland; a North-South Ministerial Council accountable to the Northern Ireland Assembly and Dáil, and suitable implementation bodies for policies agreed by this council. While the SDLP and UUP reaction to the document is generally favourable, that of Sinn Féin is less so.

18 January The LVF murders Fergal McCusker in Maghera.

19 January The INLA murders a UDA member, Jim Guiney. A Catholic taxi driver, Larry Brennan, is murdered by the UFF later that evening.

After talks with Tony Blair in London, Gerry Adams says the latest initiative does not provide a pathway to peace.

21 January Ben Hughes, a Catholic, is murdered by the UFF when leaving his motor supply shop near Donegall Road, Belfast. A Catholic taxi driver escapes a murder attempt.

23 January The UFF says it has restored its cease-fire after a 'measured military response'. In Belfast the RUC recover 300 lb of explosives in the Shankill Road area. The LVF is believed to be responsible for the murder of a Catholic man, Liam Conway, near Crumlin Road, Belfast.

24 January A Catholic taxi driver, John McColgan, is murdered in Belfast.

The River Club complex in Enniskillen is destroyed by a 300 lb Continuity IRA bomb. There are a number of bomb scares at other hotels in the Belfast area.

26 January The UDP withdraws from the talks process in London. Later in the day the party is formally expelled from the talks, because the UFF has breached the Mitchell Principles.

The British and Irish governments later present a paper on North-South structures. The paper is criticised by David Trimble for its references to the Frameworks Document (which had been rejected by unionists), though he adds that unionists have 'nothing to fear' from the new paper. The following day the UUP MP Jeffrey Donaldson tears up a copy of the document at a press conference, saying, 'We as a party will not put our hand to any agreement based on the Framework Document.'

9 February Brendan Campbell is murdered by 'Direct Action Against Drugs' on the Lisburn Road, Belfast.

10 February A loyalist, Robert Dougan, is murdered by republicans in Dunmurry. On 13 February, Mo Mowlam reveals that the RUC Chief Constable has informed her that the IRA was involved in both the Campbell and Dougan murders.

18 February The body of a Lurgan man, Kevin Conway, is found at a derelict farmhouse at Aghalee, Co. Antrim. On 11 March a government statement says he was murdered by local IRA elements.

20 February Sinn Féin is temporarily expelled from the talks because of IRA involvement in the murders of Brendan Campbell and Robert Dougan. A 500 lb car bomb planted by the Continuity IRA explodes outside an RUC station in Moira, causing extensive damage to the village. On 23 February a 300 lb Continuity IRA bomb explodes in Portadown.

3 March In Co. Louth, gardaí discover a 600 lb car bomb believed to be in preparation for a Continuity IRA attack on Armagh.

LVF gunmen murder two lifelong friends, Philip Allen (a Protestant) and Damian Trainor (a Catholic), and injure two other men in a gun attack in a bar in Poyntzpass, Co. Armagh. Trainor was to have been Allen's best man later in the year.

7 March Leading DUP members as well as members of the LVF attend a strong loyalist rally in Portadown. Ian Paisley denies any paramilitary connection with the rally.

8 March Writing in *Ireland on Sunday,* Gerry Adams says that the ongoing talks will not lead directly to a united Ireland but says Sinn Féin will view 'any agreement in this phase as being part of a traditional process of Irish unity.' He says his party's 'bottom line' includes powerful cross-border bodies operating independently of a Northern Ireland Assembly, policing and the courts coming within the remit of the new all-Ireland institutions, the disbanding of the RUC, withdrawing the army, releasing all paramilitary prisoners, and the retention of the territorial claim to Northern Ireland in the Constitution of Ireland.

Though entitled to return to the talks the following day, Sinn Féin says it will not do so until its leaders meet Tony Blair. (The meeting takes place on 12 March.) The party eventually returns to the talks on 23 March.

9 March Newspapers report that the LVF has issued a statement warning church leaders, politicians, leaders of industry and commerce and those in the paramilitary world who it says are 'colluding in a peace/surrender process designed to break the Union and establish the dynamic for Irish unity, within an all-Ireland Roman Catholic, Gaelic, Celtic state. In our fight to maintain the Union, the role of these collaborators will not be forgotten.' The LVF supports Ian Paisley's rejection of the peace process, stating, 'He has warned that this process is all about giving the Irish government a greater say in the affairs of Northern Ireland and more and more people are realising he is spot on.'

The Home Secretary, Jack Straw, announces that, for health reasons, Róisín McAliskey will not be extradited to Germany. In April she is released and returns to her family home in Co. Tyrone.

10 March Republicans launch a mortar bomb attack on Armagh RUC station.

15 March David Keys, one of four men charged with the murders of Philip

Allen and Damian Trainor, is murdered in his cell in the LVF wing of the Maze Prison. More than a dozen LVF prisoners are later charged with involvement in the murder. Unionists again call for the resignation of the Security Minister, Adam Ingram, and senior prison management. A prison officers' spokesman also calls for resignations. The following day Ingram says the issue is not a resigning matter and that the situation that prevails in the Maze Prison is unique.

17 March At a meeting in Washington, President Clinton reportedly urges David Trimble to meet Gerry Adams for negotiations. The UUP say it is not interested in a 'stunt meeting' with Adams.

22 March Three people are questioned by Gardaí after an almost completed 1,300 lb car bomb is discovered in Dundalk. The car bomb, similar to those used at Canary Wharf and Manchester in 1996, was expected to be detonated in a Northern Ireland town.

23 March A report by the House of Commons Select Committee on Northern Ireland Affairs says there is enough evidence to suggest that electoral malpractice is a serious problem in Northern Ireland. The committee draws attention to problems with the system of absent voting as well as 'a serious level of multiple registration' in some areas.

24 March Republicans fire four mortar bombs at an army base in Forkhill, Co. Armagh. The Chief Constable of the RUC, Ronnie Flanagan, says that members of the Provisional IRA may be offering their expertise to other terrorist groups.

27 March A leaked government document indicates that the NIO was considering the selective use of government-commissioned opinion poll material (with other material being withheld) and non-political public figures to help sell a political settlement to the Northern Ireland public.

A former RUC reservist, Cyril Stewart, is shot dead by the INLA at a shopping centre in Armagh.

1 April A UN investigator's report, welcomed by human rights organisations, concludes that members of the RUC have engaged in 'activities which constitute intimidation, harassment [and] hindrance' of defence solicitors. The report calls for an independent inquiry into the murder of the solicitor Pat Finucane in 1989.

The RUC agrees to a new 'peace line' being built in the White City area of north Belfast in an attempt to halt sectarian violence in the area.

2 April Five people are arrested by Gardaí after a car containing 1,000 lb of home-made explosive is intercepted at Dún Laoghaire as it is about to be loaded onto the Holyhead ferry.

After Bertie Ahern says there will be 'no more concessions' by the Irish side, the UUP negotiator, Reg Empey, replies that 'unless the Irish Government is prepared to make accommodations, there'll be no agreement' (*Belfast Telegraph,* 3 April).

3 April After the third meeting between the Prime Minister and Taoiseach in as many days, British sources say that differences between the governments are narrowing, though 'there is still work to be done.'

7 April As the talks deadline approaches, George Mitchell tables a paper aimed at helping the parties reach agreement. The rejection by the unionist parties of the paper (described by one UUP member as 'a Sinn Féin wish list') brings the process close to collapse. Tony Blair flies to Belfast in an attempt to save the talks. Before a meeting with David Trimble, he says, 'I feel the hand of history upon our shoulder.'

8 April A loyalist, Trevor Deeney, is shot dead by the INLA at his home in the Waterside area of Derry.

On the eve of the talks deadline, having just attended his mother's funeral, Bertie Ahern joins other participants at Castle Buildings, Belfast. During tense negotiations, David Trimble argues for a more 'unionist-friendly' model of north-south co-operation based on a shadow Assembly, with Tony Blair providing Trimble with decisive support.

9 April On the final official day of the talks, bilateral discussions continue. Though often on the point of breakdown, the talks continue to make slow progress. At 6 p.m. David Trimble briefs the UUP Executive, which gives him its whole-hearted support. Later that evening Sinn Féin threatens to leave the talks.

At 11 p.m. nearly 150 DUP protesters, who had earlier heckled Trimble outside the UUP head office, enter the grounds of Parliament Buildings. At a press conference at Castle Buildings an hour later, Ian Paisley and other party leaders are harangued by PUP supporters, one of whom is pulled from the scene by the PUP spokesman, David Ervine.

10 April Overnight concessions are made to Sinn Féin to keep it involved in the talks; these include a two-year limit (rather than three) for the release of prisoners and the use of vaguer language on the issue of decommissioning. In response to this issue, David Trimble receives a letter from Tony Blair stating: 'I understand [that] your problem with Paragraph 25 of Strand 1 is that it requires decisions on those who should be excluded or removed from office in the Northern Ireland Executive to be taken on a cross-community basis. This letter is to let you know that if, during the course of the first 6 months of the Shadow Assembly or the Assembly itself, these provisions have been shown to be ineffective, we will support changes to these provisions to enable them to be made properly effective in preventing such people from holding office. Furthermore, I confirm that in our view the effect of the decommissioning section of the Agreement, with decommissioning schemes coming into effect in June, is that the process of decommissioning should begin straight away.'

Twenty hours after the official deadline, negotiators reach agreement on a political settlement. A worrying sign, however, is the fact that the UUP negotiator, Jeffrey Donaldson, refuses to endorse the agreement.

The Belfast Agreement includes provision for a 108-member Assembly, with six members from each of the eighteen constituencies elected by PR. The Assembly, headed by an Executive Committee, will have legislative powers, but its first responsibility will be to set up a North-South Ministerial Council to direct co-operation on a number of issues. The intention of paragraph 25, which states that 'those who hold office should use only democratic, non-violent means, and those who do not should be excluded or removed from office ...' remains an area of dispute between unionists and republicans.

Votes in the Assembly on important decisions will require either a majority of both unionist and nationalist members voting in favour or, alternatively, a weighted majority of 60 per cent, with at least 40 per cent of both nationalists and unionists present voting in favour. As a safeguard for nationalist concerns, the Assembly will be suspended if the North-South body is not established within a year.

The Irish government agrees to recommend an amendment to articles 2 and 3 of the Constitution of Ireland. The revised article 2 will state: 'It is the entitlement of every person born in the island of Ireland … to be part of the Irish nation.' Article 3 will state: 'It is the firm will of the Irish nation, in harmony and friendship, to unite all the people who share the territory of the island of Ireland, in all the diversity of their identities and traditions, recognising that a united Ireland shall be brought about only by peaceful means with the consent of a majority of the people, democratically expressed, in both jurisdictions of the island.' The British government agrees to replace the Government of Ireland Act.

A British-Irish Council will be established, with members drawn from the Northern Ireland Assembly, the Dáil, and the new Scottish Parliament and Welsh Assembly.

The governments agree to the early release of prisoners convicted of terrorist offences, with the last prisoners being released after two years. The participants agree to use their influence to achieve the decommissioning of all paramilitary weapons within two years of referendums in Northern Ireland and the Republic endorsing the agreement.

The agreement should lead to the development of a police service representative of the community as a whole. An independent commission will be established to make recommendations for future policing arrangements in a report to be produced no later than the summer of 1999. The numbers and role of the armed forces in Northern Ireland will be reduced and emergency powers removed.

The Belfast Agreement

Though there had been many suggestions for a political agreement during the course of the Troubles, after the publication of the 'heads of agreement' document in January it was clear that the only settlement on offer was one consisting of balanced constitutional change by the British and Irish, a Northern Ireland Assembly, a replaced Anglo-Irish agreement, a British-Irish Council linking the Assembly to other United Kingdom bodies, and North-South structures.

Given the conflicting agendas and mutual suspicions of those involved in the talks, it was hardly surprising that the final agreement was characterised by safeguards, vetoes, and some areas of ambiguity. The core of the agreement, however, was unambiguous: the Union of Great Britain and Northern Ireland would continue as long as it was supported by a majority of the people of Northern Ireland. In return for this acceptance by the British and, crucially, also by the Irish government and other nationalists, unionists were required to accept power-sharing and cross-border co-operation. Perhaps the most difficult area for unionists, however, was that, in return for the ending of the IRA campaign of violence and *de facto* acceptance of the legitimacy of the North's position within the United Kingdom, they had to allow Sinn Féin a 'soft landing'. In practice this soft landing was likely to focus on the contentious issues of the release of prisoners and the decommissioning of weapons.

It soon became clear, however, that while nationalists and republicans overwhelmingly supported the deal, unionists, as with the Sunningdale agreement in 1973, were split. At first roughly half were in favour, a quarter against, and a quarter undecided. Since the effective operation of the agreement made it imperative that a majority of unionists backed the deal, much effort was expended by politicians in an attempt to win over the 'soft no' unionist vote, personified by the Ulster Unionist MP Jeffrey Donaldson.

In the weeks leading up to the referendum in Northern Ireland, attention focused not on the 'political' settlement—the institutional arrangements of the deal—but rather on the elements of the 'peace' settlement contained in the agreement involving the release of prisoners, decommissioning of weapons, and the reform of the RUC.

In this area the release of the Balcombe Street gang in time to attend a Sinn Féin ardfheis on 10 May was to have a near-disastrous impact. Television film of the triumphal reception afforded the prisoners confirmed moderate unionists in their opinion that the agreement was intended to meet the demands of extremists at the expense of 'law-abiding citizens'. As it became evident just how much damage this, and the subsequent appearance of Michael Stone at a UDP rally, had done to the 'yes' vote among unionists, government attempts to woo them back became almost frantic. Tony Blair made frequent visits to Northern Ireland and gave numerous assurances, while other British political leaders as well as international figures such as Nelson Mandela spoke in favour of the agreement. Perhaps the most telling indicator of who the main targets of the campaign were, however, came in President Clinton's statement during a 'G8' summit meeting in Birmingham when he claimed to be an Irish Protestant and said that if he lived in Ireland he would vote in favour of the agreement. Despite this, the unionist middle ground seemed far from convinced by the agreement, and it remained unclear whether the agreement would be, as Séamus Mallon famously remarked, 'Sunningdale for slow learners' or, suffering the same fate as it predecessor, merely Sunningdale in slow motion.

11 April The Belfast Agreement passes its first test when the UUP Executive endorses it by 55 votes to 23, though two MPs, William Ross and William Thompson, openly oppose it.

12 April Gerry Adams tells a republican rally at Carrickmore, Co. Tyrone, that the conclusion of the talks has brought to an end 'another phase of our struggle.' An IRA statement read out at the rally says the organisation will 'carefully study' the agreement 'against its potential to move us towards our primary objective, a 32-county democratic socialist republic' (*Irish Times,* 13 April 1998).

14 April The Irish government's decision to give early release to nine IRA prisoners (one of whom was not due to be freed until 2005) is criticised by unionists as well as the Garda Representative Association.

15 April After a meeting in Belfast, the Grand Orange Lodge says it cannot recommend the agreement to its members without clarification.

17 April Tony Blair attempts to calm unionist concerns by stating that the RUC will not be disbanded and that only prisoners whose organisations are not involved in violence will be released, and even then only on licence.

A taxi driver, Mark McNeill, is shot dead in west Belfast. The murder is believed to have been committed by the INLA.

18 April At a crucial meeting of the Ulster Unionist Council, delegates vote by 540 to 210 (72 per cent) in favour of the Belfast Agreement. The result is welcomed by Gerry Adams at the Sinn Féin ardfheis in Dublin, though the party delays a decision on the agreement. David Trimble later describes Adams's praise as a 'poisoned chalice'.

21 April A Catholic man, Adrian Lamph, is shot dead in Portadown.

23 April The Parades Commission withholds publication of a document giving its preliminary view on marches for the year after Tony Blair writes to the chairman, Alistair Graham, saying that to publish the report would risk 'overloading the political system.' Glen Barr and Tommy Cheevers, who joined the commission two months earlier, resign but deny leaving because of the document's proposals, which are rumoured to suggest banning the Drumcree parade.

Five IRA prisoners, including the members of the Balcombe Street gang, are transferred from England to Portlaoise Prison in the Republic.

A unionist anti-agreement rally in the Ulster Hall, Belfast, is addressed by six MPs, including William Thompson, William Ross and Roy Beggs of the UUP, the two DUP MPs, and Robert McCartney.

A 79-year-old man is shot in both knees and ankles in a paramilitary-style attack.

24 April The Northern Ireland Forum holds its final meeting. The UDA and UFF endorse the Belfast Agreement, saying it will not lead to a united Ireland.

25 April A Catholic student, Ciarán Heffron, is murdered at Crumlin, Co. Antrim. Loyalists are believed to be responsible for a bomb attack on a pub near Armagh.

26 April Bertie Ahern says that the British government is 'effectively out of the equation' with regard to the future of Northern Ireland.

28 April The former NIO minister and Governor of Hong Kong, Chris Patten, is named to head the commission on reform of the RUC.

30 April An IRA statement says the Belfast Agreement falls short of a basis for a lasting settlement, and that the IRA will not decommission weapons.

Army explosives experts defuse a 600 lb car bomb in the centre of Lisburn.

1 May The Orange Order says it cannot endorse the Belfast Agreement. On 7 May, Orange leaders meet Tony Blair to discuss their objections but on 13 May say they have not been persuaded to support the agreement.

2 May Newspapers report that an electronic listening device has been discovered in a house used by a Sinn Féin member, Gerry Kelly.

In Co. Wicklow a man is shot dead during an attempted robbery of a security van. The raid is believed to have been conducted by dissident IRA members later referred to as the 'Real IRA'.

4 May The route of the Belfast marathon is changed after mortar bombs are found beside part of the route.

5 May It is reported that the IRA's leadership dropped its ban on members taking part in a Northern Assembly the previous weekend.

6 May Tony Blair and John Major make a joint visit to Belfast in support of the pro-agreement campaign.

7 May The British government announces that financial assistance (estimated at £5 million) is to be provided for support schemes for the victims of violence.

The Northern Ireland (Elections) Bill, establishing an Assembly if the agreement is approved in the referendums, becomes law.

8 May A dispute erupts in the UUP after the anti-agreement MP William Thompson blames a split in the party on David Trimble and calls on him to resign as party leader.

10 May At a special Sinn Féin ardfheis in Dublin, 96 per cent of the 350 delegates vote to change the party's constitution to permit successful candidates to take their seats in a Northern Assembly. Twenty-seven republican prisoners, including the IRA commanding officer in the Maze Prison, are given temporary parole to attend the ardfheis. The ardfheis also votes to canvas for a 'yes' vote in the referendums on both sides of the border. Members of the Balcombe Street gang are greeted by Gerry Adams as 'our Nelson Mandelas' and receive a ten-minute standing ovation. Adams says of the Belfast Agreement: 'On the one hand it upholds the unionist veto over the constitutional status of the North, and, on the other hand it reduces the British territorial claim to that one hinge while it compels unionists to accept key and fundamental changes involving all-Ireland dimensions to everyday life. Our negotiating team went into the talks to get the Government of Ireland Act repealed. We succeeded in that ... There is now no indefinite commitment, no raft of Parliamentary Acts to back up an absolute claim. This is a long way from being as British as Finchley. But British rule has not ended. Neither has partition. That is why our struggle continues' (*An Phoblacht,* 14 May 1998).

Dissident republicans claiming to be the 'Real IRA' admit responsibility for an attempted mortar attack on Belleek RUC station the previous week.

12 May The Chancellor of the Exchequer, Gordon Brown, announces a £315 million investment package for Northern Ireland.

14 May In a speech in Belfast aimed at calming unionist concerns over the Belfast Agreement, Tony Blair says that if paramilitary-linked parties are to benefit from an accelerated release of prisoners and executive posts, their commitment to democratic, non-violent means must be established in a verifiable way. He says that parties that want to take up ministerial posts will have to make a clear and unequivocal commitment that violence has ended for good; for the cease-fires to be considered complete and unequivocal there must be an end to bombings, beatings, killings, and the acquisition of weapons, and the progressive dismantling of paramilitary structures. Loyalists and republicans will also be expected to co-operate fully with the independent commission on decommissioning; legislation to this effect will come before Parliament in the coming weeks. He emphasises that the agreement requires decommissioning to be completed within two years of the referendum and also notes that 'alarming stories' about the future of the RUC 'are just that—stories.'

The loyalist killer Michael Stone, on parole from the Maze Prison, receives a triumphant welcome at a UDP rally in the Ulster Hall, Belfast. Earlier in the day the UDA's leader in the Maze Prison tells the BBC that 'the war is over' and apologises to all victims of UDA and UFF violence.

15 May The LVF announces a cease-fire, and calls for a 'no' vote in the agreement referendum.

16 May Republican dissidents leave a 750 lb car bomb near an RUC station in Armagh. The bomb is defused by bomb disposal experts.

20 May Gerry Adams says IRA weapons 'have been taken out of commission and been placed in dumps.'

22 May On the morning of the referendum on the Belfast Agreement, Tony Blair writes in the *Irish News* and the *News Letter*: 'Representatives of parties intimately linked to paramilitary groups can only be in a future Northern Ireland government if it is clear that there will be no more violence and the threat of violence has gone. That doesn't just mean decommissioning but all bombing, killings, beatings, and an end to targeting, recruiting, and all the structures of terrorism.'

The highest turn-out in Northern Ireland since 1921 (81 per cent) sees a vote in favour of the agreement by 676,966 (71.1 per cent of valid votes) to 274,879 (28.9 per cent); only a few days earlier opinion polls had predicted levels of support for the agreement at less than 60 per cent. In the Republic a referendum on the agreement and on changes to articles 2 and 3 of the Constitution results in 1,442,583 (94.4 per cent) voting in favour and 85, 174 (5.6 per cent) against; the turn-out is 56 per cent.

While the single count in Belfast means that no official breakdown in the figures is possible, an exit poll conducted by Coopers and Lybrand for the *Sunday Times* finds 96 per cent of Catholics in favour of the agreement but only 55 per cent of Protestants. North Antrim is the only Westminster constituency to have a majority against the agreement (55 per cent), though Lagan Valley supports it by only 52 per cent.

Tony Blair welcomes the result as 'another giant stride along the path for peace and hope,' while Bertie Ahern says the referendum results have 'redefined Ireland. This transcends not only the Anglo-Irish Agreement but the whole 1920–21 settlement.' President Clinton says that from this day, 'peace is no longer a dream, it is a reality.'

23 May Gardaí intercept two cars containing bomb-making material near Dundalk. Two men are arrested.

25 May In a *Belfast Telegraph* interview, Tony Blair says the British and Irish governments 'will show no mercy' to anyone going back to violence, and pledges that 'there will be no fudge between democracy and terror.'

The UVF names the PUP councillor Billy Hutchinson as its contact with the arms decommissioning body. Loyalists announce that they are ending their picket of the Catholic church in Harryville, Ballymena.

The SDLP rejects calls by Sinn Féin for an electoral pact in the forthcoming Assembly election, saying that it goes against the spirit of the agreement.

26 May The MP for Lagan Valley, Jeffrey Donaldson, is refused permission by his constituency to stand in the Assembly election. Peter Robinson of the DUP calls the decision 'spiteful'.

27 May As the question of illegal weapons regains prominence, the head of the arms decommissioning body, John de Chastelain, notes that a supplied code word or appointed representative can inform the body where arms are held. Those transporting arms can be given immunity if the decommissioning body is informed in advance. Paramilitary groups can destroy weapons themselves, but this must be verified by the decommissioning body. The UDP leader, Gary McMichael, says 'it would be ambitious to expect loyalist paramilitaries to give up their weapons before the IRA has said it is prepared to give up arms.'

28 May After a meeting with Mo Mowlam, Martin McGuinness warns against 'falling into the trap of trying to make decommissioning the most important item on the agenda.' Sinn Féin also expresses concern that the British army and RUC have not been scaled down since the agreement was negotiated.

30 May Fourteen people, including eleven members of the RUC, are injured when police and nationalists clash during a protest against a Junior Orange march along the Garvaghy Road, Portadown. The RUC say that the violence accompanying the protest was orchestrated. Rioting continues in the area, as well as in Lurgan, the following night.

1 June David Alderdice, brother of Dr John Alderdice, becomes the second Alliance Party member to be elected Lord Mayor of Belfast. Derry City Council elects a DUP mayor and Sinn Féin deputy mayor.

2 June During his fourth visit to Northern Ireland in five weeks, Tony Blair meets party leaders for discussions. Jeffrey Donaldson, who had opposed the agreement, is part of the UUP delegation.

3 June Mo Mowlam names the eight members of the independent commission on the future of policing. The commission, headed by Chris Patten, includes Sir John Smith, former Deputy Commissioner of London Metropolitan Police, and Kathleen O'Toole, a senior American law enforcement figure from Boston. The two local representatives are Peter Smith QC and Dr Maurice Hayes.

In its annual report, the Police Authority says it will press for legislation to force members of the RUC to declare membership of groups such as the Orange Order.

7 June The US Commerce Secretary, William Daley, leads a trade delegation of American companies to Northern Ireland.

A shop in Royal Avenue, Belfast, is gutted in an incendiary attack.

9 June Detectives are called in to investigate the source of an NIO document leaked to Jeffrey Donaldson. The document reports that Mo Mowlam had spoken to the Sinn Féin director of publicity, Rita O'Hare, to discuss the review of the RUC. O'Hare is wanted for questioning by the RUC in connection with alleged offences, including an attempted murder in 1971. Séamus Mallon questions the loyalty of the Secretary of State's civil servants and wonders 'how the machinery of government can work at all in Northern Ireland.'

At the launch of the UUP Assembly manifesto, David Trimble rules out the formation of an Executive before 1999, saying that a shadow Executive will not be formed 'until quite some way into the transitional period.' The manifesto states that the UUP will not sit down with 'unrepentant terrorists'. For Sinn Féin and other parties linked to paramilitaries to take up ministerial posts there must be an unequivocal commitment from the paramilitaries that the 'war' is over; an end to training, weapons procurement, and punishment beatings; progressive abandonment and dismantling of paramilitary structures; complete disarmament in two years; and disclosure of the fate of disappeared victims.

Mo Mowlam announces the appointment of William Martin, former President of the Ulster Farmers' Union, and Dr Barbara Erwin to the Parades Commission to replace Tommy Cheevers and Glen Barr.

10 June Ten Unionist and Conservative MPs, including David Trimble, vote against the Northern Ireland (Sentences) Bill, which allows the early release of paramilitary prisoners, at its second reading in the House of Commons. Trimble says he is disappointed that the Prime Minister's speech on safeguards made before the referendum was more emphatic than the legislation. On 18 June six UUP MPs join Conservatives in voting against the bill's third reading. Despite a government majority of ninety-nine, the vote represents a break in the British multi-party consensus on Northern Ireland.

11 June An LVF statement says that its cease-fire is unequivocal and that it will approach the arms decommissioning body within weeks.

17 June Two days after the Parades Commission has rerouted an Orange march in north Belfast, David Trimble says the decision is a mistake and that the commission is not viable in the medium to long term.

Pádraic Wilson, the IRA's leader in the Maze Prison, tells the *Financial Times* that 'a voluntary decommissioning would be a natural development of the peace process' after the arrangements envisaged in the agreement begin to function properly. Weapons would not, however, be surrendered to the security forces.

21 June John White of the UDP says he will recommend that the UDA make the first move towards decommissioning and put pressure on the IRA to respond. He adds, however, that the UDA will not decommission unilaterally.

22 June A transcript of an interview given by the Chief Constable, Ronnie Flanagan, suggests that the RUC would be prepared to let the Orange march at Drumcree through under threat of widespread violence, even if the Parades Commission ruled against it. He later says the remarks are out of context and that he will enforce the Parades Commission's decisions.

In a speech to business leaders in Belfast, David Trimble says the people of Northern Ireland 'have a common task and a common ambition to construct in Northern Ireland a civil society that will consign coercion of any sort to the scrap-heap of history. We can now get down to the historic and honourable task of this generation, to raise up a new Northern Ireland in which pluralist unionism and constitutional nationalism can speak to each other with the civility that is the foundation of freedom' (*Belfast Telegraph*, 22 June 1998).

24 June A 200 lb INLA bomb injures five people and causes severe damage to the centre of Newtownhamilton, Co. Armagh.

25 June Elections to the Assembly return twenty-eight UUP, twenty-four SDLP, twenty DUP, eighteen Sinn Féin, six Alliance, five UKUP, two PUP, and three anti-agreement unionists. Monica McWilliams and Jane Morrice of the Northern Ireland Women's Coalition are elected, but the UDP leader Gary McMichael is not.

The result is a success for nationalist parties, with the SDLP receiving the largest number of first-preference votes, 177,963 (22.0 per cent), while Sinn Féin again wins its largest proportion of the poll (142,858 first-preference votes, 17.7 per cent). The shredding of the unionist bloc sees the UUP receive its lowest share of the vote (172,225 votes, 21.3 per cent), while the DUP receives 145,917 votes (18.0 per cent), UKUP 36,541 (4.5 per cent), PUP 20,634 (2.6 per cent), and UDP 8,651 (1.1 per cent). In the centre, Alliance receives 52,636 votes (6.5 per cent), the Women's Coalition 13,019 votes (1.6 per cent), and Labour candidates 2,729 (0.3 per cent). The turn-out is 68.8 per cent. Though the SDLP receives the largest number of first-preference votes, it is not the largest party in the Assembly: the lower turn-out in safe unionist seats, together with the way in which votes transferred between parties, means that the UUP takes the largest number of seats.

The 1998 Assembly Election

As in 1973, the result of the 1998 Assembly election revealed deep divisions within the unionist electorate. Some UUP voters, disaffected by the way in which the agreement was developing, defected to the UKUP and anti-agreement unionists; others simply did not bother to vote. The optimistic belief within loyalist parties that they were on the verge of a new era also seemed largely unfounded, with only the 'media-friendly' David Ervine and Billy Hutchinson being returned for the PUP. In all, twenty-eight anti-agreement unionists were returned, with several other UUP members deeply suspicious of the deal.

The depth of this unionist division was perhaps best illustrated in West Belfast, where a four-way split in the unionist vote meant that none of the candidates was elected. But despite the clear evidence of divisions within unionism in general and the UUP in particular, it still came as something of a surprise when Jeffrey Donaldson, during a live television interview, said that the UUP director of elections, Ken Maginnis, 'should hold his head in shame today. He has presided over one of the biggest electoral disasters for the Ulster Unionist Party in recent years.' Whether the failure of the UUP to select a larger number of 'soft no' candidates, better reflecting the party's grass-roots support, was, in the football parlance of the day, an 'own goal' was open to debate. In the short term, however, the decision provided David Trimble with a more 'loyal' group of Assembly members than Faulkner had been able to muster in 1973. While the UUP could take comfort from the fact that it would be the largest party in the Assembly, UUP voters' support for the agreement, particularly over the issues of the release of prisoners and arms decommissioning, remained fragile.

The election result also emphasised the narrowing of the gap in electoral support between Sinn Féin and the SDLP that had taken place in the nineties. In 1992 the SDLP won approximately 70 per cent of the nationalist vote, compared with Sinn Féin's 30 per cent; in 1993 it was 64 per cent to 36 per cent; in the general election of May 1997 it was 60 per cent to 40 per cent; and in the district council elections three weeks later it was 55 per cent to 45 per cent. In the 1998 Assembly election the SDLP received 552 per cent of the nationalist vote compared to Sinn Féin's 442 per cent. The election also confirmed the growth in the combined SDLP and Sinn Féin vote as a proportion of the total vote. In the May 1997 general election the total nationalist vote reached a new high point at 40.2 per cent, though the figure fell slightly, to 39.7 per cent, in the Assembly election.

29 June The Parades Commission announces that the Drumcree Orange march planned for the following Sunday will be rerouted away from the Garvaghy Road. The decision is followed by a massive police and army build-up in the area and the building of a steel wall across the Garvaghy Road. The following day the Orange Order says it will stay at Drumcree for as long as it takes to get down the Garvaghy Road.

29 June Dr John Alderdice announces that he is retiring from the leadership of the Alliance Party. On 1 July he is appointed interim Speaker of the new Northern Ireland Assembly. Seán Neeson is later elected as the new Alliance leader.

1 July At the first meeting of the Assembly the leader of the UUP, David Trimble, and deputy leader of the SDLP, Séamus Mallon, are jointly elected First Minister and Deputy First Minister, respectively. (John Hume declines the latter position because of his work load elsewhere.) The meeting is also significant in bringing together the leaders of all the main Northern Ireland parties in a single chamber. In his opening address, Trimble repeats that his party will not sit in government with 'unreconstructed terrorists' but adds: 'We have never said that simply because someone has a past they can't have a future.'

2 July Arson attacks on ten Catholic churches throughout Northern Ireland are attributed to the LVF.

3 July A Protestant man who has been under threat from loyalist paramilitaries is shot dead at his home in Bangor.

5 July The RUC and army prevent an Orange church parade returning along the Garvaghy Road in Portadown, sparking rioting in Protestant areas of Northern Ireland and another stalemate at Drumcree. The following day David Trimble says the situation has the potential to destabilise Northern Ireland but denies he threatened to resign over the issue.

6 July As rioting continues, RUC patrols are fired on in loyalist areas of Belfast. By 8 July police reports say that there have been more than four hundred attacks on the security forces, twelve shooting incidents, and twenty-five bombings.

9 July Tony Blair meets Orange leaders in London but refuses to interfere in the Parades Commission decision on Drumcree.

10 July Four people are arrested after police foil a republican attempt to launch a fire-bomb attack on central London.

11 July Indirect talks between Orange representatives and the Garvaghy Road residents' group fail to reach agreement. The Orange Order lodges an application for a march down the road on 12 July before the talks collapse, but the application is again rejected by the Parades Commission.

12 July Three brothers—Richard (11), Mark (10) and Jason (9) Quinn—are killed in a sectarian arson attack on their home in Ballymoney. In the wake of the murders Rev. William Bingham, chaplain of the Co. Armagh

Orange Order, calls for an end to the Drumcree confrontation, saying that 'no road is worth a life,' and urges Orangemen to leave Drumcree.

13 July Orange celebrations are held throughout Northern Ireland. Nationalists conduct a peaceful protest against an Orange march on the Lower Ormeau Road, Belfast. At an Orange rally in Pomeroy, Co. Tyrone, Rev. William Bingham is verbally attacked by the leader of the 'Spirit of Drumcree' group, Joel Patton, who accuses him of betraying the Portadown Orangemen.

16 July As disturbances subside, one of the two additional army battalions brought into Northern Ireland the previous week returns to England. On 23 July the NIO assesses the cost of damage resulting from the Drumcree confrontation at £3 million. This compares with £10 million of damage in 1997 and £20 million in 1996.

19 July Andrew Kearney dies after being beaten and shot in the legs and ankles by a gang at his flat on the New Lodge Road, Belfast. On 24 July the RUC says it believes the IRA is responsible for the murder.

21 July Dissident republicans make an unsuccessful attempt to launch a mortar attack on an RUC station in Newry.

27 July Two Catholic brothers are shot and wounded in a loyalist attack in Derry.

28 July In a government reshuffle, John McFall replaces Tony Worthington at the NIO.

The legislation allowing the early release of prisoners under the conditions set out in the Belfast Agreement becomes law. Despite continuing paramilitary activity, Mo Mowlam declares the IRA, UDA and UVF to be inactive, allowing prisoners from those organisations to benefit from the terms of the Northern Ireland (Sentences) Act.

30 July The government names the ten members of the commission responsible for determining the release of individual paramilitary prisoners. The joint chairmen are a former NIO permanent secretary, Sir John Blelloch, and a South African lawyer, Brian Currin.

Republican dissidents are blamed for fire-bomb attacks on three shops in Portadown.

1 August Unionists and Conservatives attack the Republic's decision to release six IRA prisoners from Portlaoise Prison. On 6 August, Thomas McMahon, convicted of the murder of Lord Mountbatten and three others in 1979, is also released.

A 500 lb bomb, claimed by the Real IRA, explodes, causing extensive damage to the centre of Banbridge.

4 August Republicans open fire on a police patrol outside an RUC station in Lurgan. The UDP leader, Gary McMichael, says that the republican attacks threaten the prospects for peace and that the security forces must deal with this threat 'fully and swiftly.'

After prolonged proximity talks, Apprentice Boys and the Bogside Residents' Group agree a compromise for a parade in Derry on 8 August. Despite this, the march itself results in scuffles between loyalists and republicans.

8 August An LVF statement says 'our war is over.' The announcement of a complete cease-fire is perceived as being influenced by the fact that the organisation's prisoners had not been included on the list of those eligible for early release under the Belfast Agreement.

10 August It emerges that £1.4 million is to be spent on reintegrating into society the four hundred paramilitary prisoners held at the Maze Prison, a cost of £3,500 per prisoner.

15 August Twenty-eight people are killed and 360 injured by a 300 lb republican car bomb attack in Omagh. The explosion takes place on a Saturday afternoon during the town's civic festival, with the result that many of those killed and injured are children. The RUC received a warning but were given the wrong location of the car bomb, with the result that they inadvertently directed people towards the device rather than away from it. A shocked local woman says, 'This is our peace. If this is peace, what's war?' Martin McGuinness of Sinn Féin says he is 'appalled and disgusted. It was an indefensible action.' The universally condemned atrocity is the largest loss of life in any incident in Northern Ireland during the Troubles.

18 August The Real IRA admits responsibility for the Omagh bomb but claims that it gave clear instructions about where the bomb had been planted. 'Despite media reports it was not our intention at any time to kill civilians. It was a commercial target, part of an ongoing war against the Brits. We offer apologies to the civilians.' UTV, which received two of the three warning calls, denies this claim and confirms that the wrong location was given. A second statement from the Real IRA later announces that it is suspending all 'military operations'.

19 August The Irish government announces its intention to introduce new anti-terrorist measures, including restricting suspects' right to silence. Under the new legislation the word of a senior Garda officer could help indict suspected members of illegal organisations.

22 August The INLA announces a 'complete cease-fire' stating. 'We acknowledge and admit faults and grievous errors in our prosecution of the war. Innocent people were killed and injured and at times our actions as a liberation army fell far short of what they should have been. For this we as republicans, as socialists and as revolutionaries do offer a sincere, heartfelt and genuine apology. It was never our intention, desire or wish to become embroiled in sectarian or internecine warfare. We have however nothing to apologise for in taking the war to the British and their loyalist henchmen. Those who preyed on the blood of nationalists paid a heavy price. However the will of the Irish people is clear. It is now time to silence the guns and allow the working classes the time and opportunity to advance their demands and their needs.'

Remembrance services are held for the victims of the Omagh bombing.

25 August In Omagh, Tony Blair announces that Parliament is to be recalled to pass a law allowing certain terrorist suspects to be imprisoned on the word of senior police officers.

28 August Leaked minutes of a meeting on 6 August between the NIO security minister, Adam Ingram, and a UUP Assembly group state that the Unionists said there was 'no chance' of an Executive being formed without an actual handing over of weapons by the IRA. Sinn Féin says the UUP is adding fresh preconditions to the agreement.

31 August An IRA spokesman tells *An Phoblacht* that the Real IRA 'should disband and they should do so sooner rather than later.'

2 September Two soldiers convicted of the murder of the Catholic teenager Peter McBride in September 1992 are released from prison on licence. The release is criticised by the victim's family.

Gerry Adams states that 'Sinn Féin is committed to exclusively peaceful and democratic means to achieve a way forward ... Sinn Féin believe the violence we have seen must be for all of us now a thing of the past, over, done with and gone.' The statement, on the eve of President Clinton's second visit to Northern Ireland, is viewed as an attempt by republicans to meet unionist demands for a declaration stating that 'the war is over.' Sinn Féin announces that Martin McGuinness has been appointed to work with the international decommissioning body.

3 September The Criminal Justice (Terrorism and Conspiracy) Bill is passed by the House of Commons. Parliament had been recalled specifically to pass the act, which gives stronger powers to deal with terrorist groups not on cease-fire. Tony Blair calls the act a 'proportionate response to deal with small and evil groups of violent men' seeking to wreck the Belfast Agreement. The UKUP MP Robert McCartney says the act introduces a system of 'two-tier' terrorism. Similar legislation is also passed in the Republic.

On a one-day visit to Northern Ireland, President Clinton tells an audience at the Waterfront Hall, Belfast, which includes Tony Blair, to grasp the opportunity for peace. 'Do not let it slip away. It will not come again in our lifetime.' Earlier, David Trimble tells the audience that he welcomes every move made by those 'crossing the bridge from terror to democracy' but that he could not reconcile positions in government with a failure to dismantle terrorist organisations. He also promises to create 'a pluralist parliament for a pluralist people.'

The President and Prime Minister also meet Assembly members at Stormont and later visit Omagh and Armagh.

5 September The death of Seán McGrath brings the number of victims of the Omagh bombing to twenty-nine.

An RUC man is seriously injured by a loyalist blast-bomb when police intervene in sectarian clashes in Portadown. Two Catholic-owned businesses are destroyed by petrol bombs after demonstrators at a 'Loyalist Right to March' rally clash with nationalists.

6 September On a BBC television programme David Trimble says the appointment of Martin McGuinness to liaise with the decommissioning commission has 'put the republican movement on a conveyor belt which will lead to actual decommissioning or it will be very clear, very quickly that they are refusing, in which case the other parties will draw the appropriate conclusions.'

7 September David Trimble and Gerry Adams meet at Stormont during round-table talks to discuss political structures.

8 September The Real IRA announces a 'complete cessation of all military activity,' leaving the Continuity IRA the only paramilitary group not to declare a cease-fire. It is reported that, on 1 September, the IRA had warned Real IRA leaders that 'action will be taken' if they did not call a cease-fire (*Belfast Telegraph,* 8 September 1998).

10 September David Trimble and Gerry Adams meet for direct discussions. It is the first official meeting between a Unionist and Sinn Féin leader in more than seventy-five years.

11 September Seven prisoners are given early release as part of the Belfast Agreement. On 18 September the first prisoner to be convicted of murder is released under the scheme.

12 September Soldiers end their patrols in the greater Belfast area.

14 September The Northern Ireland Assembly meets for the first time, in the former House of Commons chamber at Stormont. Two former Ulster Unionist members and an Independent Unionist form the United Unionist Assembly Party, led by Denis Watson.

21 September Nine men are arrested on both sides of the border in connection with the Omagh bombing.

22 September The Chief Constable announces that between three hundred and four hundred soldiers are to leave Northern Ireland in the next two weeks.

Following a meeting with David Trimble, Bertie Ahern suggests that a timetable for the handing over of IRA weapons be established.

23 September In an attempt to circumvent difficulties surrounding decommissioning, Ulster Unionists suggest that shadow Executive appointments be made but that the Executive not meet until powers are transferred.

The Conservative Party spokesman on Northern Ireland, Andrew Mackay, calls for the release of prisoners and for Sinn Féin appointments to the Executive to be halted if the IRA does not comply with the Belfast Agreement's requirements on decommissioning.

David Trimble is barracked by loyalist protesters as he leaves a meeting with Orange leaders in Portadown.

25 September Séamus Mallon and David Trimble become involved in a dispute over the issue of when a shadow Executive will be established. Mallon attacks the daily 'battle of words' over decommissioning and says the issue has 'almost become a soap opera.'

30 September Nineteen paramilitary prisoners are freed under the terms of the Belfast Agreement. In the latest series of reductions in security measures, the Chief Constable announces that a number of army installations are to be demolished and check-points removed.

6 October An RUC man, Frank O'Reilly, dies from injuries received from a loyalist blast-bomb in Portadown on 5 September. Responsibility for the murder is claimed by a new loyalist paramilitary group, the 'Red Hand Defenders'.

9 October UUP members sceptical of the Belfast Agreement launch the 'Union First' pressure group and press for a ballot of members of the Ulster Unionist Council on involvement in an Executive that includes Sinn Féin. On 12 October senior UUP Assembly members accuse the new group of trying to undermine David Trimble.

10 October An American appeal court overturns an earlier decision to return three escapers from the Maze Prison—Kevin Barry Artt, Paul Brennan, and Terence Kirby—to Northern Ireland.

The PUP spokesman, Billy Hutchinson, says the UVF and Red Hand Commando are not ready to decommission weapons and may not hand over weapons even if the IRA do so. A UUP councillor, Jim Rodgers, accuses loyalists of 'riding to the rescue' of Sinn Féin on decommissioning.

15 October In Toronto, David Trimble describes decommissioning as 'the final hurdle and one which when overcome will allow Northern Ireland to be at ease with itself and its neighbours.' He describes decommissioning as the 'litmus test' of the Belfast Agreement and says it is not a precondition but an obligation.

16 October John Hume and David Trimble are awarded the Nobel Peace Prize for their work towards finding a peaceful solution to the Troubles.

Twenty-eight prisoners, including the UDA leader in the Maze Prison, are freed under the terms of the Belfast Agreement.

19 October Tony Blair holds meetings with Martin McGuinness and David Trimble in an attempt to resolve the dispute over decommissioning.

21 October The Security Minister, Adam Ingram, tells the House of Commons that there have been fifty-four deaths related to the Troubles in the year up to 16 October. Thirty-eight of the murders were committed by republicans and sixteen by loyalists.

24 October At the UUP annual conference, David Trimble repeats his view that Sinn Féin members cannot be part of the Executive without decommissioning by the IRA. Earlier in the day the party's Assembly chief whip suggested that the UUP may have been too firm on the issue.

26 October Lieutenant-General Sir Hew Pike becomes army commander in Northern Ireland. Ronnie Flanagan announces that Whiterock army barracks in west Belfast is to close.

31 October A Catholic man, Brian Service, is murdered by the 'Red Hand Defenders' in north Belfast.

The parties fail to meet the 31 October deadline for the formation of a shadow Executive and North-South Ministerial Body, because of disagreements over decommissioning and other issues.

2 November Bertie Ahern meets pro-agreement parties at Stormont for discussions on North-South political structures.

4 November The NIO reveals that more than a thousand punishment attacks have taken place since September 1994 and warns that continued paramilitary attacks could halt the release of prisoners.

The army announces that two soldiers convicted of the murder of Peter McBride in September 1992 will be permitted to remain in the army. Mo Mowlam had said that she was against them remaining in the army.

10 November Prince Philip makes his first official visit to the Republic.

Following a meeting between Tony Blair and Gerry Adams in London, the government says it will continue to try to make progress on the Belfast Agreement.

The two-hundredth prisoner to be given early release under the Belfast Agreement is freed.

11 November The leader of the 'Spirit of Drumcree' group, Joel Patton, is expelled from the Orange Order because of his public criticism of the Co. Armagh chaplain, Rev. William Bingham, in July.

Sir David Ramsbotham's report on the Maze Prison criticises the degree of control that the prison service allowed prisoners to exercise but praises the work of the prison's staff.

At Messines Ridge in Belgium the Queen and President Mary McAleese jointly open a peace tower memorial to Irish members of the British army killed in the First World War.

13 November It is announced that a further 400 soldiers are to be withdrawn and that check-points outside Bessbrook are to be removed.

14 November At the SDLP annual conference, John Hume says there is no precondition for decommissioning in the agreement but that it is the will of the people that disarmament take place. He also asks, 'What greater unity is possible than the unity of the joint endeavours of those elected to serve in the Assembly and its Executive?'

15 November In a *Sunday Telegraph* interview the leader of the Conservative Party, William Hague, calls for a halt to the release of prisoners until decommissioning begins.

17 November The government officially accepts the validity of the LVF cease-fire, clearing the way for the early release of the organisation's prisoners.

18 November The *Irish Times* claims that a preliminary report of the Commission on Policing has suggested that the RUC be disbanded. The chairman of the commission, Chris Patten, denies there is any substance to the claim.

19 November The LVF defers its handing over of weapons, saying it was offended by comments made by Ken Maginnis in the House of Commons. He had claimed that the LVF cease-fire would last only until their prisoners were released.

The Northern Ireland Act, which makes legal provision for the implementation of the Belfast Agreement, becomes law. The act contains almost five hundred changes from the bill originally introduced in the House of Commons in July.

A report from the United Nations Committee Against Torture calls for the reconstruction of the RUC, ending the use of plastic bullets, and the closure of RUC interrogation centres.

A Union First meeting in Dunmurry, Belfast, is attended by senior DUP, UUP and UKUP members as well as the Conservative MPs David Wiltshire and Andrew Hunter. Ian Paisley says they are identifying eight UUP Assembly members to take away the cross-community support needed for further progress on the Agreement.

In Dublin, David Trimble tells the Chamber of Commerce that he looks forward to working with the Republic for the benefit of all, but not at Northern Ireland's expense. He later meets Bertie Ahern and says that agreement on the areas and structures of North-South bodies would be reached within a matter of weeks. The following night Trimble tells the Irish Association that the 'cold war' with the Republic is over but that there can be no Executive positions for Sinn Féin while their 'no, nothing, never' policy continues.

21 November Linfield football club, with a Protestant following, plays the mainly Catholic Cliftonville at the latter's home ground in north Belfast for the first time in twenty-eight years.

During an RTE radio interview, Bertie Ahern agrees with his interviewer that there is an irresistible dynamic towards a united Ireland, which will take place within twenty years. The remarks are severely criticised by unionists. However, speaking at the same time to the Irish Association, Ahern's adviser, Martin Mansergh, says the Belfast Agreement allows space for those who wish to preserve the Union on the basis of a pluralist parliament for a pluralist people.

22 November RUC statistics show that there have been 109 loyalist beatings and shootings so far in the year, with 79 similar incidents attributed to republicans.

25 November In Belfast, Tony Blair meets local politicians for talks on the peace process. The following day he becomes the first British Prime Minister to jointly address the Dáil and Seanad. He states his optimism that the peace process will continue to make progress, saying, 'We have come too far to go back now.'

28 November At the DUP conference the deputy leader, Peter Robinson, calls on Ulster Unionists to dump David Trimble rather than drag Northern Ireland 'step by step to Dublin.'

30 November As talks on the number of government departments, North-South bodies and decommissioning appear stalled, the UUP deputy leader, John Taylor, recalls the failed Sunningdale experiment and remarks: 'I see history beginning to repeat itself as Dublin and the SDLP aim too high in their ambitions for the new North-South Council. This issue could collapse the Agreement.'

2 December As Tony Blair arrives in Belfast for further negotiations, a UUP and SDLP dispute over plans for an all-Ireland body to oversee trade and business development becomes public. The following day a meeting of UUP Assembly members stresses opposition to the creation of such a body as well as the suggestion that ten departments be established rather than seven, as the UUP prefer.

3 December A crowd of up to a thousand loyalists protesting against the ban on the local Orange march clash with police at Drumcree. Loyalists have maintained a presence at Drumcree since July.

8 December Reports suggest that an IRA convention held the previous weekend decided that the conditions for allowing decommissioning of their weapons did not exist at present.

It is revealed that the arms decommissioning body has issued an arms immunity certificate to the LVF, allowing it to transport guns for decommissioning.

An NIO document leaked to the DUP reveals that the number of families forced to leave their homes because of intimidation is at its highest level since records began in 1973. The memo suggests that 60 per cent of current applications for housing relocation are from members of the security forces.

10 December In Oslo, John Hume and David Trimble receive the Nobel Peace Prize. Trimble's speech remarks that in the past, unionists, acting out of fear, had built 'a cold house for Catholics' in Northern Ireland.

11 December Reports suggest that the IRA Army Council has 'firmly' rejected decommissioning. The following day the UUP deputy leader, John Taylor, calls for an end to the early release of IRA prisoners.

12 December Loyalists, republicans and police clash during an Apprentice Boys march in Derry.

14 December It emerges that the UKUP leader, Robert McCartney, is at odds with the party's four other Assembly members over policy issues and personal differences. The main policy differences concern McCartney's insistence that UKUP members should withdraw from the Assembly if Sinn Féin takes up ministerial positions before IRA decommissioning or strong cross-border bodies are established.

17 December A blast-bomb attack on a bar in Crumlin, Co. Antrim, is claimed by the 'Orange Volunteers'. A month earlier the organisation had stated it would attack freed republican prisoners. The bomb attack is also later claimed by the 'Red Hand Defenders'.

Danny McNamee, who had been convicted of the Hyde Park bombing of July 1982, wins an appeal against his conviction for conspiracy to cause explosions on the grounds that the conviction was unsafe.

18 December SDLP and UUP negotiators agree to the creation of ten Northern Ireland departments, six North-South implementation bodies, and six North-South areas of co-operation. The six agreed implementation bodies will be responsible for inland waterways, food safety, trade and business development, special EU programmes, the Irish and Ulster Scots languages, and aquaculture and marine matters.

In the first voluntary decommissioning of weapons, the LVF hand over to the International Decommissioning Body nine guns, 350 bullets, two pipe bombs, and six detonators.

23 December 170 paramilitary prisoners are released on parole for Christmas.

28 December A loyalist blast-bomb explodes outside a house in Armagh.

DEATHS ARISING FROM THE TROUBLES: 55. SHOOTINGS: 211. BOMBS PLANTED: 243. FIREARMS FOUND: 88. EXPLOSIVES FOUND: 883 kg (1,945 lb). PERSONS CHARGED WITH TERRORIST AND SERIOUS PUBLIC ORDER OFFENCES: 459. CASUALTIES ARISING FROM PARAMILITARY ATTACKS: 216.

1999

3 January RUC detectives say they know the identity of those responsible for the Omagh bomb but have not got enough evidence to bring charges.

Bertie Ahern calls for a speedy resolution to the decommissioning issue. The following day the Tánaiste, Mary Harney, says there is no distinction between Sinn Féin and the IRA and that it is now time for them to decommission.

5 January The four UKUP Assembly members who had disagreed with the party leader, Robert McCartney, over policy issues announce that they are forming the Northern Ireland Unionist Party, leaving McCartney as the single UKUP representative. The new group is the sixth unionist party to be represented in the Assembly.

As paramilitary punishment beatings continue, two men are injured in Co. Antrim in attacks believed to have been carried out by loyalists. The following day a man is injured by a loyalist blast-bomb at Magherafelt.

7 January Arguments over decommissioning resume, with the Deputy First Minister, Séamus Mallon, saying that 'sooner or later' the UUP and Sinn Féin will have to sit together in an Executive and that it will be imperative for the IRA to hand in weapons if Sinn Féin is involved in power-sharing. UUP spokesmen angrily reject the idea of Sinn Féin involvement in an Executive before decommissioning. An IRA statement meanwhile calls on the British and Irish governments to face down unionists. The statement repeats the claim that British government and unionist attitudes led the IRA to end its 1994 cessation and warns of 'growing frustration' because of their failure to embrace 'forward political movement'. The statement is perceived by unionists as a threat that the IRA will end its cease-fire if its demands are not met. Mark Durkan of the SDLP says he can understand the unionists' perception on this point.

A UVF member sentenced to four hundred years' imprisonment for crimes including three murders and the manslaughter of a policewoman is released under the terms of the Belfast Agreement after serving ten years.

A man is wounded in a loyalist gun attack in Bangor.

10 January A PUP Assembly member, Billy Hutchinson, says David

Trimble is endangering the peace process by insisting that the IRA begin decommissioning before Sinn Féin takes its seats in the Executive.

11 January In a New Year message to Northern Ireland, Tony Blair says the key challenge of the year is to show that the Belfast Agreement is working in all its aspects. He also states that decommissioning 'would do more to create confidence between the communities than any other single step.'

13 January The Secretary of State for Northern Ireland, Mo Mowlam, says the British government will be ready to implement devolution to the Assembly on 10 March if current political problems can be resolved.

14 January Gardaí recover three anti-aircraft guns in Co. Monaghan. Four men are arrested after shots are fired at a police station in west Belfast by the Continuity IRA.

18 January As the Assembly debates an interim report on the future structures of government and North-South bodies agreed on 18 December 1998, the Deputy Leader of the UUP, John Taylor, warns that the process has only a 50 per cent chance of survival, and he states: 'Either we will go ahead without Sinn Féin or it will collapse.' A row develops after anti-agreement unionists object to the debate being guillotined. While the interim report is approved by 74 votes to 27, a UUP member, Peter Weir, votes against the report and subsequently has the party whip withdrawn.

Professor Brice Dickson is named as head of the new Northern Ireland Human Rights Commission. Unionists later complain that the commission's membership contains no Unionist representative, from either the pro-agreement or the anti-agreement camp, but several nationalist representatives.

19 January A Conservative MP, Andrew Hunter, says he will name in the House of Commons the Omagh bomber and paramilitaries suspected of punishment attacks. He postpones naming the suspects after the Chief Constable and others suggest that this might prejudice the chances of their conviction in any future trial.

20 January A man is injured in a bomb attack by the Orange Volunteers at his home in Loughinisland, Co. Down. On BBC Radio Ulster the PUP spokesman, David Ervine, claims the Orange Volunteers is largely made up of LVF members and is a combination of Protestant fundamentalists and drug dealers.

21 January In an interview in the *Belfast Telegraph,* Billy Hutchinson of the PUP says the collapse of the Belfast Agreement over decommissioning might lead to the imposition of an Anglo-Irish Agreement mark 2, which could lead to loyalists reacting by attacking the Republic's agriculture and tourism industries.

In the House of Commons the Conservative Party leader, William Hague, calls on the government to halt the release of prisoners until decommissioning begins.

22 January A former member of the PUP talks team, Lindsay Robb, is the first LVF prisoner to be given early release under the terms of the Belfast Agreement.

23 January The RUC announces that seven patrol bases along the Co. Fermanagh border will close in the following weeks.

Loyalists throw blast-bombs at the homes of two Catholic families in Larne. There are further attacks in the following months.

24 January David Trimble says the political process could be 'parked' if decommissioning does not take place, adding: 'What we don't want is for the process to have a crash-landing where it is seriously damaged.'

25 January As concern over paramilitary punishment attacks increases, the British government comes under pressure to take action. Meetings between the Secretary of State and representatives of the PUP, UDP and Sinn Féin fail to make any progress on the issue.

A meeting between the Security Minister, Adam Ingram, and relatives of IRA members killed at Loughgall in 1987 is criticised by relatives of those murdered by the IRA in the area.

Loyalists plant a pipe-bomb under the car of a Catholic man living in Greenisland, Co. Antrim.

27 January The body of a former IRA man, Éamon Collins, is found near Newry. Collins, who had written a book exposing and criticising IRA activity in south Down, had received head wounds and had been stabbed.

A Conservative Party motion calling for an end to the release of paramilitary prisoners until punishment attacks stop is defeated in the House of Commons. Later in the day Ian Paisley uses parliamentary privilege to name twenty-two people alleged to be included in a police file on the Kingsmills massacre of 1976. The RUC later denies that the information comes from a detailed police dossier.

28 January A pipe-bomb is thrown through the window of a Catholic family's house in Dungannon by the Red Hand Defenders.

30 January Seven people are injured in loyalist beatings in Newtownabbey, Co. Antrim. In Cookstown a man is shot in the leg by republicans. January is the worst month for paramilitary beatings and shootings for more than ten years.

Gerry Adams says he would be 'shocked' if the government allowed the UUP to delay devolution and the formation of the Executive.

3 February Four men, including Pearse McAuley from Strabane, plead guilty to the manslaughter of Garda Jerry McCabe in Co. Limerick in June 1996. The verdict causes an outcry in the Republic, where some believe that republican paramilitary intimidation of witnesses explained the failure of the court to bring in verdicts of murder.

The *Belfast Telegraph* reports that the North Ulster unit of the UVF has smuggled new weapons into Northern Ireland, and that the Continuity IRA has also acquired weapons.

Police clash with two hundred loyalist rioters in Portadown.

Amnesty International agrees to a request from David Trimble to investigate the issue of paramilitary punishment attacks.

4 February Nicholas Mullen, the last republican prisoner held in Britain, is freed after the Court of Appeal rules that his conviction is unsafe because the manner in which he was extradited from Zimbabwe broke international and Zimbabwean laws.

An IRA statement says that some of its weapons have been stolen by republicans opposed to the peace process.

5 February As arguments over decommissioning continue, Bertie Ahern says his Government wants to see the Belfast Agreement being implemented rather than 'parked, reviewed, or changed.' He also says that the killers of Garda Jerry McCabe will not qualify for early release under the terms of the agreement; Sinn Féin leaders disagree with this view.

8 February An opinion poll commissioned by the *Belfast Telegraph* shows 84 per cent support for immediate paramilitary decommissioning; 93 per cent of Protestants and 68 per cent of Catholics believe decommissioning should start immediately. The same poll finds 60 per cent (85 per cent of Protestants and 22 per cent of Catholics) opposed to Sinn Féin taking seats on the Executive before IRA decommissioning, while 29 per cent (7 per cent of Protestants and 63 per cent of Catholics) support Sinn Féin's inclusion without decommissioning.

An Orange Volunteers grenade explodes at a Catholic-owned bar near Toomebridge, Co. Antrim.

12 February On the tenth anniversary of the murder of the solicitor Pat Finucane, a petition signed by more than a thousand legal figures and supported by Amnesty International calls for an independent inquiry into his death.

14 February In an interview in the *Sunday Times,* Bertie Ahern says that Sinn Féin's being part of an Executive would not be possible 'without at least a commencement of decommissioning, and that would apply in the North and in the South.' Sinn Féin leaders are visible disconcerted by this statement.

16 February The Assembly votes by 77 to 29 to endorse structures of government proposed in a report presented by David Trimble and Séamus Mallon. 29 unionists vote in favour of the report and 29 against. One UUP member, Roy Beggs Jr, who considered voting against the proposals, votes in favour after receiving a private letter from Trimble believed to state that the party will not allow the appointment of Sinn Féin members to the Executive until the IRA has begun decommissioning.

The RUC recovers the largest cache of IRA arms found in west Belfast in two years. They claim that eight commercial detonators included in the cache were made in 1998, during the latest cease-fire, leading Sinn Féin to say that the RUC are pursuing a political agenda.

Gerry Adams meets Tony Blair for talks in London.

17 February UUP and Sinn Féin leaders meet for talks at Stormont. The talks fail to produce any significant progress.

19 February The RUC clash with youths in Portadown after a rally in support of the Drumcree protesters. Earlier in the week it was revealed that policing the Drumcree confrontation was still costing £10,000 a day.

21 February Seven people are held by police on both sides of the border in a series of interviews in connection with the Omagh bombing. All those questioned but not charged are released by 25 February.

24 February A Co. Armagh man living in the Republic is charged with offences relating to the Omagh bombing.

25 February The Chairman of Sinn Féin, Mitchel McLaughlin, says that even a token gesture on decommissioning could destabilise the IRA leadership, bringing unpredictable consequences.

26 February Tony Blair and Bertie Ahern hold discussions on the transfer of power to the Assembly and decommissioning during an EU heads of government meeting in Germany.

The UFF calls for Sinn Féin to be excluded from the Executive because the IRA has not signalled a permanent end to conflict. The UFF also says it will not decommission weapons, because the IRA is the most potent threat to peace in Northern Ireland.

27 February Three more people are arrested in the Republic in connection with the Omagh bombing.

3 March In an interview with the *Scotsman,* Tony Blair says that decommissioning must take place, because 'people have got to know if they are sitting down [in the Executive] with people who have given up violence for good.' Martin McGuinness had stated earlier that the issue of weapons should be dealt with 'down the road.' Mo Mowlam says her target date for devolution remains 10 March but that she will not transfer powers unless there is cross-community support.

4 March An opinion poll carried out by the BBC and Price Waterhouse

Coopers finds 41 per cent of unionists in favour of the Belfast Agreement, a fall of 14 per cent compared with a poll held on the day of the referendum.

The RUC says that paramilitary punishment attacks in February (eighteen by loyalists and seven by republicans) were half the January figure.

5 March Controversy over the issue of collusion by the British army and RUC with loyalist paramilitaries re-emerges after it is revealed that Bobby Philpott, a former UDA leader in the Maze prison, has told a BBC documentary team that he was getting so many leaked police and army intelligence reports he did not know where to store them.

The homes of two Catholic families are damaged in sectarian arson attacks in north Belfast.

7 March The *Sunday Independent* publishes a leaked republican briefing paper in which a senior figure describes Bertie Ahern as 'the biggest danger to the [peace] process—even bigger than Blair.' It quotes the same source as stating: 'We have been pushed too far. If [Ahern] believes he can push us to where he thinks he wants us to be, he will get his answer before mid-March.'

8 March The British and Irish governments sign four treaties providing the legal framework for North-South implementation bodies, the North-South Ministerial Council, the British-Irish Council, and the British-Irish Intergovernmental Conference, to replace the conference established by the Anglo-Irish Agreement.

It is revealed that the RUC has warned Gerry Adams of a threat to his life from republican dissidents.

Mo Mowlam announces that the deadline for the transfer of power to the Assembly has been postponed until 2 April. The decision is criticised by Sinn Féin and the UUP.

9 March UUP and Sinn Féin leaders meet for talks at Stormont. There is no breakthrough on political differences, but the parties agree to meet again.

Introducing the Implementation Bodies (Northern Ireland) Order in the House of Commons, the Political Development Minister, Paul Murphy, notes that the legislation is the final piece of the institutional jigsaw.

Nine families are temporarily evacuated from their homes after a pipe-bomb is thrown into a house in Portadown.

11 March In his retrial, Private Lee Clegg is acquitted of the murder of Karen Reilly in 1990 after the judge finds that it is not certain that Clegg fired the shot that killed her. Clegg is, however, found guilty of attempting to wound Martin Peake, who was shot dead in the same incident. The decision is welcomed in Britain but attacked by the Reilly family and by nationalists. In his verdict, the judge describes Clegg's version of the events surrounding the shooting as 'untruthful and incapable of belief.'

12 March A man is shot in the leg in an apparent republican punishment attack in Newry.

15 March A solicitor, Rosemary Nelson, is killed when a bomb explodes under her car in Lurgan. The incident leads to rioting by nationalist youths in the area later in the day. Among a range of professional activities, Mrs Nelson had acted as an adviser to the Garvaghy Road Residents' Association for the previous four years. She had claimed that she had been threatened by members of the RUC. Though the Red Hand Defenders say that they carried out the attack, the use of commercial explosives casts doubts on this. The RUC Chief Constable, Ronnie Flanagan, invites the Chief Constable of the Kent Constabulary, David Phillips, to oversee the investigation into the murder. The US Federal Bureau of Investigation is also asked to assist.

17 March A former member of the Red Hand Commando, Frankie Curry, is shot dead in the Shankill Road area of Belfast. The dissident loyalist group Red Hand Defenders blames the UVF for the murder. In an interview with *Sunday Life* shortly before his death (but not published until later) Curry had admitted committing sixteen murders but denied that he was involved with the Red Hand Defenders.

Thirty-eight members of the RUC are injured after rioting between nationalists and loyalists breaks out in Portadown.

In Washington, President Clinton calls on Northern Ireland's politicians to resolve their differences before the deadline of 2 April for the transfer of powers to the Assembly. David Trimble and Gerry Adams hold a thirty-minute meeting during the day.

18 March There is a further outbreak of rioting by nationalists in Portadown and Lurgan.

President Clinton, Tony Blair and Bertie Ahern issue a joint statement calling for the implementation of the Belfast Agreement in all its parts.

Ronnie Flanagan asks the Deputy Commissioner of the Metropolitan Police (London), John Stevens, to investigate new claims of collusion by the security forces in the murder of the solicitor Pat Finucane in 1989.

20 March A bomb is defused at the Belfast home of the spokesman for Families Against Intimidation and Terror, Vincent McKenna. He claims the bomb was planted by the IRA.

David Trimble is heckled at a meeting of the Ulster Unionist Council when he fails to answer a question on the quantity of IRA weapons that would have to be decommissioned before the UUP would participate in an Executive with Sinn Féin. Anti-agreement candidates do well in elections for party officerships; observers suggest that the UUC, which a year earlier was 70 per cent in favour of the agreement, is now evenly split between pro-agreement and anti-agreement members.

21 March In the latest loyalist punishment attack, a thirteen-year-old boy from Newtownards is beaten by men using baseball bats, has a gun held to his head, and is ordered to leave the country.

23 March The Home Secretary, Jack Straw, seeks a judicial review challenging the early release of four IRA prisoners (including the Brighton bomber Patrick Magee) transferred to Northern Ireland from jails in Britain. The Opposition spokesman on Northern Ireland, Andrew Mackay, says the Conservatives would have halted early releases because of the failure of the IRA to decommission and describes the timing of the judicial challenge as 'bizarre'. The Home Secretary's challenge is rejected by the High Court.

A man is injured when an Orange Volunteers grenade explodes in Castlewellan, Co. Down. There is another grenade attack by the same group at a bar outside Lurgan the following night.

24 March It is revealed that a report by the Independent Commission on Police Complaints has listed a number of 'serious concerns' about the RUC's investigation of alleged threats made against Rosemary Nelson by members of the RUC. After calls for the RUC to be removed completely from the murder investigation, the Chief Constable, Sir Ronnie Flanagan, says he will publish as much as possible of a report into alleged police threats against Mrs Nelson that has been prepared by Commander Niall Mulvihill of the Metropolitan Police (London) and submitted to the Director of Public Prosecutions.

Mo Mowlam says she will trigger the d'Hondt mechanism (which allots seats in the Executive in proportion to seats in the Assembly), allowing parties to nominate their representatives to head the various Northern Ireland departments on 2 April. David Trimble, who met Gerry Adams and Martin McGuinness the previous day, says he has done all he can to implement the terms of the agreement and that the obstacle to further progress is the intransigence of Sinn Féin.

25 March A statement by the UVF and Red Hand Commando warns that any attempt by the British and Irish governments to impose a political settlement over the heads of unionists will result in a 'retreat from all theories of process—peace or political.'

26 March The LVF warns of a 'great strain' on its cease-fire if the IRA does not begin decommissioning.

A man is shot in the legs six times in a paramilitary-style attack in the Creggan area of Derry.

27 March In Belfast, delegates to the Grand Orange Lodge of Ireland vote in favour of holding a single Twelfth of July demonstration at Drumcree if the dispute over the parade there is not resolved before then. The meeting also hears a statement, signed by Tony Blair's chief of staff, Jonathan Powell, saying that Blair holds the Orange Order in high esteem and that it could play 'an important and constructive part in the future of Northern Ireland.'

28 March In the *Observer,* Tony Blair and Bertie Ahern make a joint appeal for the Belfast Agreement to be made a living reality, stating: 'The prize is enormous, but it must be shared. There must be no winners or losers.'

The Deputy Leader of the UUP, John Taylor, says David Trimble may have to resign as First Minister later in the week if the Secretary of State triggers the d'Hondt mechanism, allocating Executive positions, and (in the event of the IRA's failure to begin decommissioning) if the SDLP refuses to support a UUP motion to exclude Sinn Féin from government.

29 March The IRA reveals that it has established the whereabouts of the bodies of nine people killed by its members and secretly buried. There is controversy over the issue in April, however, after the IRA refuses to reveal the sites unless it receives assurances that no post-mortem examinations will be carried out and that the funerals be held in private and the media barred from them.

Republicans clash with Orangemen outside the Waterfront Hall, Belfast, where an Orange cultural evening is being held.

Tony Blair and Bertie Ahern arrive in Northern Ireland to participate in the latest round of talks aimed at breaking the political deadlock over decommissioning.

A bomb explodes at the home of a Sinn Féin councillor in Ballycastle.

The RUC appoints the Deputy Chief Constable of Norfolk, Colin Port, to have day-to-day control of the investigation into the murder of Rosemary Nelson.

30 March As talks continue, there are protests by republicans and anti-agreement loyalists at Stormont. The discussions adjourn late in the evening without any agreement.

An IRA statement says the organisation supports the efforts to secure a lasting peace, but it repeats the traditional republican view that the conflict is entirely the fault of the British government and unionists.

The RUC and the Independent Commission for Police Complaints issue a ten-page 'review' based on the Mulvihill report into the murder of Rosemary Nelson; the report makes twenty recommendations for improving procedures, some of which have already been implemented. The publication of the review is criticised by nationalists as an 'exercise in damage limitation'.

31 March The Red Hand Defenders plant a pipe-bomb outside the home of a Catholic businessman in Dungannon. There is a similar attack in north Belfast.

Discussions over the decommissioning issue and the establishment of an Executive continue at Hillsborough Castle. Ian Paisley accuses David Trimble of taking part in 'surrender negotiations', and more than a hundred anti-agreement loyalists later protest outside the venue.

1 April Talks are adjourned until 13 April without agreement being reached and without the d'Hondt mechanism, activating appointments to the

Executive, being implemented. A joint declaration by the British Prime Minister and the Taoiseach at Hillsborough Castle, however, notes that against the background of the implementation of most areas of the Belfast Agreement 'there is agreement among all parties that decommissioning is not a precondition but is an obligation deriving from their commitment in the Agreement.' The statement says that the principal difficulty is the issue of the timing of decommissioning and the formation of the Executive. It proposes that on a set date parties nominate their Executive members. Within one month, on a date set by the Decommissioning Commission, 'a collective act of reconciliation will take place. This will see some arms put beyond use on a voluntary basis, in a manner which will be verified by the Independent International Commission on Decommissioning.' This would be accompanied by further reductions in security. At the same time ceremonies of remembrance of all victims of violence would be held, and about this time powers would be devolved, and other institutions associated with the Belfast Agreement would come into effect. The Decommissioning Commission would report on progress within one month of nominations being made to the Executive. If the steps suggested are not taken by that time, the nominations will not be confirmed by the Assembly.

Reacting to the Hillsborough declaration, a republican source tells the *Irish News* that 'any proposition to have Sinn Féin deliver up IRA weapons is a proposition built on sand. Sinn Féin cannot deliver weapons ... that is the bottom line.' Anti-agreement unionists also criticise the statement, with Ian Paisley calling it an 'April fool's contract'.

3 April After meetings involving senior party members, the UUP decides to reserve its position on the Hillsborough declaration pending clarification on certain points.

A leading Belfast republican, Brian Keenan, tells a rally in Inishkeen, Co. Monaghan, that the IRA will not be forced into 'surrender' masquerading as decommissioning. He describes the Hillsborough declaration as 'nothing more than an Easter bunny'.

4 April Martin McGuinness tells an Easter Rising commemoration in Dundalk that unionists are trying to 'rewrite, renegotiate and redraft the [Belfast] Agreement. It's not on, because that agreement has been endorsed by the overwhelming wish of the people of Ireland. And there is an unrealisable and unrealistic demand for a surrender by the IRA ... The result of this Hillsborough declaration, which is really only a declaration by two governments, is total and absolute confusion: there is no clarity.'

David Trimble tells the *Sunday Times* that he believes republicans will accept the Hillsborough declaration despite attempts by Sinn Féin to distance itself from it.

8 April Martin McGuinness rules out IRA decommissioning before the establishment of an Executive and says that if the governments have changed their view from the Belfast Agreement, 'we are all in very serious difficulty.'

UVF sources say they will not decommission weapons 'to get Sinn Féin into government.' The DUP spokesman Sammy Wilson says the UVF has 'joined its political bedfellows in the PUP in rescuing the IRA when it was on the ropes.'

9 April After a meeting of senior Sinn Féin members, Mitchel McLaughlin says the two governments should defend the Belfast Agreement, and that this will be the party's approach in the coming week.

The UUP deputy chief whip, Derek Hussey, becomes the third UUP Assembly member to express doubts over the Hillsborough declaration. He says he has difficulty with the proposal to nominate Sinn Féin ministers before decommissioning takes place. Despite this, the UUP Assembly team later accepts the document as a basis for negotiation.

The Irish government announces that six IRA prisoners, including the four members of the Balcombe Street gang, are to be given early release. The move is interpreted as an attempt to move Sinn Féin towards accepting the terms of the Hillsborough declaration.

10 April A man is injured when an Orange Volunteers pipe-bomb explodes at a bar near Templepatrick, Co. Antrim.

The *Belfast Telegraph* reports that there have been no republican punishment beatings in almost a month. Republican and loyalist paramilitaries are believed to be supporting schemes promoting 'restorative justice', which bring together petty criminals and their victims in an attempt to resolve problems. However, after a man is shot in both ankles in the Ardoyne area of Belfast on 12 April, Vincent McKenna of Families Against Intimidation and Terror says that beatings have continued over the past month but the victims are too frightened to report the attacks.

Loyalists again begin picketing a Catholic church in Harryville, Ballymena, heightening fears of the potential for conflict between nationalists and loyalists, especially during the Orange marching season.

12 April A report by a special rapporteur of the United Nations, Param Cumaraswamy, criticises Sir Ronnie Flanagan for 'allowing the situation to deteriorate' after a number of defence solicitors alleged harassment by the RUC. He also claims there is evidence of collusion by the security forces in the murder of Pat Finucane and calls for an independent inquiry into the case. The Chief Constable rejects the accusation of indifference, saying that he had had several meetings with the Law Society and that two complaints had been discussed. Later in the week Cumaraswamy has separate discussions with Mo Mowlam and Chris Patten, chairman of the Commission on Policing.

13 April As talks resume at Stormont, the Hillsborough declaration is rejected by both Sinn Féin and the PUP. Mo Mowlam says there will not be an Executive acceptable to both unionists and republicans under the terms of the Belfast Agreement. She adds, however, that any alternative must be acceptable to both traditions.

The release of two loyalist prisoners from the Maze prison brings the total freed under the Belfast Agreement to 257. Of the prisoners released so far, 131 are republicans, 118 are loyalists, and eight have no prison classification.

15 April There are pipe-bomb attacks on the homes of two Catholic families in Randalstown, Co. Antrim.

The Alliance Party accuses the Irish government of double standards after it is revealed that the Irish side decided not to include the killers of Detective-Garda Jerry McCabe under the early release terms of the Belfast Agreement, for fear of risking the 'public acceptability' of the agreement in the Republic.

17 April Republicans tell the BBC they have not set any preconditions on how the families of nine IRA victims, whose graves they say they have identified, should be buried.

Twenty families are evacuated from their homes during a hoax bomb scare in a Protestant area of Portadown.

Ronnie Flanagan announces that John Stevens will conduct a fresh inquiry into the murder of Pat Finucane. The decision comes after renewed allegations of collusion between security forces and loyalists in the murder.

18 April Gerry Adams says that if demands for IRA decommissioning continue, the Belfast Agreement is finished.

19 April Martin McGuinness tells the *Irish News*: 'By demanding immediate decommissioning the UUP have effectively closed down a process which represents the only possible prospect of creating the political conditions in which the gun can be removed from Irish politics ... Moreover the recent decision by the two governments to move away from the Good Friday agreement on to David Trimble's agenda is a major departure with profound implications for the Good Friday agreement. If the governments do not move away from this, and back to the letter and spirit of the agreement, then the Good Friday agreement is dead.'

19 April Tony Blair and Bertie Ahern meet Northern Ireland parties for talks in London. While there is little apparent progress, the Prime Minister and the Taoiseach say there will be no 'parking' of the process. The Taoiseach later suggests that both Sinn Féin and the UUP should give ground if talks are to achieve a successful resolution.

After the Red Hand Defenders plant a pipe-bomb at a Catholic home in north Belfast, Gerry Kelly of Sinn Féin says the latest attack is part of the loyalist version of 'ethnic cleansing' in the area.

20 April At a press conference in Stormont, Séamus Mallon says the Belfast Agreement is being 'vandalised' by Sinn Féin and the UUP and calls on the British and Irish governments to push them into movement.

The US Congress passes resolutions calling for financing of joint initiatives by the RUC and FBI to be halted because of allegations of RUC intimidation of defence lawyers. Congress also calls for an independent inquiry into the allegations of harassment of lawyers by members of the security forces.

21 April The *Belfast Telegraph* reports RUC sources as saying they believe Éamon Collins was murdered by IRA members from south Armagh, though it is unclear whether the murder was sanctioned by the IRA leadership. The police say that Collins's murderers are 'from the element that are causing problems for Adams and McGuinness.'

22 April The UUP leader, David Trimble (who is also an Orangeman) meets Pope John Paul II during a two-day seminar in Italy attended by winners of the Nobel Peace Prize.

24 April John Hume calls for parties to make a common declaration that Executive ministers whose parties or associates abandon the Belfast Agreement's commitment to peaceful means will exclude themselves from the Executive. The proposal receives a cool reaction from unionists and Sinn Féin.

25 April The Orange Volunteers throw a grenade at a house in the Legoniel area of Belfast.

27 April An opinion poll conducted by Ulster Marketing Surveys for the *Irish Times* and RTE finds that 73 per cent of respondents support the Belfast Agreement (including 58 per cent of Protestants) but only 52 per cent believe it will survive another year. While 45 per cent of respondents are prepared to accept the formation of an Executive without decommissioning, 47 per cent oppose this position; 78 per cent of Catholics accept the creation of an Executive under these conditions but 71 per cent of Protestants are against. On the question of policing, 62 per cent of Catholics support the creation of a new police force, while 76 per cent of Protestants are opposed to this.

The British and Irish governments sign an agreement to establish a three-member commission that will receive information on the site of graves of paramilitary victims and help recover their remains. The legislation will also provide immunity from prosecution in relation to evidence gathered while finding the remains or from scientific evidence.

28 April A fresh round of political talks begins in an attempt to break the impasse over the creation of an Executive.

The Northern Ireland (Location of Victims' Remains) Bill, granting a limited amnesty to those connected with identifying the sites where victims are buried, is presented in the House of Commons. Mo Mowlam says it is 'entirely designed to relieve years of suffering.' However, the measure is widely criticised by Unionists and some Conservatives. The former SDLP leader, Lord (Gerry) Fitt also criticises the bill and points out that the government has not agreed to grant immunity to witnesses preparing to give evidence to the tribunal on Bloody Sunday. Despite such criticism, the bill becomes law in late May. The first body is recovered by Gardaí in the Republic on 28 May.

A pipe-bomb planted by the Orange Volunteers explodes outside a bar near Antrim.

30 April In Belfast the UFF leader Johnny Adair is shot and wounded in the head while on parole from the Maze Prison. He claims that republicans are responsible, but newspapers suggest that loyalist rivals instigated the attack.

3 May Bertie Ahern rejects British proposals to break the deadlock over the formation of the Executive. The NIO had suggested that Executive ministers would be nominated and government programmes discussed but that power would not be devolved until decommissioning began. The Irish side say they want to see the issue resolved 'quicker rather than later.'

4 May In Craigavon, David Trimble meets local elected representatives, including the spokesman for Garvaghy Road Coalition, Councillor Breandán Mac Cionnaith, in the first of a series of meetings attempting to break the impasse over the Drumcree march. The first meeting is picketed by anti-agreement loyalists.

5 May Mo Mowlam meets members of the family of Pat Finucane, who request an independent judicial inquiry into his murder. The family raises the issue of material in a confidential Irish government report that says there is 'compelling' evidence of collusion between members of the security forces and loyalists in the murder.

In the *Irish Post,* Gerry Adams says the successful operation of the Executive could make the IRA 'irrelevant'. He also claims that unionists have taken the agreement to the 'edge of the abyss.'

In north Belfast, two boys escape injury in an apparent loyalist murder attempt outside a bookmaker's shop when the gunman's weapon jams.

6 May British and Irish government representatives meet representatives of the UUP, SDLP and Sinn Féin for talks in London. Most of those involved believe that some progress has been made.

8 May At the Sinn Féin ardfheis, Martin McGuinness and Bairbre de Brún are named as the party's nominees to the Executive. The mood of the conference is more subdued than in previous years.

9 May An alleged drugs dealer, Brendan Fegan, is shot dead in Newry. Though he had received threats from the IRA, it is not clear whether republicans were responsible for the murder.

Catholic homes are petrol-bombed in Antrim and Armagh.

10 May The Northern Ireland Law Society overturns a decision by its Council and supports calls for independent inquiries into the Finucane and Nelson murders. The decision is attacked by unionist barristers as not being even-handed.

12 May A Catholic building worker is shot and wounded in Carrickfergus; the attack is later claimed by a group calling itself the 'Protestant Liberation Force', which also claims responsibility for the abortive attack on two boys in north Belfast a week earlier. There is subsequent speculation that this may be a cover name for elements of the UFF.

The renewed loyalist picketing of Harryville Catholic church in Ballymena is called off 'until further notice.'

The Orange Order abandons a plan to hold a single rally at Drumcree on 12 July but says that individual lodges can go to Drumcree after their traditional marches.

14 May The leaders of the SDLP, Sinn Féin and UUP emerge from a further round of all-day talks in London involving the Prime Minister and the Taoiseach in a generally optimistic mood.

Gerry Adams claims that the LVF has co-operated with other loyalist groups involved in recent attacks on Catholic homes. The LVF says it has maintained a full cease-fire since 15 May 1998.

15 May Tony Blair sets 30 June as the date for agreement on terms leading to the devolution of power to the Assembly, and says the deadline is 'absolute'. (Power is also due to be devolved to the Scottish Parliament and the Welsh Assembly on 1 July.) The latest package aimed at resolving the deadlock over decommissioning and the formation of the Executive requires Sinn Féin and other parties 'to do what they can' to achieve the decommissioning of paramilitary weapons by May 2000. The d'Hondt mechanism would be triggered if the head of the International Decommissioning Body, John de Chastelain, reported that 'progress' was being made. It is reported that Trimble's view is that this would mean that decommissioning was actually taking place. Though the other participants in the talks believe that agreement has been reached and that Trimble has given an undertaking to persuade his party to agree to the package, a meeting of Assembly members later in the day fails to endorse it, with up to eight UUP members said to oppose the proposals. UUP members say Trimble's position is based on the party's principle of 'no guns, no government.' Blair expresses his 'disappointment' at the outcome.

Northern Ireland, 1968–1999: An Overview

For thirty years Northern Ireland was trapped in a conflict centred around the constitutional dispute over whether it should remain part of the United Kingdom or be incorporated into the Republic of Ireland. As a result of the violence associated with this dispute more than 3,600 people died and nearly 40,000 were injured, the vast majority of these within Northern Ireland itself. The outcome of the May 1998 referenda on the Belfast Agreement, in which 71 per cent in the North and 95 per cent in the Republic voted in favour of an agreed political package (although on a low turn-out in the latter), appeared to have finally resolved this dispute. Most of the political actors were at last prepared to settle for what they could live with rather than what they said they needed.

Despite this, two potential problem areas that could undermine the Agreement remained: grey areas of the Agreement might be interpreted in such a way as to undermine the support of those who had initially backed the Agreement, while the actions of some of those who had opposed the Agreement from the outset might also work to undermine support.

Whatever the fate of the Belfast Agreement, the political landscape of Northern Ireland in 1999 was significantly different from what it had been three decades earlier. The landmark Downing Street Declaration of August 1969, a joint statement from the Westminster and Stormont governments, stated that Northern Ireland affairs were entirely a matter for the United Kingdom, that the border was not an issue, and that Northern Ireland would remain part of the United Kingdom so long as the people of Northern Ireland wished it to remain so. By 1999 most of these views were no longer applicable. The major participants were now, as they had been since at least 1985, London and Dublin, or at best there was a three-cornered London-Dublin-Belfast axis. Northern Ireland was no longer perceived as an entirely United Kingdom domestic issue (if it ever truly had been); this had also been made clear by the Anglo-Irish Agreement. By the late 1990s other external actors, most prominently the United States and the European Union, also played significant roles in the situation. The question of partition, which in reality had always been an issue, remained so, though in a less antagonistic form than at the outset of the Troubles. The existence of Northern Ireland was now accepted by most nationalists by means of the concept of 'an agreed Ireland', an Ireland that would be, for the foreseeable future, politically divided.

Significantly, one principle enunciated in the 1969 Downing Street Declaration remained unchanged: that the consent of the people of Northern Ireland was necessary for any change in its constitutional position. Thus, while republican paramilitaries had not been defeated militarily they had failed to attain their prime political objective, a united Ireland achieved through the use of force.

Of the civil rights issues championed by NICRA, most had been satisfactorily resolved, although issues such as employment and policing remained highly sensitive and contested. Whether the proposed Northern Ireland Human Rights Commission, the Equality Commission and the report of the Patten Commission on policing would successfully resolve those outstanding issues remained to be seen.

Another area in which there had been a significant change was in demography. At the start of the Troubles the Catholic proportion of the population was just over 30 per cent; by 1999 the figure was estimated at approximately 40 per cent. This had obvious repercussions in the growth of the joint nationalist-republican share of the overall vote but also in day-to-day issues, such as tensions in competition for jobs and territory. While it was widely believed that the Catholic proportion of the population would continue to rise, it was also considered unlikely that this increase would lead to a Catholic majority within Northern Ireland for decades, and even in these circumstances a united Ireland was by no means a foregone conclusion.

The political world in which Northern Ireland was located at the end of the twentieth century was also significantly different from that which had existed in 1968. The countries of the European Union, a body that itself was much changed from the European Economic Community joined by the United Kingdom and Ireland in 1973, appeared to be moving towards a Europe of the regions, making Northern Ireland less of an anomaly than it had been decades earlier. On a less positive note, the ethnic conflicts that emerged in the wake of the collapse of the Soviet bloc, most notably in Yugoslavia, also made Northern Ireland seem less anomalous than in 1968.

The change in the political culture of the Republic was also significant. In the early years of the Troubles elements of the Irish government had gone as far as to consider invading areas of Northern Ireland, while the acquisition of arms by northern republicans had also been indirectly funded. By the late 1990s the Republic was prepared to leave its irredentist claims behind, having realised many years earlier that a united Ireland imposed in the face of unionist opposition would have disastrous consequences for the island as a whole.

The improvement in North-South relations was perhaps less novel than it appeared. On 11 December 1967, in the wake of the meeting at Stormont between Terence O'Neill and Jack Lynch, a press release from the Irish Government Information Bureau noted that in the course of a general discussion, 'Captain O'Neill, Mr Faulkner and Major Chichester-Clark reviewed with Mr Lynch the progress which had been made in such areas of consultation and co-operation as tourism, electricity supply and trade. The discussion also covered measures taken by both Governments to prevent the spread of foot-and-mouth disease from Britain. Satisfaction was expressed on both sides at the close co-operation, to date, between the two Departments of Agriculture, which would be carried further in the near future by a meeting of the two Ministers to review the position.' (Quoted in *Keesing's Contemporary Archives*, p. 224–56.) By mid-1999 North-South co-operation appeared, in some ways at least, to be coming full circle.

While the success of the peace process may be partly attributed to realism and to 'war weariness', the significance of individual effort in moving forward the peace process should not be discounted. John Hume played a significant role in helping to bring republicans in from the political wilderness and, with Albert Reynolds and Bertie Ahern, helped keep them there for most of the period after 1994. The personal interest of Bill Clinton also clearly played a part, for the American role in the peace process went far beyond the pragmatic response required to retain the support of the Irish-American lobby. However, it was perhaps the much-maligned John Major who invested most personal and political capital in Northern Ireland. Major continued to put Northern Ireland at the top of his agenda when at times it would have been comparatively easy to sideline the issue. He faced criticism from unionists on the issue of talks with Sinn Féin and even stronger criticism from nationalists and republicans, who believed (incorrectly) that his cautious attitude towards bringing Sinn Féin fully into the political process was dictated solely by his need to maintain unionist support for a dwindling Conservative majority at Westminster. While the new Labour government, backed by a massive Westminster majority, was able to quicken the pace of negotiations after 1997, any attempt to do so at an earlier stage would most probably have collapsed the entire process through lack of any unionist support.

The question of why the IRA decided to end its campaign has continued to be a matter of debate. Were the Provisionals looking for 'peace with honour' by ending their military campaign or (as many unionists believed) temporarily turning off the tap of violence to create a pan-nationalist front, which could exert greater political pressure, with the threat of a return to 'military operations' if the republican agenda was not met? Despite this, for some traditional republicans the suspicion remained that repeated statements that 'the IRA has not been defeated' were made precisely to disguise the fact that, on the political level at least, the IRA had lost the argument.

The position of the loyalist paramilitaries was somewhat clearer. For their political elite the Union was safe, and this was due, at least partly in their view, to their success in 'terrorising the terrorists' and to loyalist paramilitary harassment of the 'pan-nationalist front'. As with the republican paramilitaries, however (though arguably to a greater degree), there were those who did not believe that the Belfast Agreement signalled the end of the 'war' and who wished to continue their campaigns for purely sectarian reasons or because of the financial benefits of criminal activity in areas such as extortion and peddling drugs.

Despite this, and despite continuing disputes over decommissioning, Drumcree and RUC reform, by June 1999 there was still some cause for optimism. Most of the political actors were in general agreement over the way in which Northern Ireland would be governed, though how this was to be implemented was still a matter of often heated debate.

Although the official unemployment figure still stood at 54,000 (7.3 per cent) in May, public attention was overwhelmingly focused on the peace process. In this context the result of the European Parliamentary election (held on 10 June) sent conflicting messages. Ian Paisley again topped the poll, with 192,762 first-preference votes (28.4 per cent), while John Hume finished second, with 190,731 votes (28.1 per cent). The Ulster Unionist Jim Nicholson finished third, with 119,507 first-preference votes (17.6 per cent), just ahead of Mitchel McLaughlin of Sinn Féin, with 117,643 votes (17.3 per cent). Of the other candidates, David Ervine (PUP) received 22,494 votes (3.3 per cent), Robert McCartney (UKUP) 20,283 (3.0 per cent), Seán Neeson (Alliance) 14,391 (2.1 per cent), and James Anderson

(Natural Law) 998 (0.2 per cent). Paisley and Hume were elected on the first count and Nicholson on the third count. The turnout was 57.8 per cent. The outcome showed overwhelming support for candidates supporting the Belfast Agreement, though a majority of unionist first-preference votes went to candidates opposed to the Agreement. In the event it was also unclear to what extent the outcome was dictated by voters' attitude to the Agreement or to other factors — some unionists, for example, undoubtedly voted for Paisley to prevent John Hume topping the poll, though they may not necessarily have been fundamentally opposed to the Agreement.

On 15 June Tony Blair commenced another round of discussions aimed at achieving devolution in July with a speech in Belfast in which he noted that 'the Good Friday Agreement is the one chance Northern Ireland has got.' The speech came against a background of continuing disputes over policing, parades, decommissioning, the formation of the Executive, internal arguments in the Ulster Unionist Party leadership, the murder of the alleged drugs dealer Paul Downey (almost certainly by republicans) in Newry and continuing loyalists attacks on Catholic homes and property.

By 30 June, despite the fact that arguments between Sinn Féin and the Ulster Unionists over the formation of the Executive and decommissioning had clearly reached an impasse, the British and Irish governments unwisely chose to push ahead with their own plans. *The Way Forward*, launched on 2 July, proposed the establishment of an Executive on 15 July with power being devolved three days later. Where the question of illegal weapons was concerned, the Decommissioning Body would specify when decommissioning would commence, though all paramilitary arms would still have to be decommissioned by May 2000. If commitments under this plan were not met, the operation of all institutions set up by the Agreement would be suspended.

From the outset it was clear that the *Way Forward* proposals had little chance of success as they were met with scepticism from republicans and rejection by unionists. A so-called 'fail-safe' bill introduced by the government in an attempt to meet unionists' concerns over the plan also proved too weak to win over unionist support. Though the Orange marches of July passed off relatively quietly, the triggering of the d'Hondt mechanism on 15 July merely led to a fiasco in which only SDLP and Sinn Féin members were nominated to the Executive and the entirely nationalist body was immediately rejected. The same day saw Séamus Mallon resign his position as Deputy First Minister designate. In the wake of the debacle the government announced that a narrowly focused review of the Agreement, chaired by George Mitchell, was to commence in September. By August 1999, however, it was still unclear whether unionists and republicans were slowly moving towards an agreed compromise on decommissioning and the establishment of an Executive or whether the limit to which they were prepared to compromise had already been reached and no agreement was possible.

Bibliography

Adams, Gerry, *Before the Dawn: An Autobiography,* London: Heinemann 1996.

Annual Register, Harlow (Middx): Longman 1968–98.

Bardon, Jonathan, *A History of Ulster,* Belfast: Blackstaff Press 1992.

Bell, Robert, Johnstone, Robert, and Wilson, Robin (eds.), *Troubled Times: Fortnight Magazine and the Troubles in Northern Ireland, 1970–91,* Belfast: Blackstaff Press 1991.

Bew, Paul, Gibbon, Peter, and Patterson, Henry, *The State in Northern Ireland, 1921–72,* Manchester: Manchester University Press 1979.

Bew, Paul, Gibbon, Peter, and Patterson, Henry, *Northern Ireland, 1921–1996: Political Forces and Social Classes,* London: Serif 1996.

Bew, Paul, and Gillespie, Gordon, *The Northern Ireland Peace Process, 1993–1996: A Chronology,* London: Serif 1996.

Bew, Paul, and Patterson, Henry, *The British State and the Ulster Crisis,* London: Verso 1985.

Bew, Paul, Patterson, Henry, and Teague, Paul, *Northern Ireland: Between Peace and War: The Political Future of Northern Ireland,* London: Lawrence and Wishart 1997.

Bishop, Patrick, and Mallie, Eamonn, *The Provisional IRA,* London: Heinemann 1987.

British and Irish Communist Organisation, *Against Ulster Nationalism* (second edition), Belfast: BICO 1977.

Cadogan Group, *Rough Trade: Negotiating a Northern Ireland Settlement,* Belfast: Cadogan Group 1998.

Crossman, Richard, *The Diaries of a Cabinet Minister, vol. 3: 1968–70,* London: Hamish Hamilton 1977.

Cunningham, Michael, *British Government Policy in Northern Ireland, 1968–89: Its Nature and Execution,* Manchester: Manchester University Press 1991.

Deutsch, Richard, and Magowan, Vivien, *Northern Ireland: A Chronology of Events, vols. 1–3, 1968–74,* Belfast: Blackstaff Press 1973, 1974, 1975.

Devlin, Bernadette, *The Price of my Soul,* London: André Deutsch 1969.

Devlin, Paddy, *The Fall of the Northern Ireland Executive,* Belfast: author 1975.

Devlin, Paddy, *Straight Left: An Autobiography,* Belfast: Blackstaff Press 1993.

Duignan, Seán, *One Spin on the Merry-Go-Round,* Dublin: Blackwater Press 1995.

Elliott, Sydney, and Bew, Paul, 'The prospects for devolution', *Studies,* vol. 80, no. 318, summer 1991.

Elliott, Sydney, and Smith, F., *Northern Ireland: The District Council Elections of 1989: A Computer Analysis,* Belfast: Queen's University 1992.

Farrell, Michael, *Northern Ireland: The Orange State,* London: Pluto 1976.

Faulkner, Brian, *Memoirs of a Statesman,* London: Weidenfeld and Nicolson 1978.

Fay, Marie-Therese, Morrissey, Mike, and Smyth, Marie, *Northern Ireland's Troubles: The Human Costs,* London: Pluto 1999.

FitzGerald, Garret, *All in a Life: An Autobiography,* Dublin: Gill and Macmillan 1991.

Flackes, W., and Elliott, Sydney, *Northern Ireland: A Political Directory, 1968–1993,* Belfast: Blackstaff Press 1994.

Forum for Peace and Reconciliation, *Paths to a Political Settlement in Ireland: Policy Papers Submitted to the Forum for Peace and Reconciliation (Dublin),* Belfast: Blackstaff Press 1995.

Gallagher, Eric, and Worrall, Stanley, *Christians in Ulster, 1968–80,* Oxford: Oxford University Press 1982.

Gillespie, Gordon, 'The Sunningdale agreement: lost opportunity or an agreement too far?', *Irish Political Studies,* vol. 13 (1998).

Hadfield, Brigid (ed.), *Northern Ireland: Politics and the Constitution,* Buckingham: Open University Press 1992.

Hall, Michael, *Twenty Years: A Concise Chronology of Events in Northern Ireland from 1968 to 1988,* Newtown Abbey: Island Publications 1988.

Hamill, Desmond, *Pig in the Middle: The Army in Northern Ireland, 1969–1985,* London: Methuen 1986.

Hermon, John, *Holding the Line: An Autobiography,* Dublin: Gill and Macmillan 1997.

Hickman, Mary (ed.), *Northern Ireland—What Next?: Conference Report,* London: University of North London Press 1995.

Hume, John, *Personal Views: Politics, Peace and Reconciliation in Ireland,* Dublin: Town House 1996.

Institute for Representative Government, *Fair Employment or Social Engineering,* Belfast: Institute for Representative Government 1988.

Jarman, Neil, and Bryan, Dominic, *Parade and Protest: A Discussion of Parading Disputes in Northern Ireland,* Coleraine: Centre for the Study of Conflict 1996.

Jay, Richard, and Wilford, Rick, 'Fair employment in Northern Ireland: a new initiative', *Irish Political Studies,* vol. 6 (1991).

Kearney, Richard, *Myth and Motherland* (Field Day pamphlet no. 5), Derry: Field Day 1984.

Keesing's Contemporary Archives, London: Keesing's Publications 1968–98.

Lawson, Nigel, *The View From No. 11: Memoirs of a Tory Radical,* London: Bantam 1992.

McCann, Eamonn, *War and an Irish Town,* London: Pluto Press 1974.

McIntyre, Anthony, 'Modern Irish republicanism: the product of British state strategies', *Irish Political Studies,* vol. 10 (1995).

Mallie, Eamonn, and McKittrick, David, *The Fight for Peace: The Secret Story Behind the Irish Peace Process,* London: Heinemann 1996.

Mansergh, Martin, 'The background to the peace process', *Irish Studies in International Affairs,* 6 (1995), 145–58.

Mitchell, George, *Making Peace,* London: Heinemann 1999.

Mullan, Don (ed.), *Eyewitness Bloody Sunday,* Dublin: Wolfhound Press 1997.

Needham, Richard, *Battling for Peace,* Belfast: Blackstaff Press 1998.

New Left Review, 55 (May–June 1969).

O'Clery, Conor, *Phrases Make History Here: A Century of Political Quotations on Ireland, 1886–1987,* Dublin: O'Brien Press 1986.

O'Clery, Conor, *The Greening of the White House: The Inside Story of How America Tried to Bring Peace to Ireland,* Dublin: Gill and Macmillan 1996.

O'Leary, Cornelius, Elliott, Sydney, and Wilford, R., *The Northern Ireland Assembly, 1982–1986: A Constitutional Experiment,* London: Charles Hurst 1988.

O'Malley, Pádraig, *Northern Ireland: A Question of Nuance,* Belfast: Blackstaff Press 1990.

Patterson, Henry, *The Politics of Illusion,* London: Hutchinson 1989.

Purdy, Ann, *Molyneaux: The Long View,* Antrim: Greystone Books 1989.

Rees, Merlyn, *Northern Ireland: A Personal Perspective,* London: Methuen 1985.

Rose, Richard, *Northern Ireland: A Time of Choice,* London: Macmillan 1976.

Routledge, Paul, *John Hume: A Biography,* London: Harper-Collins 1997.

Rowan, Brian, *Behind the Headlines: The Story of the IRA and Loyalist Ceasefires,* Belfast: Blackstaff Press 1995.

Seitz, Raymond, *Over Here,* London: Weidenfeld and Nicolson 1998.

Sinn Féin, *Setting the Record Straight,* Belfast: Sinn Féin 1993.

Smith, Graham, and Ripley, Tim, *Inside the SAS,* London: Bloomsbury 1992.

Smyth, Jim, 'Weasels in a hole: ideologies of the Irish conflict' in Yonah Alexander and Alan O'Day (eds.), *The Irish Terrorism Experience,* Aldershot: Dartmouth Publishing Company 1991.

Stringer, Peter, and Robinson, Gillian (eds.), *Social Attitudes in Northern Ireland* (1990–91 edition), Belfast: Blackstaff Press 1991.

Sunday Times Insight Team, *Ulster,* London: Penguin 1972.

Sutton, Malcom, *Bear in Mind These Dead . . .: An Index of Deaths from the Conflict in Ireland 1969–1993,* Belfast: Beyond the Pale Publications 1994.

Taylor, Peter, *Beating the Terrorists?,* London: Penguin 1980.

Teague, Paul (ed.), *Beyond the Rhetoric: Politics, the Economy and Social Policy in Northern Ireland,* London: Lawrence and Wishart 1987.

Thatcher, Margaret, *The Downing Street Years,* London: Harper Collins 1993.

White, Barry, *John Hume: Statesman of the Troubles,* Belfast: Blackstaff Press 1984.

Whitelaw, William, *The Whitelaw Memoirs,* London: Aurum Press 1989.

Wilford, Rick, and Mitchell, Paul (eds.), *Politics in Northern Ireland,* Colorado: Westview Press 1999.

Newspapers and magazines

Belfast Telegraph

Daily Mail (London)

Daily Telegraph (London)

Economist (London)

Financial Times (London)

Fortnight (Belfast)

Guardian (London)

Independent (London)

Independent on Sunday (London)

Irish Independent (Dublin)

Irish News (Belfast)
Irish Press (Dublin)
Irish Times (Dublin)
Magill (Dublin)
Mail on Sunday (London)
Marxism Today (London)
News Letter (Belfast)
New Society (London)
New Statesman (London)
NI Brief (Belfast)
Northern Star (Belfast)
Observer (London)
Parliamentary Brief (London)
An Phoblacht/Republican News (Dublin and Belfast)
Sunday Business Post (Dublin)
Sunday Express (London)
Sunday Independent (Dublin)
Sunday Life (Belfast)
Sunday News (Belfast)
Sunday Press (Dublin)
Sunday Telegraph (London)
Sunday Times (London)
Sunday Tribune (Dublin)
Times (London)

Official publications

BELFAST

Parliamentary Debates: Official Report [Hansard], House of Commons, Belfast: HMSO 1968–72.

Disturbances in Northern Ireland [Cameron Report] (Cmd 532), Belfast: HMSO 1969.

Report of the Advisory Committee on Police in Northern Ireland [Hunt Report] (Cmd 535), Belfast: HMSO 1969.

Report of Review Body on Local Government in Northern Ireland [Macrory Report] (Cmd 546), Belfast: HMSO 1970.

A Record of Constructive Change (Cmd 558), Belfast: HMSO 1971.

Violence and Civil Disturbances in Northern Ireland in 1969 [Scarman Report] (Cmd 566), Belfast: HMSO 1972.

Northern Ireland Assembly, *Official Report of Debates,* Belfast: HMSO 1973–4.

Frameworks for the Future, Belfast: HMSO 1995.

Independent Review of Parades and Marches Report [North Report], Belfast: Stationery Office 1997.

Police Authority for Northern Ireland, *Chief Constable's Annual Report, 1970–97,* Belfast: Police Authority for Northern Ireland 1971–98.

DUBLIN

Dáil Debates.

Forum for Peace and Reconciliation: Report of Proceedings of Public Sessions, Dublin: Stationery Office 1995–6.

International Body on the Decommissioning of Arms, *Report of the International Body* [Mitchell Report], Belfast and Dublin: International Body on the Decommissioning of Arms 1996.

LONDON

Report of the Enquiry into Allegations Against the Security Forces of Physical Brutality in Northern Ireland Arising out of Events on 9th August, 1971 [Compton Report] (Cmnd 4823), London: HMSO 1971.

Report of the Committee of Privy Councillors Appointed to Consider Authorised Procedures for the Interrogation of Persons Suspected of Terrorism [Parker Report] (Cmnd 4901), London: HMSO 1972.

Report of the Commission to Consider Legal Procedures to Deal with Terrorist Activities in Northern Ireland [Diplock Report] (Cmnd 5185), London: HMSO 1972.

The Future of Northern Ireland, London: HMSO 1972.

Report of the Tribunal Appointed to Inquire into the Events of Sunday, 30th January 1972 which Led to Loss of Life in Connection with the Procession in Londonderry on That Day [Widgery Report] (HC 220 1971–72), London: HMSO 1972.

Northern Ireland Constitutional Proposals, London: HMSO 1973.

Anglo-Irish Law Enforcement Commission Report (Cmnd 5627), London: HMSO 1974.

The Northern Ireland Constitution (Cmnd 5675), London: HMSO 1974.

Report of the Northern Ireland Constitutional Convention, London: HMSO 1975.

Report of a Committee to Consider, in the Context of Civil Liberties and Human Rights, Measures to Deal with Terrorism in Northern Ireland [Gardiner Report] (Cmnd 5847), London: HMSO 1975.

Report of the Committee of Inquiry into Police Interrogation Procedures in Northern Ireland [Bennett Report] (Cmnd 7497), London: HMSO 1979.

The Government of Northern Ireland: A Working Paper for a Conference (Cmnd 7763), London: HMSO 1979.

The Government of Northern Ireland: Proposals for Further Discussion (Cmnd 7950), London: HMSO 1980.

Northern Ireland: Ground Rules for Substantive All-Party Negotiations (Cm 3232), London: HMSO 1996.

Parliamentary Debates: Official Report [Hansard], House of Commons (fifth and sixth series), London: HMSO 1968–98.

Northern Ireland Act (1998), London: Stationery Office 1998.

The Belfast Agreement: An Agreement Reached at the Multi-Party Talks on Northern Ireland (Cm 3883), London: Stationery Office 1998.

Television programmes

BBC (Belfast), 'The View from the Castle', 1988.

Index